Tartan For Me!

Suggested Tartans for Scottish, Scotch-Irish, Irish, and North American Surnames with Lists of Clan, Family, and District Tartans

Expanded Sixth Edition

By Philip D. Smith

Heritage Books, Inc.

Also by the same author:

District Tartans
with Dr. D. Gordon Teall

Published 1994 by

HERITAGE BOOKS, INC.
1540-E Pointer Ridge Place,
Bowie, Maryland 20716
(301) 390-7709

ISBN 0-7884-0137-8

A Complete Catalog Listing Hundreds of Titles
on Genealogy, History, and Americana
Available Free on Request

DEDICATION

To Ethel and the late Herbert MacNeal, MD, founders of the Council of Scottish Clans and Associations and of the Scottish Harp Society of America. Supporters of the International Gatherings of the Clans and dedicated to assisting their friends on the Island of Barra, they helped thousands in Scotland and in North America to appreciate more fully their Scottish heritage.

TABLE OF CONTENTS

FOREWORD

Tartan is a living textile art form with a tradition that began in the Highlands of Scotland about the same time that Europeans discovered both their own minority cultures and the New World. Over the centuries the "Pride o' Tartan" has grown while the exodus of Scots to new homes throughout the world continues even today. Millions throughout the world look to Scotland or North Ireland as their point of cultural heritage. Tartan is the living, visible symbol of this identification.

This sixth edition of **Tartan For Me!** presents the latest in a series of tools for the person seeking or giving information on the selection of tartan appropriate to a given surname. The lists of clan, family and district tartans is current; the master list of names has been revised and expanded. The early editions of **Tartan For Me!** awoke an interest in the district tartans, many now seen for the first time in decades. Families and geographic areas continue to record new tartans. Although not long associated with Irish tradition, tartans are now being recorded for Irish surnames and regions. Some English counties and other Celtic areas in Europe--Wales, Cornwall, the Isle of Man, and Galicia (Spain)--have tartans to link their peoples with the Celtic tradition.

After each printing of **Tartan For Me!** correspondents throughout the world have written with suggestions, new names, and new spellings. I am indebted to these interested friends and hope that they will continue to help me to expand and correct my lists. I hope that my work helps people to discover links of blood and tradition. In the words of K. Leroy Irvis, "We do not know who we are until we know who we were."

> Philip D. Smith, Jr.
> Fellow of the Scottish Tartans Society,
> Member of the Guild of Tartan Scholars

TARTAN FOR ME!

SUGGESTING TARTANS

It should be understood from the outset that a person may wear any tartan of his or her choice--the exceptions being personal tartans, tartans restricted by copyright or trademark, and those reserved for members of the Royal Family. The term "suggested tartan" is exactly what it says, a tartan suggested as appropriate for a person with a given surname. It does not imply that persons may not choose another tartan if they so wish.

In no way should the Name-Tartan list in **Tartan For Me!** be regarded as a list of clan or family names. That is quite a different matter. Clan or Family membership comes about by one of three means: Birth, as generally understood as having one of the surnames traditionally associated with a Clan or Family; Marriage, although a woman may choose to wear her own tartan; Adoption, this last process continues as evidenced by The Lord Strathspey's recognition in 1977 that the descendants of John More are members of Clan Grant. More had been a tenant on Drumcork Farm in Strathspey before emigrating to America in 1741.

Some clans and families encourage friends and admirers to adopt and wear their tartan. It is an old Highland custom to so honour your host. Other families wish their tartan to be worn only by persons bearing or related to a specific name or spelling. In example, the Fleming family wear the Murray tartan in recognition of a long friendship between the two families while other clans and families may prefer that their tartan be worn only by those bearing the name or associated by marriage.

Persons wishing to establish clan or family relationships should contact the clan, preferably through the Clan or Family Society rather than directly to the Chief. One is always best advised to select a tartan associated with their own surname before choosing a tartan associated with a name acquired by marriage or through a maternal ancestor.

"Scotland of Old" was divided into two distinct social systems, the clan, with a blood or marriage relationship, and the feudal land-rent society. Despite a romantic preference for the clan, feudalism predominated and eventually prevailed. In 1704 the Chief of Clan Grant directed that his tenants named "MacDonald" were required to wear tartan in the Grant colours.

By the 1700's the majority of Scots lived in non-Gaelic speaking areas with territorial or land-rent obligations more important than a mythical common ancestry. They were expected to follow their lord, whatever his name might be. On the Borders, men were required by the March Law to identify with one of the major families and be a "clannit man" no matter what their own surname. The alternative was to be an "outlaw."

A person has the right to wear the tartan associated with his or her name. Individuals with a clan or family tartan may also wish to wear an appropriate "district" tartan (if there is one) or one of the "national" tartans as an alternative or second tartan.

A person with a surname associated with several clans, families, or districts should try to identify with one and select that tartan, rather than acquiring and wearing items of differing tartans. Specific suggestions are given later for helping persons make reasonable choices among several possible tartans.

Many of the tartans included in **Tartan For Me!** are based upon clan or family associations. In cases where district tartans are suggested, the choice is based upon early documentation of members of that surname living in the district. In one case a family tartan is suggested for an area that was formerly controlled by a feudal overlord, i.e. a "family" tartan is used as a "district" tartan. The Orkney and Shetland Islands were never in the "tartan area" but were under the influence of the Sinclairs. Hence the "Sinclair" tartan is suggested for names with origins in these islands. In earlier editions of **Tartan For Me!** this approach was more widely used but has become unnecessary with the identification or development of appropriate district tartans.

In cases where the name has proven to be untraceable to a particular area or is clearly a recent importation, the "Caledonia" tartan is suggested. This lovely tartan is appropriate for all Scots and friends of Scotland.

SOURCES

Tartans listed in **Tartan For Me!** are most often from the collections of the Scottish Tartans Society and of members of The Guild of Tartan Scholars supplemented by personal knowledge and contact with the industry. Sources of names in the lists come from a wide variety of published and unpublished sources. Chief among these are Black's **Surnames of Scotland**, MacLysaght's **Surnames of Ireland**, and Bell's **The Book of Ulster Surnames**. Earlier editions used research in Scotland, Nova Scotia, the United States and northern England. Included in the Sixth Edition is recent work in Perthshire. Clan and family societies and several chiefs and heads of families have been most kind and have supplied extensive materials. Hundreds of letters of suggestions, additions, and corrections have been received since the first publication (1981).

The major weakness of earlier Name-Tartan lists, apart from their brevity, was that they were compiled from records available in the late nineteenth century. Intervening research and scholarship has resulted in the publication of hundreds of additional documents from the seventeenth and eighteenth centuries -- ship lists, parish records, military records, and tombstones among them.

Earlier lists ignored variations in spelling resulting from population shifts and urbanization at a time when most persons were just becoming literate. Perhaps a million Scots, many Gaelic speakers, arrived in North America directly or via Ulster in the period 1720-1820. Many early functionaries and census takers wrote these Scottish names with unique phonetics. The result was hundreds of names not known in Scotland. Australian, South African, and New Zealand migrations came later after the development of standardized spelling.

Modern variations of traditional names come from a variety of sources, wherever names appear in print. A number of works have recently appeared in Canada and the United States which contain long lists of immigrants and early settlers. North American telephone directories, census, and military records never fail to reveal new variations of Scottish names. A knowledge of the Gaelic language and the insights into predictable sound changes provided by training as a linguist have proven useful in identifying the original names underlying many modern variations.

By its very nature, a list of this type is incomplete. More names will be added as they are encountered. Additional tartans are recorded every year. The resources available, continuing travels to Scottish areas, and the good will of many Scots and descendents of Scots will continue to furnish new information.

MAC OR *Mc* ?

Mac, Gaelic for "son", is the most common element of Scottish and Irish surnames. In both countries, *Mc* is always an abbreviation of *Mac*. There is absolutely no truth to the American myth that *Mac* is Scottish and *Mc* is Irish. *Mac* used to be abbreviated *M'* although this spelling is not common now. At times, all three versions can be seen. In an early book on Highland music, the author spelled his own family name three different ways on the first two pages -- "MacDonald", "McDonald", and "M'Donald."

Black's **The Surnames of Scotland** and MacLysaght's **The Surnames of Ireland** both treat *Mac* in the same way--as the only and original spelling. Persons seeking a name spelled "Mc" are expected to know that it is a conventional abbreviation for *Mac*. This same approach is used in **Tartan For Me!** To find "McDeal" look for "MacDeal."

Mac is always considered an addition to a name. Before there was a "Donald's Son" there was a "Donald". In both Scotland and Nova Scotia, names beginning with *Mac* were traditionally alphabetized under the first letter of the second name -- *MacArthur* under "A", *MacZeal* under "Z". Many Scots dropped "Mac" as they became Anglicized or emigrated, "Mac Wyeth" becoming simply "Wyeth". "Kinzie" is from "MacKenzie". The one notable exception is the Innes and MacInnes families, each quite distinct. The Innes family have Pictish roots and are from the east coast of Scotland with a red tartan. The MacInnes are of Gaelic origin from the west coast and wear a green tartan.

Mac takes a variety of pronunciations. In Islay Gaelic, *Mac* is pronounced like /mek/. In the United States one hears it as "mick". Preceding a /k/ or /g/ sound, the final /k/ of *Mac* disappears. It became the practice in both the south of Scotland and in Ireland to write two words as one (MacGill to Magill; MacHale to Makale). In other names the /k/ sound of *Mac* is duplicated and attached to the front of a following word if it begins in a vowel (MacArter to MacCarter). The reverse also occurs. If the second name begins with a /k/ or /g/, producing two /k/ sounds together, one may disappear (MacGill to Magill; MacKenzie to MacEnzee). *Mac* is at times pronounced "muck" and written that way (Mac 'il Roy to Muckleroy).

SPELLING DIFFERENCES

Spelling differences among names are usually trivial no matter how much pride a person has in a particular version. Many of our ancestors were illiterate until recently, especially if they were Gaelic speakers. Most Gaels were not taught to read or write their own language. In contrast with English, Gaelic speakers place more emphasis on the spoken language than on the written form. This means that Gaelic spelling is constantly being modified to match the spoken form, the latest major revision in 1982. In addition,

Gaelic speakers did not need nor use family names until they began to interact with the English speaking culture. The Gaelic naming system is quite different and either shows a person's lineage or some personal attribute. "Donald of the race of Donald". "Donald, Son of John", and "Donny Little" all might be the same person.

Land holders were known by the name of their holdings--"Locheil", "Corriemony", "Keppoch", Family heads often had a patronymic, a stylized name referring to an ancestor --*Mac 'ic Ailein*, "the Grandson of Allan" is Mac Donald of Clanranald; *Mac Phadruig*, "Son of Patrick" is Grant of Glenmoriston. Other folk were identified by their characteristics and/or their pedigree--"Dark John the son of John (who was the) son of Allan" (*Iain Dubh Mac Iain 'ic Ailein)* is in English simply "John MacDonald". The Gaels refer to two of their great poets simply as "Mary the daughter of Red-haired Alastair" (*Mairi Nighean Alisdair Ruadh*) and "Big Mary of the Songs" (*Mairi Mhor nan Oran*)-- she was a stout lady. Neither Gaelic name had any relationship to their English language surnames, "Mary MacLeod" and "Mary MacPherson". Lady Grant of Glenmoriston was known to her tenants as *A'Bhean Bhreac*, "The Speckled Woman."

Most persons first had their names written for them by others--ministers, school masters, government officials or ship captains. There people wrote as they heard the name, often differently from one time to the next. MacLysaght, in **The Surnames of Ireland** tells of one family of six buried in adjacent graves under six different versions of the family name, five in Irish and one in English.

A name like *Mac Gille Ruaidh* (Son of the Red Headed Servant) can be variously seen as "MacGilroy", "MacKilroy", "MacIlroy", "MacElroy" and "Muckleroy". It also appears as "MacKelra" and "MacGilra". The *Mac* can be shortened to *Mc* to double the spellings. *Mac* can be dropped to form "Gilroy" and "Kilroy". There are more than fifty spellings each of "MacFie", "MacKay" and "MacAulay".

In modern spellings one can find the second part of the surname capitalized or in lower case, "MacDonald" and "Macdonald". This style was adopted in the nineteenth century to distinguish between a person who was actually the son of a man named Donald (Mac Donald) or one of the general clan surname (Macdonald). Of course, the son of "Mac Donald" may not have later changed the spelling--he is now the grandson of Donald, not the son--and the difference quickly lost any meaning. In Gaelic, "MacDonalds" are not called "MacDonald" but *Domhnullach*--"People of Donald."

Gaelic pronunciation rules account for many variations that seem unexplainable to the non-Gael. One example will illustrate . Á Gaelic *n* is an /n/ unless it follows a *c*--it is then pronounced like /r/. *Cnoc*, "rounded hillock", is pronounced like the English word "crock". The name "Nichol" is pronounced like "nickle" until the word *Mac* is prefixed. Then the name is "MacNichol" and the *n*, now follows a /k/ sound, is pronounced like /r/. "Nichol" is like "nickle" but "MacNichol" is pronounced like "MacRickle"--and may have been written that way by the local rent collector two centuries ago.

Non-Scots should remember that Scottish names are not always pronounced the same way abroad or even from one part of Scotland to another--as many visitors find out when they try to pronounce local place names. "Forbes" is often two syllables and one finds the variations "Forbus" and "Forbush". "Menzies" can be heard as "MEEN-us", "MING-us" and "MEN-zies."

When using name lists such as **Tartan For Me!**, encourage people to accept equivalent or near spellings of their names. There is no difference between *-ie* and *-y* at the end of a name; *-ie* is the older Scottish spelling, *-y* is more common in Ulster and North America. "Ogilvy" is "Olgivie". Final *-s* can disappear; "Figgins" and "Figgin" are the same. Often when a name is written phonetically, the original name will appear. One should not try to explain spelling changes unless he is a philologist. Many defy explanation.

Writing is, after all, only a poor representation of what people say. English speakers are keenly aware of the lack of agreement between the spoken and written language. Until about 1800 people wrote English as they heard and spoke it. There was wide variation in spelling even among educated men. Shakespeare wrote his own name several different ways during his lifetime. One of his own spellings is not more "correct" than another. Early Nova Scotia records show phonetic spellings of many well known Scottish names -- MacKenzee, Southerland, Munrow, Gorden, Shey, and Richords. In the United States, census takers in Indiana in 1850 wrote "McOlive" for "MacAuliffe", "McOnion" for "MacCunnion", and "MacDonald" as "McDolnold."

THE TERM "SEPT"

"Sept" is a term borrowed from Irish culture in the nineteenth century to explain the use of a variety of surnames by members of a single clan. In Ireland, "sept" is roughly synonymous with the Scottish "clan" and refers to an intra-related family. Where Scots would refer to "MacGregor and his clan" an Irish historian might say "O'Neill and his sept." Only in the case of larger clans with distinct and sometimes widely separated sub-families is the term "sept" appropriate in Scotland. The various branches of Clan Donald, for example, all using the name "MacDonald of ..." or "MacDonell of ..." may properly be viewed as septs. The many other names of Clan Donald are just that--names of Clan Donald.

The variety of surnames within a Scottish clan do not represent separate and definable sub-clans but instead reflect the vagaries of transition of the Gaels into the English naming system as well as marriages, migrations and occupations. The main family itself may have developed a variety of surnames. The preferred modern usage is to avoid the use of the term "sept" and to simply describe these names as what they are -- surnames of the family and of allied or dependent families. It is preferable to speak of "The names and families of Clan X" rather than to call a name "a sept of Clan X".

NON-TRADITIONAL SCOTTISH NAMES

Persons of many national origins live, and have lived, within Scotland. It has always been a nation of immmigrants from the earlier invasions of Scots, Northumbrians, Vikings, and Norman French through the more peaceful nineteenth and twentieth century influxes from Ireland, England, the Continent, and Asia. Many speakers with a Scottish accent have Polish, Italian, German, Pakistani, or Chinese surnames. These "new" Scots also identify with their nation through tartan be it for a wedding or a school picture. What tartan should these Scots wear?

Aside from the obvious answer, "Whatever tartan they wish", Scots with non-traditional names can choose from district, school, corporate, or national tartans. Many may choose to wear the tartan of a local clan or family. Others can select the tartan associated with the name of a relative or friend. In all cases, they wear tartan with pride.

"STEWART" OR "STUART" ?

"Stuart" is a spelling variation of "Stewart." The original word is the English title "Steward." The spelling difference is due to the presence of the /w/ sound in the middle of the name. Until late in the history of the English alphabet there was no letter *w* although the sound /w/ existed in many dialects. In Scotland the /w/ sound was written with the two-letter combination *qu* as in "Balquidder", /bal-wid-der/.

Literacy came to Scotland primarily through Latin, the language of most early records and documents, and secondarily through Norman French, Continental French, and Gaelic. None of these languages has the letter *w*. Latin and French spell the sound /w/ as *u* or *ou* (as in French *oui*). Gaelic spells the /w/ sound with the letter combinations *bh* and *mh* as in *Mac Gobhain* "MacGowan" and *Mac Amhlaigh* "MacAulay." "Stewart" is spelled *Stiùbhard* in Scottish Gaelic.

The spelling "Stuart" was adopted by some "Stewarts", especially the Lowland branches of the family, under French spelling influence. Cultural, military, and commercial contact was strong with France, particularly in the 1500's as literacy became more general. Mary, Queen of Scots, was, until the premature death of her husband, also Queen Marie of France and resided there.

Persons with the surname "Stewart" or "Stuart" should be advised that it is not correct to wear the "Royal Stewart" as their clan tartan. The "Royal Stewart" is an attractive, classic, and easily obtained design. It is, however, the tartan of the sovereign and the honour of wearing it is granted to select individuals and groups at the pleasure of the sovereign. The "Dress Stewart" is a white variation of the "Royal Stewart."

Neither is the "Hunting Stewart" properly a Clan Stewart tartan. It is one of several "national" tartans and can be worn by anyone who wishes to wear Scottish dress. Why it is called the "Hunting Stewart" when it has been a "national" tartan for almost two hundred years is one of the many mysteries facing tartan scholars.

The correct tartan for those with the surname "Stewart" is the blue and green pattern known as the "Old Stewart" or "Clan Stewart." "Stewarts" who know their Highland connection can choose to wear one of the tartans of the Stewarts of Appin, Ardshiel or Atholl.

Those who spell the name "Stuart" can choose either the "Old Stewart" or the "Stuart of Bute" tartans.

DISTRICT TARTANS

The identification of tartan with territory or place may be more ancient than its association with clan or family. In one of the earliest descriptions of the Highlanders, Martin Martin, himself a Highlander, wrote in the early 1600's, "Every isle differs from each other in their fancy of making plads so as to the stripes in breadth and colours. The humour is as different thro the main land of the Highlands in so far that they who have seen those places are able at first view of a man's Plad, to guess the place of his residence."

There has been considerable discussion over Martin's use of the word "guess." He was himself very familiar with the northwest Highlands and the Hebrides both as a native and as the factor of the MacLeod estates. Some believe that Martin meant that identification of a man with his place of residence by seeing his "plad" was purely a matter of chance. Others believe that Martin meant that a person was able to state a person's place of residence with some degree of certainty, perhaps allowing for reused clothing or variations among local craftsmen. Surely the latter is more accurate. Martin would not have troubled to say anything at all if regional identification by the sett of the tartan were truly a matter of conjecture. There would be no reason to write that a person could "guess" the place of a man's residence "at first view" if identification were solely a matter of chance. "Guess" meant "to state with some (but not total) certainty" in seventeenth century English.

General Stuart of Garth, an early historian of the Highlanders, bridged the gap between the eighteenth and nineteenth centuries. A serving officer in the Black Watch, he knew men who had been born before the "Forty-Five" and the 1747 proscription of the tartan. In his classic **Sketches of the Highlanders** he wrote, "In dyeing and arranging the various colours of their tartans they displayed no small art and taste, preserving at the same time the distinctive patterns (or setts as they were called), of the different clans, tribes, families, and districts. Thus a MacDonald, a Campbell, a Mackenzie, etc. was known by his plaid: and in like manner, the Athole, Glen Orchy, and other colours of different districts were easily distinguishable."

Regional identification makes sense in the context of world cultures. Tribal societies are often distinguished by the variations of folk costume and are usually separated from other sub-groups by distinct geographic boundaries. In the world of the Scottish Gael, surnames were not widely used and loyalty was often defined in terms of land. The Gael had a strong life-long sense of identification with place, **mo dhuthaich-fhìn**, "my land," The mountainous water-divided terrain provided isolation and protection and almost militated identification with place. To this day a Gael is identified by place of origin--"a Lewis man", "a Skye man."

Residents of the same area used the product of local weavers. These in turn employed local dyestuffs and catered to local preferences in their weaving. Traces of this can still be seen today in that the majority of older clan tartans from the west of Scotland are predominately variations in blue, black, and green--MacLeod, MacNeil, MacDonald, MacLean, Campbell. A number of neighbouring clans in the northeast, where there was closer contact with the Continent, use variations of the same pattern of black or dark blue and green stripes on a red ground -- Mackintosh, Robertson, Grant, MacGillivray, Murray and Drummond. A very few closely located clans have a distinctive azure stripe.

If tartan identification was first with **duthaich**, "homeland", it should also be recognized that most people in isolated areas would also have been related by blood and marriage.

The first recorded uniform "clan" tartan is that of the Grants (1704) when the Laird of Grant ordered all eligible men, no matter what their name, to wear red and green tartan, "broad springed", when called to military service. It was a natural transition from identification with a place to that of service to the prominent family of the district. The "Hunting MacPherson" was earlier "The gray Plaid of Badenoch" and the "Murray of Atholl" was first the "Atholl District " sett.

A listing of "district" tartans follows. Many are well known; others less so but deserving of more attention. Some are old, others of recent design. Sometimes a clan and a district have the same name but distinct tartans -- Sutherland, Dunbar, and Moffat. In the Name-Tartan list these are clearly distinguished; "Dunbar" (Family) but "Dunbar Dist."

There are several recorded setts of "Lochaber" tartans. "Arran" has been rediscovered and the "Roxburgh" was woven at the Museum of Scottish Tartans in 1985 for the first time in over a century. A number of the district tartans are recorded in the late eighteenth century and early nineteenth century pattern books of Wilson's of Bannockburn, early tartan manufacturers.

Other district tartans are of royal origin, worn by the nobility in their roles as territorial sub-rulers. The "Inverness", "St. Andrews", "Fife" and others come from patterns worn by the earls of those districts. "Strathspey" and "Argyll" have military origins. The "Lennox" may well be the oldest recorded tartan, taken from a portrait of the Countess of Lennox dated to the mid- to late 1500's. "Falkirk", "Cumbernauld", and "Caithness" are very recent designs intended to foster a bond with the district where no district tartan existed before.

The reorganization of Scotland's administrative units in the 1970's has led to both the realignment of traditional boundaries--Argyll is now in "Strathclyde"--and in the creation of new regional names such as "Tayside" and "Banff and Buchan." The redistricting has encouraged the creation of new tartans. Recent new designs are "Perthshire District Council" and "Banff and Buchan" when older "Perthshire" and "Buchan" district tartans already existed. These recent tartans are not yet included in **Tartan For Me!** since, when possible, the author encourages the use of older designs.

From the Act of Proscription

"XVII. ...from and after the first day of August, 1747, no man or boy, within Scotland, other than such as shall be employed as officers and soldiers...shall... wear or put on the clothes commonly called Highland clothes,the plaid, philibeg,or little kilt, trowse, shoulder belts ... and that no tartan, or partly colored plaid shall be used for great coats, or for upper coats ..every person so offending...shall suffer imprisonment,without bail, for the space of six months... and being convicted for a second offense shall be liable to be transported...beyond the seas...for the space of seven years."

Individuals with no clan or family tartan and should be encouraged to wear a district tartan appropriate to a locale of origin, residence, or affection. The accompanying cap badge can be any with a Scottish theme, perhaps the cross of St. Andrew, a thistle, or the badge of a particular county or city.

A LIST OF DISTRICT TARTANS

Aberdeen	Edinburgh	Lorne
Angus	Eglinton	Mar
Applecross	Ettrick	Mentieth
Argyll	Falkirk	Moffat
Arran	Fife	Montrose
Atholl	Ft. William	Mull
Ayrshire	Gala Water	Musselburgh
Berwick-upon-Tweed	Galloway	Nithsdale
Blair Logie	Glasgow	Paisley
Buchan	Glen Lyon	Perthshire
Caithness	Glen Orchy	Rothesay
Carrick	Glen Tilt	Roxburgh
Crieff	Glen Trool	St. Andrews
Culloden	Huntly	Stirling
Cumbernauld	Inverary	& Bannockburn
Deeside	Inverness	Strathclyde
Drumlithie	Largs	Strathearn
Dunbar	Lennox	Strathspey
Dunblane	Lochaber	Sutherland
Dundee	Loch Laggan	Tweedside
East Kilbride	Loch Rannoch	Tyneside

In addition to the more traditional Scottish district tartans, a number of other locales have official and unofficial tartans. The "Durham" dates from 1819 or before; the "Tyneside" from 1914. Beginning with the "Nova Scotia" in 1953, Canadian provinces and other locales have recorded tartans. A number of states of the United States have followed suit.

For an illustration and the history of each of these and other district tartans, including those from both the British Isles and overseas, see **District Tartans** by D.Gordon Teall and Philip D. Smith (London: Shepheard-Walwyn, 1992. ISBN 0-85683-085-2).

DISTRICT TARTANS

THE SCOTTISH NATIONAL TARTANS

There are many Scots and friends of Scotland for whom there may be no ready clan, family, or district tartan. In addition, there are cases where it may be inappropriate for a group to wear a variety of tartans and a uniform pattern is desired. Examples include bands, guides at national monuments, schools, and groups which represent all of Scotland. For these individuals and groups, one of the Scottish "national" tartans is a good choice.

In the past two hundred years there have been several attempts to create a single "all Scottish" or "Scottish national" tartan. Historically, such attempts have failed as the Scottish people, themselves, have chosen the "Hunting Stewart", the "Caledonia" or the "Black Watch" as their national tartans.

The "Hunting Stewart". a green tartan with black, yellow, and red overstripes, has served as the "universal" Scottish tartan since at least the early 1800's. The "Hunting Stewart" is not regarded as a Clan Stewart sett. Indeed, it is a mystery as to why it is called by the Stewart name. "Hunting Stewart" is the uniform tartan of the Royal Scots Regiment as representative of all Scotland and can be seen in daily use by the guides at Edinburgh Castle.

The "Caledonia" is a complex red tartan dating from at least 1800. Named for Scotland, it is widely used as a national tartan.

The "Government" or "Black Watch" tartan has been used by the British Army since the 1740's and by a number of clans and individuals since that time or even earlier. This tartan is regularly worn by the Grants, Munros, and Campbells. Many clan tartans are variations of the "Black Watch", often with an added colour overstripe. In lighter shades the tartan is the "Sutherland District" tartan; in darker shades it is the tartan of the Argyll and Sutherland Regiment. Since the design is used by clans and regiments from Argyll in the southwest to Sutherland in the far northeast, there is considerable reason for its popularity as a "national" tartan or a universal "Highland" tartan.

Any person may choose one of these universal Scottish tartans as a preferred tartan or as a second sett to complement a clan, family, or district pattern: the green "Hunting Stewart", the red "Caledonia, or the darker "Black Watch".

IRISH TARTANS

Irish historians agree that tartan was not a part of traditional Irish garb. Irish pipe bands, dancers, and atheletes often wear the plain saffron kilt or the kilt in blue, rose, or green. Civilian Irish pipe bands have at times adopted Scottish tartans or had special tartans designed for them ("St. Patrick", "Dunoon Irish"). Some family tartans can be shared by both Scottish and Irish families of the same name ("MacNaughten", "MacGuire"). One Irish tartan, the "Ulster", has a truly historic basis (1600 or before). Recently, it has become fashionable for Irish families ("Forde", "MacDonough", "O'Carroll/Clan Cian") to adopt tartan.

The "Ulster Tartan", provides for those names from both in Northern Ireland and the Republic, the "Oriel" for those from the southern part of Ulster; the "Connacht Tartan" for those from that district. Both the "Tara/Murphy" and "Clodagh" tartans are appropriate for all Irish names but names from central Ireland might choose the "Tara" while names from southern Ireland could choose the "Clodagh." Several hundred Irish names are included on the **Name-Tartan** list.

TARTANS FOR NON-SCOTS

Any person may wear tartan. Both Scots and non-Scots can wear the "District" and "National" tartans. There are a number of other tartans that might be selected by citizens of other nations as an alternative to any clan or family tartan.

UNITED KINGDOM: There are a number of tartans for parts of England and the United Kingdom: "Tyneside", "Durham", "Somerset", "Cornish National", "St. Piran", "Ulster Tartan", "Welsh National", or "Manx National".

IRELAND: See "Irish Tartans" (above).

CANADA: The "Canadian Centennial Tartan" serves as a "national" tartan for all Canadians. Each Province and Territory has its own official tartan. The attractive but asymmetrical "Maple Leaf" tartan is often seen in ladies clothing but is not recommended for the kilt due to the difficulty of properly pleating the sett.

AUSTRALIA: The "Australia" tartan.

UNITED STATES: A number of the states have official or unofficial tartans -- "Maine", "Carolina", "Georgia", "Ohio", "Idaho", "Washington", "Indiana", "Texas Blue Bonnet", "New Hampshire", and "Pennsylvania". One city, "Tulsa", has adopted a tartan. There is a little known tartan designed for all citizens of the United States, the "America", and several military associated and university setts: "West Point", "The Citadel", "Leatherneck".

SOUTH AMERICANS might consider wearing the "Cochrane" tartan in honour of the naval hero who founded the navies of several nations (Brazil, Argentina, and Chile).

SPAIN: Spaniards with Celtic roots can choose the "Galicia" tartan. Others might select the "Wellington" tartan in honour of the Duke who directed the Allied armies in the Peninsula against the forces of Napoleon. Wellington held the rank of Field Marshall in the Spanish army. Recently, tartans have been designed for several northern provinces of Spain. It is believed that the "Jacobite" tartan had its origins in Barcelona and is an appropriate choice for Catalans.

PORTUGAL: The Duke of Wellington began his brilliant Peninsular campaign from Portugal with the title of "Commander-in-Chief." The "Wellington" tartan is a good choice.

FRANCE: The French supported the Stuart cause for decades and the "Jacobite" tartan is a wise choice. French regulars fought to the last at Culloden Moor after the clans had broken and the "Culloden" tartan would honour those brave soldiers.

AUSTRIA: Austrians could choose the "Leslie" tartan to remember the Scottish expatriate soldier who rose to become a general in the Hapsburg army.

GERMANY: Prince Albert, lover of the Highlands and himself a tartan designer, was a German. The "Coburg" tartan was designed to commemorate the Prince Consort and is an attractive choice. Some Pennsylvania Germans ("Dutch") have chosen to wear a plain kilt in Jaeger green.

THE NETHERLANDS: The "Dutch" tartan simultaneously represents the House of Orange and the MacKay family who have been prominent citizens of both Scotland and the Netherlands for many generations.

RUSSIA: Russians might choose the "Muskova" or the "Gordon" in honour of the Scottish general who modernized the army of Peter the Great.

SCANDINAVIA: The "Munro" and "MacKay" tartans are appropriate to represent the thousands of mercenary Scots from those clans who served the Swedish kings. There are several native Scandinavian tartans recorded by the Scottish Tartans Society.

ITALY: The "Prince Charles Edward Stuart" tartan is a good choice. "Bonnie Prince Charley" was born, lived most of his life, died, and is buried in Rome.

LOCATING UNCOMMON TARTANS

Many of the tartans for smaller clans, families, and districts may not be carried as stock items by Scottish vendors. This is not surprising since kilt makers cannot be expected to invest in extensive inventories of tartans for which there is limited demand. About two-thirds of the tartans listed in **Tartan For Me!** are stock items from one or several mills, regularly woven and available on order. The balance can always be obtained through special order.

Some manufacturers will weave tartan in as few as four or five yard lengths, enough for a full kilt (the kilt maker will cut the yardage in half lengthwise to obtain double the length). Costs are understandably higher for specially woven tartan but not prohibitive. The life expectancy of tartan garments always makes them a good investment.

The patterns for most tartans can be obtained from The Scottish Tartans Society or the International Association for Tartan Studies. Both endeavor to keep records of all known tartans. Any individual or the most modest Scottish vendor can obtain the pattern or "sett" in the form of the number of thread ends of various colours. The sett is then supplied to the weaving mill which will manufacture the tartan. A number of craftsmen and women will also make hand woven tartan sashes or short lengths of yardage to order.

Often the best answer to the question, "What does this tartan look like?" is to have a sash woven before making the larger investment of more expensive yardage or of having garments made that are not to taste. Coloured drawings, photos in tartan books, computer screens, and small swatches are nice but can never duplicate the blends and possible kiltings (pleating) of several yards of material.

An order for tartan should always specify the tones (shades) of the basic colours. The following section explains the four major types of colour tone available.

Family and district tartans included for the first time in this edition of **Tartan For Me!**:

Akins	Hallingdale	MacPhedran	Drennan
Beaton	Henry	MacVeen	Fullerton
Bethune	Hogg	Maxton	Glen Trool
Brough	Hudson	Milne	MacInery
Casely	Hynde	Myron	MacLulich
Clayton	Inches	Paget	Paten
Connacht	Keeper	Raibert	Connor
Kilburnie	Stephenson	Crosser	Lee
Spencer	Dalglish	MacBride	Swan
Dallas	MacCaughan	Williams	MacNiven
Sawyer	Wishart	Young	Lynch

TARTAN COLOUR

First time buyers are often misled by the term "ancient" as applied to tartan, assuming that it somehow designates an older, more authentic version of the tartan. To the contrary, "ancient" actually is more modern than "modern." "Ancient" does not refer to the age of a tartan but rather to the shades of coloured thread used in the weaving. A tartan designed today can be woven as the "Ancient Mac X" if the weaver selects shades to try to imitate the colours of natural dyes used before 1860. It is not correct to refer to these as "vegetable" dyes since some were made of animal matter or minerals.

Tartan is woven in four shades: (1) the brighter "modern" hues made possible by new dyes after 1860, (2) the softer "ancient" or "old" colours, (3) the shades known as "muted", and (4) "reproduction" or "weathered" colours in imitation of tartan long exposed to sun and rain. For simple visual identification, the red is an orange colour when called "ancient"; blues and greens are woven as gray and brown in the "reproduction".

The key to tartan identification is in the pattern. A single pattern can be woven in large or smaller scale in each of the four colour possibilities. These eight variations will visually appear to be very different but are, in reality, all correct representations of the same tartan. It is the pattern, not the width of the sett nor the shade of colour which identifies the tartan. The so-called "Ancient Smith" and "Smith" tartans are the same, simply different colour versions of the pattern.

There are a small number of tartans which research has found to be older than the pattern usually worn by the clan or family. Here the term "old" is used. The "Old Stewart" is truly more ancient than other "Stewart" tartans and is properly the "Clan Stewart" pattern. To avoid confusion, standardization of tartan terminology is important. Persons giving advice on tartan should use the system suggested by John R. Dalgety, FSTS, in his article "Failte do Bhreacan", **Highlander**, 21.2, pp.42-47.

1.   All words BEFORE the clan/family name refer to the design or pattern (sett) and might include: "Clan", "Hunting", "Dress", "Chief", and "Old". A colour can be used before the clan/family name only to distinguish the tartan from the standard clan/family sett. Examples include "Dress MacDonald", "Hunting MacPherson", "Old Stewart" and "Red Campbell" since the standard "Clan Campbell" tartan is black, green, and blue.

2.   All words AFTER the clan/family name refer only to the colour shades with which it is woven. Examples are "Modern" or "Ordinary", "Ancient", "Muted", "Reproduction" or "Weathered". Absence of any colour descriptor implies "modern" colours.

For example, "Red Gordon, Ancient colours" indicates a red tartan woven in soft shades which is distinct from the usual green "Gordon" tartan. "Red Gordon" would indicate the same tartan but in brighter "Modern" colours. If there are two or more clan/family tartans with similar characteristics, it is usual to indicate the branch of the family. "Red Gordon" might mean either of two tartans, the "Gordon of Abergeldy" or the "Gordon of Fyvie".

WEARING TARTAN

The "proper" wearing of tartan in informal dress has been overemphasized. On the other hand, one can see variations in Scottish dress which go beyond good taste and common sense. It is certain that early Highlanders, often poor, wore whatever they could get their hands on. Scots have become more constrained and conservative as time has passed. Fashions in Highland dress come and go just as in other garments. The box pleated kilt, once popular with gentlemen, lost to the heavier and easier to make knife pleat under the pressure of military mass production. The box pleated kilt is now seen once again, especially suitable for warm climates and evening wear. Early portraits clearly show folds across the front of the garment although none are worn today.

For specific guidance on the wearing of modern Highland dress, the reader should refer to J.C. Thompson's informative book **So You're Going to Wear the Kilt.**

Almost any time is a good time to wear tartan; a tie is appropriate when the kilt is not. There are a number of ways to wear tartan that have evoked some discussion and disagreement over the years. The first is the wearing of two different tartans at the same time, the second is the proper shoulder for the lady's sash.

Early portraits clearly show Scottish notables wearing several different tartans at the same time. These are invariably tartans of the same colour combinations. It is now considered questionable taste to wear two tartans simultaneously, even if they are from the same family or clan. One does not usually wear the kilt and tie or sash and skirt of two different setts, or even sizes of setts or colour variations. It is never good practice to mix "Clan", "Hunting", and "Dress" setts. Many so-called "Dress" and "Dress-Hunting" colour variations are recent weavers inventions to increase sales, especially among female Highland dancers, and are not recognized by clan chiefs or clan societies at all.

The designation of the proper pattern to be used as the "clan" or "family" tartan is one of the few absolute prerogatives left to the Scottish chief. The selection is final and may be changed at his or her discretion.

The single exception to the wearing of only one tartan at a time occurs when a gentleman in informal or "day" dress wears the kilt and a separate plaid, across the body or in the blanket form. In this case, Thomas Innes, a former Lord Lyon, advised that the clan/family tartan should be shown as the shoulder plaid while the kilt could be in either the appropriate "district" tartan or of one of the recognized sub-divisions of the clan/family. A lady might wear "district" tartan or an "arisaid" (woman's white) tartan if the family has one.

In such cases, the two tartans should always be of the same colour tones, "Modern", "Ancient", "Muted", or "Reproduction".

Even if purchased from the same supplier, tartan may be different in shade and sett size from one time to the next. Persons who plan to have both kilt and plaid or who wish an entire group to match should purchase all items from the same supplier at the same time.

The lady's sash is conventionally worn over the right shoulder. Many believe that the sash on the left shoulder is an honour reserved for women who are chiefs, wives of chiefs, and the wives of colonels of Scottish regiments (*de facto* wives of chiefs). However, Scottish country dancers wear the sash on the left shoulder, permitting freer right arm movement. Harpers wear the sash and brooch on a shoulder that will not mar their instrument.

The white-grounded "Dress" tartans made popular in the nineteenth century and now especially created for Highland dancers are based upon "arisaid" tartans originally intended for women. They are not so popular among men as they once were. Men traditionally wore the tartan on a large scale, often ten to twelve inches across. Women often wore the patterns on a smaller scale. Since it is less expensive to make quantities of material in only one sized pattern, the large sett almost disappeared. It is more often seen in recent years and makes the man's kilt especially attractive.

RECORDING TARTANS

Individuals reporting new finds of older tartans should send all possible information to the Scottish Tartans Society, Port-na-Craig Road, Pitlochry, Perthshire, Scotland. Be sure to include a sample, a colour photograph or drawing large enough to show a complete repeat of the pattern in both directions. Older tartans were not always the same in warp and weft. Never cut a piece from an antique tartan! Lend the item to the Society for analysis. If this is inconvenient, a tartan specialist can call in person to obtain the pattern.

If it is not possible to contact a specialist, then make a cross-sectional drawing of the pattern, counting the number of threads in each colour stripe, Again, be sure to continue this process to give enough counts to show the entire width of the pattern as illustrated below.

Recognized heads of families wishing to record a new tartan should seek the advice of tartan specialists to avoid unknowing duplication of another tartan. It is better to modify a clan/family or district tartan with which the family already has some historic connection than to design a new pattern.

The Scottish Tartans Society or the International Association for Tartan Studies can also provide guidance in the choice of colours and arrangements. Often a pattern which looks well on paper may not transfer well into woven cloth. There are physical limitations on weaving of which the designer may not be aware. The weaving process, for example, may limit the number of different colours which can be used. Some patterns are beautiful in blanket or sash but look quite different when pleated. Knowledgeable tartan specialists shy away from the recent symbolic use of colour in tartan ("Blue for the sky, red for the blood of heroes..."). Instead, they are more interested in historic antecedents and in the visual effect.

A tartan pattern may be "restricted". This indicates that the pattern is recorded in the master file but is not released without the specific permission of the proprietor. Such restrictions are carefully honoured. A tartan may also be copyrighted.

Patterns are normally kept in the form of thread or "end" counts. The smallest number of threads that can be woven in tartan is two. Larger numbers are usually reduced to a sub-multiple of two and later expanded by the weaver to fit the loom. One half of the pattern is sufficient for a weaver since most tartan patterns are a series of reversing arrangements. Notice in the illustration below that the number of threads of various colours reads the same in either direction from the center of the "ground" colour.

A TARTAN PATTERN OR "SETT"

Tartan repeats itself from right to left and then from left to right. The points at which it begins to repeat itself in the opposite direction is called the "pivot." Thread counts are always in multiples of two, and can be expanded by the weaver by multiplying the count to fit the desired width of the pattern.

A cross section of the "Sawyer" tartan, illustrated below, shows how the tartan goes out in identical stripes from the central green "pivot" to the narrow red stripes. There it again begins to reverse itself.

The "Sawyer" Tartan

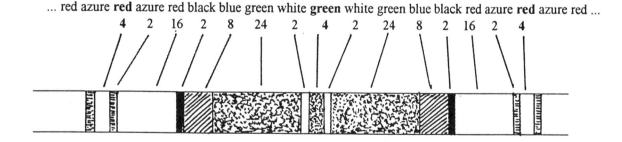

... red azure **red** azure red black blue green white **green** white green blue black red azure **red** azure red ...

4 2 16 2 8 24 2 4 2 24 8 2 16 2 4

HOW TO USE THE NAME-TARTAN LIST

The **Name-Tartan** list of **Tartan For Me!** is almost self-explanatory. There may be times when the reader is asked to help a novice select an appropriate tartan. It will prove useful to follow these suggestions:

1. *BEFORE YOU EVEN BEGIN ...* Read all of the introductory material carefully including a look at the "Examples" which follow this section. Be sure to read the "Helpful Clues" which follow.

2. Check the name to be researched against the **Name-Tartan** list. If found, there may be one or several suggested tartans. If more than one, a person can select from among the suggestions but should have a reasonable basis for such a selection.

If a person knows from what area of Scotland their particular family originated, select the clan/family/district tartan closest to that area (see a good clan/family map). If there is no known locale suggest that the individual read about the several clans/families and select the one with which he or she wishes to identify. Stress that the individual should choose ONE clan/family, not several. A person is a member of Clan X, not of Clans X, Y, and Z.

If an individual has a surname identifiable with two clans, one in the east of Scotland and another in the west and knows the point of recent residence, use that as a basis for selection. Internal Scottish migration has largely been north to south. If recent family traditions are in Edinburgh, choose the eastern clan/family; if Glasgow then choose the western tartan.

3. If you regularly give advice on tartan selection, become thoroughly familiar with Scottish geography and at least superficially knowledgeable of Scottish and colonial North American history. Settlement patterns in South Africa, Australia, and New Zealand are not as useful in identifying origins of name variations as are those of the early United States and Canada.

4. If a name is not on the **Name-Tartan** list, look under other possible spelling variations: "Lezly" as "Leslie". "Gil" may have been shortened to "Il" or "El"--and *vice versa*. Review the materials presented earlier under "*Mac or Mc*" and "Spelling Differences". A name that once began with "n" may now begin with "r" and the final "c" of "Mac" may have been duplicated into a second "c" or a "k" (MacOmber-MacComber; MacIntosh-Mackintosh).

Many spelling variations are anticipated in the **Name-Tartan** list but not all could be forseen.

Since Gaelic requires sound changes when "Mac" is prefixed, try pronouncing the new name aloud substituting a new first letter on the second part of the name, and you may hear the original.

"b" or "m" for a "v"   *MacVean* to *MacBean, MacVickle* to *MacMichael*
"p" for an "f"   *MacFall* to *MacPaul*
"d" for "g" or "t"   *MacGonell* to *MacDonell, MacLout* to *MacLeod*
Gaelic "f" becomes silent after "Mac"; try reinserting it--*MacLetcher* to *MacFletcher*.

18

5. If a person disagrees with the suggested tartan, don't argue! They may have been given conflicting information. They may have a long held (if erroneous) family tradition. Some individuals go from tartan specialist to tartan specialist seeking confirmation of already held notions. The majority of people are grateful for any suggestions that you can give.

6. If a person believes that his or her family came from Scotland but the name is not on the list, consult the "District Tartan Map" and suggest an appropriate district tartan or the tartan of a major clan/family of the area. Record the name for future reference.

7. Many individuals are disappointed to learn that their surname has no clan or family affiliation but that a district tartan is suggested. Explain that the most populous two-thirds of Scotland was under the Anglo-Norman feudal, not the clan, system. Point out that the majority of Scots were not "Highlanders" nor Gaelic speakers and did not historicly wear tartan. Tartan is now the national dress of Scotland (since 1700), worn and appreciated by all. Many district tartans are older than the majority of clan/family tartans.

8. Do not let a person go away disappointed that there is no tartan for them. There are many Scots whose families moved to Scotland for economic reasons and there are even recent Highland family resettlements to avoid the violence in Northern Ireland. Always suggest one of the "national" tartans or a "district" tartan from an area in which they have lived, visited or particularly enjoyed. Do not overlook tartans earlier suggested for non-Scots.

SPECIFIC INSTRUCTIONS

Here are some specific helps for suggesting tartans:

1. Always suggest that a person first purchase the established clan/family tartan in either "modern/ordinary" or "ancient" colours before they choose sub-family or other variations. The clan/family tartan in "modern" colours is acceptable on any occasion; other variations are not always appropriate.

2. There are many "MacDonald" tartans. Suggest that a person first purchase the general "Clan MacDonald" tartan.

3. "Stewarts" should wear the blue and green "Old Stewart".

4. Tactfully inform "Stewarts" and "Stuarts" that they should NOT wear the "Royal Stuart" as their clan tartan.

5. The "Cairns" wear the "Grant" tartan although they are not of the clan by line or marriage. They have simply aligned themselves with the Grants over many generations and are, of course, welcome members of the Clan Grant Society.

6. The Flemings wear the "Murray" tartan through friendship with that clan.

7. The name "Bowie" can be either "Grant" or "MacDonald". If from the east, "Grant", the west "MacDonald". If Protestant, "Grant", if Roman Catholic, possibly "MacDonald";

Only "MacDonald" Bowies should wear the "Bowie" tartan, a variation of the "MacDonald" tartan.

8. The present trend in Clan MacPherson is to wear the gray "Hunting MacPherson" as the clan tartan and the "Dress MacPherson" for evening and formal wear.

9. In the 1800s the "Russells", "Galbraiths", "Hunters", and "Mitchells" all selected the identical tartan. If a member of one of these clans cannot locate his or her sett, it can be purchased under one of the other names--and the name-tag removed.

10. The "Argyll District" tartan and the "MacCorquodale" are sold under "Campbell of Cawdor, Ancient Colours".

11. The "Hunting Grant" and "Hunting Munro" in "ancient colours" are sold as "Campbell" or "Black Watch, Ancient Colours".

12. The "Sutherland District" is sold as "Black Watch" or "Campbell", in "Ancient Colours".

13. Do not confuse the "Edinburgh District" with its Gaelic namesake and look-alike, the "Dunedin" (Florida, USA) tartan.

14. Be sure that so-called "dress" tartans have the acceptance of the clan or family. Few do. An example is the "White Rose", not accepted by the clan. Many "dress" tartans are of very recent origin and have no status. They are simply fashion designs, primarily for female Highland dancers.

15. The prefered tartan for "Shaws" is the "Shaw of Tordarroch." It more authentically illustrates the family's historic ties to Clan Mackintosh. The dark "Shaw" tartan is taken from an imprecise rendering on a posthumous portrait of a soldier wearing the early "Black Watch" uniform.

16. There are two "Bell" tartans. One represents the Highland "Bell" family, part of Clan MacMillan. The other is the tartan of the "Bell" family who lived in the Western March, the "Bells of the Borders". These are distinguished in the Name-Tartan list as "Bell" and "Bell of the Borders".

Both "Bell" tartans are recent designs; prior to 1985 Bells were universally advised to wear the "MacMillan" tartan. Bells who do not know the general locale of their origin will have to choose between the two tartans and clans--the west Highland "MacMillan" or the "Bell of the Borders". It is not proper to wear both or to alternate. Bells must choose.

17. Highland Scots named "Smith" are traditionally part of Clan MacPherson and wear those tartans. The attractive "Smith" tartan, designed in the 1880s, is a variation of the "MacLeod" tartan and is only appropriate for Smiths with a Hebridean background. *Gobh*, "Gow", is Gaelic for "Smith" and is a traditional alternative tartan for the "Smiths."

READING THE NAME-TARTAN LIST

In order to conserve space, the **Name-Tartan** list uses conventions to combine spellings into a single entry.

DAL(L)OCH indicates that name may be spelled either DALOCH or DALLOCH.

GOWIE,-Y indicates that the name may be either GOWIE or GOWY. The alternative endings -Y and -IE are shown together unless they will appear separated by other names when alphabetized. Then the two spellings are given separately.

GOW(D)IE,-Y(S) provides for GOWIE, GOWDIE, GOWY, GOWDY, GOWIES, GOWYS, GOWDIES, and GOWDYS variations.

DONIVAN, -EN provides for DONIVAN and DONIVEN.

The names of some tartans have been abreviated.

MAC DONALD OF ARDNAMURCHAN	MAC DON ARDNAMURCHAN
MAC DONALD OF CLANRANALD	MAC DON CLANRANALD
MAC DONALD OF GLENALADALE	MAC DON GLENALADALE
MAC DONALD OF GLENCOE	MAC DON OF GLENCOE
MAC DONALD OF KINGSBURGH	MAC DON KINGSBURGH
MAC DONALD OF KEPPOCH	MAC DON KEPPOCH
MAC DONELL OF GLENGARRY	MAC DONELL GLENGARY
MAC NEILL OF GIGHA AND COLONSAY	MAC NEIL GIGHA/COLONSAY
MAC LEAN OF KINGAIRLOCH	MAC LEAN KINGAIRLOCH

A name may be repeated. Such entries indicate that the person might select any one (and stress the **one**) of the tartans in the right hand column, depending on personal choice or other insights. Generally, there is no preference implied although the choice might be in order of **clan/family, sub-family/clan,** and **district** as illustrated below. The choice should be left to the individual.

SMITH	MAC PHERSON
SMITH	GOW
SMITH (Hebridean)	SMITH

Many names appear both in Scotland and in Ireland. The person selecting a tartan will have to choose between names such as LYNCH (Scot) and LYNCH (Irish).

A LIST OF CLAN AND FAMILY TARTANS

There are a large number of clan and family tartans currently recorded. A number have several variations in size and pattern as recorded at different times from different weavers. Only the name of each clan/family tartan, not the variations, are listed here. Not all of the tartans listed are woven by every manufacturer but each is available through special order unless the tartan is one of the few "restricted" setts.

Each clan or family with a tartan is listed only once. Many clans and families have several tartans, sometimes styled "clan", "hunting", "dress" or by the predominant colour (eg. "Blue Wallace", "Red Gordon.") No attempt is made to list these variants separately. Once associated with the clan or family society, individuals will learn which of the several variations they wish to wear.

Every edition of **Tartan For Me!** attempts to keep this list current. These are the clan or family tartans known to the author as of September, 1994.

An asterisk (*) Indicates that the tartan may be restricted and not for general use.

1 Abercrombie	32 Black	63 Campbell of Glen Lyon
2 Agnew	33 Blackstock	64 Campbell of Loch Awe
3 Ainslie	34 Blair	65 Campbell of Loch Nell
4 Akins	35 Blue	66 Campbell of Loudon
5 Alexander	36 Bonnar	67 Carmichael
6 Allison	37 Borthwick	68 Carnegie
7 Anderson	38 Bowie	69 Casely
8 Anderson of Kinneddar*	39 Boyd	70 Cathcart
9 Arbuthnot	40 Brodie	71 Cheape
10 Armstrong	41 Bronte	72 Childers
11 Arrol	42 Brooke	73 Chisholm
12 Asman	43 Brough	74 Christie
13 Atlin	44 Brown	75 Clan Chattan
14 Austin	45 Bruce	76 Clan Cian (Carroll)
15 Ayrton	46 Bruce of Kinnaird	77 Clark/Clerk
16 Baillie	47 Bryce	78 Clarke of Ulva
17 Baillie of Lamington	48 Buchanan	79 Clayton
18 Baillie of Polkmet	49 Buckleigh	80 Cleland
19 Baird	50 Buie	81 Cochrane
20 Baker	51 Bullman	82 Cockburn
21 Balfour	52 Burnett	83 Colquhoun
22 Barclay	53 Burnett of Leys	84 Connel
23 Baxter	54 Burns	85 Conner
24 Beaton	55 Callum	86 Conroy
25 Beaverbrook	56 Cameron	87 Cooper
26 Bell (of Clan MacMillan)	57 Cameron of Locheil	88 Cowan
27 Bell (of the Borders)	58 Campbell	89 Cowper
28 Bethune	59 Campbell of Argyll	90 Craig
29 Birral/Burrell	60 Campbell of Braemar	91 Craigmoor
30 Birse	61 Campbell of Breadalbane	92 Craik
31 Bissett	62 Campbell of Cawdor	93 Crail

94 Cranstock	146 Forsyth	198 Hogarth
95 Cranstoun	147 Foster	199 Hogg
96 Crawford	148 Frame	200 Home
97 Cree	149 Fraser	201 Hope-Vere
98 Crosser	150 Fraser of Altyre	202 Hopetoun
99 Cruickshank	151 Fraser of Lovat	203 Hudson
100 Cumming	152 Fullerton	204 Hunnisett*
101 Cunningham	153 Galbraith	205 Hunter
102 Currie	154 Galt	206 Hunter of Bute
103 Currow	155 Gammell	207 Hunter of Hunterston
104 Dalglish	156 Gary*	208 Hurd
105 Dallas	157 Gayre	209 Hynde
106 Dalmany	158 Geddes	210 Hyndman
107 Dalrymple	159 Gemmall	211 Ikleman
108 Dalzell	160 Gibbs/Gibson	212 Inches
109 Davidson	161 Gillespie	213 Inglis
110 Davidson of Tulloch	162 Gillies	214 Innes
111 Deas	163 Gillis	215 Innes of Cowie
112 Denholme	164 Gladstone	216 Irvine
113 Denny	165 Gordon	217 Jardine
114 Dewar	166 Gordon of Abergeldy	218 Jardine of Castlemilk
115 Douglas	167 Gordon of Esselmont	219 Johnston(e)
116 Dowling	168 Gordon of Fyvie	220 Justice
117 Drennan	169 Gow	221 Justus
118 Drummond	170 Grady	222 Keeper
119 Drummond of Logie	171 Graham of Mentieth	223 Keirnan
120 Drummond of Perth	172 Graham of Montrose	224 Keith
121 Drummond of Strathallan	173 Grant	225 Kennedy
122 Dunbar	174 Gray	226 Kennedy (Irish)
123 Duncan	175 Greer	227 Kennison
124 Dundas	176 Gunn	228 Kerr
125 Dunlop	177 Guthrie	229 Kidd
126 Dyce	178 Hackston	230 Kiernan
127 Elliot	179 Haig	231 Kierson
128 Elphinstone	180 Hall	232 Kilburnie
129 Engleheart	181 Hallingdale	233 Kilgour
130 Erskine	182 Hamilton	234 Kincaid
131 Estes	183 Hamilton of Brandon	235 Kinnison
132 Farquharson	184 Hamilton of Clayton	236 Kinnoull
133 Ferguson	185 Hannay/Hannah	237 Kinross
134 Ferguson of Balquhidder	186 Harkness	238 Kyle/Kile
135 Ferguson of Atholl	187 Harvey	239 Lamont
136 Fiddes	188 Harvie	240 Lauder
137 Finnegan	189 Hay	241 Leakie
138 Fitzgerald	190 Hayes	242 Leask
139 Fitzpatrick	191 Henderson	243 Ledford
140 Fletcher	192 Henry	244 Lee
141 Fletcher of Dunans	193 Hepburn	245 Leighton
142 Forbes	194 Herbage of Laggan	246 Leith
143 Forbes of Druminnor	195 Herd	247 Lendrum
144 Forde	196 Heslop	248 Lennie
145 Forrester	197 Hodgkinson	249 Leonard
		250 Leslie

251 Lindsay	302 MacDonald of Loch Maddy	353 MacLean of Duart
252 Little	303 MacDonald of Sleat	354 MacLean of Kingairloch*
253 Livingstone	304 MacDonald of Staffa	355 MacLeay
254 Lloyd	305 MacDonald of the Isles	356 MacLeish
255 Lobban	306 MacDonell of Glengarry	357 MacLellen/MacClellen
256 Logan	307 MacDougall	358 MacLennan
257 Longmount	308 MacDuff	359 MacLeod
258 Louden/Loudoun	309 MacEachain	360 MacLeod of Assynt
259 Lumsden	310 MacEdward	361 MacLeod of Gesto
260 Lumsden of Kintore	311 MacEwen	362 MacLeod of Raasay
261 Lynch	312 MacFadyen/MacFadden	363 MacLeod of Skye
262 Mac Gaughan	313 MacFadzean	364 MacLoughlin
263 MacAart*	314 MacFarlane	365 MacLulich
264 MacAlister	315 MacFie	366 MacMaster
265 MacAlister of Glenbarr	316 MacGill	367 MacMichael
266 MacAlpine	317 MacGillivray	368 MacMillan
267 MacAn	318 MacGlashan	369 MacNab
268 MacArthur	319 MacGowan	370 MacNaughten
269 MacAskill	320 MacGregor	371 MacNeil
270 MacAulay	321 MacGregor of Balquhidder	372 MacNeil of Barra
271 MacBain	322 MacGregor of Cardney	373 MacNeil of Gigha & Colonsay
272 MacBean	323 MacGregor of Deeside	374 MacNiven
273 MacBeth	324 MacGregor of Glen Strae	375 MacOrrell
274 MacBride	325 MacGregor of Glenlyle	376 MacPhail
275 MacBrier	326 MacGregor, Rob Roy	377 MacPhedran
276 MacByrd	327 MacGuire	378 MacPherson
277 MacCallum	328 MacHardie	379 MacPherson of Pitmain
278 MacCallum of Berwick	329 MacInery	380 MacQuarrie
279 MacCandlish	330 MacInnes	381 MacQueen
280 MacCanish	331 MacInroy	382 MacRae
281 MacCaughan	332 MacInroy of Lude	383 MacRae of Conchra
282 MacClintock	333 MacIntyre	384 MacRae of Inverinate
283 MacClure	334 MacIntyre of Glenorchy	385 MacRea
284 MacColl	335 MacIver	386 MacRory
285 MacConnell	336 MacKay	387 MacRurie
286 MacCorqudale	337 MacKay of Strathnaver	388 MacSheehy
287 MacCoul	338 MacKean	389 MacSporran
288 MacCraig	339 MacKeller	390 MacStrumer
289 MacCullough	340 MacKendrick	391 MacTaggart
290 MacCullough	341 MacKenzie	392 MacTavish
291 MacDay	342 MacKerral	393 MacThomas
292 MacDermaid	343 MacKillop	394 MacTier
293 MacDona/MacDonough	344 MacKinlay	395 MacWhirter
294 MacDonald	345 MacKinnon	396 MacWilliam
295 MacDonald of Ardnamurchan	346 MacKirdy	397 Mackintosh
296 MacDonald of Boisdale	347 MacLachlan	398 Mair
297 MacDonald of Clanranald	348 MacLaggan	399 Maitland*
298 MacDonald of Glenaladale	349 MacLaine of Lochbuie	400 Malcolm
299 MacDonald of Glencoe	350 MacLaren	401 Manson
300 MacDonald of Keppoch	351 MacLaurin	402 Mar Tribe
301 MacDonald of Kingsburgh	352 MacLean	403 Marshall
		404 Martin

405	Matheson	457	Penman	509	Stewart of Urrand
406	Maxton	458	Pitcairn	510	Stinson
407	Maxwell	459	Platt	511	Stuart of Bute
408	Melville	460	Pollock	512	Sturrock
409	Menzies	461	Porteous	513	Sutherland
410	Merrilees	462	Rae/Ray	514	Swan
411	Metcalf	463	Raeburn	515	Taylor
412	Middleton	464	Raibert	516	Teall
413	Milne*	465	Ramsay	517	Tennant
414	Minnick	466	Rankin	518	Thain
415	Mitchell	467	Rattray	519	Thompson
416	Moffat	468	Reid	520	Turnberry
417	Moncrieffe	469	Rennie	521	Turnbull
418	Montgomery	470	Renwick	522	Tyndrum
419	Montmorency	471	Ritchie	523	Urquhart
420	Montrose	472	Robbins/Robinson	524	Vipont
421	Moran*	473	Robertson	525	Waggerall
422	Mordente	474	Robertson of Kindeace	526	Walker
423	Morgan	475	Rollo	527	Wallace
424	Morris	476	Rose	528	Wallace of Dundee
425	Morrison	477	Ross	529	Watson
426	Mowat	478	Rowan	530	Weir
427	Mowbray	479	Russell	531	Wellington
428	Muir	480	Rust	532	Wemyss
429	Mulholland	481	Ruthven	533	Westergaard*
430	Munro	482	Sawyer	534	Whitson
431	Murdoch	483	Scott	535	Williams
432	Murphy ("Tara")	484	Scrymegeour	536	Wilson
433	Murray	485	Selkirk	537	Wisehart
434	Murray of Abercairney	486	Sellar/Siller	538	Witherspoon
435	Murray of Atholl	487	Service	539	Young
436	Murray of Elibank	488	Seton		
437	Murray of Tulibardine	489	Shaw		
438	Myron	490	Shaw of Tordarroch		
439	Nairn	491	Simpson (Campbell-Simpson)		
440	Napier	492	Sinclair		
441	Newlands	493	Skene		
442	Nicholson/MacNichol	494	Smeaton		
443	Nisbet	495	Smith		
444	O'Farrel	496	Snodgrass		
445	O'Keefe	497	Somerville		
446	O'Neil	498	Spencer		
447	Ochiltree	499	Spens		
448	Ochterlonie*	500	Stephenson		
449	Ogilvie	501	Stevenson		
450	Ogilvie of Skye	502	Stewart (Clan)		
451	Oliphant	503	Stewart of Appin		
452	Oliver	504	Stewart of Ardshiel		
453	Paget	505	Stewart of Atholl		
454	Parr	506	Stewart of Fingask		
455	Paten	507	Stewart of Galloway		
456	Pearson	508	Stewart of Rothesay		

APPROXIMATE LOCATIONS OF SOME MAJOR CLANS AND FAMILIES

26

THE NAME-TARTAN LIST

NOTA BENE: Since there are often several entries for a name, be sure to check for the continuation of a name at the top of a following column or on the following page.

NAME	TARTAN	NAME	TARTAN
		ACHINFOUR	GALLOWAY DIST
		ACHINS	GORDON
A		ACHINWALL	EDINBURGH DIST
		ACHLES	ST. ANDREWS DIST
		ACHLOCH	ANGUS DIST
		ACHMOUR	GLASGOW DIST
AB(B)E	MAC NAB	ACHMUT(T)IE,-Y	FIFE DIST
AB(B)OT(T)	MAC NAB	ACHNACH	STRATHSPEY DIST
ABBEY	MAC NAB	ACKINHEVIE,-Y	PERTHSHIRE DIST
ABBIE,-Y	MAC NAB	ACKL(E)Y	INVERNESS DIST
ABBOTSON	MAC NAB	ACKLIES	INVERNESS DIST
ABBOTTOUN	ST. ANDREWS DIST	ACKROYD	ST. ANDREWS DIST
ABE	MAC NAB	ACKWAITH	ABERDEEN DIST
ABEL(L)	GALLOWAY DIST	ACKWARCHIE,-Y	ABERDEEN DIST
ABER	ABERDEEN DIST	ACLAND	ST. ANDREWS DIST
ABERACH	MAC KAY	ACOCK	ANGUS DIST
ABERCHIRDER	HUNTLY DIST	ACREE	INVERNESS DIST
ABERCORN	EDINBURGH DIST	ACTON	INVERNESS DIST
ABERCROMBIE,-Y	ABERCROMBIE	ACUFF	ROXBURGH DIST
ABERDALGIE,-(E)Y	PERTHSHIRE DIST	ACULTAN(E)	GALLOWAY DIST
ABERDEEN,-ENE	ABERDEEN DIST	AD(D)IE,-Y	GORDON
ABERDEIN,-INE	ABERDEEN DIST	AD(D)ISCOTT	PERTHSHIRE DIST
ABERDORE	FIFE DIST	AD(D)ISON	MAC DONALD
ABERDOUN	FIFE DIST	ADAIR	MAXWELL
ABERIGH	LOCHABER DIST	ADAM(S)	GORDON
ABERKIRDER	HUNTLY DIST	ADAM(S)	HUNTLY DIST
ABERLADY	DUNBAR DIST	ADAMISTON(E)	GORDON
ABERNATHY	FRASER	ADAMSON	GORDON
ABERNATHY	LESLIE	ADAMSON	HUNTLY DIST
ABERNETHY,-IE	FRASER	ADAMSON	MACKINTOSH
ABERNETHY,-IE	LESLIE	ADAN	ABERDEEN DIST
ABERNYTE,-IGHT	FIFE DIST	ADDISON	GORDON
ABLE	GALLOWAY DIST	ADEN	ABERDEEN DIST
ABRACH	LOCHABER DIST	ADERSON(E)	EDINBURGH DIST
ABRACH	MAC KAY	ADIE	GORDON
ABRAHAM	STRATHEARN DIST	ADIELL	ABERDEEN DIST
ABRAHAMSON	PERTHSHIRE DIST	ADINSTON	HEPBURN
ABRAM	STRATHEARN DIST	ADMISTON	GALA WATER DIST
ABRICK	LOCHABER DIST	ADNAUCHTAN	FIFE DIST
ABROCH	LOCHABER DIST	ADOLIE,-Y	EDINBURGH DIST
ABSOLON,-M	ROXBURGH DIST	ADOUGAN	GALLOWAY DIST
ABURDENE	ABERDEEN DIST	ADOWELL	CARRICK DIST
ACCO	EDINBURGH DIST	ADUNNALE	PAISLEY DIST
ACH	MAC ALPINE	ADZELL	LESLIE
ACHESON	GORDON	AF(F)EX	ANGUS DIST
ACHESON	HUNTLY DIST	AFFLECK	LINDSAY
ACHILD	TYNESIDE DIST	AFRIN	FT. WILLIAM DIST
ACHINCLOCH,-ACH	PAISLEY DIST	AGAR	STRATHSPEY DIST
ACHINDACHY,-IE	KEITH	AGATE	ABERDEEN DIST

27

NAME	TARTAN	NAME	TARTAN
AGGEY,-IE	PAISLEY DIST	ALDOWIE,-Y	MAC LEAN OF DUART
AGLIE,-Y	DUNDEE DIST	ALDOWNIE,-Y	CAMERON
AGNEW	AGNEW	ALDOWNIE,-Y	LAMONT
AGNEW	DOUGLAS	ALDOWNIE,-Y	MAC GREGOR
AHANNAY	HANNA	ALDOWNIE,-Y	MAC LEAN OF DUART
AICHMAN	ANGUS DIST	ALDRED	ROXBURGH DIST
AICHNACH	ABERDEEN DIST	ALDRICH	STRATHCLYDE DIST
AIDIE,-Y	FERGUSON	ALDYO(U)	ANGUS DIST
AIDIE,-Y	GORDON	ALEESE	STEWART OF APPIN
AIDNIE,-Y	GORDON	ALEHOUSE	ABERDEEN DIST
AIKEN(S)	GORDON	ALEX	INVERNESS DIST
AIKENHEAD	STRATHCLYDE DIST	ALEXANDER	ALEX. OF KILCONQUHAR
AIKERS	STRATHCLYDE DIST	ALEXANDER	MAC ALISTER
AIKMAN	STRATHCLYDE DIST	ALEXANDER	MAC DONALD
AILILL	DALZELL	ALEXANDER	MAC DONELL GLENGARRY
AILMER	ROXBURGH DIST	ALEXANDERSON	ABERDEEN DIST
AIMER	DUNDEE DIST	ALEXSONE	MAR DIST
AIMERLAND	PERTHSHIRE DIST	ALFORD	ABERDEEN DIST
AINLIE,-Y	AINSLIE	ALFRED	ST. ANDREWS DIST
AIR	ANGUS DIST	ALGEO	PAISLEY DIST
AIRD	AYRSHIRE DIST	ALGIE,-Y	PERTHSHIRE DIST
AIRDS	GALLOWAY DIST	ALICE	DUNBLANE DIST
AIRIE	GALLOWAY DIST	ALICESON(E)	TWEEDSIDE DIST
AIRLAND	GALLOWAY DIST	ALIDIEL	DALZELL
AIRLIE,-EY	OGILVIE	ALIE	EDINBURGH DIST
AIRNES	GALLOWAY DIST	ALISEN	ALLISON
AIRRES	TWEEDSIDE DIST	ALISON	ALLISON
AIRTH	GRAHAM	ALISON	GRANT
AIRTH	MENTIETH DIST	ALISON	MAC ALISTER
AISDAILL	EGLINTON DIST	ALISON	MAC DONALD
AITCHISON	GORDON	ALISON	MAC FARLANE
AITH	INVERNESS DIST	ALISS	DUNBLANE DIST
AITKENHEAD	STRATHCLYDE DIST	ALISTAIR	MAC ALISTER
AITKENS,-INS	GORDON	ALISTAIR	MAC DONALD
AITKENS,-INS	HUNTLY DIST	ALISTAIR	MAC DONELL GLENGARRY
AITON,-TOUN	HOME	ALISTER	MAC ALISTER
AITOWN	HOME	ALIX	INVERNESS DIST
AKERS	DUNDEE DIST	ALLAN	GRANT
AKINS	AKINS	ALLAN	MAC DONALD
AKINSTALL	EDINBURGH DIST	ALLAN	MAC FARLANE
ALANE	DUNBLANE DIST	ALLAN	MAC KAY
ALARD	ANGUS DIST	ALLANACH	GRANT
ALASTAIR	MAC ALISTER	ALLANACH	MAC FARLANE
ALBA	ANGUS DIST	ALLANACH	STEWART OF ATHOLL
ALBAIN	MAC ALPINE	ALLANSHAW	EDINBURGH DIST
ALBANACH	MAC ALPINE	ALLANSON	ABERDEEN DIST
ALBERT	DUNDEE DIST	ALLARDYCE,-ICE	GRAHAM
ALBIN	MAC ALPINE	ALLASON	ALLISON
ALBORN(E)	FIFE DIST	ALLASON	GRANT
ALBOURNE	FIFE DIST	ALLASON	MAC DONALD
ALBURN	FIFE DIST	ALLASON	MAC FARLANE
ALCOCK	GRANT	ALLASON	MAC PHERSON
ALCOCK	MAC DON CLANRANALD	ALLATHAN	ABERDEEN DIST
ALCORN	ANGUS DIST	ALLAWAY	CARRICK DIST
ALDAN	STRATHCLYDE DIST	ALLEIS	ABERDEEN DIST
ALDANSTO(U)N	GALLOWAY DIST	ALLEN	GRANT
ALDEN	STRATHCLYDE DIST	ALLEN	MAC DONALD
ALDERSTOUN	HAY	ALLEN	MAC FARLANE
ALDIE	STRATHEARN DIST	ALLEN	MAC KAY
ALDINSTOUN	GALLOWAY DIST	ALLENBY	GALLOWAY DIST
ALDIS	PAISLEY DIST	ALLERDYCE	GRAHAM
ALDJO	ANGUS DIST	ALLGATE	ROXBURGH DIST
ALDOCH	EDINBURGH DIST	ALLHUSEN	INVERNESS DIST
ALDOWIE,-Y	CAMERON	ALLIARD	ANGUS DIST
ALDOWIE,-Y	LAMONT	ALLINGHAM	INVERNESS DIST
ALDOWIE,-Y	MAC GREGOR	ALLISEN	ALLISON

NAME	TARTAN	NAME	TARTAN
ALLISON	ALLISON	ANNANDALE	GALLOWAY DIST
ALLISON	GRANT	ANNAT	INVERNESS DIST
ALLISON	MAC DONALD	ANNECOMBE	ROXBURGH DIST
ALLISON	MAC FARLANE	ANNISTON	STRATHCLYDE DIST
ALLISON	MAC PHERSON	ANSDELL	TYNESIDE DIST
ALLISTER	MAC ALISTER	ANSON	FIFE DIST
ALLISTER	MAC DONALD	ANSTIE,-Y	INVERNESS DIST
ALLISTER	MAC DONELL GLENGARRY	ANSTRUTHER	FIFE DIST
ALLMAN	TWEEDSIDE DIST	ANTHONY	ST. ANDREWS DIST
ALLOWAY	CARRICK DIST	ANTON	ABERDEEN DIST
ALLPHIN	MAC ALPINE	APLINDENE	NITHSDALE DIST
ALLUM	MALCOLM	APPEL	INVERNESS DIST
ALLY (Irish)	CLAN CIAN	APPLE	EDINBURGH DIST
ALMAN	TWEEDSIDE DIST	APPLEBY,-IE	EDINBURGH DIST
ALMER	GALLOWAY DIST	APPLEGARTH	GALLOWAY DIST
ALMON	TWEEDSIDE DIST	APPLETON	NITHSDALE DIST
ALMOND	CRIEFF DIST	ARBECKIE	ANGUS DIST
ALONKS	MAC DONALD KINGSBURGH	ARBIGLAND	GALLOWAY DIST
ALPIN(E)	MAC ALPINE	ARBLASTER	EDINBURGH DIST
ALROUNIE,-Y	ABERDEEN DIST	ARBROATH	ANGUS DIST
ALSOP	ABERDEEN DIST	ARBUCKLE	ANGUS DIST
ALSTEN	STRATHEARN DIST	ARBUTHNOT	ARBUTHNOT
ALSTON	ROXBURGH DIST	ARCHBELL	MAC PHERSON
ALTON	ROXBURGH DIST	ARCHBOLD	MAC PHERSON
ALTRILLIE,-Y	INVERNESS DIST	ARCHER	ANGUS DIST
ALUERTON,-UN	PERTHSHIRE DIST	ARCHES	GLASGOW DIST
ALVA(H)	STIRLING DIST	ARCHIBALD	MAC PHERSON
ALVES	INVERNESS DIST	ARCHIBALDSON	MAC PHERSON
ALWART	CALEDONIA TARTAN	ARCHIE	MAC PHERSON
ALWAY	LYONS	ARCHIESON	MAC PHERSON
ALWETH	STIRLING DIST	ARCHMORE,-OUR	GLASGOW DIST
ALWIN	LENNOX DIST	ARD	INVERNESS DIST
ALWOOD	TYNESIDE DIST	ARDA(U)CH	GALLOWAY DIST
ALWYN	LENNOX DIST	ARDERNE	ST. ANDREWS DIST
ALYE	EDINBURGH DIST	ARDES	GRAHAM
ALYNTON	GALA WATER DIST	ARDINCAPLE	LENNOX DIST
ALYTH	PERTHSHIRE DIST	ARDIST	FIFE DIST
AMBLER	ROXBURGH DIST	ARDLER	ANGUS DIST
AMBROSE	STRATHCLYDE DIST	ARDOCK	GALLOWAY DIST
AMISFIELD	GALLOWAY DIST	ARDROSS	FIFE DIST
AMOUR(S)	FIFE DIST	ARDROSSAN	BARCLAY
ANALYN	DUNDEE DIST	ARDSO(U)N	CLAN CHATTAN
ANAND	NITHSDALE DIST	ARDSO(U)N	MAC HARDIE
ANCROFT	DUNBAR DIST	ARDUTHIE,-Y	FIFE DIST
ANCRUM	GLASGOW DIST	ARGENT	EDINBURGH DIST
ANDERSON	ANDERSON	ARGO	ABERDEEN DIST
ANDERSON	ANDERSON KILCONQUHAR	ARICARI	ABERDEEN DIST
ANDERSON	MAC DONALD	ARIES	GALLOWAY DIST
ANDERSON	ROSS	ARKIN	GALLOWAY DIST
ANDIE	ANDERSON	ARKLAY	ANGUS DIST
ANDIRSTON	ANDERSON	ARKLE	GALLOWAY DIST
ANDISON	ANDERSON	ARKLE	ROXBURGH DIST
ANDISON	ROSS	ARKLEY	ANGUS DIST
ANDREW(S)	ROSS	ARMALIE,-Y	CREIFF DIST
ANDREWSON	ANDERSON	ARMIT(T)	DUNBLANE DIST
ANDSON	FIFE DIST	ARMO(U)R	ANGUS DIST
ANEWITH	ROXBURGH DIST	ARMSTRANGE	ARMSTRONG
ANGUS	ANGUS DIST	ARMSTRONG	ARMSTRONG
ANGUS	MAC INNES	ARNEIL	GLASGOW DIST
ANGUSSON	MAC INNES	ARNOLD	GALLOWAY DIST
ANISO(U)N	GALLOWAY DIST	ARNOT(T)	AYRSHIRE DIST
ANKERS	DUNDEE DIST	ARNOT(T)	FIFE DIST
ANKRET	ABERDEEN DIST	ARNOULD	GALLOWAY DIST
ANNA	HANNA		
ANNAL(L)	FIFE DIST		
ANNAN(D)	NITHSDALE DIST		

29

NAME	TARTAN	NAME	TARTAN
ARRANTHREW	PAISLEY DIST	AUCHINVOLE	EDINBURGH DIST
ARRAT	ANGUS DIST	AUCHNIEVE	ABERDEEN DIST
ARRELL	HAY	AUCHTER	PERTHSHIRE DIST
ARROL(L)	ARROL	AUCHTER	STRATHEARN DIST
ARROL(L)	HAY	AUCHTERARDER	PERTHSHIRE DIST
ARROWSMITH	MAC GREGOR	AUCHTERBARNE	ABERDEEN DIST
ARSIL	ABERDEEN DIST	AUCHTERLONIE,-Y	ANGUS DIST
ARSIL	ANGUS DIST	AUCHTERLONIE,-Y	OCHTERLONIE
ARTHUR	CAMPBELL	AUCHTERMONIE	EDINBURGH DIST
ARTHUR	MAC ARTHUR	AUE	HAY
ARTHURLEE	PAISLEY DIST	AUFRAYS	INVERNESS DIST
ARTHURSON	MAC ARTHUR	AUGHMUTY,-IE	FIFE DIST
ARTLIE,-Y	PERTHSHIRE DIST	AUGIE	INVERNESS DIST
ARTO(W)N	ANGUS DIST	AULAY	MAC AULAY
ASH	DUNDEE DIST	AULAY	MAC LEOD
ASHBRIDGE	STIRLING DIST	AULD	PERTHSHIRE DIST
ASHBY	EDINBURGH DIST	AULDJO	ANGUS DIST
ASHCROFT	FIFE DIST	AULDJO	EDINBURGH DIST
ASHER	INVERNESS DIST	AULDMILL	EDINBURGH DIST
ASHFORD	DUNDEE DIST	AULDOCH,-TH	EDINBURGH DIST
ASHKIRK	GLASGOW DIST	AULDSON	FIFE DIST
ASHTON	FIFE DIST	AULDTON	ROXBURGH DIST
ASHWORTH	CREIFF DIST	AULICH	ATHOLL DIST
ASKALO(K)	GALLOWAY DIST	AULNOY	GLASGOW DIST
ASKBIE,-Y	DUNBAR DIST	AULT	PERTHSHIRE DIST
ASKEBY	DUNBAR DIST	AUMBLER	ROXBURGH DIST
ASKHAM	INVERNESS DIST	AUSTEN	KEITH
ASKIE,-EY	MAC ASKILL	AUSTIE	KEITH
ASKIE,-EY	MAC LEOD	AUSTIN	KEITH
ASKING	MAC ASKILL	AUTRAY	ANGUS DIST
ASKING	MAC LEOD	AUTRIE,-Y	ANGUS DIST
ASMAN	ASMAN	AVEN	FIFE DIST
ASPINALL	DUNDEE DIST	AVENER	DUNBLANE DIST
ASPLEN,-IN	STIRLING DIST	AVERY	EDINBURGH DIST
ASTIE	GALLOWAY DIST	AWELL	ANGUS DIST
ASTINE	KEITH	AWLOCH(E)	ATHOLL DIST
ASTON	KEITH	AXON	PAISLEY DIST
ATCHESON	GORDON	AY	HAY
ATHERAY	STIRLING DIST	AYCOCK	ANGUS DIST
ATHERSTONE	FIFE DIST	AYE	CLAN CHATTAN
ATHERTON	FIFE DIST	AYE	MAC BAIN
ATHOLL	MURRAY OF ATHOLL	AYER(S)	HAY
ATHOLL	ROBERTSON	AYLEBET,-OT	PERTHSHIRE DIST
ATHOLL	STEWART OF ATHOLL	AYLIES	HUNTLY DIST
ATKINS	GORDON	AYR(E)	ANGUS DIST
ATKINS	HUNTLY DIST	AYR(E)	AYRSHIRE DIST
ATKINS(S)ON	GORDON	AYRE(S)	TWEEDSIDE DIST
ATKINS(S)ON	HUNTLY DIST	AYRTON	AYRTON
ATLIN	ATLIN	AYSON	MAC KAY
AUCHAN(E)SON	CARRICK DIST	AYSON	MACKINTOSH
AUCHENBRUCK	STRATHSPEY DIST	AYSTON	MACKINTOSH
AUCHENCRAW	TWEEDSIDE DIST	AYTO(U)N	HOME
AUCHENLECK	LINDSAY		
AUCHIE	STIRLING DIST		
AUCHILTREE	OCHILTREE		
AUCHILTREE	STEWART		
AUCHINACHIE,-Y	ABERDEEN DIST		

B

NAME	TARTAN
AUCHINCLOSS	AYRSHIRE DIST
AUCHINHOVE	ABERDEEN DIST	BA(A)D	STIRLING DIST
AUCHINLEEK	LINDSAY	BACHOP(E)	GALLOWAY DIST
AUCHINLOCKY	GRAHAM	BACK	STIRLING DIST
AUCHINMA(I)D(E)	EGLINTON DIST	BACKIE(S)	CAITHNESS TARTAN
AUCHINROSS	LENNOX DIST	BACKUP	GALLOWAY DIST
AUCHINTORE,-URE	PAISLEY DIST	BACKY(S)	CAITHNESS TARTAN
AUCHINTOUR	PAISLEY DIST	BAD	STIRLING DIST
AUCHINVALE	EDINBURGH DIST	BAD(D)IE,-Y	ABERDEEN DIST
		BAD(D)LIE,-Y	ROXBURGH DIST
		BADBAE	SUTHERLAND DIST

NAME	TARTAN	NAME	TARTAN
BADD(E)LIE,-Y	ABERDEEN DIST	BALDRED	BISSET
BADDEN	ARGYLL DIST	BALDRO	ANGUS DIST
BADDENACH	MAC PHERSON	BALDSON	MAC PHERSON
BADDENOCH	CUMMING	BALDWIN	GALLOWAY DIST
		BALDY	MAC PHERSON
BADDILIE,-Y	ROXBURGH DIST	BALE	BELL
BADDIN	ARGYLL DIST	BALE(S)	BELL of the Borders
BADE	STIRLING DIST	BALE(S)	MAC MILLAN
BADENACH	MAC PHERSON	BALERNO	EDINBURGH DIST
BADENOCH	CUMMING	BALFOUR	BALFOUR
BADENOCH	LAGGAN DIST	BALFOUR	FIFE DIST
BADENOCH	MAC PHERSON	BALGAIK	GALBRAITH
BADGER	GALLOWAY DIST	BALGARVIE,-Y	FIFE DIST
BADICHIEL	HUNTLY DIST	BALGONIE,-Y	ABERDEEN DIST
BADIE,-Y	ABERDEEN DIST	BALGREEN	PAISLEY DIST
BAER	EDINBURGH DIST	BALHARDIE,-Y	PERTHSHIRE DIST
BAGGAT(T)	ROXBURGH DIST	BALHARRIE,-Y	PERTHSHIRE DIST
BAGLEY	ULSTER TARTAN	BALINHARD	CARNEGIE
BAGNALL,-ELL	GLASGOW DIST	BALINMAN	PERTHSHIRE DIST
BAGRA	HAY	BALKENWALL	FIFE DIST
BAIKIE,-Y	ANGUS DIST	BALL	CAMERON
BAIL(L)(E)(S)	BELL	BALL	MACKINTOSH
BAIL(L)(E)(S)	BELL of the Borders	BALLACH	MAC DONALD
BAIL(L)(E)(S)	MAC MILLAN	BALLAGH	MAC DONALD
BAILDON	INVERNESS DIST	BALLANIE	EDINBURGH DIST
BAILEY	BAILLIE	BALLANTYNE,-INE	CAMPBELL
BAILLIE	BAILLIE	BALLANTYNE,-INE	STUART OF BUTE
BAILLIE	BAILLIE of POLKMET	BALLANWALL	FIFE DIST
BAIN(E)(S)	MAC BAIN	BALLANY	EDINBURGH DIST
BAIN(E)(S)	MAC KAY	BALLARD	ST. ANDREWS DIST
BAIR	BAIRD	BALLARDIE,-Y	FIFE DIST
BAIRD	BAIRD	BALLCANWALL	FIFE DIST
BAIRDEN	GALLOWAY DIST	BALLENIE,-Y	EDINBURGH DIST
BAIRDIE	BAIRD	BALLEW	ABERDEEN DIST
BAIRDON(E)	GALLOWAY DIST	BALLEWEN	GRAHAM
BAIRDY	BAIRD	BALLINDALLOCH	STRATHSPEY DIST
BAIRNER	GALLOWAY DIST	BALLINDINE,-YNE	STUART OF BUTE
BAIRNSFEATHER	DUNBAR DIST	BALLINGALL	FIFE DIST
BAIRNSFEATHER	FALKIRK DIST	BALLINGSHALL	FIFE DIST
BAIRNSON	MATHESON	BALLINTYNE,-INE	STUART OF BUTE
BAISLER	MUSSELBURGH DIST	BALLIOL	PAISLEY DIST
BAIT(S)	FIFE DIST	BALLOCH	MAC DONALD
BAITY	MAC BETH	BALMAHAY	FIFE DIST
BAITY	MAC DONALD	BALMAIN	ABERDEEN DIST
BAKER	BAKER	BALMAIN	ANGUS DIST
BAKEY	ANGUS DIST	BALMAKIN	FIFE DIST
BAKKER	BAKER	BALMANO	PERTHSHIRE DIST
BALBIRNIE,-Y	FIFE DIST	BALMARNO	PERTHSHIRE DIST
BALCAIRN,-IE,-Y	PERTHSHIRE DIST	BALMER	ROXBURGH DIST
BALCANQUALL	FIFE DIST	BALMOSSIE,-Y	ANGUS DIST
BALCANWELL	FIFE DIST	BALMYLE(S)	ANGUS DIST
BALCASKIE,-Y	FIFE DIST	BALNDENNIE,-Y	FIFE DIST
BALCATHIE,-Y	ANGUS DIST	BALNEAVES,-IS	MURRAY
BALCHRISTIE,-Y	MUSSELBURGH DIST	BALNEVIS	MURRAY
BALCHRO	ANGUS DIST	BALO(U)GH	MAC DONALD
BALCOMIE,-EY	FIFE DIST	BALQUHIDDER	MAC LAREN
BALCUMLIE,-Y	ABERDEEN DIST	BALQUHIDDER	STEWART
BALD	TWEEDSIDE DIST	BALRAM	FIFE DIST
BALDERNIE,-Y	ABERDEEN DIST	BALVAIRD	FIFE DIST
BALDERSTO(U)N	FALKIRK DIST	BALWEARIE,-Y	FIFE DIST
BALDIE	MAC PHERSON	BALWIDDER	STEWART
BALDISON	MAC PHERSON	BANE	MAC BAIN
BALDOWNIE,-Y	ANGUS DIST	BANE(S)	MAC KAY
BALDRA(I)NIE,-Y	EDINBURGH DIST	BANK(E)S	TWEEDSIDE DIST
		BANKER	STIRLING DIST
		BANKHEAD	AYRSHIRE DIST

NAME	TARTAN	NAME	TARTAN
BANNATIE,-Y	FIFE DIST	BASILLIE,-Y	FIFE DIST
BANNATYNE,-INE	CAMPBELL	BASKEN,-IN	BUCHAN DIST
BANNATYNE,-INE	STUART OF BUTE	BASSENDE(A)N	DUNBAR DIST
BANNER	CAMPBELL	BASTOW	INVERNESS DIST
BANNERMAN	FORBES	BATCHELOR	MUSSELBURGH DIST
BANNON	ULSTER TARTAN	BATCHELOR	TWEEDSIDE DIST
BAPTIE,-Y	TWEEDSIDE DIST	BATE(S)	MAC FARLANE
BARA	MAC NEIL	BATEY	MAC BETH
BARBER	MONTGOMERY	BATHGATE	ROXBURGH DIST
BARBOUR	MONTGOMERY	BATHLE	PERTHSHIRE DIST
BARCLAY	BARCLAY	BATTEN	ARGYLL DIST
BARCLET	BARCLAY	BATTLE	GALLOWAY DIST
BARD	BAIRD	BAUCHOP(E)	DUNBLANE DIST
BARDNARD	TYNESIDE DIST	BAWN(E)	MAC KAY
BARDNER	EDINBURGH DIST	BAXTER	BAXTER
BARENER	GALLOWAY DIST	BAXTER	MAC MILLAN
BARFOOT	PAISLEY DIST	BAY	MAC LEAN
BARGARNIE,-Y	DUNBAR DIST	BAYLES	BELL
BARGILL	GLASGOW DIST	BAYLES	BELL of the Borders
BARHAM	ABERDEEN DIST	BAYLES	MAC MILLAN
BARHILL	LENNOX DIST	BAYLOON	INVERNESS DIST
BARKER	STIRLING DIST	BAYN(E)(S)	MAC KAY
BARKLIE,-EY	BARCLAY	BAYNE(S)	MAC BAIN
BARLACK	STIRLING DIST	BAYSLER	MUSSELBURGH DIST
BARLAS(S)	PERTHSHIRE DIST	BEAGRIE,-Y	HAY
BARLET(T)	MAC FARLANE	BEAL(L)(S)	BELL
BARLOCH	STIRLING DIST	BEAL(L)(S)	BELL of the Borders
BARN(A)BIE,-Y	ROXBURGH DIST	BEAL(L)(S)	MAC MILLAN
BARNES	CAMPBELL	BEALLIE,-Y	MAC GREGOR
BARNET(T)	BURNETT	BEAM(E)	MAC BAIN
BARNETSON	CAITHNESS TARTAN	BEANSTO(U)N	DUNBAR DIST
BARNIE,-Y	CAITHNESS TARTAN	BEARD	BAIRD
BARNIESON	CAITHNESS TARTAN	BEATH	MAC BETH
BARNS	CAMPBELL	BEATH	MAC DONALD
BARNSDALE	ANGUS DIST	BEATON	BEATON
BARNSFEATHER	DUNBAR DIST	BEATON	MAC BETH
BARNSFEATHER	FALKIRK DIST	BEATON	MAC DONALD
BARNTON	MUSSELBURGH DIST	BEATON	MAC LEAN
BARNWELL	GALLOWAY DIST	BEATSON	MAC LAINE
BARON	ROSE	BEATTIE,-Y	MAC BETH
BARR	PAISLEY DIST	BEATTIE,-Y	MAC DONALD
BARRA	MAC NEIL	BEAUMONT	FIFE DIST
BARRACK	ABERDEEN DIST	BEAVERBROOK	BEAVERBROOK
BARRACLOUGH	BARCLAY	BEB(B)ER	EDINBURGH DIST
BARRAT(T)	ABERDEEN DIST	BECHER	INVERNESS DIST
BARRE	PAISLEY DIST	BECK	GALLOWAY DIST
BARRET	BURNETT	BECKETT	ROXBURGH DIST
BARRETT	CONNACHT TARTAN	BECKTON	GALLOWAY DIST
BARRIE,-Y	FARQUHARSON	BED(E)FORD	GLASGOW DIST
BARRIE,-Y	GORDON	BEDDIE,-Y	ANGUS DIST
BARRIE,-Y	HUNTLY DIST	BEDE	BUCHAN DIST
BARRON	ROSE	BEDSON	FIFE DIST
BARTELL	MAR DIST	BEE	ANGUS DIST
BARTH	MAC FARLANE	BEECHAM,-EM	LOCHABER DIST
BARTHOLOMEW	MAC FARLANE	BEECHER	LOCHABER DIST
BARTIE,-Y	MAC FARLANE	BEEDLES	ABERDEEN DIST
BARTILL	MAR DIST	BEEL(E)(S)	BELL
BARTL(E)Y	MAC FARLANE	BEEL(E)(S)	BELL of the Borders
BARTLAM	INVERNESS DIST	BEEL(E)(S)	MAC MILLAN
BARTLE	MAR DIST	BEEN	MAC BAIN
BARTLEMAN	EDINBURGH DIST	BEER	EDINBURGH DIST
BARTLET(T)	MAC FARLANE	BEESTON	EDINBURGH DIST
BARTLIE	MAC FARLANE	BEGBIE,-Y	ROXBURGH DIST
BARTON	PAISLEY DIST	BEGGS	DRUMMOND
BARTY	MAC FARLANE	BEGGS	ULSTER TARTAN
BASETT(E)	BISETT	BEGLEY	ULSTER TARTAN
BASETT(E)	GRANT	BEGLIE,-Y	CAITHNESS TARTAN

NAME	TARTAN	NAME	TARTAN
BEIGHTON	MAC LAINE	BETT	MAC BETH
BEIL(L)	BELL	BETT	MAC DONALD
BEIL(L)	BELL of the Borders	BETTON	MAC BETH
BEIL(L)	MAC MILLAN	BETTON	MAC DONALD
BELCHES	ROXBURGH DIST	BETTON	MAC LEAN
BELFORD	TWEEDSIDE DIST	BETTRIDGE	FT. WILLIAM DIST
BELFRAGE	FIFE DIST	BEVERIDGE	FIFE DIST
BELHELVIE,-Y	ABERDEEN DIST	BEVERLIE,-Y	TWEEDSIDE DIST
BELL	BELL	BEW(E)S	CAITHNESS TARTAN
BELL	MAC MILLAN	BEWICK	PAISLEY DIST
BELL (Borders)	BELL OF THE BORDERS	BEY	MAC LEAN
BELL (Borders)	DOUGLAS	BICHAM	LOCHABER DIST
BELLENDEN	SCOTT	BICHENO	STRATHSPEY DIST
BELLEW	ABERDEEN DIST	BICKERTON	ROXBURGH DIST
BELLHOUSE	GLASGOW DIST	BICKET(T)	GALA WATER DIST
BELLIE	ANGUS DIST	BIDDIE,-Y	ABERDEEN DIST
BELLIE,-Y	BELL	BIDIE	ABERDEEN DIST
BELLINGHAM	TYNESIDE DIST	BIDUN(E)	ROXBURGH DIST
BELLMAN	DUNBLANE DIST	BIE	ANGUS DIST
BELSHES	ROXBURGH DIST	BIGBIE,-EE,-Y	ROXBURGH DIST
BELTEN	DUNBAR DIST	BIGGAR(S)	STRATHCLYDE DIST
BELTIE	ABERDEEN DIST	BIGGART	PAISLEY DIST
BELTIN	DUNBAR DIST	BIGHAM	EDINBURGH DIST
BELTMAKER	EDINBURGH DIST	BIGLIE,-Y	EDINBURGH DIST
BELTON	DUNBAR DIST	BILE(S)	BELL
BELTY	ABERDEEN DIST	BILE(S)	BELL of the Borders
BEN(N)ISON	FIFE DIST	BILE(S)	MAC MILLAN
BENDLOW	ABERDEEN DIST	BILHAM	LOCHABER DIST
BENE	MAC BAIN	BILL(S)	BELL
BENEST	MAC KENZIE	BILL(S)	BELL of the Borders
BENHAM	MAR DIST	BILL(S)	MAC MILLAN
BENIGAN	EDINBURGH DIST	BILL(S)	STRATHCLYDE DIST
BENISTON(E)	FIFE DIST	BILLET	PERTHSHIRE DIST
BENNET(T)	ROXBURGH DIST	BILLHOPE	ROXBURGH DIST
BENNIE,-Y	MAC BAIN	BILLIE,-Y	TWEEDSIDE DIST
BENNOCH	GALLOWAY DIST	BILLSLAND	MONTGOMERY
BENSON	ROXBURGH DIST	BILSTON(E)	ARGYLL DIST
BENT	STRATHCLYDE DIST	BILSTUN(E)	ARGYLL DIST
BENTON	ABERDEEN DIST	BINGHAM	ULSTER TARTAN
BENVIE(S),-Y(S)	DUNDEE DIST	BINNIE,-Y	MAC BAIN
BENZIE(S),-Y(S)	ABERDEEN DIST	BINNING(S)	MAC BAIN
BER(E)FORD	FALKIRK DIST	BINNS	MAC BAIN
BERE	EDINBURGH DIST	BIRCH	EDINBURGH DIST
BERMINGHAM	CONNACHT TARTAN	BIRD	EDINBURGH DIST
BERNARD	CLAN CIAN	BIRKENSHAW	PAISLEY DIST
BERNARD	MURRAY	BIRKMEIR	GALLOWAY DIST
BERNARDSON	MURRAY	BIRKMYRE,-IRE	GALLOWAY DIST
BERNER	FIFE DIST	BIRNAM	PERTHSHIRE DIST
BERNHAM	TWEEDSIDE DIST	BIRNHAM	PERTHSHIRE DIST
BERNIE,-Y	MATHESON	BIRNIE,-EY	MATHESON
BERRIE,-Y	FORBES	BIRRAL(L)	BURRELL
BERRILL	FIFE DIST	BIRRELL	BURRELL
BERRY	EDINBURGH DIST	BIRSE	BIRSE
BERWICK	TWEEDSIDE DIST	BISCUT(T)	GLASGOW DIST
BEST	EDINBURGH DIST	BISER	FRASER
BET	MAC BETH	BISET(T)	GRANT
BET	MAC DONALD	BISHOP	INVERNESS DIST
BETAGH	GALLOWAY DIST	BISSET(T)	BISETT
BETH	MAC BETH	BISSET(T)	FRASER
BETH	MAC DONALD	BISSET(T)	GRANT
BETH	MAC LAINE	BISSIE,-Y	BISETT
BETHAIR	MAC BETH	BISSIE,-Y	FRASER
BETHEL(L)	INVERNESS DIST	BISSIE,-Y	GRANT
BETHUNE	BETHUNE	BLABER	ABERDEEN DIST
BETHUNE	MAC BETH	BLABIRN,-URN	FIFE DIST
BETHUNE	MAC DONALD		
BETHUNE	MAC LEOD		

NAME	TARTAN	NAME	TARTAN
BLACK	BLACK	BOA	GALA WATER DIST
BLACK	LAMONT	BOA	ROXBURGH DIST
BLACK	MAC GREGOR	BOAG	STIRLING DIST
BLACK	MAC LEAN	BOAL	ULSTER TARTAN
BLACKADDER	TWEEDSIDE DIST	BOARTY	ULSTER TARTAN
BLACKALL	ABERDEEN DIST	BOASE	INVERNESS DIST
BLACKBURN	TWEEDSIDE DIST	BOATH	ANGUS DIST
BLACKET(T)	GALLOWAY DIST	BODDEN	GALLOWAY DIST
BLACKFORD	MURRAY	BODDIE	ABERDEEN DIST
BLACKHALL	ABERDEEN DIST	BODELL	STRATHCLYDE DIST
BLACKIE	LAMONT	BODIE,-Y	ABERDEEN DIST
BLACKLAW	GALLOWAY DIST	BOE	TWEEDSIDE DIST
BLACKLIE,-EY	GALLOWAY DIST	BOG	TWEEDSIDE DIST
BLACKLOCK	GALLOWAY DIST	BOG(G)AN,-EN	ULSTER TARTAN
BLACKMAN	GALLOWAY DIST	BOGGS	EDINBURGH DIST
BLACKSHAW	GALLOWAY DIST	BOGIE	STRATHCLYDE DIST
BLACKSTOCK	BLACKSTOCK	BOGLE	FIFE DIST
BLACKSTOCK	DOUGLAS	BOGRIE,-Y	GALLOWAY DIST
BLACKSTOCK	MAXWELL	BOGUE	ULSTER TARTAN
BLACKSTONE	GALLOWAY DIST	BOHANON	BUCHANAN
BLACKSTONE	PAISLEY DIST	BOID(E)	BOYD
BLACKTON	EDINBURGH DIST	BOKE	STIRLING DIST
BLACKWATER	ABERDEEN DIST	BOL(L)AN	ARGYLL DIST
BLACKWOOD	DOUGLAS	BOL(L)EN,-IN	ARGYLL DIST
BLACKY	LAMONT	BOLAM	ROXBURGH DIST
BLAELOCK	DOUGLAS	BOLAND	CLAN CIAN
BLAIKIE,-Y	LAMONT	BOLD	GALA WATER DIST
BLAIN(E)	GALLOWAY DIST	BOLDON	LOCHABER DIST
BLAIR	BLAIR	BOLE(S)	ABERDEEN DIST
BLAIR	GRAHAM OF MENTIETH	BOLMAR,-ER	GLASGOW DIST
BLAIR (Irish)	CLAN CIAN	BOLT	GALA WATER DIST
BLAKE(Y)	LAMONT	BOLTON	EDINBURGH DIST
BLAKER	LAMONT	BONALLIE,-Y	EDINBURGH DIST
BLALOCK	DOUGLAS	BONAR	GRAHAM OF MONTROSE
BLALOCK	DOUGLAS	BONASS (Irish)	CLAN CIAN
BLAMIRE	GALLOWAY DIST	BONE	PAISLEY DIST
BLANCE	CALEDONIA TARTAN	BONE (Irish)	CLAN CIAN
BLANCHARD	ROXBURGH DIST	BONELLY	EDINBURGH DIST
BLANCHE	CALEDONIA TARTAN	BONHILL	GLASGOW DIST
BLANE	GALLOWAY DIST	BONK	INVERNESS DIST
BLANK(E)	CAITHNESS TARTAN	BONNAR	BONNER
BLANKIN	ANGUS DIST	BONNAR	GRAHAM OF MONTROSE
BLANTYRE	STRATHCLYDE DIST	BONNER	BONNER
BLAW	FIFE DIST	BONNER	GRAHAM OF MONTROSE
BLAWET(T)	CALEDONIA TARTAN	BONNIEVILLE	BUCHAN DIST
BLAYLOCK	DOUGLAS	BONNINGTON	FALKIRK DIST
BLEL(L)OCK	PERTHSHIRE DIST	BONNYMAN	ANGUS DIST
BLENKINSOP	TWEEDSIDE DIST	BONTHRON(E)	FIFE DIST
BLEW	BLUE	BONTIEN	GRAHAM OF MENTIETH
BLEW	MAC MILLAN	BONTINE	GRAHAM OF MENTIETH
BLEYLOCK	DOUGLAS	BONVILLE	BUCHAN DIST
BLIGH(E)	DUNDEE DIST	BOOG	STIRLING DIST
BLINDSELL,-EIL	ABERDEEN DIST	BOOK	FIFE DIST
BLOCKER	FALKIRK DIST	BOOKLESS	ROXBURGH DIST
BLOKKER	FALKIRK DIST	BOOSIE,-EY	FIFE DIST
BLOMFIELD	DUNDEE DIST	BOOTH	ABERDEEN DIST
BLOOD	CLAN CIAN	BOR(R)IE	PERTHSHIRE DIST
BLOW	FIFE DIST	BORHILL	STRATHCLYDE DIST
BLOWER	STRATHCLYDE DIST	BORLAND,-UND	PAISLEY DIST
BLUE	BLUE	BORRIE,-Y	PAISLEY DIST
BLUE(S)	MAC MILLAN	BORROWMAN	ANGUS DIST
BLUEFIELD	INVERNESS DIST	BORROWMAN	STIRLING DIST
BLUND,-T	ST. ANDREWS DIST	BORTHWICK	BORTHWICK
BLYTH(E)	TWEEDSIDE DIST	BOSTACK,-ICK	EDINBURGH DIST
BLYTHESWOOD	APPLECROSS DIST	BOSTON	ROXBURGH DIST
BLYTHMAN	CAMPBELL	BOSWALL,-ELL	TWEEDSIDE DIST

NAME	TARTAN	NAME	TARTAN
BOTH	ANGUS DIST	BRANDEN	ULSTER TARTAN
BOTHIE,-Y	ABERDEEN DIST	BRANDER	HUNTLY DIST
BOTHWELL	STRATHCLYDE DIST	BRANDIN,-ON	ST. ANDREWS DIST
BOUEY	GRANT	BRANIGAN	ULSTER TARTAN
BOUEY	MAC DONALD	BRANKIN	DUNDEE DIST
BOUND	MAR DIST	BRANNAN,-ON	DUNDEE DIST
BOURNE	CAMPBELL	BRANSON	GLASGOW DIST
BOUSIE,-Y	PERTHSHIRE DIST	BRANZEAN	DUNBLANE DIST
BOW(E)	STRATHEARN DIST	BRASH	STIRLING DIST
BOWDEN	TWEEDSIDE DIST	BRASS	ABERDEEN DIST
BOWEN	CLAN CIAN	BRATNEY,-IE	GALLOWAY DIST
BOWER(S)	MAC GREGOR	BRATTON	GALLOWAY DIST
BOWES	STRATHSPEY DIST	BRAUN(E)	BROWN
BOWICK	BORTHWICK	BRAY	ABERDEEN DIST
BOWIE	GRANT	BRAYDEN,-ON	GALLOWAY DIST
BOWIE	MAC DONALD	BRAYNE	ABERDEEN DIST
BOWIE	MAC LEAN	BREAD	ST. ANDREWS DIST
BOWIE (Mac Donald)	BOWIE	BREADING	ROTHESAY DIST
BOWLBIE,-Y	LOCHABER DIST	BREAKENRIG	ARGYLL DIST
BOWMAKER	MAC GREGOR	BREAKHAUGH	INVERNESS DIST
BOWMAN	FARQUHARSON	BREAKHAWK	INVERNESS DIST
BOWSIE,-Y	FIFE DIST	BREAKIE,-Y	INVERNESS DIST
BOY	FORBES	BREBNER	FARQUHARSON
BOYACK	DUNDEE DIST	BRECHIN	ANGUS DIST
BOYCE	FORBES	BRECK	GALLOWAY DIST
BOYD	BOYD	BRECKINRIDGE	ARGYLL DIST
BOYD	STEWART	BRECKINRIDGE	STRATHCLYDE DIST
BOYDEN	ROXBURGH DIST	BRECKLIE,-EY	BARCLAY
BOYE(S)	FORBES	BREE	DUNDEE DIST
BOYLAN(D)	ULSTER TARTAN	BREEDEN	DUNDEE DIST
BOYLE	GALLOWAY DIST	BREEN	DUNDEE DIST
BOYLE	ULSTER TARTAN	BREMNER	ABERDEEN DIST
BOYMAN	BOYD	BREMNER	PAISLEY DIST
BOYNE	BUCHAN DIST	BREN(N)AN,-EN	CONNACHT TARTAN
BOYSE	FORBES	BRENDON	ULSTER TARTAN
BOYT(E)	BOYD	BRESLIN	ULSTER TARTAN
BOYTER	FIFE DIST	BRESSACK	ANGUS DIST
BRACE	GALLOWAY DIST	BRETNACH	GALBRAITH
BRACHELL	PAISLEY DIST	BREWER	DRUMMOND
BRACK	DUNBAR DIST	BREWHOUSE	PERTHSHIRE DIST
BRACKEN	BRACKEN	BREWSTER	FRASER
BRACKENRIDGE	STRATHCLYDE DIST	BREWSTER	FRASER
BRACKHAWK	ABERDEEN DIST	BREYMER	MAR DIST
BRACO	DUNBLANE DIST	BRIAN	GALLOWAY DIST
BRADIE	DUNDEE DIST	BRICE	BRYCE
BRADING	ROTHESAY DIST	BRICK	DALZELL
BRADLEY,-IE	ROXBURGH DIST	BRICKLIE,-Y	BARCLAY
BRADNER	EDINBURGH DIST	BRIDGE(S)	GALLOWAY DIST
BRADSHAW	EDINBURGH DIST	BRIDIN	INVERNESS DIST
BRADY	CLAN CIAN	BRIDSON	GALLOWAY DIST
BRADY	DUNDEE DIST	BRIEN	CLAN CIAN
BRADY	ULSTER TARTAN	BRIER	MAC BRIER
BRAID	EDINBURGH DIST	BRIEVE	MORRISON
BRAIDEN	GALLOWAY DIST	BRIGG(S)	ABERDEEN DIST
BRAIDFOOT(E)	GALLOWAY DIST	BRIGHAM	DUNBAR DIST
BRAIDING	PAISLEY DIST	BRIM(M)ER	FIFE DIST
BRAIDON	GALLOWAY DIST	BRIM(S)	SUTHERLAND DIST
BRAIDWOOD	DUNDEE DIST	BRINGHURST	TYNESIDE DIST
BRAIN	ABERDEEN DIST	BRINTON	STRATHCLYDE DIST
BRAITHWAITE	EDINBURGH DIST	BRISBANE	PAISLEY DIST
BRAKHAUGH	ABERDEEN DIST	BRISTOW	INVERNESS DIST
BRALAND	AYRSHIRE DIST	BRITTAN,-ON	GALBRAITH
BRAMBIE,-(E)Y	HUNTLY DIST	BROA	PAISLEY DIST
BRAN	GALLOWAY DIST	BROAD	AYRSHIRE DIST
BRAN(N)AN	DUNDEE DIST	BROADFOOT	NITHSDALE DIST
BRANCH	ABERDEEN DIST	BROADLIE,-(E)Y	INVERNESS DIST
BRAND	IRVINE	BROBBEL,-LE	EDINBURGH DIST
		BROCK	MURRAY OF ATHOLL

NAME	TARTAN	NAME	TARTAN
BROCKET(T)	STRATHCLYDE DIST	BUCHANAN,-ON	BUCHANAN
BROCKHOUSE	EDINBURGH DIST	BUCHLYRIE,-Y	GRAHAM
BROCKIE,-Y	ANGUS DIST	BUCHNER	INVERNESS DIST
BROCUS	MURRAY OF ATHOLL	BUCK	BUCHAN DIST
BRODERICK	INVERNESS DIST	BUCKALEW	BUCCLEUGH
BRODIE,-Y	BRODIE	BUCKALEW	SCOTT
BROE	DRUMMOND	BUCKANON	BUCHANAN
BROE	MURRAY	BUCKHANON	BUCHANAN
BROG	ST. ANDREWS DIST	BUCKHOLM	ROXBURGH DIST
BROGAN	ABERDEEN DIST	BUCKIE,-Y	BUCHAN DIST
BROGAN	CLAN CIAN	BUCKIE,-Y	STIRLING DIST
BROGAN	CONNACHT TARTAN	BUCKLE	EDINBURGH DIST
BROKE(Y)	MURRAY OF ATHOLL	BUCKLER	ABERDEEN DIST
BROKUS	ANGUS DIST	BUCKLEW	BUCCLEUGH
BRON	BROWN	BUCKLEW	SCOTT
BRON	LAMONT	BUCKNER	INVERNESS DIST
BRONTE	BRONTE	BUDERICK	ARRAN DIST
BROOK(E)(S)	ABERDEEN DIST	BUDGE	CAITHNESS TARTAN
BROOK(E)(S)	BROOKE	BUEA	MAC DONALD
BROOM	GALLOWAY DIST	BUGES	EDINBURGH DIST
BROOMFIELD	EDINBURGH DIST	BUGLASS	TWEEDSIDE DIST
BROOMHILL	GALLOWAY DIST	BUICK	ANGUS DIST
BROOMSIDE	ANGUS DIST	BUIE	BUIE
BROON(E)	BROWN	BUIE	GRANT
BROTCHIE,-Y	SUTHERLAND DIST	BUIE	MAC DONALD
BROTHERS	MUSSELBURGH DIST	BUIK	FIFE DIST
BROTHERSTON	GALA WATER DIST	BUISSLAND	STIRLING DIST
BROUGH	BROUGH	BUIST	FIFE DIST
BROUGH	DRUMMOND	BUITTLE	GALLOWAY DIST
BROUGH	MURRAY	BULKENWALL	FIFE DIST
BROUN(E)	BROWN	BULL(S)	INVERNESS DIST
BROUN(E)	LAMONT	BULL(S)	PAISLEY DIST
BROUN(E)	MAC MILLAN	BULLEN(S)	EDINBURGH DIST
BROW	DRUMMOND	BULLERSWELL	ROXBURGH DIST
BROW	MURRAY	BULLIANS	PERTHSHIRE DIST
BROWN	DOUGLAS	BULLIN(S)	PERTHSHIRE DIST
BROWN(E)	BROWN	BULLION(S)	STIRLING DIST
BROWN(E)	LAMONT	BULLMAN	BULLMAN
BROWN(E)	MAC MILLAN	BULLMAN	GRAHAM OF MENTIETH
BROWNFIELD	ROXBURGH DIST	BULLOCH,-K	MAC DONALD
BROWNHILL(S)	EDINBURGH DIST	BULMAR,-ER	GLASGOW DIST
BROWNING	ABERDEEN DIST	BULSON	ROXBURGH DIST
BROWNLIE,-LEE,-Y	STRATHCLYDE DIST	BUNCH	PERTHSHIRE DIST
BRUCE	BRUCE	BUNCHRAW	INVERNESS DIST
BRUCE	BRUCE OF KINNAIRD	BUNCLE	HOME
BRUN(E)	BROWN	BUNKLE	HOME
BRUNELL,-ILL	ARGYLL DIST	BUNTAIN	GRAHAM OF MENTIETH
BRUNLIE,-Y	EDINBURGH DIST	BUNTING	GRAHAM
BRUNTFIELD	EDINBURGH DIST	BUNTING	GRAHAM OF MENTIETH
BRUNTON,-TOUN	ANGUS DIST	BUNY	EDINBURGH DIST
BRYANT	CARRICK DIST	BUNYAN	ABERDEEN DIST
BRYANT	CLAN CIAN	BUNYIE	EDINBURGH DIST
BRYCE	BRYCE	BUNZEON	ABERDEEN DIST
BRYDE	BRODIE	BUOEY	GRANT
BRYDEN	ROTHESAY DIST	BUOEY	MAC DONALD
BRYDEN,-ON	ROXBURGH DIST	BURAND	DALZELL
BRYDIE,-Y	BRODIE	BURBANK	DUNBLANE DIST
BRYDON	ROXBURGH DIST	BURBONE	EDINBURGH DIST
BRYER	MAC BRIER	BURCH	EDINBURGH DIST
BRYMAN	DUNDEE DIST	BURD	EDINBURGH DIST
BRYSON	STRATHCLYDE DIST	BURDEN,-ON	LAMONT
BUBB	ANGUS DIST	BURGESS	ABERDEEN DIST
BUCCLEUGH	BUCCLEUGH	BURGHER	INVERNESS DIST
BUCCLEUGH	SCOTT	BURK(E)	DUNDEE DIST
BUCH	INVERNESS DIST	BURKE	CONNACHT TARTAN
BUCHAN	BUCHAN DIST	BURN(E)	TWEEDSIDE DIST
BUCHAN	CUMMING	BURN(E)VILLE	GALLOWAY DIST

NAME	TARTAN	NAME	TARTAN
BURNES(S)	CAMPBELL	CAIL	MAC DOUGALL
BURNETT	BURNETT	CAIN	MAC DONALD
BURNETT (Western)	CAMPBELL	CAIRD	MAC GREGOR
BURNETT(E)	BURNETT OF LEYS	CAIRG	GALLOWAY DIST
BURNFIELD	GLASGOW DIST	CAIRNCROSS	ANGUS DIST
BURNHAM	PERTHSHIRE DIST	CAIRNIE,-Y	GALLOWAY DIST
BURNHAM,-EM	MAR DIST	CAIRNIE,-Y	PERTHSHIRE DIST
BURNIE,-Y	MATHESON	CAIRNS	GRANT
BURNS	BURNS OF MONTROSE	CAITHNESS	CAITHNESS TARTAN
BURNS	CAMPBELL	CAL(L)UM	CALUM
BURNSIDE	ANGUS DIST	CAL(L)UM	MALCOLM
BURR	ABERDEEN DIST	CALAN	MAC DONALD
BURR	MAR DIST	CALBRAITH	GALBRAITH
BURRELL	BURRELL	CALD(E)COTT	GALA WATER DIST
BURROWS	INVERNESS DIST	CALDER	CAMPBELL OF CAWDOR
BURT	FIFE DIST	CALDERHEAD	STRATHCLYDE DIST
BURTNETT	BURNETT	CALDERWOOD	STRATHCLYDE DIST
BUSBIE,-Y	PAISLEY DIST	CALDOW	HAMILTON
BUTCHART	ABERDEEN DIST	CALDWELL	PAISLEY DIST
BUTCHART	ANGUS DIST	CALE	KILE
BUTCHER	ABERDEEN DIST	CALEY	FIFE DIST
BUTCHER	ANGUS DIST	CALHOUN	COLQUHOUN
BUTHE	INVERNESS DIST	CALL(E)Y,-IE	FIFE DIST
BUTLER	FALKIRK DIST	CALLACK	GALLOWAY DIST
BUTTER(S)	PERTHSHIRE DIST	CALLAGHAN	ULSTER TARTAN
BUTTERCASE	ST. ANDREWS DIST	CALLAM	MALCOLM
BUTTRESS	INVERNESS DIST	CALLAN	GRANT
BUY	STRATHEARN DIST	CALLAN	MAC DONALD
BUYERS	LINDSAY	CALLAN	MAC FARLANE
BUYTH	INVERNESS DIST	CALLANACH	STEWART OF APPIN
BUZBY	PAISLEY DIST	CALLANAN	CONNACHT TARTAN
BYARS	LINDSAY	CALLANDAR,-ER	MAC FARLANE
BYATS	EDINBURGH DIST	CALLAWAY	MAC FARLANE
BYDON(E)	ROXBURGH DIST	CALLEN(D)	GRANT
BYE	ANGUS DIST	CALLENDAR	MAC GREGOR
BYERS	LINDSAY	CALLEY	FIFE DIST
BYOOT	GLASGOW DIST	CALLIN	GRANT
BYRAN	CLAN CIAN	CALLIN	MAC FARLANE
BYRES	LINDSAY	CALLOWAY	MAC FARLANE
BYRNES	CAMPBELL	CALPIN(E)	MAC ALPINE
		CALTON	GALLOWAY DIST
		CALUM	CALUM
		CALUM	MALCOLM
		CALVERT	ANGUS DIST
		CALVIE,-Y	FIFE DIST

C

NAME	TARTAN	NAME	TARTAN
CABEL	ANGUS DIST	CAMBELL	CAMPBELL
CABLE	ANGUS DIST	CAMBIE,-Y	GALLOWAY DIST
CACHIE,-Y	MAC DONALD	CAMBL(E)Y	MAC AULAY
CACHIE,-Y	MAC EACHAIN	CAMBLE	CAMPBELL
CAD(D)ELL	CAMPBELL	CAMBO	FIFE DIST
CADDEN	GORDON	CAMBRIDGE	MAC DONALD
CADDER	CAMPBELL OF CAWDOR	CAME	MAC DONALD OF SLEAT
CADDIN	GORDON	CAMELL	CAMPBELL
CADDO(W)	HAMILTON	CAMERON	CAMERON
CADENHEAD	GALLOWAY DIST	CAMERON	CAMERON OF LOCHEIL
CADGER	PERTHSHIRE DIST	CAMERON	LOCHABER DIST
CADY,-IE	DOUGLAS	CAMES	MAC DONALD OF SLEAT
CADZEON	DUNBLANE DIST	CAMMOCK	GALLOWAY DIST
CADZOW	HAMILTON	CAMP	CAMPBELL
CAFFRAY	PERTHSHIRE DIST	CAMPBELL	CAMPBELL
CAHILL	CONNACHT TARTAN	CAMPBELL	MAC ARTHUR
CAHOON	COLQUHOUN	CAMPSIE,-Y	STIRLING DIST
CAHOUN(E)	COLQUHOUN	CAN(AN)ICH	MAC PHERSON
CAIG	FARQUHARSON	CAN(N)ADY	KENNEDY
CAIG	MAC LEOD	CAN(N)OCH	DUNBLANE DIST

NAME	TARTAN	NAME	TARTAN
CANANACH	MAC PHERSON	CARRACH	ARRAN DIST
CANAVAN	CONNACHT TARTAN	CARRAHER	FARQUHARSON
CANDEL(L)	TWEEDSIDE DIST	CARRAN	STIRLING DIST
CANDEN,-IN	ABERDEEN DIST	CARRE	KERR
CANDLISH	GALLOWAY DIST	CARREN(S)	GRANT
CANDO	AYRSHIRE DIST	CARREY	PAISLEY DIST
CANDON	ABERDEEN DIST	CARRICK	CARRICK DIST
CANDWELL	ARGYLL DIST	CARRICK	KENNEDY
CANDY	KENNEDY	CARRIE,-Y	PAISLEY DIST
CANE	MAC DONALD	CARRIG	CARRICK DIST
CANNAN,-IN	GALLOWAY DIST	CARRIG	KENNEDY
CANNING	ULSTER TARTAN	CARRIGLE	DRUMMOND
CANNON	GALLOWAY DIST	CARRINGTON	EDINBURGH DIST
CANSO(W)	DUNDEE DIST	CARRIOCK	NITHSDALE DIST
CANT	DOUGLAS	CARROCH	ANGUS DIST
CANTLAY	ABERDEEN DIST	CARROL(L) (Scot)	DUNBLANE DIST
CANTLEY,-IE	ABERDEEN DIST	CARROL(L) (Irish)	CLAN CIAN
CAPEL	PERTHSHIRE DIST	CARRON(ES)	MAC DONELL GLENGARRY
CAPPAR	ABERDEEN DIST	CARROONS	MAC DONELL GLENGARRY
CAR(R)ON	STIRLING DIST	CARRUBER	MUSSELBURGH DIST
CARABINE	FT. WILLIAM DIST	CARRUTH	GLASGOW DIST
CARAN	STIRLING DIST	CARRUTHERS	BRUCE
CARBERRY	EDINBURGH DIST	CARRUTHERS	NITHSDALE DIST
CARCARIE,-Y	PERTHSHIRE DIST	CARS(E)	PERTHSHIRE DIST
CARDNEY,-IE	MAC GREGOR	CARSLAW	GALLOWAY DIST
CAREY,-IE	PAISLEY DIST	CARSON	GALLOWAY DIST
CAREY,-IE	STIRLING DIST	CARSTAIRS	STRATHCLYDE DIST
CAREY,-IE	TYNESIDE DIST	CARSTARPHEN	FORRESTER
CARGILL	DRUMMOND	CARSWELL	ROXBURGH DIST
CARISTAN,-ON	SKENE	CART	MAC ARTHUR
CARKETTLE	EDINBURGH DIST	CARTER (Isles)	MAC ARTHUR
CARL(E)(S)	ABERDEEN DIST	CARTER (South)	GALLOWAY DIST
CARL(E)TON	MAC KERREL	CARUS	BRUCE
CARLAW	MAC KENZIE	CARUTH	BRUCE
CARLIN	ULSTER TARTAN	CARVEL	ANGUS DIST
CARLISLE	BRUCE	CARVILL(E)	CLAN CIAN
CARLOCK	MAC KENZIE	CARWOOD	STRATHCLYDE DIST
CARLYLE	BRUCE	CARY	PAISLEY DIST
CARMAC(K)	ANGUS DIST	CAS(S)EY	ABERDEEN DIST
CARMAIG	ANGUS DIST	CASE	PAISLEY DIST
CARMAN	ROXBURGH DIST	CASELY	CASELY
CARMELL	CARMICHAEL	CASEY	CLAN CIAN
CARMEN	ROXBURGH DIST	CASH	MAC TAVISH
CARMENT	FIFE DIST	CASKIE,-Y	MAC ASKILL
CARMICHAEL,-IL	CARMICHAEL	CASKIE,-Y	MAC LEOD
CARMICHAEL,-IL	STEWART	CASSELL (Irish)	CLAN CIAN
CARMICKLE	CARMICHAEL	CASSELS	KENNEDY
CARMICKLE	STEWART	CASSIDY	ULSTER TARTAN
CARMMAN,-ON	EDINBURGH DIST	CASSIE	PAISLEY DIST
CARMONT	ROXBURGH DIST	CASSILLIS	KENNEDY
CARN(E)S	GRANT	CASSY	AYRSHIRE DIST
CARNABY,-IE	TYNESIDE DIST	CASTEL(L)	KENNEDY
CARNBEE,-IE,-Y	FIFE DIST	CASTLE	KENNEDY
CARNEGIE,-Y	CARNEGIE	CASTLELAW	GALLOWAY DIST
CARNEIL	FIFE DIST	CASTLES (Irish)	CLAN CIAN
CARNET	CARNET	CASTRAL(L)	INVERNESS DIST
CARNEY,-IE	CLAN CIAN	CATANACH	CLAN CHATTAN
CARNIE,-Y	SKENE	CATCHIE,-Y	MAC DONALD
CARNIGAL,-UL	ABERDEEN DIST	CATCHIE,-Y	MAC EACHAIN
CARNOCK	GALLOWAY DIST	CATE	KEITH
CAROLAN(D)	ULSTER TARTAN	CATHAL	MAC DONALD
CAROLANG	ULSTER TARTAN	CATHAN	DUNBLANE DIST
CAROON	MAC DONELL GLENGARRY	CATHCART	PAISLEY DIST
CARPENTER	PERTHSHIRE DIST	CATHER	LENNOX DIST
CARPOL	GLASGOW DIST	CATHERWOOD	STRATHCLYDE DIST
CARR	KERR	CATHIE,-(E)Y	MAC FIE

NAME	TARTAN	NAME	TARTAN
CATHIL	MAC DONALD	CHREE	CREE
CATHIN	EDINBURGH DIST	CHREE	GORDON
CATHNAL(L)	MAC DONALD	CHRISHOLM	CHISHOLM
CATHRO	DUNDEE DIST	CHRISTIAN	GALLOWAY DIST
CATTAN(N)ACH	CLAN CHATTAN	CHRISTIE	CHRISTIE
CATTELL	CAMPBELL OF CAWDOR	CHRISTIE	FARQUHARSON
CATTEN	GORDON	CHRISTISON	FARQUHARSON
CATTERSON	LORNE DIST	CHRISTOPHER	OGILVIE
CATTIE,-Y	MAC FIE	CHRISTY	CHRISTIE
CATTO	BUCHAN DIST	CHRISTY	FARQUHARSON
CATTON	CLAN CHATTAN	CHRYSTAL	BUCHAN DIST
CAUDILL	CAMPBELL OF CAWDOR	CIARAN(S)	GRANT
CAUDLE	CAMPBELL OF CAWDOR	CIDERBO	MOFFAT DIST
CAULDLAW	DOUGLAS	CIMMON	CUMMING
CAVAN	DOUGLAS	CLACHLAN(E)	MAC LACHLAN
CAVANA(U)GH	ULSTER TARTAN	CLAGHORN	STEWART
CAVEN(S)	GALLOWAY DIST	CLAMP	GALLOWAY DIST
CAVERHILL	TWEEDSIDE DIST	CLANACHAN,-AHAN	MAC LEAN
CAVERS	DOUGLAS	CLANCHY	CLAN CIAN
CAVERTON	ROXBURGH DIST	CLANCY	CLAN CIAN
CAVIE	SUTHERLAND DIST	CLANNIE,-Y	AYRSHIRE DIST
CAVISH	MAC TAVISH	CLAPPERTON	BUCHAN DIST
CAW	STEWART	CLAPPERTON	EDINBURGH DIST
CAWSELL	BUCHAN DIST	CLARK(E)	CLAN CHATTAN
CAY	MAC KAY	CLARK(E)	CLARK
CAYMAN	MAC KAY	CLARK(E)	CLARK OF ULVA
CEARD	STRATHSPEY DIST	CLARK(E)	MAC PHERSON
CEARL	GALLOWAY DIST	CLARK(E)	MACKINTOSH
CERAS,-ES	FIFE DIST	CLARKE	CAMERON
CESSFORD	KERR	CLARKIN	CLAN CHATTAN
CHALMERS	CAMERON	CLARKIN	CLARK
CHAMBERLAIN	EDINBURGH DIST	CLARKSON	CLAN CHATTAN
CHAMBERS	CAMERON	CLARKSTON	GLASGOW DIST
CHAMPNESS	GLASGOW DIST	CLASON	MAC NICOL
CHANCELLOR	AYRSHIRE DIST	CLATHAN	STIRLING DIST
CHANDLER	GLASGOW DIST	CLATHIE,-Y	MAC FIE
CHANEY,-AY	CUMMINGS	CLATT	ABERDEEN DIST
CHANEY,-AY	SUTHERLAND	CLAVERING	TYNESIDE DIST
CHANNON	MAC DONALD	CLAWSON	PERTHSHIRE DIST
CHANTRY,-IE	CALEDONIA TARTAN	CLAY	STEWART OF APPIN
CHAPLE	STEWART	CLAYHILLS	DUNDEE DIST
CHAPLIN	ABERDEEN DIST	CLAYPOOL,-POLE	GALLOWAY DIST
CHAPMAN	ANGUS DIST	CLAYTON	CLAYTON
CHAPP	BUCHAN DIST	CLAYTON	WELSH NATIONAL
CHAPPEL(L)	STEWART	CLEARY,-IE	CAMERON
CHARLES	MAC KENZIE	CLEARY,-IE	CLAN CHATTAN
CHARLESON,-STON	MAC KENZIE	CLEARY,-IE	MAC PHERSON
CHARLESWORTH	TYNESIDE DIST	CLEARY,-IE	MACKINTOSH
CHARLSON	MAC KENZIE	CLECKIN	ULSTER TARTAN
CHARLTON	TYNESIDE DIST	CLEEL(L)AND	MAC LELLEN
CHARTER(S)	GALLOWAY DIST	CLEGHORN	STEWART
CHARTERIS	ROXBURGH DIST	CLEL(L)AND	CLELAND
CHATTO	ROXBURGH DIST	CLEL(L)AND	MAC LELLEN
CHEAP(E)	CHEAPE	CLEL(L)AND	MAC NAB
CHERRIE,-Y	PAISLEY DIST	CLEM	LAMONT
CHEYNE(Y)	CUMMING	CLEMENT	LAMONT
CHEYNE(Y)	SUTHERLAND	CLEMINSON	CAITHNESS TARTAN
CHIESLEY	EDINBURGH DIST	CLEMMER	GALLOWAY DIST
CHILD(S)	DRUMMOND	CLENDENING	DOUGLAS
CHILDRESS	GALLOWAY DIST	CLENDINING	DOUGLAS
CHIRNSIDE	DUNBAR DIST	CLENHILL	TWEEDSIDE DIST
CHIRNSIDE	TWEEDSIDE DIST	CLEPHANE	GALA WATER DIST
CHISHOLM	CHISHOLM	CLERIHEW(S)	ABERDEEN DIST
CHISM	CHISHOLM	CLERK(E)	CLAN CHATTAN
CHIVAS,-ES	ABERDEEN DIST	CLERK(E)	CLARK
CHOUN	COLQUHOUN	CLERK(E)	MAC PHERSON

NAME	TARTAN	NAME	TARTAN
CLERK(E)	MACKINTOSH	COHRAN	COCHRANE
CLEWSTON(E)	MAC DONALD	COL(E)MAN	BUCHANAN
CLIFF	INVERNESS DIST	COL(L)YEAR	ROBERTSON
CLINCH	CLAN CIAN	COLDEN	EDINBURGH DIST
CLINE	CAITHNESS TARTAN	COLDINHAM	TWEEDSIDE DIST
CLINKSCALES	TWEEDSIDE DIST	COLDLAW	DOUGLAS
CLINKSKILL	TWEEDSIDE DIST	COLDSTREAM	TWEEDSIDE DIST
CLINTON	GALLOWAY DIST	COLDWELL	GALLOWAY DIST
CLINTS	EDINBURGH DIST	COLE(S)	MAC DOUGALL
CLOAKIE,-Y	LAMONT	COLFORD	CRAWFORD
CLOGG	DUNDEE DIST	COLHOUN,-OON	COLQUHOUN
CLOGIE,-Y	LAMONT	COLL	MAC COLL
CLOKIE,-Y	LAMONT	COLL	MAC DONALD
CLOUD	MAC LEOD	COLLEDGE	ROXBURGH DIST
CLOUDSLIE,-Y	ANGUS DIST	COLLEN	GORDON
CLOUSTON	SINCLAIR	COLLET	CAITHNESS TARTAN
CLOW(E)	STRATHEARN DIST	COLLIAR	ROBERTSON
CLOWDEN	MAC LACHLAN	COLLIE,-EY	ABERDEEN DIST
CLUB(B)	ABERDEEN DIST	COLLIER	ROBERTSON
CLUBBY	CONNACHT TARTAN	COLLIGAN	DUNDEE DIST
CLUFF	ABERDEEN DIST	COLLINGSWOOD	TYNESIDE DIST
CLUGSTON	DUNBAR DIST	COLLINS	ANGUS DIST
CLUNESS	MAC KENZIE	COLLINSON	ABERDEEN DIST
CLUNIE	MAC PHERSON	COLLISON	ABERDEEN DIST
CLUNIES,-YS	MAC KENZIE	COLMERIE,-Y	MONTGOMERY
CLUNY,-IE	MAC PHERSON	COLQUHOUN	COLQUHOUN
CLUSBY,-IE	MAC PHERSON	COLSON	MAC COLL
CLUTTON	SUTHERLAND DIST	COLSON	MAC DONALD
CLYDE	STRATHCLYDE DIST	COLSTON	MAC COLL
CLYDESDALE	STRATHCLYDE DIST	COLSTON	MAC DONALD
CLYNE	CAITHNESS TARTAN	COLT	PERTHSHIRE DIST
COAT(E)S	FARQUHARSON	COLTART	GALLOWAY DIST
COATNEY	GLASGOW DIST	COLTHERS	GALLOWAY DIST
COB(B)LER	DUNBLANE DIST	COLTON	TWEEDSIDE DIST
COBB(E)	LINDSAY	COLTRAN	GALLOWAY DIST
COBBAN	ABERDEEN DIST	COLVEN	GALLOWAY DIST
COBURN	COCKBURN	COLVILL(E)	ROXBURGH DIST
COCHERT	MAC GREGOR	COLVILLE	AYRSHIRE DIST
COCHRAN(E)	COCHRANE	COLVIN	ROXBURGH DIST
COCHRAN(E)	MAC DONALD	COLYEAR	ROBERTSON.
COCK	FIFE DIST	COMB(E)	MAC THOMAS
COCK(H)ILL	INVERNESS DIST	COMB(E)	MACKINTOSH
COCKAYNE	GLASGOW DIST	COMBICH,-ICK	STEWART OF APPIN
COCKBURN	COCKBURN	COMBIE,-Y	MAC THOMAS
COCKER	EDINBURGH DIST	COMBIE,-Y	MACKINTOSH
COCKERHAM	TWEEDSIDE DIST	COMIE	MAC THOMAS
COCKIE,-Y	ABERDEEN DIST	COMIE	MACKINTOSH
COCKING(S)	PERTHSHIRE DIST	COMMONS	CUMMING
COCKRAM	COCHRANE	COMOLQUOY	SINCLAIR
COCKRAN	COCHRANE	COMRIE	MAC GREGOR
COCKRUM	COCHRANE	COMRIE	STRATHEARN DIST
COCKS	DUNDEE DIST	COMYN(S)	CUMMING
COCORAN	COCHRANE	CON(E)SON	GLEN ORCHY DIST
COE	MUSSELBURGH DIST	CON(N)AN	GLEN ORCHY DIST
COEBOURN(E)	COCKBURN	CON(N)AN	TWEEDSIDE DIST
COEHON	COLQUHOUN	CON(N)ING	GALLOWAY DIST
COF(F)IELD	LORNE DIST	CONACHEE	MAC DOUGALL
COFFEE,-EY,-IE	MAC FIE	CONACHEE	STEWART OF ATHOLL
COFFEY	CONNACHT TARTAN	CONACHER	MAC DOUGALL
COFY	CONNACHT TARTAN	CONACHER	STEWART OF ATHOLL
COG(G)AN	TWEEDSIDE DIST	CONAHEE	MAC DOUGALL
COGBO(U)RN(E)	COCKBURN	CONAHEE	STEWART OF ATHOLL
COGHLAN,-EN	CLAN CIAN	CONAHER	MAC DOUGALL
COGHRANE	CLAN CIAN	CONAHER	STEWART OF ATHOLL
COGILL	CAITHNESS TARTAN	CONBOY	CONNACHT TARTAN
COGLE	CAITHNESS TARTAN	CONDIE,-Y	STRATHEARN DIST

NAME	TARTAN	NAME	TARTAN
CONDRICK	MAC NAUGHTEN	CORCORAN	CLAN CIAN
CONE(S)	ABERDEEN DIST	CORCORAN	ULSTER TARTAN
CONEANNON	CONNACHT TARTAN	CORDINER	ABERDEEN DIST
CONGHAL	STRATHEARN DIST	CORDWAINER	ABERDEEN DIST
CONGLE	STRATHEARN DIST	CORE	STRATHCLYDE DIST
CONGLETON	EDINBURGH DIST	COREY	CLAN CIAN
CONHEATH	GALLOWAY DIST	COREY	GALLOWAY DIST
CONKEY,-IE	ROBERTSON	CORFIELD	DALZIEL
CONLAN,-ON	ULSTER TARTAN	CORHEAD	GALLOWAY DIST
CONLAY	MAC LEAY	CORK	LENNOX DIST
CONLAY	STEWART OF APPIN	CORKRAN(E)	GALLOWAY DIST
CONLEAF	STEWART OF APPIN	CORMACK	BUCHANAN
CONLEAVE	STEWART OF APPIN	CORNELL	TWEEDSIDE DIST
CONLEAVEY,-IE	STEWART OF APPIN	CORNER	SINCLAIR
CONLEY,-IE	MAC DONALD	CORNET	DUNBAR DIST
CONN	HAY	CORNFOOT	DUNDEE DIST
CONN	MAC DONALD	CORNTON	STIRLING DIST
CONNACHIE,-Y	MAC GREGOR	CORNUELL	LENNOX DIST
CONNACHIE,-Y	ROBERTSON	CORNWALL	CORNISH TARTAN
CONNAL(L)	MAC DONALD	CORNWALL	STIRLING DIST
CONNALLY	ULSTER TARTAN	CORPHINSTONE	EDINBURGH DIST
CONNEL(L)	CONNELL	CORR	ULSTER TARTAN
CONNEL(L)	MAC DONALD	CORR	ULSTER TARTAN
CONNELLY,-IE	DUNDEE DIST	CORRIE(S)	DOUGLAS
CONNER	ULSTER TARTAN	CORRIE(S)	MAC DONALD
CONNERY	MAC DONALD	CORRIGALL	SINCLAIR
CONNET(TE)	ROSS	CORRIGAN	MAC GUIRE
CONNIGAN	CONNACHT TARTAN	CORRY	GALLOWAY DIST
CONNOCHIE,-Y	CAMPBELL	CORRY	ULSTER TARTAN
CONNOCHIE,-Y	ROBERTSON	CORS(S)AR	STIRLING DIST
CONNOLLY	ULSTER TARTAN	CORSAN(E)	GALLOWAY DIST
CONNON	GORDON	CORSE	ANGUS DIST
CONNON	HUNTLY DIST	CORSEHILL	ABERDEEN DIST
CONNOR	CLAN CIAN	CORSKIE,-Y	ABERDEEN DIST
CONNOR	CONNACHT TARTAN	CORSON	GALLOWAY DIST
CONNOR	CONNOR	CORSTON(E)	PERTHSHIRE DIST
CONNORY	MAC DONALD	CORY	CLAN CIAN
CONOCHER	MAC DOUGALL	COSALT	INVERNESS DIST
CONOCHER	STEWART OF ATHOLI	COSCRACH	BUCHAN DIST
CONROY	CLAN CIAN	COSGRAVE	CLAN CIAN
CONROY	CONROY	COSGRAVE	ULSTER TARTAN
CONRY	CLAN CIAN	COSGROVE	ULSTER TARTAN
CONSTABLE	HAY	COSH	AYRSHIRE DIST
CONSTANTINE	STRATHCLYDE DIST	COSHAM	MAC DONALD
CONVALL,-ELL	LENNOX DIST	COSSAR	TWEEDSIDE DIST
CONVET	ROSS	COSSENS,-INS	LYONS
CONWAY	CONNACHT TARTAN	COSTAIN	CALEDONIA TARTAN
CONWAY	DUNDEE DIST	COSTERMAN	TWEEDSIDE DIST
CONYER(S)	GRAHAM	COSTIE,-Y	BUCHAN DIST
CONYNGHAM(E)	CUNNINGHAM	COTHART	ARGYLL DIST
COOK(E)	MAC DONALD	COTTON	FIFE DIST
COOK(E)	STEWART	COTTRAM	TWEEDSIDE DIST
COOLEY,-IE	MAC AULAY	COTTRELL	ST. ANDREWS DIST
COOMBE (Irish)	CLAN CIAN	COTTS	GALLOWAY DIST
COON,-EY	AYRSHIRE DIST	COUBRO(UGH)	ABERDEEN DIST
COONEY	CLAN CIAN	COUGHRAN	COCHRANE
COONEY	CONNACHT TARTAN	COULL	MAC COLL
COOPER	COOPER	COULL	MAC DONALD
COOSAR,-ER	TWEEDSIDE DIST	COULSON	MAC COLL
COP(E)LAND	TWEEDSIDE DIST	COULSON	MAC DONALD
COP(E)LEY	GLASGOW DIST	COULTAR	GALLOWAY DIST
COP(P)LEY	GLASGOW DIST	COULTER	GALLOWAY DIST
COPLAY	GLASGOW DIST	COULTHARD	GALLOWAY DIST
CORBET(T)	ROSS	COUPAR,-ER	COOPER
CORBETT	DUNBAR	COUPLAND	GALLOWAY DIST
CORBIE,-Y	FIFE DIST	COURTNEY	DUNBAR DIST
CORBRIDGE	ROXBURGH DIST	COURTY	FORBES

NAME	TARTAN	NAME	TARTAN
COUSAR	TWEEDSIDE DIST	CRANSTO(U)N	CRANSTOUN
COUSINS	ABERDEEN DIST	CRANTACK,-ICK	CRANTOCK
COUSLAND	BUCHANAN	CRANTOCK	CRANTOCK
COUSTON	ANGUS DIST	CRASTER	GLASGOW DIST
COUT(T)IE,-Y	ANGUS DIST	CRAVEN(S)	GALLOWAY DIST
COUTTS	FARQUHARSON	CRAW	TWEEDSIDE DIST
COUTTS	MAC DONALD	CRAWFORD,-ERD	CRAWFORD
COVENTRY	TWEEDSIDE DIST	CRAWFORD,-ERD	LINDSAY
COVINGTON	STRATHCLYDE DIST	CRAWFURD	CRAWFORD
COW(E)	MUSSELBRUGH DIST	CRAWFURD	LINDSAY
COWAN	COLQUHOUN	CRAY	MAC RAE
COWAN	COWAN	CREA	GORDON
COWAN	MAC DOUGALL	CREA	MAC RAE
COWDEN	EDINBURGH DIST	CREAMER	ANGUS DIST
COWEN	COLQUHOUN	CREARER	MACKINTOSH
COWEN	COWAN	CREATH	MAC RAE
COWGILL	STRATHCLYDE DIST	CREE	CREE
COWIE,EY,-Y	FRASER	CREE	GORDON
COWLIE,-Y	MAC AULAY	CREE	MAC RAE
COWMAN(S)	CUMMING	CREECH	FIFE DIST
COWPER	COWPER	CREEL	FIFE DIST
COWRAN	COCHRANE	CREELMAN	GLASGOW DIST
COX(E)	ARGYLL DIST	CREEVIE,-Y	ABERDEEN DIST
COY	MAC KAY	CREIGHTON	EDINBURGH DIST
COYLE	ULSTER TARTAN	CREMON	INVERNESS DIST
COYNE	CONNACHT TARTAN	CRERAR	MACKINTOSH
CRABB(E)	ABERDEEN DIST	CREVIE,-Y	ABERDEEN DIST
CRACHET(T)	ANGUS DIST	CREWER	PERTHSHIRE DIST
CRAE	MAC RAE	CRIBB(E)S	EDINBURGH DIST
CRAELL	DUNDEE DIST	CRIBB(E)S	STRATHCLYDE DIST
CRAFFERD,-URD	CRAWFORD	CRICHTON,-OUN	EDINBURGH DIST
CRAFFORD	CRAWFORD	CRIEFF	CRIEFF DIST
CRAIB	INVERNESS DIST	CRIEVE	CRIEFF DIST
CRAIG	CRAIG	CRIGHALL	EDINBURGH DIST
CRAIG	GORDON	CRIGHTON	EDINBURGH DIST
CRAIG	HUNTLY DIST	CRIMMON(D)	MAC LEOD
CRAIGA(I)LLIE,-Y	PERTHSHIRE DIST	CRINAN	PERTHSHIRE DIST
CRAIGAN,-EN	STRATHSPEY DIST	CRINGLE	PAISLEY DIST
CRAIGEN,-EN	INVERNESS DIST	CRIPPLE	PERTHSHIRE DIST
CRAIGFORTH	STIRLING DIST	CRIRIE	MAC DONALD
CRAIGHEAD	ABERDEEN DIST	CRISPIN	NITHSDALE DIST
CRAIGHILL	PERTHSHIRE DIST	CRITCHLIE,-Y	INVERNESS DIST
CRAIGIE,-Y	AYRSHIRE DIST	CROALL	DUNDEE DIST
CRAIGIN	EDINBURGH DIST	CROCHET(T)	ANGUS DIST
CRAIGMILLER	EDINBURGH DIST	CROCKAT(T)	STRATHCLYDE DIST
CRAIGMOOR,-ORE	CRAIGMOOR	CROCKET(T	STRATHCLYDE DIST
CRAIGMYLE	ABERDEEN DIST	CROCKFORD	CRAWFORD
CRAIGNICH	ARGYLL DIST	CROG(G)AN	ARGYLL DIST
CRAIGNISH	ARGYLL DIST	CROLL	ABERDEEN DIST
CRAIGOW	PAISLEY DIST	CROLLA(GH)	GALLOWAY DIST
CRAIGTON	ANGUS DIST	CROM	MAC DONALD
CRAIK	CRAIK OF ASSINGTON	CROMAR	FARQUHARSON
CRAIK	GALLOWAY DIST	CROMARTIE,-Y	MAC KENZIE
CRAIL	FIFE DIST	CROMB	GORDON
CRAIN(E)	ANGUS DIST	CROMB	MAC DONALD
CRAINER	MAC DONALD	CROMBIE,-Y	GORDON
CRALE	FIFE DIST	CROMDALE	STRATHSPEY DIST
CRAM(B)	FIFE DIST	CROMIE,-Y	GORDON
CRAM(B)	MAC DONALD	CRON	ARGYLL DIST
CRAM(M)OND,-UND	EDINBURGH DIST	CROOK(E)(S)	PAISLEY DIST
CRAMBIE,-Y	FIFE DIST	CROOKSHANK(S)	STEWART OF ATHOLL
CRAMPSHEE	GRAHAM	CROOM(E)	GORDON
CRAMPTON	PERTHSHIRE DIST	CROSAR	ARMSTRONG
CRAMSIE,-Y	GRAHAM	CROSBIE,-Y	BRUCE
CRAN(N)	ANGUS DIST	CROSIR	ARMSTRONG
CRAN(N)ACH	BUCHAN DIST	CROSS	GALLOWAY DIST
CRANDAL(L),-IE	STRATHCLYDE DIST	CROSSAN (Irish)	ULSTER TARTAN
CRANER	MAC DONALD	CROSSAN (Scot.)	INVERNESS DIST

NAME	TARTAN	NAME	TARTAN
CROSSER	CROSSER	CURR(E)Y	MAC PHERSON
CROSSHILL	STRATHCLYDE DIST	CURRAN	AYRSHIRE DIST
CROSSHONE	INVERNESS DIST	CURRER	DUNBAR DIST
CROUCH	INVERNESS DIST	CURRIE	CURRIE OF BALILONE
CROUNER	ABERDEEN DIST	CURRIE	MAC DON CLANRANALD
CROW(E)	ROSS	CURRIE	MAC FIE
CROWNER	ABERDEEN DIST	CURRIE	MAC PHERSON
CROWTHER	MAC GREGOR	CURRIEHILL	SKENE
CROY	ROSS	CURRIER	GALLOWAY DIST
CROZ(I)ER	ARMSTRONG	CURROR	DUNBAR DIST
CRU(I)ZEAN,-ANE	EDINBURGH DIST	CURRY,-IE (Irish)	CLAN CIAN
CRUD(D)ON	BUCHAN DIST	CURSITER	SINCLAIR
CRUDEN	BUCHAN DIST	CURTIS	ANGUS DIST
CRUI(C)KSHANK(S)	CRUICKSHANK	CURWEN,-IN	ROXBURGH DIST
CRUI(C)KSHANK(S)	STEWART OF ATHOLL	CURZON	GALLOWAY DIST
CRUM(B)	MAC DONALD	CUS(S)AR,-ER	TWEEDSIDE DIST
CRUM(M)E	EDINBURGH DIST	CUSACK	DUNDEE DIST
CRUNKLETON	ROXBURGH DIST	CUSHIE,-EY	FIFE DIST
CRUS(I)ER	ARMSTRONG	CUSHIE,-EY	ROXBURGH DIST
CRYING	ABERDEEN DIST	CUSHING	TYNESIDE DIST
CRYSTAL(L)	BUCHAN DIST	CUSHNIE,-EY	INVERNESS DIST
CUB(B)IE,-Y	ANGUS DIST	CUSICK	DUNDEE DIST
CUB(B)IS(T)ON	GALLOWAY DIST	CUT(T)LER	DUNBAR DIST
CUDDIE,-Y	GALLOWAY DIST	CUTEL(L)AR,-ER	GALLOWAY DIST
CUFFIE,-Y	MAC FIE	CUTHBERT,-SON	ANGUS DIST
CULBERT	ANGUS DIST	CUTHELL,-ILL	MUSSELBURGH DIST
CULCHOEN	COLQUHOUN		
CULLEN	GORDON		
CULLIE,-Y	ROSS		
CULLISH	GALLOWAY DIST		
CULLISON	ABERDEEN DIST		
CULLOCH	MAC DONALD OF SLEAT		
CULLOCH	MUNRO		
CULLOCH	ROSS		
CULP	ABERDEEN DIST	D'AILILL	DALZELL
CULROSS	DUNBLANE DIST	D'ANNAN(D)	NITHSDALE DIST
CULROSS	FIFE DIST	D'AY(E)	HAY
CULTON	GALLOWAY DIST	DA HAY(A)	HAY
CULWEN	GALLOWAY DIST	DACKAR,-ER	ABERDEEN DIST
CUM(M)INE	CUMMING	DACKAR,-ER	ROXBURGH DIST
CUMENS	CUMMING	DACRE	ABERDEEN DIST
CUMIN(S)	CUMMING	DACRE	ROXBURGH DIST
CUMLAQUOY	SINCLAIR	DAFFAN,-EN	STRATHCLYDE DIST
CUMMIN(G)(S)	CUMMING	DAG(G)(S)	ABERDEEN DIST
CUMNOCK	PAISLEY DIST	DAG(G)(S)	MAR DIST
CUMRAY	MAC GREGOR	DAGLISH	EDINBURGH DIST
CUMRAY	STRATHEARN DIST	DAILEY	ULSTER TARTAN
CUMYN(S)	CUMMING	DAINTY	STRATHCLYDE DIST
CUN(N)INGHAM(E)	CUNNINGHAM	DAKERS	ANGUS DIST
CUNDIE,-Y	INVERNESS DIST	DALCILLE	DALZELL
CUNIGHAM(E)	CUNNINGHAM	DALCROSS	INVERNESS DIST
CUNNEGAN	CONNACHT TARTAN	DALE	PAISLEY DIST
CUNNEIN	GALLOWAY DIST	DALGARNO	ABERDEEN DIST
CUNNING	GALLOWAY DIST	DALGARNO	NITHSDALE DIST
CUNNINGHAM	CUNNINGHAM		
CUNNISON	MAC FARLANE		
CUNNISON	ROBERTSON		
CUNUNGSBY,-IE	CUNNINGHAM		
CUNYGAN	CUNNINGHAM		
CUNYINGHAM(E)	CUNNINGHAM		
CUPPLE(S)	LORNE DIST		
CURDY,-IE	MAC KIRDY		
CURLE	PAISLEY DIST		
CURR	KERR		
CURR(E)Y	CURRIE OF BALILONE		
CURR(E)Y	MAC DON CLANRANALD		
CURR(E)Y	MAC FIE		

D

NAME	TARTAN	NAME	TARTAN
DALGAT(T)IE,-Y	HAY	DAY(S)	DAVIDSON
DALGET(T)IE,-Y	HAY	DAZIEL	DALZELL
DALGINCH	DUNBAR DIST	DE HAY(A)	HAY
DALGL(E)ISH	ETTRICK DIST	DE LA HAY(E)	HAY
DALGL(E)ISH	ROXBURGH DIST	DE LESQUE	HAY
DALGLISH	DALGLISH	DE PLESSIS	HAY
DALGLISH	ROXBURGH DIST	DE QUINCY	FIFE DIST
DALHAM	GALLOWAY DIST	DE YELL	DALZELL
DALIEL	DALZELL	DE ZELL	DALZELL
DALL	CLAN CHATTAN	DE(A)VER	ULSTER TARTAN
DALLACHIE,-Y	CLAN CHATTAN	DEA(S)	DAVIDSON
DALLAS	DALLAS	DEA(S)	DEAS
DALLAS	MACKINTOSH	DEA(S)	ROSS
DALLERGHAN	ULSTER TARTAN	DEADY	CLAN CIAN
DALLING	EDINBURGH DIST	DEAL	DALZELL
DALLY,-IE	ULSTER TARTAN	DEALY	CONNACHT TARTAN
DALMAHOY	EDINBURGH DIST	DEAN(E)S	DAVIDSON
DALMENY,-IE	DALMENY	DEASON	DAVIDSON
DALRYMPLE	AYRSHIRE DIST	DEB(B)ER(S)	MAC GREGOR
DALTON	ABERDEEN DIST	DEBOYS	DUNDEE DIST
DALTON	GALLOWAY DIST	DEE (Irish)	CLAN CIAN
DALWHINNIE,-Y	LOCHABER DIST	DEE(S)	DAVIDSON
DALY,-IE	CONNACHT TARTAN	DEEL	DALZELL
DALY,-IE	ULSTER TARTAN	DEELY	CONNACHT TARTAN
DALYELL	DALZELL	DEENEY	ULSTER TARTAN
DALZEAL	DALZELL	DEER(E)	ABERDEEN DIST
DALZELL	DALZELL	DEERAN	CAITHNESS TARTAN
DALZIEL(L)	DALZELL	DEHART	FIFE DIST
DAND,-IE,-Y	DUNDEE DIST	DEHEM	DENHOLME
DANDISON	GALLOWAY DIST	DEIL	DALZELL
DANIEL(S)	MAC DONALD	DELAHAY	HAY
DANKS	DUNDEE DIST	DELAP	DUNLOP
DANSKIN	DUNDEE DIST	DELDAY	SINCLAIR
DANSON	ROXBURGH DIST	DELGAT(T)IE,-Y	HAY
DANZIEL	DALZELL	DELL	DALZELL
DARG(S)	MUSSELBURGH DIST	DEMAR	GLASGOW DIST
DARGAVELL	PAISLEY DIST	DEMPSEY,-IE	PERTHSHIRE DIST
DARGIE,-Y	ANGUS DIST	DEMPSTER	STRATHEARN DIST
DARLEITH	LENNOX DIST	DEMPSTERTON	FIFE DIST
DARLING	TWEEDSIDE DIST	DENHAM	ROXBURGH DIST
DARLINGTON	ROSS	DENHOLM(E)	DENHOLME
DARRACH	MAC DONALD	DENHOLM(E)	ROXBURGH DIST
DARRAGH	MAC DONALD	DENIVAN	STIRLING DIST
DARREL(L)	TWEEDSIDE DIST	DENNING	STRATHEARN DIST
DARRIE	ROXBURGH DIST	DENNIS	DALZELL
DARROCH	MAC DONALD	DENNISON	MAC GREGOR
DARRY,-IE	ROXBURGH DIST	DENNISON,-STON	STEWART
DARSEY,-IE	FIFE DIST	DENNY(S)	DENNY
DASH(P)ER	LORNE DIST	DENOON	CAMPBELL
DASS	CAITHNESS TARTAN	DENOON	ROSS
DAUGHERTY,-IE	MAC GREGOR	DENOVAN,-IN	STIRLING DIST
DAULZELL	DALZELL	DENSMORE	MURRAY
DAVENTRIE,-Y	EDINBURGH DIST	DENSON	MAC GREGOR
DAVENY,-IE	ABERDEEN DIST	DENTON	GALLOWAY DIST
DAVEY	DAVIDSON	DERAND	CAITHNESS TARTAN
DAVID	DAVIDSON	DERBY	ABERDEEN DIST
DAVIDSON	CLAN CHATTAN	DERM(A)ID	CAMPBELL OF BREADLABANE
DAVIDSON	DAVIDSON	DERMOND	ULSTER TARTAN
DAVIDSON	DAVIDSON OF TULLOCH	DERRICK(S)	TYNESIDE DIST
DAVIE(S)	DAVIDSON	DERRY	ULSTER TARTAN
DAVIE(S)SON	DAVIDSON	DES HAY	HAY
DAVIS	DAVIDSON	DESHAYS	HAY
DAVISON	DAVIDSON	DESKIE,-(E)Y	STRATHSPEY DIST
DAW(E)(S)	DAVIDSON	DESSON	DAVIDSON
DAWSON	DAVIDSON	DEUCHAR(S)	LINDSAY

NAME	TARTAN	NAME	TARTAN
DEUGELL,-LE	MAC DOUGALL	DIVERTIE,-Y	ABERDEEN DIST
DEVAN	CLAN CIAN	DIVILY,-IE	CONNACHT TARTAN
DEVANEY	CONNACHT TARTAN	DIVINIE,-Y	ABERDEEN DIST
DEVANEY	ULSTER TARTAN	DIXON	KEITH
DEVANIE,-Y	DUNDEE DIST	DIXSON	KEITH
DEVER(S)	LAMONT	DOAK(E)	DRUMMOND
DEVER(S)	MAC GREGOR	DOAK(E)	GLASGOW DIST
DEVETTE	DAVIDSON	DOAN	CLAN CIAN
DEVINE	DUNDEE DIST	DOANE	STEWART OF ATHOLL
DEVLIN	CONNACHT TARTAN	DOB(B)IE,-Y	ROBERTSON
DEVLIN	ULSTER TARTAN	DOBBIN(S)	ROBERTSON
DEVLIN (Scot.)	MAC DONALD	DOBBINSON	ROBERTSON
DEWAR	BUCHANAN	DOBIESON	ROBERTSON
DEWAR	MAC ARTHUR	DOBSON	ROBERTSON
DEWAR	MAC NAB	DOCHART	MAC GREGOR
DEWAR	MENZIES	DOCHARTY,-IE	MAC GREGOR
DEWIS	DAVIDSON	DOCHERT	MAC GREGOR
DEY(S)	DAVIDSON	DOCHERTIE,-Y	MAC GREGOR
DEYELL	DALZELL	DOCK	DRUMMOND
DEYELL	DALZIEL	DOCKERY	CONNACHT TARTAN
DIACK	ABERDEEN DIST	DOCKRAY	MAC GREGOR
DIAL	DALZELL	DOCTOR	GALLOWAY DIST
DIAMANT	ANGUS DIST	DODD(S)	FIFE DIST
DIAMOND	ANGUS DIST	DODD(S)	TYNESIDE DIST
DIBBS	FIFE DIST	DODDLE	MAC DONALD OF GLENCOE
DICE	DYCE	DOE	PERTHSHIRE DIST
DICE	SKENE	DOGGARD,-ERD	MAC GREGOR
DICERBO	MOFFAT DIST	DOHERTY	ULSTER TARTAN
DICK	AYRSHIRE DIST	DOHERTY,-IE	ULSTER TARTAN
DICK(I)SON	KEITH	DOIG	DRUMMOND
DICKENSON	PAISLEY DIST	DOLAN,-EN	ULSTER TARTAN
DICKER	FIFE DIST	DOLE(S)	MACKINTOSH
DICKIE,-(E)Y	DOUGLAS	DOLEPAIN	GALLOWAY DIST
DICKIE,-(E)Y	KEITH	DOLEZAL(L)	DALZELL
DICKINSON	PAISLEY DIST	DOLFIN	ROXBURGH DIST
DICSON	KEITH	DOLFINESTON(E)	ROXBURGH DIST
DICUS	STRATHCLYDE DIST	DOLL	CLAN CHATTAN
DIE	DYCE	DOLL	MURRAY OF ATHOLL
DIE	SKENE	DOLLAN,-EN	DUNDEE DIST
DIESK(E)Y	STRATHSPEY DIST	DOLLAR	STIRLING DIST
DIKE,-ER(S)	STRATHSPEY DIST	DOLLARD	INVERNESS DIST
DILL	INVERNESS DIST	DOLLASE	MACKINTOSH
DILLIDA(FF)	ABERDEEN DIST	DOLZELL	DALZELL
DILLON	CONNACHT TARTAN	DON(N)	MAR DIST
DIMMER	LOCHABER DIST	DONACHIE,-Y	ROBERTSON
DIMOND	ULSTER TARTAN	DONAGHY	ROBERTSON
DIN(N)	DUNBLANE DIST	DONAHUE	ULSTER TARTAN
DINGWALL	MUNRO	DONAL(L)	MAC DONALD
DINGWALL	ROSS	DONALD	MAC DONALD
DINNEL	GALLOWAY DIST	DONALDSON	MAC DONALD
DINNES	INNES	DONAT(T)	STRATHEARN DIST
DINNIE,-Y	MAR DIST	DONDALE	MAR DIST
DINNING(S)	STRATHEARN DIST	DONEGAN	ULSTER TARTAN
DINSMORE	MURRAY	DONELL(E)Y	ULSTER TARTAN
DINWIDDIE	MAXWELL	DONILLSON	MAC DONALD
DINWOODY	MAXWELL	DONLE(A)VY	BUCHANAN
DIPPIE,-Y	EDINBURGH DIST	DONLE(A)VY	STEWART OF APPIN
DIPPLE	INVERNESS DIST	DONNACHIE,-Y	ROBERTSON
DIRLAND	ROXBURGH DIST	DONNAL(L)	MAC DONALD
DIRLETON	EDINBURGH DIST	DONNEL(L)	MAC DONALD
DIS(E)	DYCE	DONNELLAN,-EN	CONNACHT TARTAN
DIS(S)	SKENE	DONOHOE	ULSTER TARTAN
DISE	SKENE	DONOHUE	ULSTER TARTAN
DISHART	FIFE DIST	DOOGAN	ULSTER TARTAN
DISSOCK	ROBERTSON	DOOL	DALZELL
DIVER	ULSTER TARTAN	DOORLY,-IE	CONNACHT TARTAN

NAME	TARTAN	NAME	TARTAN
DOORS	PERTHSHIRE DIST	DRIVER(S)	CAITHNESS TARTAN
DORAN	GALLOWAY DIST	DROWSER	TYNESIDE DIST
DORCY	CONNACHT TARTAN	DRUBBER	GLASGOW DIST
DORIAN	GALLOWAY DIST	DRUM	ABERDEEN DIST
DORNACH	INVERNESS DIST	DRUM	ULSTER TARTAN
DORNIE,-Y	ABERDEEN DIST	DRUMAGAHASSIE,-Y	GRAHAM
DORNOCH,-K	INVERNESS DIST	DRUMBECK	ABERDEEN DIST
DORREN	GALLOWAY DIST	DRUMELIZOR	HAY
DORSEY	CONNACHT TARTAN	DRUMLITHE	DRUMLITHE
DORTHON,-AN	ANGUS DIST	DRUMMOND	DRUMMOND
DORWARD	GORDON	DRUMMOND	DRUMMOND OF LOGIE
DORWARD	MAR DIST	DRUMMOND	DRUMMOND OF STRATHALLAN
DORY,-IE	CORNISH TARTAN	DRYB(O)URGH	ROXBURGH DIST
DOTT	ST. ANDREWS DIST	DRYBURN(E)	EDINBURGH DIST
DOUCHALL	PAISLEY DIST	DRYDEN	ANGUS DIST
DOUCHERTY,-IE	MAC GREGOR	DRYLAW	EDINBURGH DIST
DOUGAL(L)	MAC DOUGALL	DRYLIE,-Y	STRATHCLYDE DIST
DOUGALSON	MAC DOUGALL	DRYMAN,-EN	DRUMMOND
DOUGAN	GALLOWAY DIST	DRYNEN	DRUMMOND
DOUGHAN	GALLOWAY DIST	DRYSDALE	DOUGLAS
DOUGHERTY,-IE	MAC GREGOR	DRYSDEN	ANGUS DIST
DOUGHTIE,-Y	ROXBURGH DIST	DRYSEDALE	DOUGLAS
DOUGLAS(S)	DOUGLAS	DUAINE	CLAN CIAN
DOUGLAS(S)	LAMONT	DUANE	CLAN CIAN
DOUL(L)	CAITHNESS TARTAN	DUBBER	GLASGOW DIST
DOUL(L)	MAC DOUGALL	DUBHSITHE	MAC FIE
DOUNE	STEWART OF ATHOLL	DUBSIDE	MAC FIE
DOVE	BUCHANAN	DUBUCAN	ANGUS DIST
DOVE	DAVIDSON	DUCAT(T)	ABERDEEN DIST
DOVERTIE,-Y	ABERDEEN DIST	DUCHRAY	GRAHAM
DOW(E)	BUCHANAN	DUCHWRAY	GRAHAM
DOW(E)	MAC DOUGALL	DUDDING(S)TON	EDINBURGH DIST
DOWALL,-ELL	MAC DOUGALL	DUDGEON	MUSSELBURGH DIST
DOWALL,-ELL	MAC DOUGALL	DUFACIUS	MAC FIE
DOWD	CONNACHT TARTAN	DUFF	GORDON
DOWDALL,-ELL	GLASGOW DIST	DUFF	MAC DUFF
DOWDLE	MAC DOUGALL	DUFFES	GORDON
DOWIE	CAMERON	DUFFES	SUTHERLAND
DOWIE	MAC GREGOR	DUFFIE,-(E)Y	MAC FIE
DOWIE	MAC LEAN OF DUART	DUFFUS	GORDON
DOWLER,-AR	MAC DOUGALL	DUFFUS	SUTHERLAND
DOWLING	DOWLING	DUFFY	ULSTER TARTAN
DOWNEY	CLAN CIAN	DUG(G)AN	CONNACHT TARTAN
DOWNEY	CONNACHT TARTAN	DUG(G)AN	GALLOWAY DIST
DOWNIE	LINDSAY	DUGAID	ABERDEEN DIST
DOWNS	CLAN CIAN	DUGAL(D)	MAC DOUGALL
DOWNS	LINDSAY	DUGALSTON	GRAHAM
DOYLE	MAC DOUGALL	DUGETT	ABERDEEN DIST
DRAIN	MAC DONALD	DUGGIE,-Y	INVERNESS DIST
DRAINIE,-Y	INVERNESS DIST	DUGID	ABERDEEN DIST
DRAKE	STRATHSPEY DIST	DUGITT	ABERDEEN DIST
DRANE	MAC DONALD	DUGLE	MAC DOUGALL
DRAPPO	GLASGOW DIST	DUIE	CAMERON
DREDAN,-EN,-IN	GALLOWAY DIST	DUIE	MAC LEAN OF DUART
DREGHORN	PAISLEY DIST	DUIL	DALZELL
DREN(N)AN,-IN	DRENNAN	DUILACH	STEWART OF ATHOLL
DREN(N)AN,-IN	DRUMMOND	DUINEMATH	MAC GREGOR
DREVER	SINCLAIR	DUIRS	PERTHSHIRE DIST
DREW	GLASGOW DIST	DUKE	ABERDEEN DIST
DREW	STIRLING DIST		
DRIDAN,-EN	ANGUS DIST	DUL(L)Y,-IE	INVERNESS DIST
DRIMMAN,-EN	DRUMMOND	DULACK,-OCK	STEWART OF ATHOLL
DRIMMIE,-Y	PERTHSHIRE DIST	DULAP	DUNLOP
DRINNAN	DRUMMOND	DULL	DALZELL
DRIPP(S)	STRATHCLYDE DIST	DULL	MURRAY OF ATHOLL
DRISDALE	DOUGLAS	DULLEN,-IN	GALLOWAY DIST
DRISDALL	DOUGLAS	DULLIE,-Y	INVERNESS DIST
		DULLOP	DUNLOP

NAME	TARTAN	NAME	TARTAN
DUMBART	DUNBAR	DURKIN	CLAN CIAN
DUMBART	GUNN	DURLAND	ROXBURGH DIST
DUMBARTON	LENNOX DIST	DURNIE,-EY	ABERDEEN DIST
DUMBRETTON	LENNOX DIST	DURNO	ABERDEEN DIST
DUMFREYS	GALLOWAY DIST	DURRAN(D)	DUNBAR DIST
DUMFRIES	GALLOWAY DIST	DURRANS	CAITHNESS TARTAN
DUN	TWEEDSIDE DIST	DURRAR,-ER	BUCHANAN
DUNAN	CAMPBELL	DURRAR,-ER	MENZIES
DUNAN	ROSS	DURRAT	MAR DIST
DUNBAR	DUNBAR	DURREY	ANGUS DIST
DUNBAR	HOME	DURREY	DUNDEE DIST
DUNBAR	MURRAY	DURROCH	MAC DONALD
DUNBARNY,-EY	STRATHEARN DIST	DURWARD	GORDON
DUNBARTON	LENNOX DIST	DURWARD	MAR DIST
DUNBLANE	DUNBLANE DIST	DURY	CAITHNESS TARTAN
DUNCAN(SON)	DUNCAN	DUSKIE,-(E)Y	CAITHNESS TARTAN
DUNCAN(SON)	ROBERTSON	DUST	PERTHSHIRE DIST
DUNCANSON	DUNCAN	DUSTIE,-Y	PERTHSHIRE DIST
DUNCANSON	ROBERTSON	DUTCH	DUNDEE DIST
DUNCOLL	GALLOWAY DIST	DUTCH	DUTCH TARTAN
DUNDAS	DUNBAR	DUTHIE,-Y	ROSS
DUNDAS	DUNDAS	DUTHIL(L)	STRATHSPEY DIST
DUNDEE	DUNDEE DIST	DUTT	AYRSHIRE DIST
DUNDONALD	PAISLEY DIST	DUVALL	MAC DOUGALL
DUNFEE	INVERNESS DIST	DUWALL	MAC DOUGALL
DUNFIE(S)	INVERNESS DIST	DWAINE	CLAN CIAN
DUNGALSON	STRATHCLYDE DIST	DYACK	ABERDEEN DIST
DUNIPACE	STIRLING DIST	DYALL	DALZELL
DUNKELD	PERTHSHIRE DIST	DYAS	SKENE
DUNKIN	DUNCAN	DYAT(T)	EGLINTON DIST
DUNLAP	AYRSHIRE DIST	DYCE	DYCE
DUNLAP	DUNLOP	DYCE	SKENE
DUNLEAVY	MAC KINLEY	DYCUS	STRATHCLYDE DIST
DUNLOP	AYRSHIRE DIST	DYE	DAVIDSON
DUNLOP	DUNLOP	DYER	ABERDEEN DIST
DUNMIRE	CAMPBELL	DYESON	DAVIDSON
DUNMORE	CAMPBELL	DYESS	SKENE
DUNN(E)	ANGUS DIST	DYKE(S)	STRATHCLYDE DIST
DUNNACHIE,-Y	ROBERTSON	DYKER(S)	STRATHSPEY DIST
DUNNATT	CAITHNESS TARTAN	DYS(H)ART	FIFE DIST
DUNNEL	MAC DONALD	DYSE	SKENE
DUNNET(T)	CAITHNESS TARTAN	DYSON	DAVIDSON
DUNNING	STRATHEARN DIST		
DUNOON	CAMPBELL		
DUNOON	ROSS		
DUNOVAN,-EN	STIRLING DIST		
DUNPHY,-IE	INVERNESS DIST		
DUNS(E)	TWEEDSIDE DIST		
DUNS(H)IRE	STRATHCLYDE DIST		
DUNSCORE	GALLOWAY DIST		
DUNSE	TWEEDSIDE DIST		
DUNSHIE,-Y	GALLOWAY DIST	EACH	MAC DONALD
DUNSIRE	STRATHCLYDE DIST	EACH	MAC EACHAIN
DUNSLEAVE	ARGYLL DIST	EACHAN,-EN	MAC DONALD
DUNSMORE	MURRAY	EACHAN,-EN	MAC EACHAIN
DUNSMUIR	MURRAY	EAD(D)IE,-Y	GORDON
DUNSTAN	FIFE DIST	EADAILE	STRATHCLYDE DIST
DUNWOODY,-IE	MAXWELL	EAGLE(S)	ROXBURGH DIST
DUP(P)LIN	HAY	EAGLESFIELD	GALLOWAY DIST
DUPHACI(E),-Y	MAC FIE	EAGLESHAM	PAISLEY DIST
DUPLATT	DALZELL	EAGLESOME	LORNE DIST
DUR(R)IE,-Y	ANGUS DIST	EAKIN(S)	GORDON
DURAND	DUNBAR DIST	EAKS	MAC EACHAIN
DURAY	ANGUS DIST	EANR(U)IG	GUNN
DURDLE	INVERNESS DIST	EARLE	PAISLEY DIST
DURHAM	ROXBURGH DIST	EARLSON	TWEEDSIDE DIST
DURIE	DUNDEE DIST	EARLSTON	GLASGOW DIST
		EAS(S)IE	ANGUS DIST

E

NAME	TARTAN	NAME	TARTAN
EAS(S)ON	MAC KAY	ELLIS	MAC PHERSON
EAS(S)ON	MACKINTOSH	ELLISON	MAC PHERSON
EASDALE	STRATHCLYDE DIST	ELLON	ABERDEEN DIST
EASTMEAD	INVERNESS DIST	ELLUM	TWEEDSIDE DIST
EASTON	TWEEDSIDE DIST	ELMER	DUNDEE DIST
EASTWOOD	PAISLEY DIST	ELMORE	MORRISON
EATON	HOME	ELMSLIE,-Y	ABERDEEN DIST
EBAUGH	ABERDEEN DIST	ELPHIN	MAC ALPINE
EBBOT	DUNDEE DIST	ELPHINSTONE	ELPHINSTONE
ECCLES	TWEEDSIDE DIST	ELRICK	ABERDEEN DIST
ECHLIN	EDINBURGH DIST	ELSHENER	MAC DONALD
ECKFORD	ROXBURGH DIST	ELSON	MAC KAY
ECKLES	TWEEDSIDE DIST	ELWIS(E)	MULL DIST
ED(D)ELL	LINDSAY	EMM	GALLOWAY DIST
ED(D)IE,-Y	GORDON	EMSLIE,-EY	ABERDEEN DIST
EDDISLAW	EDINBURGH DIST	ENGAIN(E)	ROXBURGH DIST
EDGAR	MAXWELL	ENGELHEART	ENGELHEART
EDGAR	NITHSDALE DIST	ENGLAND	DUNDEE DIST
EDGIE	MACKINTOSH	ENGLISH	ROXBURGH DIST
EDGLAW	EDINBURGH DIST	ENLOE	EDINBURGH DIST
EDINBORO	EDINBURGH DIST	ENNIS	INNES
EDINBURGH	EDINBURGH DIST	ENR(U)IG	MAC KENDRICK
EDINGTON	TWEEDSIDE DIST	ENRICK	GUNN
EDINSTON(E)	EDINBURGH DIST	ENRICK	MAC KENDRICK
EDISON	GORDON	ENRIGHT	GUNN
EDMINSHIRE	EDINBURGH DIST	ENSLIE,-EY	AINSLIE
EDMISTON	EDINBURGH DIST	ENTWHISTLE	TYNESIDE DIST
EDMISTON	GLASGOW DIST	ENTWISLE	TYNESIDE DIST
EDMOND	ABERDEEN DIST	EPPS	LORNE DIST
EDMONDSON	ABERDEEN DIST	ERASMUSON	CALEDONIA TARTAN
EDMONDSTON(E)	LENNOX DIST	ERCILDO(U)N	TWEEDSIDE DIST
EDMUND	ABERDEEN DIST	ERGO	MAR DIST
EDNAM	ROXBURGH DIST	ERI(C)KSON	CALEDONIA TARTAN
EDNIE,-Y	FIFE DIST	ERRIDGE	SUTHERLAND DIST
EDWARD(S)	LENNOX DIST	ERROL	ARROL
EDWARDSON	LENNOX DIST	ERROLL	HAY
EDWARDSON	MAC EDWARD	ERSKINE	ERSKINE
EDWART	ROXBURGH DIST	ERVIN(E)	IRVINE
EEKS	MAC DONALD	ERWIN	IRVINE
EEKS	MAC EACHAIN	ESB(E)Y,-IE	MAC PHERSON
EEN	MAC BEAN	ESB(E)Y-IE	ULSTER TARTAN
EG(G)O	MAR DIST	ESBANK	GRAHAM
EGAN	CONNACHT TARTAN	ESP(E)Y,-IE	GILLESPIE
EGARR	MAXWELL	ESPL(E)Y,-IE	GILLESPIE
EGGIE	MACKINTOSH	ESPL(E)Y,-IE	MAC PHERSON
EGLINGBURG	EGLINTON DIST	ESPLIN(E)	STIRLING DIST
EGLINTON	EGLINTON DIST	ESS(H)LEMONT	GORDON
EIBHINN	MAC IVER	ESSIE,-Y	ANGUS DIST
EILERTON,-SON	SUTHERLAND DIST	ESSON	MAC KAY
EIVERS	MAC IVER	ESSON	MACKINTOSH
EL(L)IAS	DUNDAS	ESTBRIDGE	INVERNESS DIST
ELDER	MACKINTOSH	ESTES	ESTES
ELDRED	ROXBURGH DIST	ESTRIDGE	INVERNESS DIST
ELFORD	ABERDEEN DIST	ETBORN(E)	TWEEDSIDE DIST
ELGE(Y)	DUNDEE DIST	ETCHELL(S)	LINDSAY
ELGIN	STRATHSPEY DIST	ETELL	LINDSAY
ELIOTSON	ELLIOT	ETTALE,-ALL	ABERDEEN DIST
ELL	GALLOWAY DIST	ETTELL,-ALL	ABERDEEN DIST
ELLEM	TWEEDSIDE DIST	ETTERSHANK	ABERDEEN DIST
ELLEN	TWEEDSIDE DIST	EU(E)NSON	MAC EWEN
ELLERMAN	INVERNESS DIST	EURE	MAC IVER
ELLESLEY	STRATHEARN DIST	EUSTACE	CLAN CIAN
ELLET	DUNDAS	EVANDER	MAC IVER
ELLET	ELLIOT	EVANS	WELSH NATIONAL
ELLICE	MAC PHERSON	EVANSON	WELSH NATIONAL
ELLINGHAM	ARRAN DIST	EVER(S)	MAC IVER
ELLIOT(T)	ELLIOT	EVERETT	ANGUS DIST
		EVERLIE,-Y	PERTHSHIRE DIST

NAME	TARTAN	NAME	TARTAN
EVERSON	MAC IVER	FAREFULL	ST. ANDREWS DIST
EVIOT	ANGUS DIST	FARG	DUNBLANE DIST
EVOR(S)	MAC IVER	FARGASON	FARQUHARSON
EWAN	MAC EWEN	FARGASON	FERGUSON
EWARD,-T	DALZELL	FARGIE,-Y	FERGUSON
EWARD,-T	ROXBURGH DIST	FARIE	AYRSHIRE DIST
EWEN	MAC EWEN	FARKER	FARQUHARSON
EWER(S)	MAC IVER	FARLAN(E)	MAC FARLANE
EWING	MAC EWEN	FARLENE	MAC FARLANE
EYE	MAC KAY	FARLEY,-IE	ROSE
EYRE(S)	ROXBURGH DIST	FARMER	PERTHSHIRE DIST
		FARNAN	ANGUS DIST
		FARNELL,-ALL	ANGUS DIST
		FARNINGDON	ROXBURGH DIST
		FARNINGTON	ROXBURGH DIST
F		FARQUHAR	FARQUHARSON
		FARQUHARSON	FARQUHARSON
		FARQUHARSON	FARQUHARSON OF FINDZEAN
FAA	TWEEDSIDE DIST	FARRAN	MAC FARLANE
FABER	PERTHSHIRE DIST	FARRAR	INVERNESS DIST
FACHNIE,-EY	STRATHEARN DIST	FARRELL	O'FARRELL
FACKNEY,-IE	STRATHEARN DIST	FARRELL	ULSTER TARTAN
FAD	MAC LAREN	FARRELLY	ULSTER TARTAN
FADDEN	MAC FADYEN	FARREN	ULSTER TARTAN
FADDEN	MAC LEAN OF DUART	FARRER	INVERNESS DIST
FADYEN	MAC FADYEN	FASKIN,-EN	BUCHAN DIST
FADYEN	MAC LEAN OF DUART	FASLANE	LENNOX DIST
FAED	MAC LAREN	FASLANE,-AIN	LENNOX DIST
FAH(E)Y	CONNACHT TARTAN	FASSINGTON	EDINBURGH DIST
FAH(S)	TWEEDSIDE DIST	FAUBUS	FORBES
FAHERTY	CONNACHT TARTAN	FAUCETT	CARRICK DIST
FAICHNIE,-EY	STRATHEARN DIST	FAULDS	EDINBURGH DIST
FAILL	MAC KAY	FAULE(S)	AYRSHIRE DIST
FAILL	MAC PHAIL	FAULKNER	ULSTER TARTAN
FAIN,-E (S)	AYRSHIRE DIST	FAW(E)(S)	TWEEDSIDE DIST
FAIR	ROSS	FAWCETT	CARRICK DIST
FAIRBAIN	ARMSTRONG	FAWNS	TWEEDSIDE DIST
FAIRBAIRN	ARMSTRONG	FAWSIDE,-YDE	EDINBURGH DIST
FAIRFIELD	FIFE DIST	FEAR	ROSS
FAIRFULL	ST. ANDREWS DIST	FEARN(S)	ROSS
FAIRGRIEVE	TWEEDSIDE DIST	FEATHERS	FIFE DIST
FAIRHAIR	FARQUHARSON	FEATHERSTON(E)	FIFE DIST
FAIRHAR	FARQUHARSON	FECHNIE,-Y	STRATHEARN DIST
FAIRHAUGH	DUNBAR DIST	FEDDES,-IS	FIDDES
FAIRHOLM	STRATHCLYDE DIST	FEDERITH	SUTHERLAND
FAIRHURST	CALEDONIA TARTAN	FEE	MAC FIE
FAIRIE,-Y	AYRSHIRE DIST	FEEHENY	CONNACHT TARTAN
FAIRINGTON	ROXBURGH DIST	FEENEY,-IE	PAISLEY DIST
FAIRLEY,-LIE	ROSE	FELDIE,-Y	ST. ANDREWS DIST
FAIRSERVICE	STRATHCLYDE DIST	FELL	DUNDEE DIST
FAIRWEATHER	PERTHSHIRE DIST	FELLOW(E)S	STRATHSPEY DIST
FALA	EDINBURGH DIST	FEMISTER	INVERNESS DIST
FALASTONE	ROBERTSON	FEND(E)	GALLOWAY DIST
FALAY	GALLOWAY DIST	FENDER	EDINBURGH DIST
FALCONER,-OR	KEITH	FENTON	CHISHOLM
FALDS	EDINBURGH DIST	FENWICK	ROXBURGH DIST
FALKIRK	STIRLING DIST	FER(R)IAR	LENNOX DIST
FALL	MAC KAY	FERGIE	FERGUSON
FALL(S)	TWEEDSIDE DIST	FERGUS	FERGUSON
FALLA	EDINBURGH DIST	FERGUSON	FERGUSON
FALLAS	STRATHCLYDE DIST	FERGUSON	FERGUSON BALQUHIDDER
FALLEN	CONNACHT TARTAN	FERME,-A	STRATHCLYDE DIST
FALLON	CONNACHT TARTAN	FERN	SUTHERLAND DIST
FALTON	ARGYLL DIST	FERNIE,-Y	FIFE DIST
FAMILTON	DUNBAR DIST	FERQUHAR	FARQUHARSON
FARAHAR	FARQUHARSON	FERRAL(L)	O'FARRELL
FARCHAIR	FARQUHARSON	FERRET	FARQUHARSON
FARE	ROSS		

NAME	TARTAN	NAME	TARTAN
FERRIE(S),-Y(S)	FARQUHARSON	FITCHET	DUNDEE DIST
FERRIE(S),-Y(S)	FERGUSON	FITCHIE,-Y	BUCHAN DIST
FERRIER	ANGUS DIST	FITGERALD	FITZGERALD
FERRILL	O'FARRELL	FITHIE,-Y	ANGUS DIST
FERRIS(S)	FERGUSON		
FERSEN,-ON	MAC PHERSON	FITZPATRICK	FITZPATRICK
FETTERS	FIFE DIST	FITZSIMMONS	ULSTER TARTAN
FETTES	FIDDES	FIVE,-Y	ANGUS DIST
FEY	MAC FIE	FLACK	LINDSAY
FID(D)LER	STRATHCLYDE DIST	FLANAGAN,-EN	CONNACHT TARTAN
FIDDES	FIDDES	FLANELLY	CONNACHT TARTAN
FIDDISON	GALLOWAY DIST	FLANIGAN	ULSTER TARTAN
FIFE	FIFE DIST	FLANNERY	CONNACHT TARTAN
FIFE	MAC DUFF	FLAWS	SINCLAIR
FIL(L)AN(S)	STRATHEARN DIST	FLECK(E)	LINDSAY
FILMORE	LENNOX DIST	FLEDG(E)CARE	MAC GREGOR
FILP	ANGUS DIST	FLEMING	MURRAY OF ATHOLL
FILSHIE,-Y	LENNOX DIST	FLESHER	ABERDEEN DIST
FIMISTER	STRATHSPEY DIST	FLETCHER	FLETCHER
FIMMERTON	EDINBURGH DIST	FLETCHER	FLETCHER OF DUNANS
FIN(D)LAY	MAC KINLEY	FLETCHER	MAC GREGOR
FIN(N)	STRATHCLYDE DIST	FLETT(E)	SINCLAIR
FINAGHY	CONNACHT TARTAN	FLEX	ROXBURGH DIST
FINAN	CONNACHT TARTAN	FLINT	TWEEDSIDE DIST
FINDEN	MAR DIST	FLISK(E)	FIFE DIST
FINDLATER	HUNTLY DIST	FLOCKHART,-ERT	FIFE DIST
FINDLATER	OGILVIE	FLOOD	CLAN CIAN
FINDLAY	FARQUHARSON	FLORENCE	GALLOWAY DIST
FINDLAY	MAC KINNON	FLORIN	GLASGOW DIST
FINDLAYSON	FARQUHARSON	FLOWERS	EDINBURGH DIST
FINDLEY,-IE	FARQUHARSON	FLUCKER	FIFE DIST
FINDON	MAR DIST	FLUGG	INVERNESS DIST
FINEGAN(D)	FINEGAN	FLYNN	CONNACHT TARTAN
FINGALL	MAC DONALD	FLYNN	STIRLING DIST
FINGASK	MAC THOMAS	FOGGIE,-Y	ABERDEEN DIST
FINGLASS	ANGUS DIST	FOGGO	TWEEDSIDE DIST
FINGLE	MAC DONALD	FOLDS	EDINBURGH DIST
FINITER	STRATHSPEY DIST	FOLKHARD	GALLOWAY DIST
FINLAISON	FARQUHARSON	FOOT(E)	ANGUS DIST
FINLAISON	MAC KINLEY	FOR(E)SON	EDINBURGH DIST
FINLAISON	MAC KINNON	FORBES	FORBES
FINLAISSON	MAC KINLEY	FORBES	FORBES OF DRUMINNOR
FINLASON	FARQUHARSON	FORBISTER	CAITHNESS TARTAN
FINLASON	MAC KINLEY	FORBUSH	FORBES
FINLASON	MAC KINNON	FORD(E)	FORDE
FINLAY	FARQUHARSON	FORDELL	PERTHSHIRE DIST
FINLAY	MAC KINNON	FORDICE	FORBES
FINLAYSON	FARQUHARSON	FORDOUN	ANGUS DIST
FINLAYSON	MAC KINLEY	FORDYCE	FORBES
FINLEY	MAC KINNON	FORDYCE	FORBES
FINN	CONNACHT TARTAN	FOREHOUSE	TWEEDSIDE DIST
FINNAN	GALLOWAY DIST	FOREMAN	EDINBURGH DIST
FINNELSTON	AYRSHIRE DIST	FOREST	DOUGLAS
FINNICK	EDINBURGH DIST	FOREST	FORRESTER
FINNICK	FIFE DIST	FORET	DOUGLAS
FINNIE,-EY	ABERDEEN DIST	FORFAR	ANGUS DIST
FINNIE,-EY	GLASGOW DIST	FORGAN	FIFE DIST
FINNIESTON	GLASGOW DIST	FORGIE,-Y	ANGUS DIST
FINNISON	ABERDEEN DIST	FORGREIVE	ARGYLL DIST
FINNOCK	FIFE DIST	FORGUS	FARQUHARSON
FINTRAY,-IE	GRAHAM	FORGUS	FERGUSON
FINTRY,-IE	GRAHAM	FORK(S)	PAISLEY DIST
FIRSKIN	PERTHSHIRE DIST	FORKER	FARQUHARSON
FIRTH	ROXBURGH DIST	FORMAN	EDINBURGH DIST
FISH	EDINBURGH DIST	FORRES	STRATHSPEY DIST
FISHER	CAMPBELL	FORREST	FORRESTER
FISKEN,-IN	STRATHEARN DIST	FORREST	MAC DONALD

NAME	TARTAN	NAME	TARTAN
FORRESTER	FORRESTER	FRESER	FRASER
FORRESTER	MAC DONALD	FRESKIN,-YN	PERTHSHIRE DIST
FORRET	FIFE DIST	FRESSLY,-IE	FIFE DIST
FORSHAW	PERTHSHIRE DIST	FREW	FRASER
FORSTER	FORRESTER	FREZEL(L)(E)	FRASER
FORSTER	MAC DONALD	FRIAR	DUNDEE DIST
FORSYTH(E)	FORSYTH	FRIEL(L)	ULSTER TARTAN
FORTEITH	LORNE DIST	FRIER	DUNDEE DIST
FORTEVIOT	PERTHSHIRE DIST	FRISEAL	FRASER
FORTRIETH,-IE,-Y	ABERDEEN DIST	FRISELL(E)	FRASER
FORTUNE	MUSSELBURGH DIST	FRISKIN	PERTHSHIRE DIST
FOSSARD,-T	EDINBURGH DIST	FRISLIN(E)	EDINBURGH DIST
FOSSETT(S)	EDINBURGH DIST	FRISWELL	FRASER
FOSTER	DOUGLAS	FRIZEL(L)(E)	FRASER
FOSTER	FORRESTER	FRODSHAM	ST. ANDREWS DIST
FOSTER	FOSTER	FROG	EDINBURGH DIST
FOSTER	MAC DONALD	FROGGET	NITHSDALE DIST
FOTHERGILL	PERTHSHIRE DIST	FROOD	ROXBURGH DIST
FOTHERINGHAM	LINDSAY	FROST	ROXBURGH DIST
FOUBISTER	CAITHNESS TARTAN	FRUCTOR	MAR DIST
FOUGLER	INVERNESS DIST	FRYER	DUNDEE DIST
FOULER	TWEEDSIDE DIST	FUDGE	FT. WILLIAM DIST
FOULIS	MUNRO	FUKTOR	MAR DIST
FOUNTAIN	EDINBURGH DIST	FUL(L)TON	AYRSHIRE DIST
FOURNES	DUNDEE DIST	FULKERSON	FARQUHARSON
FOURSIDES	LAMONT	FULLAR	EDINBURGH DIST
FOW(E)L(L)	INVERNESS DIST	FULLARTON	STUART OF BUTE
FOWLER	TWEEDSIDE DIST	FULLER	EDINBURGH DIST
FOWLIE,-Y	MUNRO	FULLERTON	FULLERTON
FOWLIS	MUNRO	FULLERTON	STUART OF BUTE
FOX	GALLOWAY DIST	FULTEN	ARRAN DIST
FOYD	ANGUS DIST	FULTON	AYRSHIRE DIST
FOYER(S)	MENTIETH DIST	FURBUR	ROXBURGH DIST
FOYT	ANGUS DIST	FURBUSH	FORBES
FRAHER	FRASER	FUREY	CONNACHT TARTAN
FRAIL	LENNOX DIST	FURGURSON	FERGUSON
FRAIN	ABERDEEN DIST	FURIE,-Y	ANGUS DIST
FRAM(E)	FRAME	FURMAGE	DUNDEE DIST
FRANCE(S),-IS	STEWART	FURNIVAL	INVERNESS DIST
FRANK	EDINBURGH DIST	FURRY,-IE	ANGUS DIST
FRANK(MAN)	PERTHSHIRE DIST	FURYE	ANGUS DIST
FRASER	FRASER	FUTHIE	OGILVIE
FRASER	FRASER OF ALTYRE	FYALL	FIFE DIST
FRASER	FRASER OF LOVAT	FYF(F)E	FIFE DIST
FRASHER	FRASER	FYVIE,-Y	ANGUS DIST
FRASHIER	FRASER		
FRASHURE	FRASER		
FRASIER	FRASER		
FRASUER	FRASER		
FRASUIR	FRASER		
FRATER	GALLOWAY DIST		
FRAY	CAITHNESS TARTAN		
FRAYSER	FRASER		
FRAZAR	FRASER		
FRAZEE	FRASER		
FRAZER	FRASER	GADDIE,-Y	GEDDES
FRAZIER	FRASER	GAFFNEY	DUNDEE DIST
FRAZURE	FRASER	GAILBRAITH	MAC DONALD
FREEBAIRN	GALLOWAY DIST	GAIN(ES)	GLASGOW DIST
FREELAND,-ANE	DUNBLANE DIST	GAIR	GAYRE
FREELOVE	ABERDEEN DIST	GAIR	MAC GREGOR
FREEMAN	ROXBURGH DIST	GAIR	ROSS
FREER	TWEEDSIDE DIST	GAIRN(S)	GRANT
FREESSELL	FRASER	GAIRNER	GORDON
FREEVILLE	ANGUS DIST	GALASHAN	MAC GLASHAN
FRENCH	CONNACHT TARTAN	GALBRAITH	GALBRAITH
FRENCH	NITHSDALE DIST	GALBRAITH	MAC DONALD
		GALBRAITH	MAC FARLANE
		GALBREATH	GALBRAITH
		GALBREATH	MAC FARLANE

G

NAME	TARTAN	NAME	TARTAN
GALCHE	GUNN	GARRA(D)	HAY
GALDIE,-(E)Y	GUNN	GARRATT	NITHSDALE DIST
GALE(S)	ABERDEEN DIST	GARRAWAY	GALLOWAY DIST
GALL	MAC DONALD	GARRETT	NITHSDALE DIST
GALLACHER	DUNDEE DIST	GARRICK	GORDON
GALLAGHER	ULSTER TARTAN	GARRIGAN	DUNDEE DIST
GALLAGHRER	ULSTER TARTAN	GARRIOCK	GORDON
GALLANT	ABERDEEN DIST	GARRISON	FT. WILLIAM DIST
GALLARD	FIFE DIST	GARROW	HAY
GALLATLY,-IE	PERTHSHIRE DIST	GARROW	STEWART
GALLERY,-IE	MAC GILLIVRAY	GARROWAY	CALEDONIA TARTAN
GALLESPIE,-Y	MAC PHERSON	GARSON	CAITHNESS TARTAN
GALLETLY,-IE	ABERDEEN DIST	GARSTANG	GALLOWAY DIST
GALLIE,-(E)Y	CAITHNESS TARTAN	GARTIE,-Y	STRATHSPEY DIST
GALLIE,-(E)Y	GUNN	GARTLIE,-Y	ABERDEEN DIST
GALLIGAN	ULSTER TARTAN	GARTNEY	MAR DIST
GALLIMORE	ANGUS DIST	GARTSHORE	LENNOX DIST
GALLITIE,-Y	PERTHSHIRE DIST	GARVAN	GLASGOW DIST
GALLIWOOD	EDINBURGH DIST	GARVEY,-IE	CONNACHT TARTAN
GALLOCH	CAITHNESS TARTAN	GARVIE,-Y	MAC LEAN
GALLOGIE,-Y	MAC DONALD	GARVILL(E)	CLAN CIAN
GALLOW	EDINBURGH DIST	GARVINE	CONNACHT TARTAN
GALLOWAY	LENNOX DIST	GARVOCK,-CH	PERTHSHIRE DIST
GALLOWAY	MAC FARLANE	GARWOOD	STRATHCLYDE DIST
GALLY,-IE	GUNN	GARY	GARY
GALPIN(E)	MAC ALPINE	GARY,-IE	PAISLEY DIST
GALRIG,-CK	FIFE DIST	GASK	CRIEFF DIST
GALSTON(E)	CARRICK DIST	GASK	STRATHEARN DIST
GALT	GALT	GASKELL	MAC ASKILL
GALT	MAC DONALD	GASKELL	MAC LEOD
GALWIE,-EY	GALLOWAY DIST	GASS	GALLOWAY DIST
GALWREATH	GALBRAITH	GASTON	ROXBURGH DIST
GAMBLE	GALLOWAY DIST	GATES	LENNOX DIST
GAMELSON	STIRLING DIST	GATHERER	INVERNESS DIST
GAMILSON	STIRLING DIST	GATT	ROXBURGH DIST
GAMMACK	MAR DIST	GAUDEN,-ON	CALEDONIA TARTAN
GAMMELL	AYRSHIRE DIST	GAUL	MAC DONALD
GAMMELL	GAMMELL	GAULCHE	GUNN
GAMMERIE,-Y	BUCHAN DIST	GAULD	MAC DONALD
GAMMIE,-Y	INVERNESS DIST	GAULEY,-IE	PERTHSHIRE DIST
GAN(N)ON	DUNDEE DIST	GAULT	MAC DONALD
GANDE	SUTHERLAND DIST	GAUNSON	GUNN
GANDER	INVERNESS DIST	GAUNT	SUTHERLAND DIST
GANDY,-IE	SUTHERLAND DIST	GAVIN(E)	ROXBURGH DIST
GANE	INVERNESS DIST	GAWIE,-Y	STIRLING DIST
GANSON	GUNN	GAWNE	MANX NATIONAL
GANWORTH	GALLOWAY DIST	GAY(E)	ANGUS DIST
GAR(R)ICH	GORDON	GAY(E)	DUNDEE DIST
GARDEN	ANGUS DIST	GAYNE	GLASGOW DIST
GARDEN	JARDINE	GAYRE	GAYRE
GARDENER	JARDINE	GAYTON(E)	ABERDEEN DIST
GARDENKIRK	STRATHCLYDE DIST	GEALS	ABERDEEN DIST
GARDER	GORDON	GEAR	GAYRE
GARDIN(E)	JARDINE	GEAR	MAC GREGOR
GARDIN(S)	JARDINE	GEAR	ROSS
GARDINER	GORDON	GEARY	CLAN CIAN
GARDINO	JARDINE	GEBBIE,-Y	BUCHANAN
GARDNER	GORDON	GEDD	FIFE DIST
GARDYNE	JARDINE	GEDDER	ANGUS DIST
GARIOCH	GORDON	GEDDES	GEDDES
GARLAN(D)	MURRAY	GEDDES	GORDON
GARLEA	ANGUS DIST	GEDDES	ROSE
GARMACH,-K	ABERDEEN DIST	GEDDES	SCOTT
GARMAN	ANGUS DIST	GEDDIE(S),-Y(S)	GEDDES
GARMORY,-IE	MONTGOMERY	GEDDIE(S),-Y(S)	GORDON
GARNER	ARGYLL DIST	GEDDIE(S),-Y(S)	ROSE
GARNOCK	ABERDEEN DIST	GEDDIE(S),-Y(S)	SCOTT

NAME	TARTAN	NAME	TARTAN
GEE	MAC KAY	GILFILLAN	MAC NAB
GEEKIE,-Y	ANGUS DIST	GILGUNN	GUNN
GELLAN	ABERDEEN DIST	GILHAGIE,-Y	GLASGOW DIST
GELLATIE,-Y	PERTHSHIRE DIST	GILL	MAC DONALD
GELLATTLY,-ETTLY	ABERDEEN DIST	GILL	MAC GILL
GELLEN	ABERDEEN DIST	GILL(I)ON	MAC LEAN
GELLESPIE,-Y	MAC PHERSON	GILLAM	MAC KAY
GELLIE,-EY	FIFE DIST	GILLAN	ULSTER TARTAN
GELVRA	MAC GILLIVRAY	GILLAN(D)	MAC LEAN
GEMILSTON	GALLOWAY DIST	GILLANDER(S)	ROSS
GEMMELL,-ILL	AYRSHIRE DIST	GILLEAN	MAC LEAN
GEMMELL,-ILL	GAMMELL	GILLES	GILLIES
GENTLE(S)	DUNBLANE DIST	GILLES	MAC PHERSON
GENTLEMAN	GRAHAM OF MONTROSE	GILLESPIE,-Y	GILLESPIE
GEORGE	AYRSHIRE DIST	GILLESPIE,-Y	MAC PHERSON
GEORGESON	GUNN	GILLESPISON	MAC PHERSON
GERAN(D)	GALLOWAY DIST	GILLIAM	MAC KAY
GERARD	NITHSDALE DIST	GILLIAN(D)	MAC LEAN
GERMAN	ROXBURGH DIST	GILLICE	GILLIES
GERNON	ULSTER TARTAN	GILLICE	MAC PHERSON
GERRAN	GALLOWAY DIST	GILLIECHATTAN	CLAN CHATTAN
GERRARD	NITHSDALE DIST	GILLIES	GILLIES
GERRAY	GORDON	GILLIES	MAC PHERSON
GERRIE,-Y	GORDON	GILLIGAN	ULSTER TARTAN
GERRON	GALLOWAY DIST	GILLILAND	MAC LELLEN
GERRY	CLAN CIAN	GILLIS	GILLIES
GERRY	GORDON	GILLIS	MAC DONELL GLENGARRY
GETTY,-IE	GEDDES	GILLIS	MAC PHERSON
GETTY,-IE	HAY	GILLON	MAC DONALD
GIB(B)SON	BUCHANAN	GILLON	MAC LEAN
GIB(B)SON	GIBBS	GILMAN	DUNBAR DIST
GIBB(S)	BUCHANAN	GILMARTIN	CAMERON
GIBB(S)	GIBBS	GILMER	MORRISON
GIBBIE,-Y	BUCHANAN	GILMICHAEL	TWEEDSIDE DIST
GIBBIESON	GIBBS	GILMORE	MORRISON
GIBBON	CAMPBELL	GILMOUR	MORRISON
GIBBON(S)	BUCHANAN	GILPATRICK	COLQUHOUN
GIBBSON	BUCHANAN	GILPATRICK	DOUGLAS
GIBES	BUCHANAN	GILRAY	MAC GILLIVRAY
GIBSSON	BUCHANAN	GILROY	FRASER
GIFFARD	HAY	GILROY	GRANT
GIFFEN	AYRSHIRE DIST	GILROY	MAC GILLIVRAY
GIFFERD,-URD	HAY	GILRUTH	FRASER
GIFFORD	HAY	GILRUTH	MAC DONALD OF SLEAT
GIGHT	ANGUS DIST	GILT	STIRLING DIST
GIL(L)DART	GALLOWAY DIST	GILVRAY	MAC GILLIVRAY
GIL(L)FIMAN	MAC LENNAN	GILZEAN	MAC LEAN
GIL(L)IN	DUNBAR DIST	GIMPSIE,-Y	GALLOWAY DIST
GIL(L)KERSON	AYRSHIRE DIST	GIPSON	BUCHANAN
GILBERT	BUCHANAN	GIRDWOOD	GLASGOW DIST
GILBERTSON	BUCHANAN	GIRRARD	NITHSDALE DIST
GILBERTSON	CAMERON	GIRTY,-IE	FORBES
GILBEY,-IE	OGILVIE	GIRVAN	CARRICK DIST
GILBOY	OGILVIE	GIRWOOD	STRATHCLYDE DIST
GILBRIDE	MAC DONALD	GIVAN(S)	ROXBURGH DIST
GILBY,-IE	OGILVIE	GIVEN(S)	DUNBLANE DIST
GILCHREST	OGILVIE	GLADSTONE	GLADSTONE
GILCHRIST	MAC LACHLAN	GLAISHER	ANGUS DIST
GILCHRIST	OGILVIE	GLAMES	ANGUS DIST
GILCHRISTSON	OGILVIE	GLANCE	EDINBURGH DIST
GILCREASE	OGILVIE	GLANCY	CLAN CIAN
GILD	STIRLING DIST	GLANDY,-IE	PERTHSHIRE DIST
GILES	GILLIES	GLAS(H)BY,-IE	MAC PHERSON
GILES	MAC PHERSON	GLAS(S)	STIRLING DIST
GILFEATHER	DUNDEE DIST	GLASBORO(W)	DUNDEE DIST
GILFILL(I)AN	MAC LELLEN	GLASER	ANGUS DIST
GILFILL(I)AN	STRATHEARN DIST	GLASGO(W)	GLASGOW DIST

NAME	TARTAN	NAME	TARTAN
GLASHAN,-EN,-IN	MAC GLASHAN	GOODSIR	FIFE DIST
GLASPEY,-IE	MAC PHERSON	GOODWILLIE,-Y	FIFE DIST
GLASS	STUART OF BUTE	GOODWIN	STIRLING DIST
GLASS(I)TER	ANGUS DIST	GOODWIN	STRATHCLYDE DIST
GLASSAN,-EN	MAC GLASHAN	GOODYEAR	FIFE DIST
GLASSELL	NITHSDALE DIST	GOONERY,-IE	MONTGOMERY
GLASSFORD	STRATHCLYDE DIST	GOR(R)IE,-Y	DUNBLANE DIST
GLASSIE,-Y	DUNDEE DIST	GOR(R)IE,-Y	MAC DONALD
GLASSIN	MAC GLASHAN	GORDON,-EN	GORDON
GLAY	MAC LEAY	GORDON,-EN	GORDON OF ABERGELDY
GLAY	STEWART	GORDON,-EN	GORDON OF FIVEY
GLEAVE	MAC LEAY	GORLET(T)	GALA WATER DIST
GLEGG	ANGUS DIST	GORLEY,-IE	FIFE DIST
GLEGG	TWEEDSIDE DIST	GORLEY,-IE	LENNOX DIST
GLEN(N)	DOUGLAS	GORMAN	AYRSHIRE DIST
GLEN(N)	MACKINTOSH	GORMAN	BOYD
GLENCAIRN	NITHSDALE DIST	GORML(E)Y	CONNACHT TARTAN
GLENCAIRNIE,-Y	STRATHSPEY DIST	GORO	GLASGOW DIST
GLENCORSE	GALLOWAY DIST	GORTHIE,-Y	PERTHSHIRE DIST
GLENDAY,-EY	ANGUS DIST	GORTIE,-Y	PERTHSHIRE DIST
GLENDENING(S)	DOUGLAS	GROS(S)MAN	FIFE DIST
GLENDIE,-Y	ANGUS DIST	GOSFORD	MUSSELBURGH DIST
GLENDINNING(S)	DOUGLAS	GOTTERSON	ANGUS DIST
GLENDOCHART	MAC GREGOR	GOTTS	SINCLAIR
GLENESK	ANGUS DIST	GOUDIE,-Y	MAC PHERSON
GLENHOLM(E)	STRATHCLYDE DIST	GOUGH	MAC FARLANE
GLENISON	ABERDEEN DIST	GOUK	ANGUS DIST
GLENNIE,-Y	GRAHAM	GOULD	ANGUS DIST
GLENNIE,-Y	MACKINTOSH	GOULDIE,-Y	MAC PHERSON
GLENNIE,-Y	MAR DIST	GOURDAN,-EN,-IN	GORDON
GLESSEN	PERTHSHIRE DIST	GOURLEY,-AY	FIFE DIST
GLINN (Irish)	CLAN CIAN	GOURLIE,-Y	LENNOX DIST
GLOAG,-K(S)	STRATHEARN DIST	GOURTON	EDINBURGH DIST
GLOVER	ANGUS DIST	GOURTY	FORBES
GLYNN	CLAN CIAN	GOVAN	GLASGOW DIST
GO(O)DSMAN	ABERDEEN DIST	GOVE	GOW
GOAN	GOW	GOW	GOW
GOAR	SINCLAIR	GOW	MAC PHERSON
GOD(S)MAN	FT. WILLIAM DIST	GOWAN(S)	GOW
GODALL	ROXBURGH DIST	GOWAN(S)	MAC DONALD
GODDARD	ROXBURGH DIST	GOWAN(S)	MAC PHERSON
GODFREY(SON)	STRATHCLYDE DIST	GOWANLOCK	EDINBURGH DIST
GODRICKSON	TWEEDSIDE DIST	GOWDIE,-(E)Y	MAC PHERSON
GOGAR	EDINBURGH DIST	GOWE	GOW
GOHAN	GOW	GOWE	MAC PHERSON
GOHAN	MAC PHERSON	GOWEN(S)	GOW
GOLD	ANGUS DIST	GOWEN(S)	MAC PHERSON
GOLDEN	FIFE DIST	GOWIN(S)	GOW
GOLDER	ANGUS DIST	GOWIN(S)	MAC PHERSON
GOLDIE,-Y	GALLOWAY DIST	GOWING(S)	GOW
GOLDMAN	DUNDEE DIST	GOWMAN	MAC DONALD
GOLDSMITH	LENNOX DIST	GOWRIE,-Y	OGILVIE
GOLDY	GALLOWAY DIST	GRACIE,-EY	FARQUHARSON
GOLIGHTLY	PERTHSHIRE DIST	GRADEN	TWEEDSIDE DIST
GOLLACH	SUTHERLAND DIST	GRADY,-IE	GRADY
GOLLAN(D)	FIFE DIST	GRAEME	GRAHAM OF MENTIETH
GONNE	GUNN	GRAHAM	GRAHAM OF MENTIETH
GONNE	MANX NATIONAL	GRAHAM	GRAHAM OF MONTROSE
GOOD	CLAN CIAN	GRAHAM	MENTIETH DIST
GOOD(E)	GLASGOW DIST	GRAHAMSLAW	ETTRICK DIST
GOODALL	ROXBURGH DIST	GRAHAN	GRAHAM
GOODBODY	INVERNESS DIST	GRAINGER	ROXBURGH DIST
GOODBRAND	ABERDEEN DIST	GRAM(M)	GRAHAM
GOODFELLOW	ANGUS DIST	GRAND	GRANT
GOODLAD	STIRLING DIST	GRANDISTOUN	ANGUS DIST
GOODLATTE	STIRLING DIST	GRANEY,-IE	MAC DONALD
GOODLET	STIRLING DIST	GRANGE	CAMPBELL

NAME	TARTAN	NAME	TARTAN
GRANGER	ROXBURGH DIST	GUALTER	AYRSHIRE DIST
GRANSON	GUNN	GUAN	GOW
GRANSTON	CRANSTOUN	GUAN	MAC PHERSON
GRANT	GRANT	GUELP(H)	ABERDEEN DIST
GRANTHAM(E)	GALLOWAY DIST	GUIDING	EDINBURGH DIST
GRAS(S)ICK	FARQUHARSON	GUILD	STIRLING DIST
GRASSIE,-Y	FARQUHARSON	GULLAN(E)	MUSSELBURGH DIST
GRATNEY	MAR DIST	GULLAND	MUSSELBURGH DIST
GRAUNT	GRANT	GULLILAND	MAC LELLEN
GRAY	DUNBAR	GUNION	AYRSHIRE DIST
GRAY	GRAY	GUNN	GUNN
GRAY	SUTHERLAND	GUNNING	DUNDEE DIST
GRAYSON	MAC GREGOR	GURDEN	GORDON
GREAGH	CLAN CIAN	GURMAN	AYRSHIRE DIST
GREATHEAD	ABERDEEN DIST	GURNAY,-EY	ROXBURGH DIST
GREE	GORDON	GURNER	ROXBURGH DIST
GREEG	MAC GREGOR	GURRAN(D)	GALLOWAY DIST
GREEN(E)	ROXBURGH DIST	GURTIE,-Y	FORBES
GREENFIELD	MAC DONELL GLENGARRY	GUTHRIE	GUTHRIE
GREENHEAD	TWEEDSIDE DIST		
GREENHILL(S)	ANGUS DIST		
GREENLAW	HOME		
GREENLEA,-EE(S)	HOME		
GREENLEASE	HOME		
GREENOCK	AYRSHIRE DIST		
GREENSHIEL(D)S	GLASGOW DIST		
GREER	MAC GREGOR	# H	
GREG(G)SON	MAC GREGOR		
GREGARACH	MAC GREGOR	HACHIE,-Y	ANGUS DIST
GREGOR	MAC GREGOR	HACKETT	FIFE DIST
GREGORSON	MAC GREGOR	HACKIE,-Y	ANGUS DIST
GREGORY	MAC GREGOR	HACKING	GALLOWAY DIST
GREIG	MAC GREGOR	HACKNEY	AYRSHIRE DIST
GREIGSON	MAC GREGOR	HACKSON	DUNBLANE DIST
GREIVE	CREIFF DIST	HACKSTON(E)	HACKSTON
GRENDLEY,-IE	EDINBURGH DIST	HADDEN,-IN	GRAHAM
GRENDON	ABERDEEN DIST	HADDINGTON	GLASGOW DIST
GRESOUN	ABERDEEN DIST	HADDLE	STRATHSPEY DIST
GREUS(S)ACH	FARQUHARSON	HADDOCK	PAISLEY DIST
GREVAR,-ER	PERTHSHIRE DIST	HADDON	GRAHAM
GREWER,-AR	DRUMMOND	HADDOW	STRATHCLYDE DIST
GREWER,-AR	FRASER	HADDOWAY	STRATHCLYDE DIST
GREWER,-AR	MAC GREGOR	HADLOW	CAITHNESS TARTAN
GREY	SUTHERLAND	HADYARD	STRATHCLYDE DIST
GREYSON	MAC GREGOR	HAFFIE,-Y	MAC FIE
GRIBBEN	ULSTER TARTAN	HAG(G)ART,-Y	MAC NAB
GRIER	MAC GREGOR	HAG(G)ART,-Y	ROSS
GRIERSON	MAC GREGOR	HAGAN	ULSTER TARTAN
GRIEVE(R)	CREIFF DIST	HAGARTY	ULSTER TARTAN
GRIGG	MAC GREGOR	HAGEN	GLASGOW DIST
GRIM(M)	GRAHAM	HAGERTY	ROSS
GRIME(S)	GRAHAM	HAGERTY (Irish)	ULSTER TARTAN
GRIMMOND	DRUMMOND	HAGGAS	DUNDEE DIST
GRINDL(E)Y,-IE	EDINBURGH DIST	HAGGERSTON	ROXBURGH DIST
GRINDLAY	EDINBURGH DIST	HAGGERT(Y)	ROSS
GRINOCK	AYRSHIRE DIST	HAGGIE	STIRLING DIST
GRINTON	EDINBURGH DIST	HAGGIS	DUNDEE DIST
GROAT	CAITHNESS TARTAN	HAGOMAN	TWEEDSIDE DIST
GROSART	STRATHCLYDE DIST	HAGSTO(U)N	DUNBLANE DIST
GROSIER	ARMSTRONG	HAIG	HAIG
GROVES	TWEEDSIDE DIST	HAIG	ROXBURGH DIST
GRUBB(E)	ANGUS DIST	HAIL(E)S	EDINBURGH DIST
GRUBBET	ROXBURGH DIST	HAILEES	HAY
GRUER	DRUMMOND	HAINE(S)	MAC DONALD
GRUER	FRASER	HAINING	NITHSDALE DIST
GRUER	MAC GREGOR	HAIR	NITHSDALE DIST
GRUMBEG,-AIG	MAC KAY	HAIR(T)	AYRSHIRE DIST
		HAIRSTAINS,-ES	GALLOWAY DIST
		HAITLIE,-Y	GALLOWAY DIST
		HAL(L)IBURTON	TWEEDSIDE DIST

NAME	TARTAN	NAME	TARTAN
HALBERT	PAISLEY DIST	HANVY,-BY	ULSTER TARTAN
HALCRO(W)	SINCLAIR	HAPBURN	HEPBURN
HALCROSS	INVERNESS DIST	HAPPY	LENNOX DIST
HALDANE	GRAHAM	HAR(A)HAN	ULSTER TARTAN
HALDEN	GRAHAM	HAR(R)OLD	MAC LEOD
HALDINE	GRAHAM	HARCASE	TWEEDSIDE DIST
HALE(S)	EDINBURGH DIST	HARCUS	TWEEDSIDE DIST
HALFKNIGHT	EDINBURGH DIST	HARDCASTLE	ROXBURGH DIST
HALFORD	INVERNESS DIST	HARDEN	ROXBURGH DIST
HALFPENNY	EDINBURGH DIST	HARDIE,-Y	CLAN CHATTAN
HALHEAD	DUNDEE DIST	HARDIE,-Y	FARQUHARSON
HALKERSON	TWEEDSIDE DIST	HARDIE,-Y	MAC HARDIE
HALKERSTON(E)	FIFE DIST	HARDIE,-Y	MACKINTOSH
HALKET(T)	FIFE DIST	HARDIE,-Y	MAR DIST
HALL	HALL	HARDIN	BUCHAN DIST
HALL	SKENE	HARDING	PERTHSHIRE DIST
HALL (Irish)	CLAN CIAN	HARDL(E)Y,-IE	LORNE DIST
HALLDYKES	MAXWELL	HARDMAN,-NAN	BUCHAN DIST
HALLEY	CAL CIAN	HARDSON	MAC HARDIE
HALLIDAY	GALLOWAY DIST	HARDWICK	GLASGOW DIST
HALLIE,-EY	PERTHSHIRE DIST	HARE	AYRSHIRE DIST
HALLINGDALE	HALLINGDALE	HARE	CLAN CIAN
HALLISON	DUNBLANE DIST	HARKES(S)	TWEEDSIDE DIST
HALLIWELL	ROXBURGH DIST	HARKIN(S)	ULSTER TARTAN
HALLORAN	CONNACHT TARTAN	HARKNESS	HARKNESS
HALLSON	DUNBLANE DIST	HARKNESS	NITHSDALE DIST
HALLY	CLAN CIAN	HARLAW	HUNTLY DIST
HALLYARD	SKENE	HARLEY	CLAN CIAN
HALPINE	MAC ALPINE	HARLIE,-Y	HUNTLY DIST
HALSON	DUNBLANE DIST	HARLOW	HUNTLY DIST
HALTON	GALLOWAY DIST	HARMER	LENNOX DIST
HAM(M)	GUNN	HARNESS	HARKNESS
HAM(M)IL,-ELL	HAMILTON	HARPER	BUCHANAN
HAMBLETON	HAMILTON	HARPERFIELD	STRATHCLYDE DIST
HAMER	LENNOX DIST	HARPERSON	BUCHANAN
HAMILTON	ARRAN DIST	HARPERSON	CARRICK DIST
HAMILTON	HAMILTON	HARRES	CAMPBELL
HAMLYN	CAITHNESS TARTAN	HARRIS	CAMPBELL
HAMMAR,-ER	GLASGOW DIST	HARRISON	ANGUS DIST
HAMMEL(L)	HAMILTON	HARROW	PERTHSHIRE DIST
HAMMOND	DUNDEE DIST	HARROW	SINCLAIR
HAMPSEY,-IE	AYRSHIRE DIST	HARROWAY	EDINBURGH DIST
HAMPTON	GLASGOW DIST	HARROWER	FIFE DIST
HANAGAN	CLAN CIAN	HART (Irish)	CONNACHT TARTAN
HANAMAN	ANGUS DIST	HART(E)	ROXBURGH DIST
HANDIE,-Y	DUNDEE DIST	HARTFELL	NITHSDALE DIST
HANDLIE,-Y	GALLOWAY DIST	HARTLIE,-Y	GALLOWAY DIST
HANDYSIDE	TWEEDSIDE DIST	HARTSIDE	STRATHCLYDE DIST
HANKIN	ABERDEEN DIST	HARVEY	HARVIE
HANL(E)Y	INVERNESS DIST	HARVEY	KEITH
HANLEY,-IE	CONNACHT TARTAN	HARVIE	HARVIE
HANNA(H)	GALLOWAY DIST	HARVIE	KEITH
HANNA(H)	HANNA	HARWOOD	GALA WATER DIST
HANNAM	ROXBURGH DIST	HASBEN	ANGUS DIST
HANNAN	GALLOWAY DIST	HASSAN	GLASGOW DIST
HANNAN	HANNA	HASSELT	INVERNESS DIST
HANNAWINKLE	EDINBURGH DIST	HASSEN	GLASGOW DIST
HANNAY,-IE	GALLOWAY DIST	HASSENDEAN	ROXBURGH DIST
HANNAY,-IE	HANNA	HASTAN(E)	GALLOWAY DIST
HANNING	ROXBURGH DIST	HASTIE,-Y	GRAHAM OF MENTIETH
HANOMAN	ANGUS DIST	HASTINGS (East)	ANGUS DIST
HANRAHAN	CLAN CIAN	HASTINGS (West)	CAMPBELL
HANRALTY	ULSTER TARTAN	HASTON	GALLOWAY DIST
HANRATTY,-IE	EDINBURGH DIST	HASTY	GRAHAM OF MENTIETH
HANSEN,-SON	STRATHSPEY DIST	HASWELL	ROXBURGH DIST
HANTON	ANGUS DIST	HATCHET(T)(E)	FIFE DIST
HANTON	DUNDEE DIST	HATHAWAY	FALKIRK DIST

NAME	TARTAN	NAME	TARTAN
HATHINGTON	EDINBURGH DIST	HEFFERNAN	CLAN CIAN
HATSTON	CAITHNESS TARTAN	HEGARTY,-IE	ULSTER TARTAN
HATTEN	CLAN CHATTAN	HEGGIE	MACKINTOSH
HATTO	ROXBURGH DIST	HEGGIN(S)	EDINBURGH DIST
HATTON	CLAN CHATTAN	HEGGY,-IE	MACKINTOSH
HAUGH	FIFE DIST	HEHIR	CLAN CIAN
HAUGHIE,-Y	GLASGOW DIST	HELM(S)	ROXBURGH DIST
HAVERL(E)Y	CONNACHT TARTAN	HELY	CLAN CIAN
HAWES	CAMPBELL	HEM(M)ISTON	FT. WILLIAM DIST
HAWICK	ROXBURGH DIST	HEMMING(S)	GALLOWAY DIST
HAWK(E)(S)	FIFE DIST	HEMPHILL	CUNNINGHAM
HAWKSLEY	ABERDEEN DIST	HEMPSEED	DUNBLANE DIST
HAWORTH	TYNESIDE DIST	HENAGHAN	CLAN CIAN
HAWS	CAMPBELL	HENAGHAN	CONNACHT TARTAN
HAWSON	CAMPBELL	HENDERSON	GUNN
HAWSON	HAY	HENDERSON	HENDERSON
HAWTHORN,-E	MAC DONALD	HENDERSON	MAC DONALD
HAXON	DUNBLANE DIST	HENDIRE,-Y	MAC DONALD OF GLENCOE
HAXTON	KEITH	HENDLY,-IE	DALZELL
HAY	HAY	HENDRICKSON	HENDERSON
HAYBURN	HAY	HENDRIE,-Y	MAC DONALD OF GLENCOE
HAYDEN,-AN	HAY	HENDRIE,-Y	MAC NAUGHTON
HAYDOCK,-CH	HAY	HENEHAN	CLAN CIAN
HAYE	HAY	HENERDIE,-Y	MAC NAUGHTON
HAYENS	HAY	HENERDRIE,-Y	MAC DONALD OF GLENCOE
HAYES	HAY	HENERSON	HENDERSON
HAYFIELD	HAY	HENRIE,-Y	MAC NAUGHTEN
HAYHOE	HAY	HENRY	HENRY
HAYHURST	SUTHERLAND DIST	HENRY,-IE(S)	MAC DONALD OF GLENCOE
HAYLEES	HAY	HENRYSON	HENDERSON
HAYNE(S)	HAY	HENSCHEL	STRATHCLYDE DIST
HAYNE(S)	MAC DONALD	HENSHAW	ROXBURGH DIST
HAYNIE,-EY	HAY	HENSHILWOOD	STRATHCLYDE DIST
HAYROCK	STRATHSPEY DIST	HEPBURN	HEPBURN
HAYS	HAY	HER(R)ING	DUNBAR
HAYSON	HAY	HER(R)IOT	FIFE DIST
HAYSTO(U)N	HAY	HER(R)IOT	GALA WATER DIST
HAYTER	HAY	HER(R)SHILL	ANGUS DIST
HAYTON	ROXBURGH DIST	HER(R)YING	DUNBAR
HAYTOR	HAY	HERBERT	STIRLING DIST
HAYWARD	HAY	HERBERTSON	GLASGOW DIST
HAYWOOD	HAY	HERBERTSON	MUSSELBURGH DIST
HAZELL	INVERNESS DIST	HERD	ANGUS DIST
HE(A)LY	CONNACHT TARTAN	HERD	GALLOWAY DIST
HEA(S)	HAY	HERD	HERD
HEADER	DUNBAR DIST	HERDMAN	ANGUS DIST
HEALY	CLAN CIAN	HERKES,-IS	TWEEDSIDE DIST
HEANEY,-IE	ULSTER TARTAN	HERMISTON	ROXBURGH DIST
HEARD	HERD	HERN	STIRLING DIST
HEARIE,-Y	DUNDEE DIST	HERON	GRANT
HEARNE	CLAN CIAN	HERON	MAC DONALD
HEATHERWICK,-YCK	FIFE DIST	HERON	STEWART
HEATLIE,-Y	GALLOWAY DIST	HERON	ULSTER TARTAN
HEATLIE,-Y	TWEEDSIDE DIST	HERON (Irish)	CLAN CIAN
HEBBURN	HEPBURN	HERR(I)ES	MAXWELL
HEBERN	HEPBURN	HERRING	ROXBURGH DIST
HEBRON	DUNBLANE DIST	HERRON(S)	GRANT
HECTOR	ABERDEEN DIST	HERRON(S)	MAC DONALD
HECTORSON	STRATHSPEY DIST	HERRON(S)	STEWART
HEDDELL	INVERNESS DIST	HERSH	TWEEDSIDE DIST
HEDDER	DUNBAR DIST	HERSHELL	ANGUS DIST
HEDDERWICK	DUNBAR DIST	HERSHTON	TWEEDSIDE DIST
HEDDLE	INVERNESS DIST	HERSTON	TWEEDSIDE DIST
HEDERICK	DUNBAR DIST	HERTFORD	STEWART
HEDLEY,-IE	TYNESIDE DIST	HERVIE,-Y	HARVIE
HEDRICK	HENDERSON		
HEENEY	ULSTER TARTAN		

NAME	TARTAN	NAME	TARTAN
HERVIE,-Y	KEITH	HOLDEN	ANGUS DIST
HERVO(E)	FT. WILLIAM DIST	HOLLAND	ANGUS DIST
HERWART	TWEEDSIDE DIST	HOLLIDAY	GALLOWAY DIST
HESLOP	EDINBURGH DIST	HOLLINGER	INVERNESS DIST
HESTON	GALLOWAY DIST	HOLLINS	STEWART
HETH	MAC KAY	HOLLIWELL	ROXBURGH DIST
HEVER	INVERNESS DIST	HOLLOWAY	ROXBURGH DIST
HEWAT	ABERDEEN DIST	HOLM(E)(S)	HOME
HEWAT	GALA WATER DIST	HOLNS	HOME
HEWDEN	INVERNESS DIST	HOME	DUNBAR
HEWIE	MAC LEAN	HOME	HOME
HEWISON	MAC DONALD	HONEYMAN	FIFE DIST
HEWISTON	MAC DONALD	HOOD	ARGYLL DIST
HEWITT	ABERDEEN DIST	HOOD	EDINBURGH DIST
HEWITT	GALA WATER DIST	HOOK(E)	GALLOWAY DIST
HEWLEN,-IN	CALEDONIA TARTAN	HOOK(E)	GLASGOW DIST
HEY(S)	HAY	HOOSTEN,-IN	MAC DONALD
HEYES	HAY	HOPE	STRATHCLYDE DIST
HEYFRON	CLAN CIAN	HOPE-VERE	HOPE-VERE
HEYNE	CONNACHT TARTAN	HOPKIN(S)	DUNDEE DIST
HEYWOOD	STRATHSPEY DIST	HOPKIN(S)	GALLOWAY DIST
HICKEY,-IE	CLAN CIAN	HOPKIRK	ROXBURGH DIST
HICKS	SUTHERLAND DIST	HOPPER	TWEEDSIDE DIST
HIDDLESTON	GALLOWAY DIST	HOPTOUN	HOPTOUN
HIGGINS	CONNACHT TARTAN	HOR(R)AN,-EN	ARGYLL DIST
HIGGINS	EDINBURGH DIST	HORAN	CONNACHT TARTAN
HIGGINSON	MACKINTOSH	HORDEN	STRATHCLYDE DIST
HIGHET	GLASGOW DIST	HORL(E)Y,-IE	ABERDEEN DIST
HIGHGATE	GLASGOW DIST	HORMEL(L)	GALLOWAY DIST
HILL	ROXBURGH DIST	HORN(E)	GALLOWAY DIST
HILL(E)ARY	INVERNESS DIST	HORNELL	GALLOWAY DIST
HILLOCK	GLASGOW DIST	HORNER	ANGUS DIST
HILSON	STRATHCLYDE DIST	HORRIE,-Y	SINCLAIR
HILTON	TWEEDSIDE DIST	HORSBURGH	ANGUS DIST
HIND(E)	GLASGOW DIST	HORSBURGH	GALLOWAY DIST
HINDMAN	PAISLEY DIST	HORSLIE,-Y	TYNESIDE DIST
HINE(S)	ROXBURGH DIST	HORTON	EDINBURGH DIST
HINNEGAN	CLAN CIAN	HOSE	GALLOWAY DIST
HINSHAW	ROXBURGH DIST	HOSEASON	CALEDONIA TARTAN
HINSHILLWOOD	STRATHCLYDE DIST	HOSEY,-IE	DUNDEE DIST
HIRD	HERD	HOSSACK,-ICK	MACKINTOSH
HIRSEL(L)	TWEEDSIDE DIST	HOUGHTON	LENNOX DIST
HIRSTON	TWEEDSIDE DIST	HOULISTON	GLASGOW DIST
HISLOP	HISLOP	HOUN	ABERDEEN DIST
HITCHELL	GALLOWAY DIST	HOURRIE	SINCLAIR
HOAG	ETTRICK DIST	HOURSTON	SINCLAIR
HOBART	DUNDEE DIST	HOUSTO(U)N	MAC DONALD
HOBKIRK	ROXBURGH DIST	HOVELL	DUNDEE DIST
HOBSON	ROBERTSON	HOWATSON	EDINBURGH DIST
HOCUTT	ROXBURGH DIST	HOWATT,-ITT	MAC DONALD
HOD(G)KINSON	HODGKINSON	HOWBURN	GALLOWAY DIST
HODDAM,-EM	GALLOWAY DIST	HOWDEN	GRAHAM
HODGE(S)	GLASGOW DIST	HOWE	MAC DONALD
HODGSON	CALEDONIA TARTAN	HOWELL,-S	MAC DOUGALL
HODKINSON	INVERNESS DIST	HOWESTON	MAC DONALD
HODSON	STRATHSPEY DIST	HOWIE	CARRICK DIST
HOG	ETTRICK DIST	HOWIE,-Y	MAC AULAY
HOGAN	CLAN CIAN	HOWIE,-Y	MAC DONALD
HOGAN	DUNBLANE DIST	HOWIESON	MAC DONALD
HOGARTH	FIFE DIST	HOWNAN(E)	ROXBURGH DIST
HOGARTH	HOGARTH OF FIRHILL	HOWSON	TWEEDSIDE DIST
HOGG	ETTRICK DIST	HOWSTEN,-IN	MAC DONALD
HOGG	HOGG	HOWSTON	MAC DONALD
HOGGAN	DUNBLANE DIST	HOWTON	LENNOX DIST
HOGGARD	FIFE DIST	HOY(E)	ROXBURGH DIST
HOGGART	FIFE DIST	HOYLE	PERTHSHIRE DIST
HOGGE	ETTRICK DIST	HUBBARD,-ERD	INVERNESS DIST
HOLCOTT	ROXBURGH DIST	HUDDLESTON(E)	NITHSDALE DIST

NAME	TARTAN	NAME	TARTAN
HUDSON	HUDSON	IMLACH,-K	ABERDEEN DIST
HUDSON	MAC DONALD	IMLAY,-H	PERTHSHIRE DIST
HUESTEN,-IN	MAC DONALD	IMRIE,-EY	STRATHEARN DIST
HUESTON	MAC DONALD	INCH	INNES
HUEY	MAC LEAN	INCHES	INCHES
HUG	FIFE DIST	INCHES	ROBERTSON
HUGGAN	FIFE DIST	INCHMARTIN	PERTHSHIRE DIST
HUGH	MAC KAY	INGLES	DOUGLAS
HUGHES	CLAN CIAN	INGLES	INGLIS
HUGHES	INVERNESS DIST	INGLESTON	PERTHSHIRE DIST
HUGHIS(T)ON	MAC DONALD	INGLIS	DOUGLAS
HUGHSON	MAC DONALD	INGLIS	INGLIS
HUIE	MAC LEAN	INGRAHAM	COLQUHOUN
HULDIE,-Y	PAISLEY DIST	INGRAM	COLQUHOUN
HULEN,-IN	CALEDONIA TARTAN	INKSTER	SINCLAIR
HULK	ABERDEEN DIST	INNERWICK	DUNBAR DIST
HULME	CAITHNESS TARTAN	INNES	INNES
HULME(S)	HOME	INNES	INNES OF COWIE
HULT	ANGUS DIST	INNIE,-Y	INNES
HUME(S)	HOME	INRICK	HENDERSON
HUMPHARS(T)ON	GLASGOW DIST	INRIG	GUNN
HUMPHRAY,-EY	DUNDEE DIST	INRIG	HENDERSON
HUMPHRIES,-EYS	ABERDEEN DIST	INSCH	INNES
HUNLIE,-Y	GORDON	INSHAW	GLASGOW DIST
HUNLIE,-Y	HUNTLY DIST	INVERARITY	ANGUS DIST
HUNNISETT	HUNNISETT	IRELAND	STRATHEARN DIST
HUNT	HUNTLY DIST	IRONS	ANGUS DIST
HUNTER	HUNTER	IRONSIDE	ABERDEEN DIST
HUNTER	HUNTER OF BUTE	IRVIN(E)	IRVINE
HUNTER	HUNTER OF HUNTERSTON	IRVIN(E)	MAR DIST
HUNTINGDON	GALLOWAY DIST	IRVINE	GALLOWAY DIST
HUNTL(E)Y,-IE	GORDON	IRVING	IRVINE
HUNTL(E)Y,-IE	HUNTLY DIST	IRVING(SON)	IRVINE
HURD	HERD	IRVING(SON)	MAR DIST
HURLEY	CLAN CIAN	IRWIN	IRVINE
HURRIE,-Y	KEITH	IRWIN	MAR DIST
HUSBAND	ANGUS DIST	ISAAC(S)	CAMPBELL
HUT(T)	PERTHSHIRE DIST	ISAAC(S)	MAC DON CLANRANALD
HUTCHEON	MAC DONALD	ISBISTER	SINCLAIR
HUTCHESON	MAC DONALD	ISDALE,-LL	ROXBURGH DIST
HUTCHIN(G)S	STIRLING DIST	ISLES	MAC DONALD
HUTCHINSON	MAC DONALD	IVAR(S)	MAC IVER
HUTCHISON	MAC DONALD	IVARSON	MAC IVER
HUTSON	MAC DONALD	IVER(S)	MAC IVER
HUTTON	STRATHCLYDE DIST	IVERACH	MAC IVER
HUXL(E)Y	INVERNESS DIST	IVERACH	MAC KENZIE
HWITE	MAC GREGOR	IVERSON	CAMPBELL
HYND(E)	GLASGOW DIST	IVERSON	MAC IVER
HYNDE	HYNDE	IVERSON	MAC KENZIE
HYNDFORD	STRATHCLYDE DIST	IVERY,-IE	MAC KENZIE
HYNDMAN	HYNDMAN	IVORSON	MAC KENZIE
HYNDMAN	PAISLEY DIST	IVORY	MAC KENZIE
HYSLOP	HISLOP	IYE	MAC KAY
		IZAT(T)	IRVINE
		IZSET(T)	IRVINE

I

IBBOTSON	ROTHESAY DIST		
IBISTER	CAITHNESS TARTAN		
IDILL	ABERDEEN DIST		

J

IDVIE,-Y	ANGUS DIST	JACK(S)	ABERDEEN DIST
ILIF(F)E	FIFE DIST	JACKSON	GLASGOW DIST
ILLINGWORTH	INVERNESS DIST	JACOB(S)	ANGUS DIST
IMBART,-ERT	ROXBURGH DIST	JACOBSON	ANGUS DIST
		JAFFERY	ROXBURGH DIST

NAME	TARTAN	NAME	TARTAN
JAFFRAY	STIRLING DIST	JUPP	GORDON
JAMES	TYNESIDE DIST	JUSTICE	JUSTICE
JAMESON	GUNN	JUSTUS	JUSTUS
JAMESON	STEWART		
JAMIE	STRATHCLYDE DIST		
JAMIESON	GUNN		
JAMIESON	STEWART	# K	
JAMISON	GUNN		
JAMISON	STEWART		
JANES	ABERDEEN DIST	KACHIE,-Y	MAC DONALD
JAPP	GORDON	KACHIE,-Y	MAC EACHAIN
JARDANE	JARDINE	KAE	MAC KAY
JARDEN	JARDINE	KAILOR	MAR DIST
JARDIN(G)	JARDINE	KAIN	MAC DONALD
JARDINE	JARDINE	KAIRNES	GRANT
JARDYNE,-EEN	JARDINE	KAMBELL	CAMPBELL
JARVIS,-IE	STIRLING DIST	KANE	MAC DONALD
JEANS	ABERDEEN DIST	KARNES	GRANT
JEFF	PAISLEY DIST	KARRICK	CARRICK DIST
JEFFERI(E)S	ROXBURGH DIST	KARRICK	KENNEDY
JEFFERS	ROXBURGH DIST	KARWELL	CLAN CIAN
JEFFERSON	GALA WATER DIST	KATCHIE,-Y	MAC DONALD
JEFFERY,-IE	GALA WATER DIST	KATCHIE,-Y	MAC EACHAIN
JEFFERY,-IE	ST. ANDREWS DIST	KATY	MAC KAY
JELLY,-IE	GALLOWAY DIST	KAVANA(U)GH	ULSTER TARTAN
JEMPSON	STEWART		
JENKIN(S)	ANGUS DIST	KAY(E)	DAVIDSON
JENNER	TWEEDSIDE DIST	KAY(E)	MAC KAY
JENNETT(E)	INVERNESS DIST	KAYES	AYRSHIRE DIST
JENNINGS	CONNACHT TARTAN	KAYLE	KILE
JENSON	ANGUS DIST	KAYLOR,-ER	MAR DIST
JERDAN,-IN,-ON	JARDINE	KEAIRNS	GRANT
JERDIN(E)	JARDINE	KEAN(E)	GUNN
JERRAT,-ETT(E)	NITHSDALE DIST	KEAN(E)	MAC DONALD
JERVEY,-IE	EDINBURGH DIST	KEAN(E)	MAC IAN
JERVIS	ANGUS DIST	KEAN(E)	MAC KEAN
JESSE(I)MAN	GORDON	KEARLIE,-Y	INVERNESS DIST
JIMPSON	STEWART	KEARNEY	CLAN CIAN
JIMSON	STEWART	KEARNIE,-Y	STIRLING DIST
JOBSON	NITHSDALE DIST	KEAY	DAVIDSON
JOHNMAN	PERTHSHIRE DIST	KEAY	MAC KAY
JOHNSON	GUNN	KEDDIE,-Y	GORDON
JOHNSON	JOHNSTONE	KEE(S)	MAC KAY
JOHNSON	MAC DONALD	KEECH	KEITH
JOHNSTON(E)	JOHNSTONE	KEEFE	O'KEEFE
JOINER	MAC INTYRE	KEEGAN,-EN	MAC DONALD
JOLLIE,-Y	ANGUS DIST	KEEN(E)	GUNN
JOLLY,-IE	EDINBURGH DIST	KEEN(E)	MAC DONALD
JONES	WELSH NATIONAL	KEEN(E)	MAC IAN
JOPP	GORDON	KEEN(E)	MAC KEAN
JOPSON	NITHSDALE DIST	KEENAN	GALLOWAY DIST
JORDAN	ABERDEEN DIST	KEEPER	KEEPER
JORDAN (Irish)	CONNACHT TARTAN	KEETCH	KEITH
JOSE	FIFE DIST	KEETH	KEITH
JOSS	FIFE DIST	KEG(G)AN	MAC DONALD
JOURDEN	ABERDEEN DIST	KEHOE	CLAN CIAN
JOY(S)	INVERNESS DIST	KEIGHRAN	MAC EACHAIN
JOYCE	CONNACHT TARTAN	KEIL(L)	DUNDEE DIST
JOYCE	INVERNESS DIST	KEILLER	MAR DIST
JUDD	MORRISON	KEILOR	MAR DIST
JUDGE	MORRISON	KEIN(S)	MAC DONALD
JUN(I)OR	INVERNESS DIST	KEIR	KERR
JUN(I)OR	LORNE DIST	KEIRD	STRATHSPEY DIST
JUNER	LORNE DIST	KEIRNAN	KEIRNAN
JUNKEIN	DUNCAN	KEITH	KEITH
JUNKIN(S)	DUNCAN	KELBURN	ROTHESAY DIST

NAME	TARTAN	NAME	TARTAN
KELDAY,-IE	SINCLAIR	KERCHOPE	ANGUS DIST
KELHAM	ARGYLL DIST	KERMACK	BUCHAN DIST
KELL(S)	EDINBURGH DIST	KERN(E)Y	CLAN CIAN
KELLAR	MAC KELLAR	KERNAN	KEIRNAN
KELLAS	FARQUHARSON	KERR	KERR
KELLER	CLAN CIAN	KERRACHER	FARQUHARSON
KELLER	MAC KELLAR	KERRIE,-Y	PAISLEY DIST
KELLET	TYNESIDE DIST	KERSE	FALKIRK DIST
KELLO	HOME	KESBY,-IE	INVERNESS DIST
KELLO(U)R	HAY	KESSON,-EN	LENNOX DIST
KELLOCK,-CH	MAC DONALD	KETCHEN,-IN	MAC DON CLANRANALD
KELLOG	MAC DONALD	KETH	KEITH
KELLOW	HOME	KETTLE(S)	STRATHEARN DIST
KELLS	GALLOWAY DIST	KETTLES(T)ON	STIRLING DIST
KELLY	CONNACHT TARTAN	KEVAN,-EN	GALLOWAY DIST
KELLY,-(IE)	MAC DONALD	KEY(E)(S)	MAC KAY
KELMAN,-IN	ABERDEEN DIST	KIAR	CLAN CIAN
KELMARTIN	FIFE DIST	KIARON	CLAN CIAN
KELSO	ARRAN DIST	KIBBLE	PAISLEY DIST
KELSO	ROXBURGH DIST	KID(D)	KIDD
KELT	STIRLING DIST	KIDDER	KIDD
KELTIE,-Y	FIFE DIST	KIDDIE	GORDON
KELTON	GALLOWAY DIST	KIDSON	STIRLING DIST
KELTY,-IE	EDINBURGH DIST	KIE(S)	MAC KAY
KELVIN	GLASGOW DIST	KIELAN	INVERNESS DIST
KEMBELL	CAMPBELL	KIELTY,-IE	CLAN CIAN
KEMBO	STIRLING DIST	KIEREN,-AN	KIEREN
KEMLO(UGH)	ANGUS DIST	KIERON	CLAN CIAN
KEMMEL(L)	CAMPBELL	KILBANE,-AIN	ANGUS DIST
KEMP	CAMPBELL	KILBRIDE	MAC DONALD
KEMPIE,-Y	STIRLING DIST	KILBURN	ROTHESAY DIST
KEMPLIN	LORNE DIST	KILBURNIE	KILBURNIE
KEMPT	ABERDEEN DIST	KILBY,-IE	OGILVIE
KEN(N)	GALLOWAY DIST	KILCHRIST	OGILVIE
KENAGY	KENNEDY	KILCULLEN,-AN	ANGUS DIST
KENAPER	MUSSELBURGH DIST	KILDAY	SINCLAIR
KENDALL,-ELL	CAITHNESS TARTAN	KILDONAN	AYRSHIRE DIST
KENDRICK	MAC NAUGHTEN	KILDUFF	LAMONT
KENE	MAC DONALD	KILE	CARRICK DIST
KENLOCK,-CH	FIFE DIST	KILE	KILE
KENMOUGH	FIFE DIST	KILGORE	DOUGLAS
KENNARDY,-IE	ABERDEEN DIST	KILGORE	KILGOUR
KENNAWAY	FIFE DIST	KILGORE	MAC DUFF
KENNEDY	CAMERON	KILGOUR	DOUGLAS
KENNEDY	CARRICK DIST	KILGOUR	KILGOUR
KENNEDY	KENNEDY	KILGOUR	MAC DUFF
KENNEDY	KENNEDY (IRISH)	KILL(I)AN	MAC NAB
KENNEDY	MAC DONELL GLENGARRY	KILLEEN	CLAN CIAN
KENNETH	MAC KENZIE	KILLEEN	CONNACHT TARTAN
KENNETHSON	MAC KENZIE	KILLEN,-AN	MAC DONALD
KENNICK	MAC PHERSON	KILLIN	MAC NAB
KENNIE,-Y	MAC KENZIE	KILLO(UGH)	HOME
KENNING	FT. WILLIAM DIST	KILLO(UGH)	MAC DONALD
KENNOCK	MAC KENZIE	KILMAN	ABERDEEN DIST
KENNOWAY,-AWAY	FIFE DIST	KILMARON	FIFE DIST
KENRICK	MAC NAUGHTEN	KILMARTIN	FIFE DIST
KENT	MUSSELBURGH DIST	KILPATRICK	COLQUHOUN
KENT	STIRLING DIST	KILPATRICK	DOUGLAS
KEOGH	CLAN CIAN	KIM(M)	FRASER
KEOGH	CONNACHT TARTAN	KIMBALL,-ELL	CAMPBELL
KEOT	STIRLING DIST	KIMBLE	CAMPBELL
KEPPIE	FIFE DIST	KIMMIE,-Y	FRASER
KER(R)IGAN	CONNACHT TARTAN	KIN(N)AH	PERTHSHIRE DIST
KER(R)IGAN	MAC DONALD	KINBUCK	DUNBLANE DIST
KER(R)IGAN	MAC KERRAL	KINCAID	KINCAID
KERBACHER	FARQUHARSON	KINCAID	STIRLING DIST

NAME	TARTAN	NAME	TARTAN
KINCAIL	KINCAID	KIRSOP	LORNE DIST
KINCH	MAC INNES	KIRSOP	MULL DIST
KINCRAIGIE,-Y	ABERDEEN DIST	KISSACK,-OCK	CAMPBELL
KINDLER	DUNDEE DIST	KISSACK,-OCK	MAC DON CLANRANALD
KINEARDUNE	FIFE DIST	KITCHEN,-IN	MAC DON CLANRANALD
KING	MAC GREGOR	KITSON	STIRLING DIST
KINGARTH	STRATHEARN DIST	KNAP(P)	CAMPBELL
KINGHORN	FIFE DIST	KNATCHBULL	DALZELL
KINGLASS	CHISHOLM	KNE(E)LAND	MAC LENNAN
KINKEAD	KINCAID	KNIGHT	ANGUS DIST
KINKEAD	STIRLING DIST	KNOTTERBELT	INVERNESS DIST
KINLOCH	FIFE DIST	KNOWLEN	INVERNESS DIST
KINLOUGH	FIFE DIST	KNOWLES	ABERDEEN DIST
KINMOND	NITHSDALE DIST	KNOWLES	MAR DIST
KINMONT	NITHSDALE DIST	KNOWLIN	INVERNESS DIST
KINN(E)Y,-IE	MAC KINNON	KNOX	PAISLEY DIST
KINNABURG	GLASGOW DIST	KRAF(F)ERD	CRAWFORD
KINNACH	PERTHSHIRE DIST	KRAF(F)ORD	CRAWFORD
KINNAIRD	OGILVIE	KRAFFURD	CRAWFORD
KINNEAR	FIFE DIST	KRAHAM	GRAHAM
KINNEBURG	GLASGOW DIST	KRAIL	FIFE DIST
KINNELL	MAC DONALD	KRAMER	INVERNESS DIST
KINNESON	MAC FARLANE	KROLL	DUNDEE DIST
KINNIE,-Y	MAC KENZIE	KRON	ARGYLL DIST
KINNIESON	KINNISON	KROY	ROSS
KINNIMOND	DUNDEE DIST	KRUM(B)	MAC DONALD
KINNINGHAM	CUNNINGHAM	KULP	ABERDEEN DIST
KINNINMOND	NITHSDALE DIST	KURD	STRATHSPEY DIST
KINNISON	ANGUS DIST	KYLE	CARRICK DIST
KINNISON	KINNISON	KYLE	KYLE
KINNISTON	KINNISON	KYNOCH	MAC KENZIE
KINNOCH	PERTHSHIRE DIST	KYNOCH	PERTHSHIRE DIST
KINNOUL	HAY		
KINNOUL	KINNOUL		
KINROSS	FIFE DIST		
KINROSS	KINROSS		
KINSEY	MAC KENZIE		
KINSMAN	EDINBURGH DIST		
KINSTABLE	HAY		
KINSTABUL	HAY		
KIPP	STRATHCLYDE DIST	L'AMI	LAMONT
KIPPEN	STIRLING DIST	LABURN	ANGUS DIST
KIRBY,-IE	TWEEDSIDE DIST	LACHANN	MAC LACHLAN
KIRD	STRATHSPEY DIST	LACHIE,-Y	MAC LACHLAN
KIRDIE,-Y	MAC KIRDY	LACHIESON	MAC LACHLAN
KIRDIE,-Y	ROTHESAY DIST	LACHLAN(D)(E)	MAC LACHLAN
KIRK	MAXWELL	LACHLANSON	MAC LACHLAN
KIRKBRIGHT	GALLOWAY DIST	LACHLASON	MAC LACHLAN
KIRKBY(E)	TWEEDSIDE DIST	LACHLIESON	MAC LACHLAN
KIRKCALDIE,-Y	FIFE DIST	LACHY	MAC LACHLAN
KIRKCO	MAXWELL	LACK(E)Y,-IE	MAC GREGOR
KIRKHAUGH	MAXWELL	LACKLAND	ROXBURGH DIST
KIRKHOPE	ANGUS DIST	LAD(D)EN	ABERDEEN DIST
KIRKKALDIE,-Y	FIFE DIST	LADYARD,-URD	TWEEDSIDE DIST
KIRKLAND	MAXWELL	LAFFERTY,-IE	ULSTER TARTAN
KIRKLAND	TWEEDSIDE DIST	LAFFRIES,-YS	INVERNESS DIST
KIRKNESS	INVERNESS DIST	LAG(E)	GALLOWAY DIST
KIRKO	MAXWELL	LAG(G)AN	MAC LENNAN
KIRKOLE	MAXWELL	LAG(G)AN,-EN	LAGGAN DIST
KIRKPATRICK	COLQUHOUN	LAG(G)S	GALLOWAY DIST
KIRKPATRICK	DOUGLAS	LAGHEAD	STRATHCLYDE DIST
KIRKSIE,-Y	CALEDONIA TARTAN	LAHORE,-OAR	GLASGOW DIST
KIRKTON,-OUN	ROXBURGH DIST	LAIDLAW	SCOTT
KIRKWALL	CALEDONIA TARTAN	LAIDLAY	SCOTT
KIRKWOOD	STIRLING DIST	LAIDLER	SCOTT
KIRREN,-ON	CLAN CIAN	LAIKIE,-Y	MAC GREGOR
		LAIN(E)	MAC LAINE

NAME	TARTAN	NAME	TARTAN
LAING	COLQUHOUN	LARKIN (Irish)	CONNACHT TARTAN
LAING	GORDON	LARKIN (Scot.)	GALLOWAY DIST
LAING	LESLIE	LARMER	ULSTER TARTAN
LAING	MAC DONALD	LARMOUR	ULSTER TARTAN
LAIPER	NAPIER	LARNACH	MAC LAREN
LAIR	MAC LAREN	LARNACK	STEWART OF ATHOLL
LAIRD	TWEEDSIDE DIST	LARRIE,-Y	CLAN CHATTAN
LAKEY,-IE	MAC PHERSON	LARRIE,-Y	MAC PHERSON
LALLIE,-Y	ROXBURGH DIST	LARRIE,-Y	MACKINTOSH
LAM(M)ON	LAMONT	LARRISTON	ELLIOT
LAMACH	IRVINE	LARSON	INVERNESS DIST
LAMB	LAMONT	LARY	CLAN CHATTAN
LAMBDEN	TWEEDSIDE DIST	LARY	MAC PHERSON
LAMBERT	GALLOWAY DIST	LARY	MACKINTOSH
LAMBERTON	TWEEDSIDE DIST	LASSWADE	EDINBURGH DIST
LAMBIE,-Y	LAMONT	LATHRISK	FIFE DIST
LAME	EDINBURGH DIST	LATIMER	GALLOWAY DIST
LAMINGTON	STRATHCLYDE DIST	LATTA	PAISLEY DIST
LAMLEY,-IE	DUNBAR DIST	LATTEMORE	GALLOWAY DIST
LAMMACH	IRVINE	LATTER	INVERNESS DIST
LAMMIE,-Y	LAMONT	LATTIMER	GALLOWAY DIST
LAMOND	LAMONT	LATTO	PAISLEY DIST
LAMONDSON	LAMONT	LAUCHLAN	MAC LACHLAN
LAMONE	LAMONT	LAUDER	LAUDER
LAMONT	LAMONT	LAUDERDALE	MAITLAND
LAMP(E)	GALLOWAY DIST	LAUGHHEAD,-EED	STRATHCLYDE DIST
LANACHAN	MAC DONALD	LAUGHLAN(D)	MAC LACHLAN
LANARK	STRATHCLYDE DIST	LAUGHLIN	MAC LACHLAN
LANDALE(S)	HOME	LAUGHTON	MAC LACHLAN
LANDEL(L)S	HOME	LAURENCE	MAC LAREN
LANDER(S)	LAMONT	LAURENSON	MAC LAREN
LANDES	GLASGOW DIST	LAURIE,-Y	GORDON
LANDIN	HAMILTON	LAURISTON	ELLIOT
LANDIS,-ES	AYRSHIRE DIST	LAVAN	CONNACHT TARTAN
LANDLASS	MAC GREGOR	LAVERICK	PERTHSHIRE DIST
LANDLES	HOME	LAVERIE	DUNDEE DIST
LANDLESS	HOME	LAVEROCK	PERTHSHIRE DIST
LANDLESS	MAC GREGOR	LAVERTIE,-Y	ULSTER TARTAN
LANDON	HAMILTON	LAVERY	ULSTER TARTAN
LANDRUM	ABERDEEN DIST	LAW(S)	MAC LAREN
LANDSBURG	GALLOWAY DIST	LAWIE	GORDON
LANDSMAN	FIFE DIST	LAWLER	ST. ANDREWS DIST
LANE	MAC LAINE	LAWLESS	ANGUS DIST
LANE (Irish)	CLAN CIAN	LAWRENCE	MAC LAREN
LANEY	CLAN CIAN	LAWRIE(S)	GORDON
LANG	COLQUHOUN	LAWSON	MAC LAREN
LANG	GORDON	LAWTHER	LAUDER
LANG	LESLIE	LAWTHIE,-Y	CARRICK DIST
LANG	MAC DONALD	LAWTHIE,-Y	LAUDER
LANGAN	ULSTER TARTAN	LAWTON	MAC LAREN
LANGFORD	TYNESIDE DIST	LAXEY	MANX NATIONAL
LANGLANDS	SCOTT	LAXFIRTH	HAY
LANGMORE	AYRSHIRE DIST	LAY(S)	MAC LEAY
LANGMUIR	AYRSHIRE DIST	LAY(S)	STEWART OF APPIN
LANGSIDE	GLASGOW DIST	LAYBURN	ANGUS DIST
LANGTON	TWEEDSIDE DIST	LAYCOCK	RATTRAY
LANGWELL	ARGYLL DIST	LAYRICK	FIFE DIST
LANGWILL	GLASGOW DIST	LAYTON	LEIGHTON
LANRICK	NITHSDALE DIST	LE POER	CLAN CIAN
LANSBOROUGH	GALLOWAY DIST	LE(D)GERWOOD	TWEEDSIDE DIST
LAPPIN	ULSTER TARTAN	LEA(S)	MAC LEISH
LAPRICK,-AKE	STRATHCLYDE DIST	LEA(S)	MAC PHERSON
LAPSLIE,-(E)Y	STIRLING DIST	LEABURN	DUNDEE DIST
LAPWOOD	SUTHERLAND DIST	LEACH	MAC BETH
LARDNER	BRUCE	LEACH	MAC DONALD
LARG(S)	LARGS DIST	LEACOCK	RATTRAY
LARGE	MUIR	LEAD	STIRLING DIST
LARGUE	LARGS DIST	LEADBETTER	FALKIRK DIST

NAME	TARTAN	NAME	TARTAN
LEADHOUSE	ABERDEEN DIST	LEMMON(D)	LAMONT
LEAKIE,-Y	LEAKIE,-Y	LEMON(D)	LAMONT
LEAKIE,-Y	MAC PHERSON	LEMPITLAW	ROXBURGH DIST
LEAL	ABERDEEN DIST	LENANE	MAC LENNAN
LEAN	MAC LEAN	LENARD	LEONARD
LEAPER	NAPIER	LENDON	MAC LENNAN
LEARD	TWEEDSIDE DIST	LENDRUM	LENDRUM
LEARIE	CAMERON	LENG	GORDON
LEARIE	CLAN CHATTAN	LENG	MAC DONALD
LEARIE	MAC PHERSON	LENNIE	LENNIE
LEARIE	MACKINTOSH	LENNIE,-Y	BUCHANAN
LEARMOND	TWEEDSIDE DIST	LENNON,-AN	MAC LENNAN
LEARMONTH	TWEEDSIDE DIST	LENNOX	LENNOX DIST
LEARMOUTH	ANGUS DIST	LENNOX	MAC FARLANE
LEARY	CAMERON	LENNOX	STEWART
LEARY	CLAN CHATTAN	LENNY	LENNIE
LEARY	MAC PHERSON	LENSE	LINDSAY
LEARY	MACKINTOSH	LENTRON	ST. ANDREWS DIST
LEARY (Irish)	ULSTER TARTAN	LENZI(E)(S)	LINDSAY
LEASK(E)	HAY	LENZIES	LENNOX DIST
LEASK(E)	LEASK	LEOD	MAC LEOD
LEASON	INVERNESS DIST	LEON	INVERNESS DIST
LEAVER	DUNDEE DIST	LEONARD (Irish)	CONNACHT TARTAN
LEAVETT,-ITT	STRATHSPEY DIST	LEONARD,-ERD	MAC LENNAN
LEAVY	BUCHANAN	LERGAIN	MAC LEAN
LEAVY	MAC LEAY	LERRICK	FIFE DIST
LEAVY	STEWART OF APPIN	LESK	HAY
LEAY	MAC LEAY	LESK	LEASK
LEAY	STEWART OF APPIN	LESLEY	LESLIE
LECKIE,-Y	LEAKIE	LESLIE,-Y	LESLIE
LECKIE,-Y	MAC GREGOR	LESSELS	LESLIE
LECKIE,-Y	MAC PHERSON	LESSLIE,-Y	LESLIE
LEDDERBURROW	ARGYLL DIST	LESTEN	EDINBURGH DIST
LEDDY,-IE	CLAN CIAN	LESTER	MAC ALISTER
LEDFORD	LEDFORD	LETHAM,-EM	TWEEDSIDE DIST
LEDINGHAM	ABERDEEN DIST	LETHAN,-EM	FIFE DIST
LEDYARD,-ERD	TWEEDSIDE DIST	LETTICE	DUNDEE DIST
LEE	LEE	LETTRICK	STRATHCLYDE DIST
LEE	STRATHCLYDE DIST	LEUCHARS	FIFE DIST
LEECH	MAC BETH	LEURS	FIFE DIST
LEECH	MAC DONALD	LEV(R)INGTON	LIVINGSTONE
LEEDLE	ROXBURGH DIST	LEVACK	STEWART OF APPIN
LEEN	MAC LEAN	LEVEN	FIFE DIST
LEES	MAC LEISH	LEVERICK,-UCK	PERTHSHIRE DIST
LEES	MAC PHERSON	LEVISTON	LIVINGSTONE
LEESON	MAC LEISH	LEVY	MAC LEAY
LEESON	MAC PHERSON	LEVY	STEWART OF APPIN
LEETCH	MAC BETH	LEWARS	GALLOWAY DIST
LEETCH	MAC DONALD	LEWIS	STUART OF BUTE
LEETH	LEITH	LEY	GALLOWAY DIST
LEETIAN	FIFE DIST	LEYBURN	ROXBURGH DIST
LEGG(E)	GALLOWAY DIST	LEYDEN	TWEEDSIDE DIST
LEGG(E)	TWEEDSIDE DIST	LEYS	FARQUHARSON
LEGGAT,-ET	STIRLING DIST	LIB(B)ERTON	EDINBURGH DIST
LEICESTER	DUNDEE DIST	LIBBERT	DALZELL
LEIGHTON	FIFE DIST	LICHTY,-IE	TWEEDSIDE DIST
LEIGHTON	LEIGHTON	LIDDEL(L)	DALZELL
LEIPER	HAMILTON	LIDDEL(L)	ROXBURGH DIST
LEIPER	NAPIER	LIDDERSDALE	ETTRICK DIST
LEISH	HAY	LIDDESS	ETTRICK DIST
LEISHMAN	MAC LEISH	LIDDLE	DALZELL
LEISHMAN	MAC PHERSON	LIDDLE	ROXBURGH DIST
LEISK	BUCHAN DIST	LIDDY	CLAN CIAN
LEITCH	MAC BETH	LIDDY,-IE	TWEEDSIDE DIST
LEITCH	MAC DONALD	LIGHT	GLASGOW DIST
LEITH	LEITH (HAY)	LIGHTBODY	LENNOX DIST
LEITHEAD	EDINBURGH DIST	LIGHTNING	FT. WILLIAM DIST

NAME	TARTAN	NAME	TARTAN
LIGHTOWER	SUTHERLAND DIST	LOCKHEAD,-EED	STRATHCLYDE DIST
LIK(E)LY	ABERDEEN DIST	LOCKIE,-Y	ANGUS DIST
LIL(I)BURN	ABERDEEN DIST	LOCKIE,-Y	MAC GREGOR
LIL(I)BURN	TYNESIDE DIST	LOCKLAN(D)	MAC LACHLAN
LILE	STEWART	LOCKSMITH	GALLOWAY DIST
LILEY	STEWART	LOCKWOOD	EDINBURGH DIST
LILIE,-Y	STEWART	LODDER	LAUDER
LILLE	STEWART	LOFTUS	CLAN CIAN
LILLICO	ROXBURGH DIST	LOG(G)AN,-EN	MAC LENNAN
LILLIE,-Y	STEWART	LOG(G)IE	FIFE DIST
LIMOND,-T	LAMONT	LOG(G)IN	MAC LENNAN
LINCHY	ULSTER TARTAN	LOGUE	ULSTER TARTAN
LINCOLN	INVERNESS DIST	LOMBARD	STEWART
LIND(E)	AYRSHIRE DIST	LONERGAN	CLAN CIAN
LINDEN,-ON	MAC LENNAN	LONG	FIFE DIST
LINDOR(E)S	FIFE DIST	LONGER	ABERDEEN DIST
LINDSAY,-EY	LINDSAY	LONGMOOR,-ORE	AYRSHIRE DIST
LINE(S)	AYRSHIRE DIST	LONGMOUNT	LONGMOUNT
LINEN	STRATHCLYDE DIST	LONGMUIR	AYRSHIRE DIST
LINGO	GRAHAM	LONGSTAFF	STRATHSPEY DIST
LINIE,-EY	ANGUS DIST	LONGTON	GALLOWAY DIST
LINING	STRATHCLYDE DIST	LONIE,-EY	CAMERON
LINKLATER	SINCLAIR	LOOB	MAC ALISTER
LINKLETTER	SINCLAIR	LOOKUP	ROXBURGH DIST
LINLIE,-Y	ANGUS DIST	LOOP	MAC ALISTER
LINLIE,-Y	TYNESIDE DIST	LOOR	ANGUS DIST
LINN	AYRSHIRE DIST	LOORIE,-Y	GORDON
LINTON(S)	ROXBURGH DIST	LOP(P)ER	ANGUS DIST
LINTRON	ROXBURGH DIST	LORIMER	ANGUS DIST
LINWOOD	PAISLEY DIST	LORIMER	STRATHEARN DIST
LINZEE	LINDSAY	LORNE	CAMPBELL
LINZIE	LINDSAY	LORNE	LORNE DIST
LION(S)	FARQUHARSON	LORNE	MAC LAREN
LIPP(E)	ABERDEEN DIST	LORNE	STEWART OF APPIN
LIPPO(C)K	INVERNESS DIST	LORNIE,-Y	HAY
LIPTON	GLASGOW DIST	LORRAINE	TWEEDSIDE DIST
LISLE(S)	TYNESIDE DIST	LOTHIAN	EDINBURGH DIST
LIST	LEASK	LOTON	LOTON
LISTER	MAC ALISTER	LOTON	MAC LAREN
LISTON	FALKIRK DIST	LOUB	MAC ALISTER
LITHGOW	FALKIRK DIST	LOUD	MAC LEOD
LITSTER	MAC ALLISTER	LOUDEN,-IN	CAMPBELL
LITSTER	PERTHSHIRE DIST	LOUDEN,-IN	LOUDON
LITTLE	ANGUS DIST	LOUDON	CAMPBELL
LITTLE	DUNDEE DIST	LOUDON	LOUDON
LITTLEJOHN	GLASGOW DIST	LOUGH	GALLOWAY DIST
LITTLEJOHN	INVERNESS DIST	LOUGHEAD,-EED	STRATHCLYDE DIST
LITTLESON	ARGYLL DIST	LOUGHNAN	CLAN CIAN
LIVINGSTON(E)	LIVINGSTONE	LOUGHRAN	ULSTER TARTAN
LIZARS	ROXBURGH DIST	LOUMIS	STRATHCLYDE DIST
LLOYD	LLOYD	LOUNAN	ANGUS DIST
LLOYD	WELSH NATIONAL	LOUNTAIN	CAMPBELL
LOBBAN,-IN	LOBBAN	LOUP	MAC ALISTER
LOBBAN,-IN	MAC LENNAN	LOUPAR,-ER	ANGUS DIST
LOCH	TWEEDSIDE DIST	LOUR	ANGUS DIST
LOCHART	ROSS	LOURIE	GORDON
LOCHERBIE,-Y	DOUGLAS	LOUT(H)ET,-IT	STRATHEARN DIST
LOCHHEAD	STRATHCLYDE DIST	LOUTHRIE,-Y	GORDON
LOCHMABEN	DOUGLAS	LOUTIT(T)	STRATHEARN DIST
LOCHORE	SUTHERLAND DIST	LOVAT(T)	FRASER
LOCHRIE,-Y	DUNDEE DIST	LOVE	MAC KINNON
LOCK(E)	ROXBURGH DIST	LOVEL(L)	ROXBURGH DIST
LOCKERBY,-IE	DOUGLAS	LOVETT	FRASER
LOCKERWORT	HAY	LOW(S)	MAC LAREN
LOCKERY	DOUGLAS	LOWD	MAC LEOD
LOCKETT	SUTHERLAND DIST	LOWDEN,-ON,-IN	CAMPBELL
LOCKHART	ROSS	LOWDEN,-ON,-IN	LOUDEN
		LOWDEN,-ON,-IN	MAC LACHLAN

NAME	TARTAN	NAME	TARTAN
LOWE(S)	MAC LAREN	LYND(E)	AYRSHIRE DIST
LOWELL	MAC DONALD	LYNDON	MAC LENNAN
LOWMAN	CALEDONIA TARTAN	LYNE	TWEEDSIDE DIST
LOWNIE,-Y	HAY	LYNE (Irish)	CONNACHT TARTAN
LOWPAR,-ER	ANGUS DIST	LYNN(E)	MAC DONALD
LOWRIE,-Y	GORDON	LYON(S)	FARQUHARSON
LOWSON	MAC LAREN	LYON(S)	LYONS
LOWTH	EDINBURGH DIST	LYSAGHT	CLAN CIAN
LOWTHERN	MAC LACHLAN	LYSARS	ROXBURGH DIST
LOWTHER(S)	LAUDER		
LOXTON	EDINBURGH DIST		
LOY(E)	STEWART		
LOYNACHAN	MAC DONALD		
LUBIE,-Y	MAC ALISTER		
LUCAS	LAMONT		
LUCAS	MAC DOUGALL		
LUCK	LAMONT	MABANE	MAC BAIN
LUCK	MAC DOUGALL	MABEAN	MAC BAIN
LUCKIE,-Y	LAMONT	MABEAN	MAC LEAN
LUCKIE,-Y	MAC DOUGALL	MABEE	MAC LEAN
LUCKLAW	FIFE DIST	MABEN	GALLOWAY DIST
LUDDALE,-ALL	SINCLAIR	MABEY,-IE	MAC LEAN OF DUART
LUDDLE,-ELL	ROXBURGH DIST	MABIN,-ON	GALLOWAY DIST
LUGGIE	STRATHCLYDE DIST	MAC A	MAC KAY
LUGTON	FIFE DIST	MAC A-CHAILLIES	MAC DONALD OF SLEAT
LUIB	MAC ALISTER	MAC A-PHI	MAC FIE
LUKE	LAMONT	MAC AART	MAC AART
LUKE	MAC DOUGALL	MAC ABARD	BAIRD
LUMBARD	STEWART	MAC ABE(E)	MAC FIE
LUMGAIN(E)	KEITH	MAC ABEATHA	MAC BETH
LUMGAIR	KEITH	MAC ABEATHA	MAC DONALD
LUMIDEN	LUMSDEN	MAC ABEATHA	MAC LEAN
LUML(E)Y,-IE	STRATHCLYDE DIST	MAC ABERIE,-Y	PERTHSHIRE DIST
LUMMIS	STRATHCLYDE DIST	MAC ABI	MAC FIE
LUMSDAINE	FORBES	MAC ABOY	MAC LEAN OF DUART
LUMSDAINE	LUMSDEN	MAC ACHANNEY	ARGYLL DIST
LUMSDEN	FORBES	MAC ACHEENY	ARGYLL DIST
LUMSDEN	LUMSDEN	MAC ACHERN	MAC DON CLANRANALD
LUMSDEN	LUMSDEN OF KINTORE	MAC ACHERN	MAC EACHAIN
LUNAN	ANGUS DIST	MAC ACHIN	MAC DON CLANRANALD
LUNAR	ANGUS DIST	MAC ACHIN	MAC EACHAIN
LUNCART	MAR DIST	MAC ACHLERIE,-Y	MAC KENZIE
LUND	TWEEDSIDE DIST	MAC ACHOPICH	MAC FIE
LUNDIE,-Y	FIFE DIST	MAC ACHOUNICH	COLQUHOUN
LUNDIN(E)	FIFE DIST	MAC ACHRAN	MAC DON CLANRANALD
LUNDY	ULSTER TARTAN	MAC ACHRAN	MAC EACHAIN
LUNE	MAC DONALD	MAC ACHREN	MAC DON CLANRANALD
LUNER	ANGUS DIST	MAC ACHREN	MAC EACHAIN
LUNERGAN	CLAN CIAN	MAC ACLLION	MAC LAREN
LUNHAM	GLASGOW DIST	MAC AD(D)EN,-IN	GORDON
LUNN	DUNBLANE DIST	MAC ADAM	GORDON
LUNN	TWEEDSIDE DIST	MAC ADAM	MAC GREGOR
LUNN(E)Y	ULSTER TARTAN	MAC ADDIE,-Y	FERGUSON
LUNN(E)Y	ULSTER TARTAN	MAC ADDIE,-Y	GORDON
LUSK	GALLOWAY DIST	MAC ADDIE,-Y	MUNRO
LUSS	COLQUHOUN	MAC ADLEY,-IE	ULSTER TARTAN
LUSS	LENNOX DIST	MAC ADOO	GALLOWAY DIST
LYAL(L)(S)	STEWART	MAC ADOREY	ULSTER TARTAN
LYDER	ABERDEEN DIST	MAC ADORY,-IE	AYRSHIRE DIST
LYELL(S)	STEWART	MAC AENZIE	MAC KENZIE
LYHTE	TWEEDSIDE DIST	MAC AFEE	MAC FIE
LYLE(S)	STEWART	MAC AFFER	MAC DONALD
LYN(N)	MAC DONALD	MAC AFIE,-Y	MAC FIE
LYNAS	ULSTER TARTAN	MAC AFILICHIE,-Y	MAC LEOD
LYNCH	LYNCH	MAC AFOOS	MAC FIE
LYNCH	GLASGOW DIST	MAC AGGIE	MACKINTOSH

M

NAME	TARTAN	NAME	TARTAN
MAC AGOWN	GOW	MAC ALLA	MAC AULAY
MAC AGOWN	MAC PHERSON	MAC ALLAN	GRANT
MAC AGY	MACKINTOSH	MAC ALLAN	MAC DON CLANRANALD
MAC AHAY	MAC KAY	MAC ALLAN	MAC FARLANE
MAC AHEE	MAC KAY	MAC ALLAN	MAC KAY
MAC AI	MAC KAY	MAC ALLASTER	MAC ALISTER
MAC AICHAN	MAC DON CLANRANALD	MAC ALLECE	MAC LEISH
MAC AICHAN	MAC EACHAIN	MAC ALLEN	GRANT
MAC AIDH	MAC KAY	MAC ALLEN	MAC FARLANE
MAC AINDRA	ANDERSON	MAC ALLEN	MAC KAY
MAC AINDRA	MAC FARLANE	MAC ALLEY,-IE	MAC AULAY
MAC AINISH,-ICH	MAC GREGOR	MAC ALLIN	GRANT
MAC AINISH,-ICH	MAC INNES	MAC ALLION	CAMPBELL
MAC AIRE(Y)	MAC NAUGHTEN	MAC ALLION	GRANT
MAC AIRY,-IE	MAC NAUGHTEN	MAC ALLION	MAC DONALD CLANRANALD
MAC AKERLEY	MAC KENZIE	MAC ALLIP	MAC DON OF GLENCOE
MAC AKEY	MAC KAY	MAC ALLIP	MAC DON OF KEPPOCH
MAC AKIE	MAC KAY	MAC ALLISTER	MAC ALISTER
MAC AKMOFFET	MOFFAT	MAC ALLUM	MALCOLM
MAC AL(L)IE	MAC AULAY	MAC ALLUN	GRANT
MAC AL(L)ISTOR	MAC ALISTER	MAC ALLY	MAC AULAY
MAC ALARY	MAC PHERSON	MAC ALMAN	BUCHANAN
MAC ALASTER	MAC ALISTER	MAC ALONAN	MAC LENNAN
MAC ALAVEY	AYRSHIRE DIST	MAC ALONIE,-Y	CAMERON
MAC ALDEN	MAC LEAN OF DUART	MAC ALOON	CAMERON
MAC ALDEWY	MAC GREGOR	MAC ALOOSE	MAC LEISH
MAC ALDINE	MAC LEAN OF DUART	MAC ALORUM	GALLOWAY DIST
MAC ALDONICH	BUCHANAN	MAC ALPHINE	MAC ALPINE
MAC ALDOWNIE	MAC GREGOR	MAC ALPIN(E)	MAC ALPINE
MAC ALDOWNIE,-Y	MAC LEAN OF DUART	MAC ALRAY	GRANT
MAC ALDRIDGE	ROXBURGH DIST	MAC ALUM	MALCOLM
MAC ALDUIE	MAC GREGOR	MAC ALVAIN	MAC BAIN
MAC ALEA	STEWART OF APPIN	MAC ALVANAH	MAC DONALD
MAC ALEAR	MAC LEOD	MAC ALY	MAC AULAY
MAC ALEARIE,-Y	CAMERON	MAC AMBLIE,-Y	MAC AULAY
MAC ALEARIE,-Y	MAC PHERSON	MAC AMBROSE	MAC DONALD
MAC ALEARIE,-Y	MACKINTOSH	MAC AMES	STUART OF BUTE
MAC ALECE	STEWART OF APPIN	MAC AMHLA	MAC AULAY
MAC ALEE	STEWART OF APPIN	MAC AMIS(H)	STUART OF BUTE
MAC ALEER	MAC LEOD	MAC AN(N)	MAC DONALD
MAC ALEERIE,-Y	CLAN CHATTAN	MAC AN(N)	MAC INNES
MAC ALEERIE,-Y	MAC PHERSON	MAC AN(N)	MACAN
MAC ALEERIE,-Y	MACKINTOSH	MAC ANABB	MAC NAB
MAC ALEES(E)	MAC LEISH	MAC ANALLEN	GRANT
MAC ALENEY	GALLOWAY DIST	MAC ANALLEN	MAC DON CLANRANALD
MAC ALENON	MAC LENNAN	MAC ANALLY	ULSTER TARTAN
MAC ALESTER	MAC ALISTER	MAC ANAS	MAC CANISH
MAC ALEV(E)Y	AYRSHIRE DIST	MAC ANAS	MAC INNES
MAC ALEXANDER	MAC ALISTER	MAC ANASPEY,-IE	NITHSDALE DIST
MAC ALEXANDER	MAC DONALD	MAC ANASPY	NITHSDALE DIST
MAC ALEY	MAC AULAY	MAC ANAUL	ULSTER TARTAN
MAC ALHANY,-IE	MAC KENZIE	MAC ANDEOIR	BUCHANAN
MAC ALI(E)	MAC AULAY	MAC ANDEOIR	MAC NAB
MAC ALILLY,-IE	MAC GILL	MAC ANDIE,-Y	MAC LEOD
MAC ALIN(I)ON	MAC LENNAN	MAC ANDLES(S)	GALLOWAY DIST
MAC ALINDEN	ULSTER TARTAN	MAC ANDO	PERTHSHIRE DIST
MAC ALINO	MAC LENNAN	MAC ANDREAS	ANDERSON
MAC ALINSTER	MAC ALISTER	MAC ANDREW	ANDERSON
MAC ALINSTON	MAC ALISTER	MAC ANDREW	MACKINTOSH
MAC ALIPINE	MAC ALPINE	MAC ANDREW	ROSS
MAC ALISTAIR	MAC ALISTER	MAC ANDRIE,-Y	MACKINTOSH
MAC ALISTER	MAC ALISTER	MAC ANDRISH	ANDERSON
MAC ALISTER	MAC ALISTER OF GLENBARR	MAC ANEAVES	ULSTER TARTAN
MAC ALL	MAC COLL	MAC ANEAVEY	CONNACHT TARTAN
MAC ALL	MAC DONALD	MAC ANEERY	CONNACHT TARTAN
MAC ALL	STUART OF BUTE	MAC ANEIR	MAC NAB
		MAC ANEIR	MAC NAUGHTEN

NAME	TARTAN	NAME	TARTAN
MAC ANENA	MAC KENZIE	MAC ARTHER	MAC ARTHUR
MAC ANENIE,-Y	MAC KENZIE	MAC ARTHUR	CAMPBELL
MAC ANFIELD	MULL DIST	MAC ARTHUR	MAC ARTHUR
MAC ANGUS	MAC GREGOR	MAC ARTHUR	MAC DONALD OF SLEAT
MAC ANGUS	MAC INNES	MAC ARTHYS	ULSTER TARTAN
MAC ANIFF	MAC GREGOR	MAC ARTNIE,-Y	CLAN CHATTAN
MAC ANISH,-ICH	MAC GREGOR	MAC ARTNIE,-Y	FARQUHARSON
MAC ANISH,-ICH	MAC INNES	MAC ARTNIE,-Y	MACKINTOSH
MAC ANISTAN	ARGYLL DIST	MAC ARTOR	MAC ARTHUR
MAC ANN	MAC DONALD	MAC ARVER	ULSTER TARTAN
MAC ANN	MAC INNES	MAC ARVIE	GALLOWAY DIST
MAC ANNA	MAC KENZIE	MAC AS(S)EY	MAC ASKILL
MAC ANNANY	GALLOWAY DIST	MAC AS(S)EY	MAC LEOD
MAC ANOY	EDINBURGH DIST	MAC ASEE	MAC ASKILL
MAC ANSH	MAC GREGOR	MAC ASEE	MAC LEOD
MAC ANSH	MAC INNES	MAC ASGILL	MAC ASKILL
MAC ANSLIN(E)	BUCHANAN	MAC ASGILL	MAC LEOD
MAC ANTAFFER	GLEN LYON DIST	MAC ASH	MAC TAVISH
MAC ANTOFFER	GLEN LYON DIST	MAC ASHLAN(D)	BUCHANAN
MAC ANUFF	MAC GREGOR	MAC ASKIE,-Y	MAC ASKILL
MAC ANULLA	GALLOWAY DIST	MAC ASKIE,-Y	MAC LEOD
MAC ANULTY	ULSTER TARTAN	MAC ASKILL	MAC ASKILL
MAC AOUT	FORBES	MAC ASKILL	MAC LEOD
MAC APHIE	MAC FIE	MAC ASKIN(E)	CAMPBELL
MAC APINLACH	STEWART OF APPIN	MAC ASLAN(E)	BUCHANAN
MAC APLINE	MAC ALPINE	MAC ASLIN(E)	BUCHANAN
MAC ARA	MAC GREGOR	MAC ASPARRAN	MAC DONALD
MAC ARADY,-IE	GRADY	MAC ASPEN,-UN	GALLOWAY DIST
MAC ARAR	FARQUHARSON	MAC ASTNEY	AYRSHIRE DIST
MAC ARAVARRA	MAC NEIL	MAC ASTNEY	GALLOWAY DIST
MAC ARCHER	FARQUHARSON	MAC ASTOCKER	GALLOWAY DIST
MAC ARCHIE	MAC PHERSON	MAC ASTON	CAMPBELL
MAC ARD	MAC DONALD	MAC ATEE	GALLOWAY DIST
MAC ARD	MAC KERRAL	MAC ATEER	MAC INTYRE
MAC ARDALE	GALLOWAY DIST	MAC ATEER	MAC TIER
MAC ARDELL	GALLOWAY DIST	MAC ATILIA	ULSTER TARTAN
MAC ARDI(E)	MAC HARDIE	MAC AUGHER	GALLOWAY DIST
MAC ARDI(E)	MACKINTOSH	MAC AUGHTRIE,-Y	INVERNESS DIST
MAC ARDLE	GALLOWAY DIST	MAC AULAY,-EY	MAC AULAY
MAC ARDY	MAC HARDIE	MAC AULAY,-EY	MAC LEOD
MAC ARDY	MACKINTOSH	MAC AUSELAN(E)	BUCHANAN
MAC AREAVY	GALLOWAY DIST	MAC AUSLAN(D)	BUCHANAN
MAC AREE	MAC GREGOR	MAC AUSLAN(E)	BUCHANAN
MAC AREL(L)	MAC ORRELL	MAC AUSTIN	MAC DONALD
MAC ARI	CAMPBELL	MAC AVARD,-IE,-Y	BAIRD
MAC ARI	MAC GREGOR	MAC AVAY	MAC FIE
MAC ARIN	MAC DONELL GLENGARRY	MAC AVERIE,-Y	PERTHSHIRE DIST
MAC ARLANTIE,-Y	MAD DONALD	MAC AVEY	MAC FIE
MAC ARLIE	MAC KENZIE	MAC AVIC	MAC VICAR
MAC ARN(E)	MAC DONALD	MAC AVINNY,-IE	ULSTER TARTAN
MAC AROW	MAC RAE	MAC AVISH	MAC TAVISH
MAC AROY	GRANT	MAC AVISH	MAC THOMAS
MAC AROY	MAC GILLIVRAY	MAC AVLAY,-EY	MAC AULAY
MAC ARRA	HAY	MAC AVOY	MAC LEAN
MAC ARRA	MAC GREGOR	MAC AW(E)	MAC KAY
MAC ARRAN	MAC DONELL GLENGARRY	MAC AWARD	BAIRD
MAC ARSIE,-Y	ANGUS DIST	MAC AWBER	ARGYLL DIST
MAC ARSIE,-Y	MAC ARTHUR	MAC AWEENIE,-Y	MAC KENZIE
MAC ART	MAC AART	MAC AWHO	MAC FARLANE
MAC ART	MAC ARTHUR	MAC AY(E)	MAC KAY
MAC ART(T)ER	CAMPBELL	MAC BAIDE	GALLOWAY DIST
MAC ART(T)ER	MAC ARTHUR	MAC BAIN(E)	MAC BAIN
MAC ART(T)ER	MAC DONALD OF SLEAT	MAC BAIN(E)	MAC KAY
MAC ARTAIR	CAMPBELL	MAC BALL	CAMERON
MAC ARTAN	MAC ARTHUR	MAC BALL	MACKINTOSH
MAC ARTAN	MAC DONALD OF SLEAT	MAC BAR(R)	MAC FARLANE

NAME	TARTAN	NAME	TARTAN
MAC BARD	BAIRD	MAC BRIEVE	MORRISON
MAC BARDIE,-Y	BAIRD	MAC BRINE	MAC LEAN
MAC BARNETT(E)	SINCLAIR	MAC BRINE	MAC NAUGHTEN
MAC BARON	MAC FARLANE	MAC BRINN	MAC NAUGHTEN
MAC BARREN,-IN	MAC FARLANE	MAC BRION	MAC LEAN
MAC BARRON	O'NEILL	MAC BRIT(T)IN	GALBRAITH
MAC BARRON	ULSTER TARTAN	MAC BRITAIN	GALBRAITH
MAC BATH	MAC BETH	MAC BRODIE,-Y	BRODIE
MAC BATH	MAC DONALD	MAC BRODIN	CLAN CIAN
MAC BAW(E)	CAMERON	MAC BRODY	CLAN CIAN
MAC BAW(E)	MACKINTOSH	MAC BROLOCHAN	ARGYLL DIST
MAC BAXTER	BAXTER	MAC BROOKS	PERTHSHIRE DIST
MAC BAXTER	MAC MILLAN	MAC BROOM(E)	MAC DON CLANRANALD
MAC BAY	MAC DONALD	MAC BROON	MAC DON CLANRANALD
MAC BAY	MAC LEAN	MAC BROON	MAC DON OF GLENCOE
MAC BAY	MAC LEAN OF DUART	MAC BRUNE	MAC DON CLANRANALD
MAC BAYDGE	GALLOWAY DIST	MAC BRUODIN	CLAN CIAN
MAC BEAIN	MAC BAIN	MAC BRYAN	MAC LEAN
MAC BEAN	MAC BAIN	MAC BRYDE	MAC DONALD
MAC BEATH	MAC BETH	MAC BRYNE	MAC LEAN
MAC BEATH	MAC DONALD	MAC BRYON	MAC LEAN
MAC BEATH	MAC BEAN	MAC BUDDEN	ARGYLL DIST
MAC BEE	MAC BAIN	MAC BURIE,-Y	MAC DON CLANRANALD
MAC BEE	MAC LEAN	MAC BURNETTE	BURNETT
MAC BEEN	MAC BAIN	MAC BURNEY	MATHESON
MAC BEIDE	GALLOWAY DIST	MAC BURNIE,-Y	MATHESON
MAC BENNET(T)	ROXBURGH DIST	MAC BURROWS	ULSTER TARTAN
MAC BEOL(A)IN	MAC KENZIE	MAC BURSE	GALLOWAY DIST
MAC BEOLA(I)N	MAC KENZIE	MAC BYE	MAC DONALD
MAC BETH	MAC BAIN	MAC BYE	MAC LEAN
MAC BETH	MAC BETH	MAC BYRD	MAC BYRD
MAC BETH	MAC DONALD	MAC BYRNEY	MATHESON
MAC BETH	MAC LEAN	MAC CA(I)ODH	MAC KAY
MAC BEY	MAC DONALD	MAC CAA	MAC KAY
MAC BEY	MAC LEAN OF DUART	MAC CAAM	STUART OF BUTE
MAC BIRD	MAC BYRD	MAC CAAN	INVERNESS DIST
MAC BIRNIE,-Y	MATHESON	MAC CAAN	SUTHERLAND DIST
MAC BLACKIE,-Y	GALLOWAY DIST	MAC CABE	MAC LEOD
MAC BLAIN(E)	GALLOWAY DIST	MAC CABE	ULSTER TARTAN
MAC BLAININE	GALLOWAY DIST	MAC CABERY,-IE	PERTHSHIRE DIST
MAC BLANE	GALLOWAY DIST	MAC CACHREN	MAC NAUGHTEN
MAC BLAREN	PERTHSHIRE DIST	MAC CAD(D)IE,-Y	FERGUSON
MAC BOURNIE,-Y	MATHESON	MAC CAD(D)IE,-Y	GORDON
MAC BRACADAIR	GLEN LYON DIST	MAC CAD(D)IE,-Y	MUNRO
MAC BRACHTER	GLEN LYON DIST	MAC CADDEN,-IN(S)	GORDON
MAC BRADY	ULSTER TARTAN	MAC CAEME	STUART OF BUTE
MAC BRAIRE	MAC BRIER	MAC CAENE	MAC DONALD
MAC BRAITY	ULSTER TARTAN	MAC CAFFER	MAC DONALD
MAC BRANNAN	CONNACHT TARTAN	MAC CAFFERTIE,-Y	MAC FIE
MAC BRATNIE,-Y	GALBRAITH	MAC CAFFIE,-Y	MAC FIE
MAC BRAYER	MAC BRIER	MAC CAFFREY	MAC FIE
MAC BRAYN(E)	MAC DONALD	MAC CAGE	FARQUHARSON
MAC BRAYN(E)	MAC NAUGHTEN	MAC CAGHERTIE,-Y	EDINBURGH DIST
MAC BREAIRTIE,-Y	STUART OF BUTE	MAC CAGUE	FARQUHARSON
MAC BREARTIE,-Y	STUART OF BUTE	MAC CAGUE	MAC LEOD
MAC BREATIE,-Y	STUART OF BUTE	MAC CAGUE (Irish)	ULSTER TARTAN
MAC BRECK	PERTHSHIRE DIST	MAC CAHREN	MAC DONELL GLENGARRY
MAC BREEN	MAC NAUGHTEN	MAC CAID(H)	MAC KAY
MAC BRETON	GALBRAITH	MAC CAIG	FARQUHARSON
MAC BRIAN	MAC LEAN	MAC CAIG	MAC LEOD
MAC BRIDE	MAC BRIDE	MAC CAIGNIE,-Y	PERTHSHIRE DIST
MAC BRIDE	MAC DONALD	MAC CAIL	MAC DOUGALL
MAC BRIDGE	MAC DONALD	MAC CAIL	MAC PHAIL
MAC BRIEF(F)	MORRISON	MAC CAINISH	MAC GREGOR
MAC BRIEN	MAC LEAN	MAC CAIR(E)	ULSTER TARTAN
MAC BRIER	GALLOWAY DIST	MAC CAIRN(E)Y	GRANT
MAC BRIER	MAC BRIER	MAC CAIRN(S)	GRANT

NAME	TARTAN	NAME	TARTAN
MAC CAIRN(S)	MAC DONALD	MAC CAMLIE,-Y	MAC AULAY
MAC CAIRN(S)	STUART OF BUTE	MAC CAMMAN(T)	BUCHANAN
MAC CAIRTER	MAC ARTHUR	MAC CAMMEL	CAMPBELL
MAC CAISE	MAC TAVISH	MAC CAMMEN(T)	BUCHANAN
MAC CAISH	MAC TAVISH	MAC CAMMON(T)	BUCHANAN
MAC CALDAN,-EN,-IN	MAC LEAN OF DUART	MAC CAMMOND	BUCHANAN
MAC CALE	MAC DOUGALL	MAC CAMNACK	CARRICK DIST
MAC CALE	ROTHESAY DIST	MAC CAMPBELL	CAMPBELL
MAC CALEB(B)	MAC DON OF KEPPOCH	MAC CANANACH	MAC PHERSON
MAC CALEP(S)	MAC DON OF GLENCOE	MAC CANASPIE,-Y	AYRSHIRE DIST
MAC CALEP(S)	MAC DON OF KEPPOCH	MAC CANCE	MAC GREGOR
MAC CALEP(S)	MAC KILLOP	MAC CANCE	MAC INNES
MAC CALIDEN	STRATHEARN DIST	MAC CANCH	GALLOWAY DIST
MAC CALIP(S)	MAC DON OF KEPPOCH	MAC CANCHIE,-Y	GALLOWAY DIST
MAC CALIP(S)	MAC KILLOP	MAC CANDLISS,-SH	GALLOWAY DIST
MAC CALIPP	MAC DON OF GLENCOE	MAC CANDRES	ANDERSON
MAC CALIPP	MAC KILLOP	MAC CANDRIE,-Y	MACKINTOSH
MAC CALKEN,-IN	ARGYLL DIST	MAC CANDY	MACKINTOSH
MAC CALL	MAC COLL	MAC CANENY,-IE	BUCHANAN
MAC CALL	STUART OF BUTE	MAC CANFIEL(D)	MULL DIST
MAC CALLA	MAC AULAY	MAC CANISH	MAC CANISH
MAC CALLA	MAC CALL	MAC CANISH	MAC INNES
MAC CALLACHY,-IE	DUNDEE DIST	MAC CANN	MAC DONALD
MAC CALLAN	GRANT	MAC CANN	MAC INNES
MAC CALLAN	MAC DON CLANRANALD	MAC CANN	ULSTER TARTAN
MAC CALLAN	MAC FARLANE	MAC CANNA	MAC KENZIE
MAC CALLAN	MAC KAY	MAC CANNAMANT,-D	BUCHANAN
MAC CALLAND	MAC LELLEN	MAC CANNEL(L)	MAC DONALD
MAC CALLEN	GRANT	MAC CANQUELL	DUNBLANE DIST
MAC CALLEN	MAC DON CLANRANALD	MAC CANSKIE,-Y	EDINBURGH DIST
MAC CALLEN	MAC FARLANE	MAC CANTS	MAC INNES
MAC CALLEN	MAC KAY	MAC CAP(P)IE,=Y	MAC ALPINE
MAC CALLIE	MAC AULAY	MAC CAPPIN(E)	MAC ALPINE
MAC CALLIEN	GRANT	MAC CAR(R)ACHER	FARQUHARSON
MAC CALLIG	MAC DONALD	MAC CAR(R)AHER	FARQUHARSON
MAC CALLIG,-K	ULSTER TARTAN	MAC CAR(R)OL(L)	MAC DONALD
MAC CALLIN	CAMPBELL	MAC CAR(R)OL(L)	CLAN CIAN
MAC CALLIN	GRANT	MAC CAR(S)	ULSTER TARTAN
MAC CALLIN	MAC DONALD CLANRANALD	MAC CARA	MAC GREGOR
MAC CALLION	CAMPBELL	MAC CARAR	FARQUHARSON
MAC CALLION	MAC DON CLANRANALD	MAC CARAS	ULSTER TARTAN
MAC CALLISTER	MAC ALISTER	MAC CARAVARRA	MAC NEIL
MAC CALLON	GRANT	MAC CARBERRY	ULSTER TARTAN
MAC CALLON	MAC DONALD	MAC CARCLE	MAC CORQUODALE
MAC CALLOUGH	MAC DONALD OF SLEAT	MAC CARD	MAC HARDIE
MAC CALLOUH	MAC AULAY	MAC CARD	MACKINTOSH
MAC CALLUM	MAC CALLUM	MAC CARDELL	GALLOWAY DIST
MAC CALLUM	MAC CALLUM OF BERWICK	MAC CARDIE,-Y	MAC HARDIE
MAC CALLUM	MALCOLM	MAC CARDIE,-Y	MAC KIRDY
MAC CALMAN	BUCHANAN	MAC CARDIE,-Y	MACKINTOSH
MAC CALMONT	BUCHANAN	MAC CARDIE,-Y	STUART OF BUTE
MAC CALMONT	LAMONT	MAC CARDLE	GALLOWAY DIST
MAC CALOP	MAC DON OF KEPPOCH	MAC CARDNIE,-Y	FARQUHARSON
MAC CALOP	MAC KILLOP	MAC CARDNIE,-Y	MACKINTOSH
MAC CALPIN(E)	MAC ALPINE	MAC CARE	ULSTER TARTAN
MAC CALVIN	BUCHANAN	MAC CARG	GALLOWAY DIST
MAC CAM(B)LIE,-EY	MAC AULAY	MAC CARGAR	GALLOWAY DIST
MAC CAM(E)Y	STUART OF BUTE	MAC CARGILL	PERTHSHIRE DIST
MAC CAM(M)ANT	BUCHANAN	MAC CARGO	GALLOWAY DIST
MAC CAM(M)IE,-Y	STUART OF BUTE	MAC CARL(E)Y	MAC KENZIE
MAC CAM(M)ON	BUCHANAN	MAC CARLICH	ARGYLL DIST
MAC CAMBLIE,-Y	EDINBURGH DIST	MAC CARLIE,-Y	MAC KENZIE
MAC CAMBRIDGE	MAC DONALD	MAC CARMICH	MAC LAINE LOCH BUIE
MAC CAMBRY	MAC AULAY	MAC CARMICK	BUCHANAN
MAC CAME	STUART OF BUTE	MAC CARN(S)	GRANT
MAC CAMERON	CAMERON		

NAME	TARTAN	NAME	TARTAN
MAC CARN(S)	MAC DONALD	MAC CASKIN	CAMPBELL
MAC CARNE	GRANT	MAC CASKIN	MAC ASKILL
MAC CARNE	MAC DONALD	MAC CASKIN	MAC LEOD
MAC CARNIE,-Y	CLAN CHATTAN	MAC CASLAN(D)	BUCHANAN
MAC CARNOCHAN	GALLOWAY DIST	MAC CASTER	ABERDEEN DIST
MAC CARPIN	MAC ALPINE	MAC CASTON	BUCHANAN
MAC CARRA	HAY	MAC CASTOR	ABERDEEN DIST
MAC CARRAGHAN	ULSTER TARTAN	MAC CATCHIE,-Y	CARRICK DIST
MAC CARRAN,-EN	MAC DONELL GLENGARRY	MAC CATHAIL	MAC DOUGALL
MAC CARRER	MAC DONELL GLENGARRY	MAC CATHAY	MAC FIE
MAC CARRICK	CARRICK DIST	MAC CATHERN(E)	MAC DON CLANRANALD
MAC CARRIE,-Y	MAC NAUGHTEN	MAC CATHERN(E)	MAC EACHAIN
MAC CARRIE,-Y	MAC RAE	MAC CATHEY	MAC FIE
MAC CARRIG	CARRICK DIST	MAC CATHIE,-Y	MAC FIE
MAC CARRIN	MAC DONELL GLENGARRY	MAC CATHRON	MAC DON CLANRANALD
MAC CARRISON	GALLOWAY DIST	MAC CATHRON	MAC EACHAIN
MAC CARROL(L)	MAC DONALD	MAC CATMONT	GORDON
MAC CARROL(L)	MAC KERRAL	MAC CATTY,-IE	CLAN CHATTAN
MAC CARRON	MAC DONELL GLENGARRY	MAC CAUD	MAC KAY
MAC CARROW	MAC KERRAL	MAC CAUGAN	MAC CAUGHAN
MAC CARROW	MAC KERRAL	MAC CAUGAN	MAC EACHAIN
MAC CARROWER	FARQUHARSON	MAC CAUGHAN	MAC CAUGHAN
MAC CARRY,-IE	CAMPBELL	MAC CAUGHIE,-(E)Y	ULSTER TARTAN
MAC CARSE	ULSTER TARTAN	MAC CAUGHLEY	MAC AULAY
MAC CARSER	MAC ARTHUR	MAC CAUGHTER	GALLOWAY DIST
MAC CARSIE,-Y	ANGUS DIST	MAC CAUGNAN	MAC EACHAIN
MAC CARSON	MAC PHERSON	MAC CAUL	MAC COLL
MAC CART(T)	MAC ARTHUR	MAC CAUL(L)EY	MAC AULAY
MAC CARTA(I)N	MAC ARTHUR	MAC CAULAND	MAC AULAY
MAC CARTA(I)N	MAC DONALD OF SLEAT	MAC CAULE,-IE	MAC AULAY
MAC CARTAIR	MAC ARTHUR	MAC CAULY	MAC AULAY
MAC CARTAIR	MAC DONALD OF SLEAT	MAC CAUSE	MAC FARLANE
MAC CARTELL,-LE	GALLOWAY DIST	MAC CAUSE	MAC TAVISH
MAC CARTER	CAMPBELL	MAC CAUSLAN(D)	BUCHANAN
MAC CARTER	MAC ARTHUR	MAC CAVANA	ULSTER TARTAN
MAC CARTER	MAC DONALD OF SLEAT	MAC CAVANAUGH	ULSTER TARTAN
MAC CARTHA	MAC ARTHUR	MAC CAVAT(T)	DAVIDSON
MAC CARTHAR,-ER	MAC ARTHUR	MAC CAVE	ULSTER TARTAN
MAC CARTHUS	MAC ARTHUR	MAC CAVELL	MAC GREGOR
MAC CARTIN	MAC ARTHUR	MAC CAVEY,-IE	MAC FIE
MAC CARTIN	MAC DONALD OF SLEAT	MAC CAVILL	MAC GREGOR
MAC CARTLE	GALLOWAY DIST	MAC CAVISH	MAC TAVISH
MAC CARTNAY	MACKINTOSH	MAC CAVIT	GALLOWAY DIST
MAC CARTNEY,-IE	MACKINTOSH	MAC CAVOR	MAC IVER
MAC CARTNIE,-Y	CLAN CHATTAN	MAC CAW(S)	MAC KAY
MAC CARTNIE,-Y	FARQUHARSON	MAC CAW(S)	MAC TAVISH
MAC CARTNIE,-Y	MACKINTOSH	MAC CAW(S)	STUART OF BUTE
MAC CARTUR(E)	MAC ARTHUR	MAC CAWELL	CAMPBELL
MAC CARTUR(E)	MAC DONALD	MAC CAWELL	MAC COLL
MAC CARUS	ULSTER TARTAN	MAC CAWIL	MAC COLL
MAC CARVER	ULSTER TARTAN	MAC CAWISH	ARGYLL DIST
MAC CARVILLE	MAC GREGOR	MAC CAWL	MAC DONALD
MAC CASE	MAC KAY	MAC CAWSE,-IE	MAC TAVISH
MAC CASH	MAC TAVISH	MAC CAY(E)	MAC KAY
MAC CASHIE,-Y	DUNDEE DIST	MAC CAY(E)	SHAW
MAC CASHIN	CAMPBELL	MAC CEACHAN	MAC DONALD
MAC CASHLAND	BUCHANAN	MAC CEACHAN	MAC EACHAIN
MAC CASHLIN(E)	BUCHANAN	MAC CEALLAICH	MAC DONALD OF SLEAT
MAC CASHNIE,-Y	DUNDEE DIST	MAC CEDDY	GORDON
MAC CASKEN	CAMPBELL	MAC CEDDY	MUNRO
MAC CASKEN	MAC ASKILL	MAC CEE	MAC KAY
MAC CASKEN	MAC LEOD	MAC CEG	FARQUHARSON
MAC CASKIE,-Y	MAC ASKILL	MAC CEG	MAC LEOD
MAC CASKIE,-Y	MAC LEOD	MAC CELIE,-Y	GALLOWAY DIST
MAC CASKILL	MAC ASKILL	MAC CELLEN(S)	MAC LELLEN

71

NAME	TARTAN	NAME	TARTAN
MAC CELOG	MAC DONALD	MAC CLAMMIE,-Y	GALLOWAY DIST
MAC CELOGIE,-Y	MAC DONALD	MAC CLAMRACH,-OCH	MAC KAY
MAC CERRIE,-Y	MAC KERRAL	MAC CLANA(C)HAN	MAC LENNAN
MAC CEUN	MAC EWEN	MAC CLANAGHAN	CLAN CIAN
MAC CHAD(D)IE,-Y	FERGUSON	MAC CLANALD	MAC DON CLANRANALD
MAC CHAD(D)IE,-Y	GORDON	MAC CLANCY	CLAN CIAN
MAC CHAD(D)IE,-Y	MUNRO	MAC CLAND(R)ISH	ANDERSON
MAC CHANBLE,-Y	AYRSHIRE DIST	MAC CLANE	MAC LAINE
MAC CHANEY	MAC DON ARDNAMURCHAN	MAC CLANSBURGH	EDINBURGH DIST
MAC CHANEY	MAC DON OF GLENCOE	MAC CLARAEN	MAC LAREN
MAC CHANNENIE	BUCHANAN	MAC CLARD	MAC DONALD
MAC CHAPMAN	PERTHSHIRE DIST	MAC CLARDIE,-Y	MAC DONALD
MAC CHARLATIE,-Y	CAMPBELL	MAC CLARE	CLAN CHATTAN
MAC CHARLES	MAC KENZIE	MAC CLARE	MAC PHERSON
MAC CHARLIE,-(E)Y	ARGYLL DIST	MAC CLAREN,-IN	MAC LAREN
MAC CHEINE	CUMMING	MAC CLARENCE	MAC LAREN
MAC CHERAN	GRANT	MAC CLARIE,-Y	CLAN CHATTAN
MAC CHERAN	MAC DONALD	MAC CLARIE,-Y	MAC PHERSON
MAC CHESNIE,-(E)Y	CUMMING	MAC CLARIE,-Y	MACKINTOSH
MAC CHEWER	MAC CLURE	MAC CLARIN	MAC LAREN
MAC CHEYNE	CUMMING	MAC CLARKEN,IN	CLAN CHATTAN
MAC CHEYNE	SUTHERLAND	MAC CLARNEN	MAC LAREN
MAC CHISHOLM	CHISHOLM	MAC CLARON	MAC LAREN
MAC CHISSON	CHISHOLM	MAC CLARTIE,-Y	MAC DONALD
MAC CHISSUM	CHISHOLM	MAC CLASER	MAC GLASHAN
MAC CHLEARIE,-Y	CAMERON	MAC CLASSAR	MAC GLASHAN
MAC CHLEARIE,-Y	CLAN CHATTAN	MAC CLASSEY,-IE	MAC GLASHAN
MAC CHLEARIE,-Y	MAC PHERSON	MAC CLATCHER	GALLOWAY DIST
MAC CHLEARIE,-Y	MACKINTOSH	MAC CLATCHIE,-Y	CARRICK DIST
MAC CHLERY	MACKINTOSH	MAC CLATCHIE,-Y	PAISLEY DIST
MAC CHOITER	MAC GREGOR	MAC CLAUCHIE	GALLOWAY DIST
MAC CHORD	GALLOWAY DIST	MAC CLAVE	MAC LEAY
MAC CHREE	GORDON	MAC CLAVE	STEWART OF APPIN
MAC CHRISTEN	GALLOWAY DIST	MAC CLAVERTY,-IE	PAISLEY DIST
MAC CHRISTIAN	FARQUHARSON	MAC CLAWSON	PERTHSHIRE DIST
MAC CHRISTIE,-Y	FARQUHARSON	MAC CLAY	MAC LEAY
MAC CHRISTIN	GALLOWAY DIST	MAC CLAY	STEWART OF APPIN
MAC CHRISTON	GALLOWAY DIST	MAC CLAYMORE	STEWART OF APPIN
MAC CHRUIE	GORDON	MAC CLE	STEWART OF APPIN
MAC CHRUITER	BUCHANAN	MAC CLE(A)D	MAC LEOD
MAC CHRYSTAL	BUCHANAN	MAC CLEA	MAC LEAY
MAC CHUBHSITHE	MAC FIE	MAC CLEA	STEWART OF APPIN
MAC CHURG	GALLOWAY DIST	MAC CLEACAN(S)	LEAKIE
MAC CIANNAN	MAC KINNON	MAC CLEAD	MAC LEOD
MAC CIE	MAC KAY	MAC CLEAF	MAC LEAY
MAC CIM(E)	FRASER	MAC CLEAF	STEWART OF APPIN
MAC CIMLIN,-ON	GALLOWAY DIST	MAC CLEAKERIE,-Y	EDINBURGH DIST
MAC CIN	MAC KINNON	MAC CLEAKIN(S)	LEAKIE
MAC CINSTEY	MAC KENZIE	MAC CLEALLICH	MAC DONALD
MAC CINTY,-IE	MAC KENZIE	MAC CLEAN	MAC LEAN
MAC CITY	HAY	MAC CLEAR	CAMERON
MAC CIVY,-IE	MAC IVER	MAC CLEAR	CLAN CHATTAN
MAC CLAB(B)	MAC LEAN	MAC CLEAR	MAC PHERSON
MAC CLACKUON	MAC NAUGHTEN	MAC CLEAR	MACKINTOSH
MAC CLADDIE,-Y	MAC DONALD	MAC CLEARIE,-Y	CAMERON
MAC CLAF(F)	MAC LEAY	MAC CLEARIE,-Y	CLAN CHATTAN
MAC CLAF(F)	STEWART OF APPIN	MAC CLEARIE,-Y	MAC PHERSON
MAC CLAFERTIE,-Y	GLASGOW DIST	MAC CLEARIE,-Y	MACKINTOSH
MAC CLAFLIN	MAC LACHLAN	MAC CLEAT(T)Y,-IE	ULSTER TARTAN
MAC CLAINE	MAC LAINE	MAC CLEAVE	MAC LEAY
MAC CLAIR(E)	CLAN CHATTAN	MAC CLEAVE	STEWART OF APPIN
MAC CLAIR(E)	MAC PHERSON	MAC CLEAY	MAC LEAY
MAC CLAIREN,-ON	MAC LAREN	MAC CLEAY	STEWART OF APPIN
MAC CLALIN	MAC LELLEN	MAC CLEDDY,-IE	ULSTER TARTAN
MAC CLAM(E)	MAC LAINE	MAC CLEE	ARGYLL DIST
MAC CLAMERACH	MAC KAY		

NAME	TARTAN	NAME	TARTAN
MAC CLEEKIN(S)	LEAKIE	MAC CLUCKIE,-Y	LAMONT
MAC CLEERIE,-Y	CLAN CHATTAN	MAC CLUE	STEWART OF APPIN
MAC CLEERIE,-Y	MAC PHERSON	MAC CLUER	MAC CLURE
MAC CLEERIE,-Y	MACKINTOSH	MAC CLUMPHA	GALLOWAY DIST
MAC CLEIR	MACKINTOSH	MAC CLUN(E)Y	MAC KENZIE
MAC CLEISH	MAC PHERSON	MAC CLUNE	AYRSHIRE DIST
MAC CLEISTER	MAC ALISTER	MAC CLUNG	GALLOWAY DIST
MAC CLELLAN(D)	MAC LELLEN	MAC CLURAN	MAC LAREN
MAC CLELLIN	MAC LELLEN	MAC CLURE	MAC CLURE
MAC CLEM(M)	LAMONT	MAC CLUREN	MAC LAREN
MAC CLEMENT(S)	LAMONT	MAC CLURG	CLAN CHATTAN
MAC CLENA(G)HAN	GALLOWAY DIST	MAC CLURI(E)CH	MAC PHERSON
MAC CLENAGHAN	CLAN CIAN	MAC CLURIN	MAC LAREN
MAC CLENE	MAC LEAN	MAC CLURKIN	CLAN CHATTAN
MAC CLENNAN	MAC LENNAN	MAC CLURKIN	MAC PHERSON
MAC CLENNIE,-Y	MAC LENNAN	MAC CLURN	MAC LAREN
MAC CLENNON	MAC LENNAN	MAC CLURON	MAC LAREN
MAC CLERAN,-EN	MAC LAREN	MAC CLUSKIE,-Y	MAC DONALD
MAC CLERICH,-K	MAC PHERSON	MAC CLUTCHEON	MAC DONALD
MAC CLERMED,-ID	LAMONT	MAC CLUTCHION	MAC DONALD
MAC CLERN	MAC LAREN	MAC CLYMOND(S)	LAMONT
MAC CLERNON	MAC LENNAN	MAC CLYMONT(S)	LAMONT
MAC .CLERY	MACKINTOSH	MAC COACH	CARRICK DIST
MAC CLESKIE,-Y	MAC ASKILL	MAC COAL	MAC NAUGHTEN
MAC CLESKIE,-Y	MAC LEOD	MAC COAN	COLQUHOUN
MAC CLESTER	MAC ALISTER	MAC COAN	MAC DONELL GLENGARRY
MAC CLEW	STEWART OF APPIN	MAC COAN	MAC EWEN
MAC CLEWISTON	MAC DONALD	MAC COARD	CARRICK DIST
MAC CLEY	MAC LEAY	MAC COBB	STEWART OF APPIN
MAC CLEY	STEWART OF APPIN	MAC COBIUS	ARGYLL DIST
MAC CLILAN(S)	MAC LELLEN	MAC COCKHILL	MAC CORQUODALE
MAC CLIMAN	LAMONT	MAC COD(D)	MAC KAY
MAC CLINDEN	MAC DONALD	MAC CODRUM	MAC DONALD
MAC CLINDEN	MAC LENNAN	MAC COE	MAC KAY
MAC CLINE	MAC LEAN	MAC COFEE,-Y	MAC FIE
MAC CLINGAN,-EN	GALLOWAY DIST	MAC COGHLAN	CLAN CIAN
MAC CLINNIE	MAC LENNAN	MAC COICH	MAC FIE
MAC CLINTIC(K)	COLQUHOUN	MAC COID(E)	MAC FIE
MAC CLINTIC(K)	MAC CLINTOCK	MAC COIG	MAC FIE
MAC CLINTIC(K)	MAC DOUGALL	MAC COIK	ARRAN DIST
MAC CLINTOCK	COLQUHOUN	MAC COIL	MAC COLL
MAC CLINTOCK	MAC CLINTOCK	MAC COIL	MAC DONALD
MAC CLINTOCK	MAC DOUGALL	MAC COIN	MAC EWEN
MAC CLINTON	GALLOWAY DIST	MAC COISH	MAC DONALD
MAC CLISH	MAC LEISH	MAC COISH	MAC FIE
MAC CLISH	MAC PHERSON	MAC COISHIM	MAC INTYRE
MAC CLIVE	STEWART OF APPIN	MAC COIST	MAC DONALD
MAC CLONE	MAC LEAN	MAC COL(L)UM	MALCOLM
MAC CLONVEY	CAMERON	MAC COL(L)Y	STRATHSPEY DIST
MAC CLOO	MAC LEAY	MAC COLASH	INVERNESS DIST
MAC CLOO	STEWART OF APPIN	MAC COLD	MAC DOUGALL
MAC CLOOR	MAC CLURE	MAC COLE	MAC COLL
MAC CLORAN,-EN	MAC LAREN	MAC COLGAN(G)	AYRSHIRE DIST
MAC CLORGAN	GALLOWAY DIST	MAC COLGAR	ULSTER TARTAN
MAC CLORIE,-Y	GALLOWAY DIST	MAC COLINN	MALCOLM
MAC CLOSKY	ULSTER TARTAN	MAC COLL	MAC COLL
MAC CLOTHEN,-IN	MAC LACHLAN	MAC COLL	MAC DONALD
MAC CLOTHIN	MAC LACHLAN	MAC COLL	STEWART OF APPIN
MAC CLOUD	MAC LEOD	MAC COLL(E)N	CAMPBELL
MAC CLOUGHRIE,-Y	CARRICK DIST	MAC COLLA	GALLOWAY DIST
MAC CLOUNIE,-Y	GALLOWAY DIST	MAC COLLAM(E)	MALCOLM
MAC CLOW	MAC LEOD	MAC COLLAN	CAMPBELL
MAC CLOWD	MAC LEOD	MAC COLLAN	MAC LELLEN
MAC CLOWIE,-Y	ARGYLL DIST	MAC COLLEM	CALUM
MAC CLOWTHEN,-IN	MAC LACHLAN	MAC COLLEM	MAC CALLUM
MAC CLOY	STUART OF BUTE	MAC COLLEM	MALCOLM
MAC CLOYD	MAC LEOD	MAC COLLIE,-Y	MAC AULAY

NAME	TARTAN	NAME	TARTAN
MAC COLLIM	MALCOLM	MAC CONAWAY	INVERNESS DIST
MAC COLLIN(S)	MAC DONALD	MAC CONAY	INVERNESS DIST
MAC COLLISTER	MAC ALISTER	MAC CONBILE	MAC DONALD
MAC COLLOCH	MAC DONALD OF SLEAT	MAC CONCHER	MAC DOUGALL
MAC COLLOCH	MAC DOUGALL	MAC CONCHIE	CAMPBELL
MAC COLLOCH	MUNRO	MAC CONDACH	ROBERTSON
MAC COLLOCH	ROSS	MAC CONDICH	ROBERTSON
MAC COLLUM,-OM	CALUM	MAC CONDIE,-Y	MAC FARLANE
MAC COLLUM,-OM	MALCOLM	MAC CONDIE,-Y	MAC GREGOR
MAC COLLY,-IE	MAC AULAY	MAC CONDOCHIE	GRANT
MAC COLM	CALUM	MAC CONDOCHIE	ROBERTSON
MAC COLM	CAMPBELL	MAC CONE	COLQUHOUN
MAC COLM	MALCOLM	MAC CONE	MAC DONELL GLENGARRY
MAC COLM	STEWART OF APPIN	MAC CONE	ULSTER TARTAN
MAC COLMA	BUCHANAN	MAC CONECHY	ROBERTSON
MAC COLMAN	BUCHANAN	MAC CONICO	GRANT
MAC COLMBE	CAMPBELL	MAC CONICO	ROBERTSON
MAC COLOUGH	MAC DONALD OF SLEAT	MAC CONIE,-Y	MAC GREGOR
MAC COLOUGH	MAC DOUGALL	MAC CONKIE,-Y	ROBERTSON
MAC COLOUGH	MUNRO	MAC CONLIE,-Y	MAC DONALD
MAC COLOUGH	ROSS	MAC CONLOQUE	GRANT
MAC COLPIN(E)	MAC ALPINE	MAC CONLOQUE	ROBERTSON
MAC COLTON	ULSTER TARTAN	MAC CONN	MAC DONALD
MAC COLUM	MALCOLM	MAC CONNACH	MAC KENZIE
MAC COLVER	ULSTER TARTAN	MAC CONNAL	MAC DONALD
MAC COLVIN	ROXBURGH DIST	MAC CONNECH,-K	MAC KENZIE
MAC COLWAN	BUCHANAN	MAC CONNECHY,-IE	CAMPBELL
MAC COM	MAC THOMAS	MAC CONNEL(L)	MAC CONNELL
MAC COMAC	MAC LAINE	MAC CONNEL(L)	MAC DONALD
MAC COMAS	MAC TAVISH	MAC CONNICH,-K	MAC KENZIE
MAC COMAS	MAC THOMAS	MAC CONNOLL	MAC DONALD
MAC COMAS	MACKINTOSH	MAC CONNOLL	MAC DOUGALL
MAC COMAS(H)	GUNN	MAC CONNOLL	ROBERTSON
MAC COMB(S)	MAC THOMAS	MAC CONNON	MAC KINNON
MAC COMB(S)	MACKINTOSH	MAC CONOCHER	MAC DOUGALL
MAC COMBE	STEWART OF APPIN	MAC CONOCHIE,-Y	CAMPBELL
MAC COMBER	STEWART OF APPIN	MAC CONOCHIE,-Y	GRANT
MAC COMBICH	STEWART OF APPIN	MAC CONOMY,-IE	ULSTER TARTAN
MAC COMBIE,-Y	MAC THOMAS	MAC CONRY	CLAN CIAN
MAC COMBIE,-Y	MACKINTOSH	MAC CONRY	CONNACHT TARTAN
MAC COMBIE,-Y	STEWART OF APPIN	MAC CONSER	ARGYLL DIST
MAC COMBISH	MAC THOMAS	MAC CONSIDINE	CLAN CIAN
MAC COMBISH	MACKINTOSH	MAC CONVAY	ULSTER TARTAN
MAC COME	MAC THOMAS	MAC CONVEY	ULSTER TARTAN
MAC COME	MACKINTOSH	MAC CONVILLE	MAC DONALD
MAC COMI(N)SKIE	EDINBURGH DIST	MAC COO	MAC DONALD
MAC COMIE,-EY	MAC THOMAS	MAC COO	MAC KAY
MAC COMIE,-EY	MACKINTOSH	MAC COO	MAC LEOD
MAC COMIE,-Y	STEWART OF APPIN	MAC COOCHAM	MAC DONALD
MAC COMISH	MAC THOMAS	MAC COOE(Y)	MAC KAY
MAC COMISH	MACKINTOSH	MAC COOGAN	ULSTER TARTAN
MAC COMISKIE,-Y	CAMPBELL	MAC COOISH	MAC DON CLANRANALD
MAC COMISTRY,-IE	GALLOWAY DIST	MAC COOK	MAC DONALD
MAC COMLIE,-EY	MAC AULAY	MAC COOKWEIRS	ULSTER TARTAN
MAC COMMON	BUCHANAN	MAC COOL(E)	MAC COUL
MAC COMPSIE,-Y	CAMPBELL	MAC COOL(E)	MAC LEOD
MAC COMPSIE,-Y	STEWART OF APPIN	MAC COOM(E)(S)	MAC THOMAS
MAC COMSIE,-EY	STEWART OF APPIN	MAC COOM(E)(S)	MACKINTOSH
MAC COMSIE,-Y	CAMPBELL	MAC COOMB(E)(S)	MAC THOMAS
MAC CONACHER	ARGYLL DIST	MAC COOMB(E)(S)	MACKINTOSH
MAC CONACHIE,-Y	CAMPBELL	MAC COON	MAC EWEN
MAC CONACHIE,-Y	ROBERTSON	MAC COONDOCHIE,-Y	MAC FARLANE
MAC CONAGHY	ROBERTSON	MAC COOSHAM	MAC INTYRE
MAC CONARTY	ULSTER TARTAN	MAC COOWATT	FORBES
MAC CONATHA	HANNA	MAC COPLA(I)N	MAC ALPINE
MAC CONATHAY	ROBERTSON	MAC COPPIN(E)	MAC ALPINE

NAME	TARTAN	NAME	TARTAN
MAC COR(R)AL	MAC ORRELL	MAC COURIE,-Y	MAC QUARRIE
MAC CORAIGH	MAC QUARRIE	MAC COURK(E)Y	MAC CORQUODALE
MAC CORAN	CAMPBELL	MAC COURT	CARRICK DIST
MAC CORBA	ARGYLL DIST	MAC COURT (Irish)	ULSTER TARTAN
MAC CORBEY	ARGYLL DIST	MAC COURTEREY	GALLOWAY DIST
MAC CORCAL	MAC CORQUODALE	MAC COURTIE	MAC KIRDY
MAC CORD	CARRICK DIST	MAC COURTIE	STUART OF BUTE
MAC CORISKEN(E)	ERSKINE	MAC COURTUEY	GALLOWAY DIST
MAC CORK(H)ILL	GUNN	MAC COUSKY,-IE	MAC LEOD
MAC CORK(H)ILL	MAC CORQUODALE	MAC COVER	ULSTER TARTAN
MAC CORKADALE	MAC CORQUODALE	MAC COVEY	ULSTER TARTAN
MAC CORKELL	GUNN	MAC COWAN,-EN	COLQUHOUN
MAC CORKELL	MAC CORQUODALE	MAC COWAN,-EN	COWAN
MAC CORKELL	MAC LEOD	MAC COWAN,-EN	MAC DONELL GLENGARRY
MAC CORKENDALE	MAC CORQUODALE	MAC COWAN,-EN	MAC DOUGALL
MAC CORKIE,-Y	MAC CORQUODALE	MAC COWAT(T)	GLASGOW DIST
MAC CORKINDALE	MAC CORQUODALE	MAC COWELL	MAC DOUGALL
MAC CORKLE	GUNN	MAC COWIR	MAC IVER
MAC CORKLE	MAC CORQUODALE	MAC COWIS	MAC FIE
MAC CORKLE	MAC LEOD	MAC COWLE	MAC DOUGALL
MAC CORLY	MAC KENZIE	MAC COWLIE,-EY	MAC AULAY
MAC CORMA	BUCHANAN	MAC COY	MAC KAY
MAC CORMA	MAC LAINE	MAC COYD	MAC KAY
MAC CORMAC(K)	BUCHANAN	MAC COYLE	MAC DOUGALL
MAC CORMAC(K)	MAC LAINE	MAC COYNISH	MAC QUEEN
MAC CORMICK	MAC LAINE	MAC CRA	MAC RAE
MAC CORMICK	MAC LEAN	MAC CRACH	MAC RAE
MAC CORN	CAMPBELL	MAC CRACK	GALLOWAY DIST
MAC CORNACK,-OCK	BUCHANAN	MAC CRACKAN(S)	MAC NAUGHTEN
MAC CORNACK,-OCK	MAC LAINE	MAC CRACKEN(S)	GALLOWAY DIST
MAC CORPIN(E)	MAC ALPINE	MAC CRACKEN(S)	MAC LEAN
MAC CORQUHDALE	MAC CORQUODALE	MAC CRACKEN(S)	MAC NAUGHTEN
MAC CORQUODALE	MAC CORQUODALE	MAC CRACKIN(G)(S)	GALLOWAY DIST
MAC CORRAN	MAC NEIL GIGHA/COLONSAY	MAC CRACKIN(G)(S)	MAC NAUGTEN
MAC CORREL(L)	MAC ORRELL	MAC CRACKTIN	MAC NAUGHTEN
MAC CORRIE,-Y	MAC ORRELL	MAC CRAE	MAC RAE
MAC CORRIE,-Y	MAC QUARRIE	MAC CRAEV(E)Y,-IE	MAC DONALD OF SLEAT
MAC CORRISTAN	MAC DONALD	MAC CRAFT	GALLOWAY DIST
MAC CORRY	ULSTER TARTAN	MAC CRAIG	MAC CRAIG
MAC CORSE(Y)	MAC ORRELL	MAC CRAIN	MAC DONALD
MAC CORVIE,-(E)Y	ARGYLL DIST	MAC CRAING	MAC LEAN
MAC CORWIS	ARGYLL DIST	MAC CRAITH	MAC RAE
MAC COSGRAVE	ULSTER TARTAN	MAC CRALEY	ULSTER TARTAN
MAC COSGROVE	ULSTER TARTAN	MAC CRAN(N)	MAC DONALD
MAC COSH	MAC INTYRE	MAC CRANDELL	MAC DON CLANRANALD
MAC COSHAM,-EM,-IM	MAC DONALD	MAC CRANE	MAC DONALD
MAC COSKER	GLASGOW DIST	MAC CRANER	ARGYLL DIST
MAC COSKERY,-IE	GALLOWAY DIST	MAC CRANK	MAC LEAN
MAC COSKEY,-IE	MAC ASKILL	MAC CRANOR	ARGYLL DIST
MAC COSKEY,-IE	MAC LEOD	MAC CRARY	MAC RAE
MAC COSKREY	MAC ASKILL	MAC CRATE	MAC RAE
MAC COSTELLO	CONNACHT TARTAN	MAC CRATH	MAC RAE
MAC COTTER	MAC DONALD	MAC CRAV(E)Y	MAC DONALD OF SLEAT
MAC COU	MAC KAY	MAC CRAVEN(S)	GALLOWAY DIST
MAC COUBRIE,-Y	BUCHANAN	MAC CRAVIE,-Y	GALLOWAY DIST
MAC COUGAN	ULSTER TARTAN	MAC CRAW	MAC RAE
MAC COUH	MAC KAY	MAC CRAY	MAC RAE
MAC COUK	ARRAN DIST	MAC CRE(E)RIE,-Y	MAC DONALD
MAC COUL(L)	MAC COUL	MAC CREA	MAC RAE
MAC COUL(L)	MAC DOUGALL	MAC CREADH	MAC RAE
MAC COULESKIE,-Y	ARGYLL DIST	MAC CREADIE,-Y	GALLOWAY DIST
MAC COULF	MAC DOUGALL	MAC CREANOR	ARGYLL DIST
MAC COUN	GOW	MAC CREANOR	GALLOWAY DIST
MAC COUN	MAC DOUGALL	MAC CREAR	PERTHSHIRE DIST
MAC COUN	MAC EWEN	MAC CREATH	MAC RAE
MAC COUN	MAC PHERSON	MAC CREAVER	MAC DONALD
MAC COURBREY,-IE	BUCHANAN	MAC CREDDAN	GALLOWAY DIST
MAC COURICH,-K	MAC PHERSON	MAC CREDIE,-Y	GALLOWAY DIST

NAME	TARTAN	NAME	TARTAN
MAC CREE	GORDON	MAC CRUAR	DRUMMOND
MAC CREE	MAC RAE	MAC CRUAR	DUNBLANE DIST
MAC CREEDIE,-Y	GALLOWAY DIST	MAC CRUD(D)EN,-IN	MAC GREGOR
MAC CREEHAN	ULSTER TARTAN	MAC CRUDDEN	DUNDEE DIST
MAC CREEL	MAC NEIL	MAC CRUITER	BUCHANAN
MAC CREEN	MAC QUEEN	MAC CRUM(B)	MAC DONALD
MAC CREESH	MAC GREGOR	MAC CRUMMIN,-EN	MAC LEOD
MAC CREETH	MAC RAE	MAC CRUSKER	DUNDEE DIST
MAC CREIG	MAC DONALD	MAC CRYSTAL	BUCHAN DIST
MAC CREIGH	MAC RAE	MAC CUAG	FARQUHARSON
MAC CREIGHT	MAC RAE	MAC CUAG	MAC DONALD
MAC CREIL	MAC NEIL	MAC CUAG	MAC LEOD
MAC CRELAR(S)	CAMPBELL	MAC CUAICH	MAC DONALD
MAC CRELAR(S)	MAC KELLAR	MAC CUAIG	FARQUHARSON
MAC CRELLAS,-IS	CAMPBELL	MAC CUAIG	MAC DONALD
MAC CRELLIS	MAC NEIL	MAC CUAIL	MAC GREGOR
MAC CRERIE,-Y	MAC DONALD	MAC CUAN	MAC EWEN
MAC CRETON	ULSTER TARTAN	MAC CUBBIE,-Y	BUCHANAN
MAC CRIBBON	GRAHAM OF MENTIETH	MAC CUBBIN(E)(S)	BUCHANAN
MAC CRICKARD	ABERDEEN DIST	MAC CUBBIN(G)(S)	BUCHANAN
MAC CRIDDY	GALLOWAY DIST	MAC CUDDEN	GORDON
MAC CRIDGE	ULSTER TARTAN	MAC CUDDIE,-Y	BUCHANAN
MAC CRIE	GORDON	MAC CUDDIN	GORDON
MAC CRIE	MAC RAE	MAC CUDIE,-Y	ROXBURGH DIST
MAC CRIERICK	NITHSDALE DIST	MAC CUDRIE,-Y	LENNOX DIST
MAC CRIGHT	MAC INTYRE	MAC CUE	MAC KAY
MAC CRIL(L)Y	ULSTER TARTAN	MAC CUEN	MAC EWEN
MAC CRILL	MAC RAE	MAC CUFFIE,-Y	MAC FIE
MAC CRILLY	ULSTER TARTAN	MAC CUGAN	ULSTER TARTAN
MAC CRIMLISK	ARGYLL DIST	MAC CUIAG	MAC LEOD
MAC CRIMMON(D)	MAC LEOD	MAC CUID	MAC KAY
MAC CRIMMOR	MAC LEOD	MAC CUIDDIE,-Y	MAC KENZIE
MAC CRIND	MAC DONALD	MAC CUIDHEAN	MAC EWEN
MAC CRINDELL	MAC DON CLANRANALD	MAC CUIL(I)KEN	MAC DONALD
MAC CRINDLE	MAC DON CLANRANALD	MAC CUIR	MAC IVER
MAC CRINK	MAC LEAN	MAC CUISH	MAC DONALD
MAC CRIR(R)ICK	GALLOWAY DIST	MAC CUISH	MAC FIE
MAC CRIRIE,-Y	GALLOWAY DIST	MAC CUIST(I)ON	MAC DONALD
MAC CRISTIE,-IN	GALLOWAY DIST	MAC CUITHAN	MAC DONALD OF SLEAT
MAC CRITE	MAC INTYRE	MAC CUITHAN	MAC EWEN
MAC CROBBIE,-Y	ROBERTSON	MAC CUITHEIN	MAC DONALD OF SLEAT
MAC CROCKEN	MAC NAUGHTEN	MAC CUITHEIN	MAC EWEN
MAC CROCKET(T)	STIRLING DIST	MAC CUL(L)OUGH	MAC DONALD OF SLEAT
MAC CRODDAN,-EN	DUNDEE DIST	MAC CULASKY,-IE	ARGYLL DIST
MAC CRODDIE,-Y	GALLOWAY DIST	MAC CULIP	MAC DON OF KEPPOCH
MAC CROFT	GALLOWAY DIST	MAC CULIP	MAC KILLOP
MAC CROHAN	DUNDEE DIST	MAC CULIVRAY	MAC GILLIVRAY
MAC CROM	CAMPBELL	MAC CULL(E)Y	GALLOWAY DIST
MAC CRONE	GALLOWAY DIST	MAC CULLA	MAC DONALD OF SLEAT
MAC CRORIE,-Y	MAC DONALD	MAC CULLAG(A)(H)	MAC DONALD OF SLEAT
MAC CRORIE,-Y	MAC LAREN	MAC CULLAM	MALCOLM
MAC CROSKIE,-Y	STRATHEARN DIST	MAC CULLANE	MAC LAINE
MAC CROSS	ROSS	MAC CULLAR(S)	CAMPBELL
MAC CROSSAN,-EN	STRATHEARN DIST	MAC CULLAR(S)	MAC KELLAR
MAC CROSSIN	INVERNESS DIST	MAC CULLEN	ULSTER TARTAN
MAC CROSTIE,-Y	STRATHEARN DIST	MAC CULLIE,-Y	GALLOWAY DISTST
MAC CROTTER	BUCHANAN	MAC CULLIE,-Y	GUNN
MAC CROUDER	DRUMMOND	MAC CULLIE,-Y	MAC AULAY
MAC CROUDER	MAC GREGOR	MAC CULLIE,-Y	ROSS
MAC CROUTER	DRUMMOND	MAC CULLITER	MAC ALISTER
MAC CROUTHER	MAC GREGOR	MAC CULLOCH,-K	MAC DONALD OF SLEAT
MAC CROW	MAC RAE	MAC CULLOCH,-K	MAC DOUGALL
MAC CROWDER	DRUMMOND	MAC CULLOCH,-K	MUNRO
MAC CROWDER	MAC GREGOR	MAC CULLOCH,-K	ROSS
MAC CROWTHER	DRUMMOND	MAC CULLOCK,-ICK	MAC CULLOUGH
MAC CROWTHER	MAC GREGOR	MAC CULLON	MAC LELLEN
MAC CROY	MAC RAE		

NAME	TARTAN	NAME	TARTAN
MAC CULLONY,-IE	INVERNESS DIST	MAC DARRAN,-EN	ROXBURGH DIST
MAC CULLOUGH	MAC CULLOUGH	MAC DAVID	DAVIDSON
MAC CULLOW	MAC DONALD OF SLEAT	MAC DAVIE	CONNACHT TARTAN
MAC CULLOY	GALLOWAY DIST	MAC DAVIS	DAVIDSON
MAC CULP	MAC DON OF GLENCOE	MAC DAVIT(T)	DAVIDSON
MAC CUMBER	STEWART OF APPIN	MAC DAW(E)	DAVIDSON
MAC CUMISKY	GORDON	MAC DAW(E)Y	DAVIDSON
MAC CUMISY	GORDON	MAC DAY	MAC DAY
MAC CUMMIN(S)	CUMMING	MAC DEE	DAVIDSON
MAC CUMMING(S)	CUMMING	MAC DERM(A)ID	CAMPBELL OF BREADLABANE
MAC CUMRID	MONTGOMERY	MAC DERM(A)ID	MAC DERMAID
MAC CUNE	MAC EWEN	MAC DERMIERD	CAMPBELL OF BREADLABANE
MAC CUNEO	AYRSHIRE DIST	MAC DERMIERD	MAC DERMAID
MAC CUNN	MAC EWEN	MAC DERMIT(T)	CAMPBELL OF BREADLABANE
MAC CUNNEGAN	CUNNINGHAM	MAC DERMIT(T)	MAC DERMAID
MAC CUNNIE,-Y	GALLOWAY DIST	MAC DERMODY,-IE	ULSTER TARTAN
MAC CUNNIN	MAC KINNON	MAC DERMOLTRA	CONNACHT TARTAN
MAC CUR(R)	EDINBURGH DIST	MAC DERMONT	CAMPBELL OF BREADALBANE
MAC CUR(R)ICH	MAC PHERSON	MAC DERMOT (Irish)	CONNACHT TARTAN
MAC CURBIN	ULSTER TARTAN	MAC DERMOT	CAMPBELL OF BREADLABANE
MAC CURDIE,-Y	MAC KIRDY	MAC DERMUT(E)	CAMPBELL OF BREADLABANE
MAC CURDIE,-Y	STUART OF BUTE	MAC DESON	DAVIDSON
MAC CURE	MAC IVER	MAC DEVITT	DAVIDSON
MAC CUREITH	MAC QUARRIE	MAC DEWAR	MAC GREGOR
MAC CURL	MAC ORRELL	MAC DEWEL(L)	MAC DOUGALL
MAC CURLAN(G)	MAC DONALD	MAC DEWY	MAC GREGOR
MAC CURLEY,-Y	MAC DONALD	MAC DHUBHSITHE	MAC FIE
MAC CURNIN	ARGYLL DIST	MAC DICK	KEITH
MAC CURRA(G)HER	ROXBURGH DIST	MAC DICKEN,-IN(S)	KEITH
MAC CURRACH,-GH	MAC DON CLANRANALD	MAC DICKIE,-Y	KEITH
MAC CURRACH,-GH	MAC PHERSON	MAC DICKMIE,-MY	EDINBURGH DIST
MAC CURRICH	MAC PHERSON	MAC DICKON(S)	KEITH
MAC CURRIE,-Y	MAC DON CLANRANALD	MAC DICKSON	KEITH
MAC CURRIE,-Y	MAC GREGOR	MAC DIER	DUNDEE DIST
MAC CURRIE,-Y	MAC PHERSON	MAC DIFFIE,-Y	MAC FIE
MAC CURTAIN	GRAHAM OF MENTIETH	MAC DILL	MAC DOUGALL
MAC CURTAIN	MAC DONALD OF SLEAT	MAC DILLIDA(F)	ABERDEEN DIST
MAC CURTHIE,-Y	MAC KIRDY	MAC DIRMIT	CAMPBELL OF BREADALBANE
MAC CURTHIE,-Y	STUART OF BUTE	MAC DIRMIT	MAC DERMAID
MAC CURWIE,-Y	MAC QUARRIE	MAC DOCHERY	CONNACHT TARTAN
MAC CUSBAIG	MAC KENZIE	MAC DOFFY,-IE	MAC FIE
MAC CUSBAKE	MAC KENZIE	MAC DOIR	INVERNESS DIST
MAC CUSH	MAC DONALD	MAC DOLE	MAC DOUGALL
MAC CUSH	MAC INTYRE	MAC DOLNOLD	MAC DONALD
MAC CUSKER	GLASGOW DIST	MAC DOLOTHE	MAC DOUGALL
MAC CUSKIE(E)Y	MAC LEOD	MAC DON(N)ACH	ROBERTSON
MAC CUSPIC	MAC KENZIE	MAC DON(N)IE	MAC DONALD
MAC CUSPIC,-(K)	PERTHSHIRE DIST	MAC DONA	MAC DONA
MAC CUTCHE(O)N	MAC DONALD	MAC DONACHIE,-Y	CAMPBELL
MAC CUTCHEN,-AN	MAC DONALD	MAC DONACHIE,-Y	MAC GREGOR
MAC CUTCHEON	MAC DONALD	MAC DONACHIE,-Y	ROBERTSON
MAC CUTHAN	MAC DONALD OF SLEAT	MAC DONAGH	MAC DONA
MAC CUTHEN	MAC DONALD OF SLEAT	MAC DONAL(L)	MAC DONALD
MAC DADE	DAVIDSON	MAC DONAL(L)	MAC DONELL GLENGARRY
MAC DAGNIE,-Y	DAVIDSON	MAC DONALD	MAC DON ARDNAMURCHAN
MAC DAID	DAVIDSON	MAC DONALD	MAC DON CLANRANALD
MAC DAIR	GALLOWAY DIST	MAC DONALD	MAC DON OF BOISDALE
MAC DAIRM(A)ID	MAC DERMAID	MAC DONALD	MAC DON OF GLENCOE
MAC DAIRMID	CAMPBELL OF BREADLABANE	MAC DONALD	MAC DON OF KEPPOCH
MAC DANATO	TWEEDSIDE DIST	MAC DONALD	MAC DON OF KINGSBURGH
MAC DANEL	MAC DONELL GLENGARRY	MAC DONALD	MAC DONALD
MAC DANIEL(L)	MAC DONELL GLENGARRY	MAC DONALD	MAC DONALD GLENALADALE
MAC DANNALD	MAC DONALD	MAC DONALD	MAC DONALD OF LOCHMADDY
MAC DARBY	ULSTER TARTAN	MAC DONALD	MAC DONALD OF SLEAT
MAC DARIS	AYRSHIRE DIST	MAC DONALD	MAC DONALD OF STAFFA
MAC DARLEY	ULSTER TARTAN	MAC DONART	GALLOWAY DIST
MAC DARMODY	ULSTER TARTAN	MAC DONEGAN	ULSTER TARTAN

NAME	TARTAN	NAME	TARTAN
MAC DONELL,-ALL	MAC DONELL GLENGARRY	MAC EANHIE,-Y	MACKINTOSH
MAC DONLE(A)VY	BUCHANAN	MAC EANLAIG	MAC NEIL
MAC DONLEAVY	STEWART OF APPIN	MAC EAR(R)ACHER	FARQUHARSON
MAC DONLEVY(Irish)	ULSTER TARTAN	MAC EAR(R)ACHER	MAC FARLANE
MAC DONNA(H)	MAC DONA	MAC EARACHAR	FARQUHARSON
MAC DONNEL(L)	MAC DONELL GLENGARRY	MAC EARCHON	MAC EACHAIN
MAC DONNER	MAC DONA	MAC EDDIE,-Y	GORDON
MAC DONOUGH,-TH	MAC DONA	MAC EDDIE,-Y	MUNRO
MAC DOOL	MAC DOUGALL	MAC EDWARD(S)	MAC EDWARD
MAC DOOM	GALLOWAY DIST	MAC EDWARDS	MAC IVER
MAC DOOR	INVERNESS DIST	MAC EGAN	CONNACHT TARTAN
MAC DORFF	ABERDEEN DIST	MAC EICHAN	MAC EACHAIN
MAC DORMAN(D)	CAMPBELL	MAC ELAN,-EN	MAC LELLEN
MAC DORMAN(D)	MAC DERMAID	MAC ELATIN(E)	GALLOWAY DIST
MAC DORRAN,-EN	ROXBURGH DIST	MAC ELCHATTAN	CLAN CHATTAN
MAC DORTAN,-IN	AYRSHIRE DIST	MAC ELDOWNIE,-Y	MAC LEAN OF DUART
MAC DOUALL	GALLOWAY DIST	MAC ELDUIE	MAC GREGOR
MAC DOUALL	MAC DOUGALL	MAC ELEARIE,-Y	CLAN CHATTAN
MAC DOUGAL(L)	MAC DOUGALL	MAC ELEARIE,-Y	MAC PHERSON
MAC DOUGALD	MAC DOUGALL	MAC ELENIE,-Y	EDINBURGH DIST
MAC DOUGH	MAC DUFF	MAC ELFRESH,-ISH	MAC DONALD
MAC DOUGLAS(S)	LAMONT	MAC ELGUNN	GUNN
MAC DOUGLE	MAC DOUGALL	MAC ELHATTAN,-ON	CLAN CHATTAN
MAC DOUL(L)	MAC DOUGALL	MAC ELHATTEN	CLAN CHATTAN
MAC DOUNIE,-Y	EDINBURGH DIST	MAC ELHERAN	GRANT
MAC DOWALL	MAC DOUGALL	MAC ELHERAN	MAC DONALD
MAC DOWELL	MAC DOUGALL	MAC ELHERON	GRANT
MAC DOWNIE,-Y	EDINBURGH DIST	MAC ELHERON	MAC DONALD
MAC DRANE	MAC DONALD	MAC ELHILL	GLASGOW DIST
MAC DRIAN	MAC DONALD	MAC ELHINNEY	ULSTER TARTAN
MAC DUEL(L)	MAC DOUGALL	MAC ELHONE	GLASGOW DIST
MAC DUF(F)SON	MAC DUFF	MAC ELLER,-AR	CAMPBELL
MAC DUFF	MAC ALPINE	MAC ELLER,-AR	MAC KELLAR
MAC DUFF	MAC DUFF	MAC ELLICHER	ARRAN DIST
MAC DUFFIE,-Y	MAC FIE	MAC ELLIGER	ARRAN DIST
MAC DUFFYE	MAC FIE	MAC ELLIGOT(T)	ELLIOT
MAC DUFTHI	MAC FIE	MAC ELLIS(H)	ULSTER TARTAN
MAC DUGALD	MAC DOUGALL	MAC ELLOT	ULSTER TARTAN
MAC DUGALL	MAC DOUGALL	MAC ELMEEL	GLASGOW DIST
MAC DULL	MAC DOUGALL	MAC ELNAY	EDINBURGH DIST
MAC DULOTHE	MAC DOUGALL	MAC ELNICK	MAC DONALD
MAC DUNCAN	ROBERTSON	MAC ELNIE,-Y	EDINBURGH DIST
MAC DUNLEVY	ULSTER TARTAN	MAC ELPRANG	MAC ALPINE
MAC DUNN	AYRSHIRE DIST	MAC ELQUHAM	GLASGOW DIST
MAC DUPHE	MAC FIE	MAC ELRAVY,-IE	MAC DONALD
MAC DURKAN,-IN	CONNACHT TARTAN	MAC ELREE,-Y	GRANT
MAC DURMET	CAMPBELL OF BREADALBANE	MAC ELREE,-Y	MAC GILLIVRAY
MAC DURMIT(T)	CAMPBELL OF BREADLABANE	MAC ELREVIE,-Y	MAC DONALD
MAC DURMIT(T)	MAC DERMAID	MAC ELROY	GRANT
MAC DYER,-RE	DUNDEE DIST	MAC ELROY	MAC GILLIVRAY
MAC EACH	SHAW	MAC ELVAR	MAC KELLAR
MAC EACHAIN	MAC DON CLANRANALD	MAC ELVEEN	MAC BAIN
MAC EACHAIN	MAC EACHAIN	MAC ELVENTIE,-Y	MAC KENZIE
MAC EACHAN,-EN	MAC DON CLANRANALD	MAC ELVERY	CAMPBELL
MAC EACHAN,-EN	MAC EACHAIN	MAC ELVIE,-Y	CAMPBELL
MAC EACHERN	MAC DON CLANRANALD	MAC ELVIE,-Y	MAC KELLAR
MAC EACHERN	MAC EACHAIN	MAC ELVOGUE	ULSTER TARTAN
MAC EACHIN	MAC DON CLANRANALD	MAC ELWAIN	MAC BAIN
MAC EACHIN	MAC EACHAIN	MAC ELWANE	MAC BAIN
MAC EACHRAN,-ON	MAC DON CLANRANALD	MAC ELWAYNE	MAC BAIN
MAC EACHRAN,-ON	MAC EACHAIN	MAC ELWEE	CAMPBELL
MAC EACHRUN	MAC DON CLANRANALD	MAC ELWIN	MAC BAIN
MAC EACHRUN	MAC EACHAIN	MAC ELYA	CAMPBELL
MAC EACHUN	MAC DON CLANRANALD	MAC ELYEA	CAMPBELL
MAC EACHUN	MAC EACHAIN	MAC EMLIN(N)(E)	ARRAN DIST
MAC EAGH	SHAW	MAC ENDARFER	ULSTER TARTAN

NAME	TARTAN	NAME	TARTAN
MAC ENDO(E)	BUCHANAN	MAC FALLIN,-ON	MAC FARLANE
MAC ENDOLLAR	ULSTER TARTAN	MAC FARCHARD	FARQUHARSON
MAC ENEAN(E)Y	ULSTER TARTAN	MAC FARLAN(D)	MAC FARLANE
MAC ENEAS	MAC INNES	MAC FARLANE	MAC FARLANE
MAC ENENEY	MAC KINNON	MAC FARLANG	MAC FARLANE
MAC ENHILL	DUNDEE DIST	MAC FARLENE	MAC FARLANE
MAC ENLAKE	MAC KINLAY	MAC FARLIN(G)(S)	MAC FARLANE
MAC ENNIE,-Y	MAC KENZIE	MAC FARQUHAR	FARQUHARSON
MAC ENTEE	MAC KENZIE	MAC FARQUHAR	LAMONT
MAC ENTIRE	MAC INTYRE	MAC FARQUHAR	MAC FARLANE
MAC ENTYRE	MAC INTYRE	MAC FARRAN,-EN	MAC FARLANE
MAC EOGHAN	MAC EWEN	MAC FAT(T)ER	MAC LAREN
MAC EONE	MAC EWEN	MAC FATE	MAC LAREN
MAC ER(R)ACHER	FARQUHARSON	MAC FATRICK	LAMONT
MAC ER(R)ACHER	LAMONT	MAC FATRICK	MAC LENNAN
MAC ERCHAR	FARQUHARSON	MAC FATRIDGE	MAC LEAN
MAC ERICH	MAC DON CLANRANALD	MAC FATTIN	MAC FADYEN
MAC ERIGAN	ULSTER TARTAN	MAC FAUL(L)	MAC KINNON
MAC ERLAIN(E)	MAC DONALD	MAC FAULD(S)	MACKINTOSH
MAC ERLAIN(E)	MAC LAINE	MAC FAULT(S)	MACKINTOSH
MAC ERLANE	MAC DONALD	MAC FAWN	GALLOWAY DIST
MAC ERLEAN	MAC DONALD	MAC FAYDEN	MAC FADYEN
MAC ERNOCH,-K	ARGYLL DIST	MAC FEA	MAC FIE
MAC ERVIN(E)	IRVINE	MAC FEAD	MAC LAREN
MAC ERWIN	IRVINE	MAC FEARGUS	FERGUSON
MAC ETH	MAC KAY	MAC FEAT	MAC LAREN
MAC ETT(E)RICK	MAXWELL	MAC FEDDEN,-IN	MAC FADYEN
MAC EUR(E)	MAC IVER	MAC FEDDES	FIDDES
MAC EVANNY	ULSTER TARTAN	MAC FEE	MAC FIE
MAC EVER	CAMPBELL	MAC FEEL	CAMERON
MAC EVER,-S	MAC IVER	MAC FEEL	MAC PHAIL
MAC EVILIE,-Y	MAC IVER	MAC FEEL	MACKINTOSH
MAC EVILLY (Irish)	CONNACHT TARTAN	MAC FEELIE,-Y	CAMERON
MAC EVILLY,-IE	MAC KEEVER	MAC FEELIE,-Y	MAC PHAIL
MAC EVIT(T)Y	ULSTER TARTAN	MAC FEELIE,-Y	MACKINTOSH
MAC EVOY	ULSTER TARTAN	MAC FEET	MAC LAREN
MAC EWEN,-AN	MAC DOUGALL	MAC FEGGAN(S)	ARGYLL DIST
MAC EWEN,-AN	MAC EWEN	MAC FEITHE	MAC FIE
MAC EWIN(S)	MAC DOUGALL	MAC FEND	SINCLAIR
MAC EWIN(S)	MAC EWEN	MAC FERCHAR	FARQUHARSON
MAC EWING(S)	MAC DOUGALL	MAC FERGUS	FERGUSON
MAC EWING(S)	MAC EWEN	MAC FERRAN,-EN	INVERNESS DIST
MAC EYE	MAC KAY	MAC FERRIES	FERGUSON
MAC FADDEN,-AN,-IN	MAC FADYEN	MAC FERRIN	INVERNESS DIST
MAC FADDEN,-AN,-IN	MAC LAINE LOCH BUIE	MAC FERSHAR	FARQUHARSON
MAC FADE	MAC LAREN	MAC FERSON	MAC PHERSON
MAC FADIEN	MAC FADYEN	MAC FERY	INVERNESS DIST
MAC FADIEN	MAC LAINE LOCH BUIE	MAC FETRICK	LAMONT
MAC FADIN(E)	MAC FADYEN	MAC FETRICK	MAC LENNAN
MAC FADIN(E)	MAC LAINE LOCH BUIE	MAC FETRIDGE	MAC LEAN
MAC FADYEN	MAC FADYEN	MAC FETTER(S)	MAC GREGOR
MAC FADYEN	MAC LAINE LOCH BUIE	MAC FEYDEN	MAC FADYEN
MAC FADYEN	MAC LEAN	MAC FEYE	MAC FIE
MAC FADZEAN	MAC FADYEN	MAC FIDDES	FIDDES
MAC FADZEAN	MAC LAINE LOCH BUIE	MAC FIE	MAC FIE
MAC FAGAN	GALLOWAY DIST	MAC FIELD	CAMERON
MAC FAGGEN	GALLOWAY DIST	MAC FIG(G)AN(S)	ARGYLL DIST
MAC FAIDEN	MAC FADYEN	MAC FILANE	ARGYLL DIST
MAC FAIDEN	MAC LAINE LOCH BUIE	MAC FILLAN	STRATHEARN DIST
MAC FAIL	CAMERON	MAC FILLECHAIR	INVERNESS DIST
MAC FAIL	MAC PHAIL	MAC FINLA	MAC KINLAY
MAC FAIL	MACKINTOSH	MAC FIRBIS	FORBES
MAC FAIR	ULSTER TARTAN	MAC FIRBIS (Irish)	CONNACHT TARTAN
MAC FAIRESH	FERGUSON	MAC FOD	DUNDEE DIST
MAC FAIT	MAC LAREN	MAC FOIL	ARGYLL DIST
MAC FALL	CAMERON	MAC FOL(L)AN	STRATHEARN DIST
MAC FALL	MACKINTOSH	MAC FOYLE	ARGYLL DIST

NAME	TARTAN	NAME	TARTAN
MAC FREDERICK,-OCK	GALLOWAY DIST	MAC GAWLIE,-Y	MAC AULAY
MAC FREE	ULSTER TARTAN	MAC GAWN	GOW
MAC FRUCTER,-OR	MAR DIST	MAC GAWN	MAC PHERSON
MAC FRUNK	ULSTER TARTAN	MAC GAWRIE,-Y	MAC QUARRIE
MAC FRY(E)	DUNDEE DIST	MAC GAWRIS	MAC QUARRIE
MAC FUN(N)	MAC ARTHUR	MAC GAY(E)	MAC KAY
MAC FURLON(G)	MAC FARLANE	MAC GEACH	MAC GREGOR
MAC GAA	MAC DONALD	MAC GEACHAN	MAC DONALD
MAC GAA	MAC KAY	MAC GEACHIE,-Y	GALLOWAY DIST
MAC GACHAN,-IN	MAC DONALD	MAC GEAN	MAC DON OF GLENCOE
MAC GACHIE,-Y	MAC DONALD OF SLEAT	MAC GEAN	MAC KEAN
MAC GADIE,-Y	GORDON	MAC GEATH	KEITH
MAC GAF	MAC KAY	MAC GEDRIE,-Y	MAC DONALD
MAC GAFFIE,-Y	MAC FIE	MAC GEE	MAC DONALD
MAC GAFIC(K)	MAC FIE	MAC GEE	MAC KAY
MAC GAGH	MAC KAY	MAC GEECHAN	MAC DON ARDNAMURCHAN
MAC GAHA	MAC DONALD	MAC GEECHAN	MAC KEAN
MAC GAHA	MAC KAY	MAC GEEHAN	MAC DON OF GLENCOE
MAC GAHAN	GOW	MAC GEEHAN	MAC KEAN
MAC GAHAN	MAC PHERSON	MAC GEEHEE	MAC KAY
MAC GAHEY	MAC KAY	MAC GEEHIE,-Y	MAC KAY
MAC GAIN	GLASGOW DIST	MAC GEEIN	MAC DON OF GLENCOE
MAC GAIR(E)	MAC GUIRE	MAC GEEIN	MAC KEAN
MAC GAIRTIE,-Y	MAC ARTHUR	MAC GEEL	MAC GILL
MAC GALE(Y)	MAC AULAY	MAC GEEN	MAC DON OF GLENCOE
MAC GALL	MAC COLL	MAC GEEN	MAC KEAN
MAC GALL	MAC DONALD	MAC GEEVER	MAC IVER
MAC GALLERIE,-Y	MAC GILLIVRAY	MAC GEGHAEN	DUNDEE DIST
MAC GALLERIE,-Y	MAC LEAN	MAC GEHE(E)	MAC KAY
MAC GALLIARD	SKENE	MAC GELVRA	MAC GILLIVRAY
MAC GALLOGLY,-IE	MAC DONALD	MAC GENN	GLASGOW DIST
MAC GALLOWAY	MAC FARLANE	MAC GEOCH	GALLOWAY DIST
MAC GAN(N)	GOW	MAC GEOGEGHAN	DUNDEE DIST
MAC GAN(N)	MAC KENZIE	MAC GEOGHIE,-Y	DUNDEE DIST
MAC GAN(N)	MAC PHERSON	MAC GEORAIDH	MAC DONALD
MAC GANELL	MAC DONALD	MAC GEORGE	BUCHANAN
MAC GANNET	GALLOWAY DIST	MAC GEORGE	MAC NAB
MAC GANNON	CONNACHT TARTAN	MAC GEORIE,-Y	MAC DONALD
MAC GAR(R)ITY	EDINBURGH DIST	MAC GEOUGH	DUNDEE DIST
MAC GARDIE,-Y	FARQUHARSON	MAC GERAGHTY	CONNACHT TARTAN
MAC GARDLE	GALLOWAY DIST	MAC GERTIE,-Y	FORBES
MAC GARIE,-Y	MAC QUARRIE	MAC GETTIE,-Y	HAY
MAC GARMORY	MONTGOMERY	MAC GETTIGAN	ANGUS DIST
MAC GARNIE,-Y	MAC DON CLANRANALD	MAC GHIE	MAC KAY
MAC GARRACHAN	GALLOWAY DIST	MAC GHOIL	MAC DOUGALL
MAC GARRELL	GALLOWAY DIST	MAC GIBBIE,-Y	INVERNESS DIST
MAC GARRIE	MAC QUARRIE	MAC GIBBON	CAMPBELL
MAC GARRIGLE	GALLOWAY DIST	MAC GIBBON	GRAHAM OF MENTIETH
MAC GARROW	CAMPBELL	MAC GIBBON(S)	BUCHANAN
MAC GARROW	STEWART	MAC GIBBONY,-IE	CAMPBELL
MAC GARRY	MAC QUARRIE	MAC GIBSON	INVERNESS DIST
MAC GARTIE,-Y	MAC ARTHUR	MAC GIE	MAC KAY
MAC GARVA	GALLOWAY DIST	MAC GIFF	GALLOWAY DIST
MAC GARVIE,-Y	GALLOWAY DIST	MAC GIFFORD	HAY
MAC GARVOCK	ANGUS DIST	MAC GIL	MAC GILL
MAC GAUGHRIN	MAC EACHAIN	MAC GIL(LE)GLASS	MAR DIST
MAC GAUHY	MAC KAY	MAC GILANDRICE	ANDERSON
MAC GAULIE,-Y	MAC AULAY	MAC GILBERT	BUCHANAN
MAC GAUNE	GOW	MAC GILCHRIST	MAC LACHLAN
MAC GAUNE	MAC PHERSON	MAC GILCHRIST	OGILVIE
MAC GAVIC(K)	MAC VICAR	MAC GILERA	MAC GILLIVRAY
MAC GAVIGAN	EDINBURGH DIST	MAC GILERDRICE	ANDERSON
MAC GAVIN	GOW	MAC GILEVRAIE,-Y	MAC GILLIVRAY
MAC GAVIN	MAC PHERSON	MAC GILFILLAN	MAC LELLEN
MAC GAVRANGALL	EDINBURGH DIST	MAC GILGUNN	GALLOWAY DIST
MAC GAVROCK	ANGUS DIST	MAC GILHOOLY	ULSTER TARTAN
MAC GAW	STUART OF BUTE	MAC GILIVRAY,-IE	MAC GILLIVRAY
MAC GAW(E)	MAC KAY		

NAME	TARTAN	NAME	TARTAN
MAC GILLIVRAY	MAC GILLIVRAY	MAC GILVIE,-Y	CLAN CHATTAN
MAC GILLIVRAY	MAC LAINE LOCH BUIE	MAC GILVIE,-Y	MAC GILLIVRAY
MAC GILLONIE	CAMERON	MAC GILVOIR	MORRISON
MAC GILLRAVIE,-Y	MAC DONALD OF SLEAT	MAC GILVOYLE	MORRISON
MAC GILLREVIE,-Y	MAC GILLIVRAY	MAC GILVRA,-Y	MAC GILLIVRAY
MAC GILLVRAY	MAC GILLIVRAY	MAC GILWHINNIE	STUART OF BUTE
MAC GILLY	MAC PHERSON	MAC GIMPSIE,-Y	GALLOWAY DIST
MAC GILMARTIN	ULSTER TARTAN	MAC GINELLY	ULSTER TARTAN
MAC GILMICHAEL	STUART OF BUTE	MAC GING	ULSTER TARTAN
MAC GILMORE,-OUR	MORRISON	MAC GINLAY,-EY	ULSTER TARTAN
MAC GILNEW	ROTHESAY DIST	MAC GINN	ULSTER TARTAN
MAC GILNOA	CAMERON	MAC GINNIS	MAC INNES
MAC GILOVRAY	CLAN CHATTAN	MAC GINTIE,-Y	GLASGOW DIST
MAC GILOVRAY	MAC GILLIVRAY	MAC GINTY	ULSTER TARTAN
MAC GILP	MAC DON OF GLENCOE	MAC GIRL	MAC ORRELL
MAC GILP	MAC DON OF KEPPOCH	MAC GIRR	GALLOWAY DIST
MAC GILP	MAC KILLOP	MAC GIRTIE,-Y	FORBES
MAC GILPATRICK	COLQUHOUN	MAC GIVEN(S)	CAMPBELL
MAC GILPIN	CONNACHT TARTAN	MAC GIVEN(S)	GRAHAM OF MENTIETH
MAC GILRAY,-RA	GRANT	MAC GIVERN	MONTGOMERY
MAC GILREY,-RIE	GRANT	MAC GIVERSON	MAC IVER
MAC GILRICK	FRASER	MAC GLADDY,-IE	ULSTER TARTAN
MAC GILROY	GRANT	MAC GLADE	MAC LEOD
MAC GILROY	MAC GILLIVRAY	MAC GLADERIE,-Y	EDINBURGH DIST
MAC GILTON	CARRICK DIST	MAC GLADREY	EDINBURGH DIST
MAC GILVANE	MAC BAIN	MAC GLADRIE,-Y	EDINBURGH DIST
MAC GILVEIL	CAMERON	MAC GLAGAN	MAC LAGGAN
MAC GILVERNOCK	GRAHAM OF MENTIETH	MAC GLAM(M)IE	GALLOWAY DIST
MAC GILVERY,-IE	MAC GILLIVRAY	MAC GLAME	GALLOWAY DIST
MAC GILIVREY	MAC GILLIVRAY	MAC GLAMYN	LAMONT
MAC GILKER	CAMPBELL	MAC GLARKEN,-IN(S)	CLAN CHATTAN
MAC GILL	MAC DONALD	MAC GLASARICH,-K	CAMPBELL
MAC GILL	MAC GILL	MAC GLASARICH,-K	MAC DON OF KEPPOCH
MAC GILLAN	MAC DONALD	MAC GLASARICH,-K	MAC IVER
MAC GILLANDERS	CARRICK DIST	MAC GLASHAM	CLAN CHATTAN
MAC GILLAWAY	MAC GILLIVRAY	MAC GLASHAM	MAC GLASHAN
MAC GILLE	MAC DONALD	MAC GLASHAN,-EN	CLAN CHATTAN
MAC GILLECHALUM	MAC LEOD OF RAASAY	MAC GLASHAN,-EN	MAC GLASHAN
MAC GILLEDOW	LAMONT	MAC GLASHAN,-EN	MACKINTOSH
MAC GILLEGLASS	CLAN CHATTAN	MAC GLASHAN,-EN	ROBERTSON
MAC GILLEM	MAC DONALD	MAC GLASHAN,-EN	STEWART OF ATHOLL
MAC GILLEMILL	MAC MILLAN	MAC GLASHAW	MAC GLASHAN
MAC GILLEN	MAC DONALD	MAC GLASHING(S)	CLAN CHATTAN
MAC GILLENEIL	O'NEILL	MAC GLASHING(S)	MAC GLASHAN
MAC GILLERAGH	MAC GILLIVRAY	MAC GLASHON(S)	CLAN CHATTAN
MAC GILLERY,-IE	CAMERON	MAC GLASHON(S)	MAC GLASHAN
MAC GILLESPIE	MAC PHERSON	MAC GLASS	CLAN CHATTAN
MAC GILLEWIE	LAMONT	MAC GLASS	MAC GLASHAN
MAC GILLIARD,-G	AYRSHIRE DIST	MAC GLATCHIE,-Y	CARRICK DIST
MAC GILLICH	MAC PHERSON	MAC GLATHERY,-IE	EDINBURGH DIST
MAC GILLIE(S),-Y	GILLIES	MAC GLATIN(E)	GALLOWAY DIST
MAC GILLIE(S),-Y	MAC PHERSON	MAC GLAUGHON	MAC LACHLAN
MAC GILLIGAN	MACKINTOSH	MAC GLEAVE	CAMPBELL
MAC GILLIGAN	ULSTER TARTAN	MAC GLEAVE	MAC LEAY
MAC GILLILAN(D)	MAC LELLEN	MAC GLEAVE	STEWART OF APPIN
MAC GILLIN	MAC DONALD	MAC GLEISH	MAC LEISH
MAC GILLIS	GILLIES	MAC GLEISH	MAC PHERSON
MAC GILLIS	MAC DONELL GLENGARRY	MAC GLEN(N)(S)	CAMERON
MAC GILLIS	MAC PHERSON	MAC GLEN(N)(S)	GALLOWAY DIST
MAC GILLIUARY	MAC GILLIVRAY	MAC GLEN(N)(S)	MACKINTOSH
MAC GILLIVANTIC(K)	MAC DON OF KEPPOCH	MAC GLEW	STEWART OF APPIN
MAC GILLIVERAY	CLAN CHATTAN	MAC GLIMCHIE,-Y	EDINBURGH DIST
MAC GILLIVERAY	MAC GILLIVRAY	MAC GLINCHIE,-Y	GLASGOW DIST
MAC GILLIVERAY	MAC LAINE LOCH BUIE	MAC GLINN(S)	CAMERON
MAC GILLIVRARY	MAC LEAN	MAC GLINN(S)	MACKINTOSH
MAC GILLIVRAY	CLAN CHATTAN	MAC GLOGAN	MAC LENNAN

NAME	TARTAN	NAME	TARTAN
MAC GLOHAN	DUNDEE DIST	MAC GRAIN	MAC DONALD
MAC GLOIN(E)	GALLOWAY DIST	MAC GRALL	ULSTER TARTAN
MAC GLOM	GALLOWAY DIST	MAC GRANAHAN	EDINBURGH DIST
MAC GLONE	GALLOWAY DIST	MAC GRANDLE	MAC DON CLANRANALD
MAC GLOSSEN,-ON	MAC GLASHAN	MAC GRANE	MAC DONALD
MAC GLOTHLON	MAC LACHLAN	MAC GRATH	MAC RAE
MAC GLOTTEN,-IN	MAC LACHLAN	MAC GRAVIE,-Y	MAC DONALD OF SLEAT
MAC GLOUTHLIN	MAC LACHLAN	MAC GRAW	MAC RAE
MAC GLUICHEY	CARRICK DIST	MAC GRAY	MAC RAE
MAC GLUKEN	MAC DON CLANRANALD	MAC GREACHA(I)N	MAC NAUGHTEN
MAC GLYN(N)(S)	CAMERON	MAC GREAL	MAC NEIL
MAC GLYN(N)(S)	GALLOWAY DIST	MAC GREEN(E)	GALLOWAY DIST
MAC GLYN(N)(S)	MACKINTOSH	MAC GREESKIN(E)	EDINBURGH DIST
MAC GOEY	MAC KAY	MAC GREEVIE,-Y	MAC DONALD OF SLEAT
MAC GOF(F)	MAC FIE	MAC GREEVY (Irish)	CONNACHT TARTAN
MAC GOHAN	GOW	MAC GREGOR	MAC ALPINE
MAC GOHAN	MAC PHERSON	MAC GREGOR	MAC GREGOR
MAC GOIL	MAC DOUGALL	MAC GREGOR	MAC GREGOR BALQUHIDDER
MAC GOLASH	MAC GLASHAN	MAC GREGOR	MAC GREGOR OF CARDNEY
MAC GOLDRICK	EDINBURGH DIST	MAC GREGOR	MAC GREGOR OF DEESIDE
MAC GOLDRICK	GLASGOW DIST	MAC GREGOR	MAC GREGOR OF GLEN LYLE
MAC GOMERY	MONTGOMERY	MAC GREGOR	MAC GREGOR OF GLENSTRAE
MAC GONIGAL,-LE	ULSTER TARTAN	MAC GREGOR	ROB ROY
MAC GONIGLE	ULSTER TARTAN	MAC GREIGOR	MAC GREGOR
MAC GONLDRICK	DUNDEE DIST	MAC GREUSICH	BUCHANAN
MAC GOOKIE,-Y	MAC FIE	MAC GREUSICH	MAC FARLANE
MAC GOON	MAC EWEN	MAC GREW	MAC GREGOR
MAC GOR(R)IE,-Y	LAMONT	MAC GREWAR,-ER	DRUMMOND
MAC GOR(R)IE,-Y	MAC QUARRIE	MAC GREWAR,-ER	FRASER
MAC GORLICK	GALLOWAY DIST	MAC GREWAR,-ER	MAC GREGOR
MAC GORMAN	ULSTER TARTAN	MAC GRIBBON	GRAHAM OF MENTIETH
MAC GORNAHAN	GORDON	MAC GRIGOR	MAC GREGOR
MAC GORRIE,-Y	MAC DONALD	MAC GRIME	GRAHAM OF MENTIETH
MAC GOUCHTRAY	AYRSHIRE DIST	MAC GRIMEN	GRAHAM OF MENTIETH
MAC GOUGAN,-EN	MAC NEIL GIGHA/COLONSAY	MAC GRIMEN	MAC LEOD
MAC GOUGH	MAC DUFF	MAC GRINDER	MAC DON CLANRANALD
MAC GOUGHAN	MAC NEIL GIGHA/COLONSAY	MAC GRODAN	MAC LEAN
MAC GOUGHTRY,-IE	AYRSHIRE DIST	MAC GROGAN	MAC LEAN
MAC GOUIRK	LENNOX DIST	MAC GRONE	MAC DONALD
MAC GOUIRK	MAC FARLANE	MAC GROON	MAC DONALD
MAC GOUN	MAC DONALD	MAC GRORIE,-Y	MAC LAREN
MAC GOUN	MAC PHERSON	MAC GRORIE,-Y	MAC RORY
MAC GOURLY	ULSTER TARTAN	MAC GROSSAN	GALLOWAY DIST
MAC GOURTY,-IE	FORBES	MAC GROT(T)IE,-Y	DRUMMOND
MAC GOVAN,-EN	GOW	MAC GROUTHER	DRUMMOND
MAC GOVAN,-EN	MAC PHERSON	MAC GROUTHER	MAC GREGOR
MAC GOVERN	ULSTER TARTAN	MAC GRUAR	DUNBLANE DIST
MAC GOW	GOW	MAC GRUAR	FRASER
MAC GOW	MAC DONALD	MAC GRUDER	DRUMMOND
MAC GOW	MAC PHERSON	MAC GRUDER	MAC GREGOR
MAC GOWAN,-EN	GOW	MAC GRUE	MAC GREGOR
MAC GOWAN,-EN	MAC DONALD	MAC GRUEN	MAC EWEN
MAC GOWAN,-EN	MAC PHERSON	MAC GRUER	DRUMMOND
MAC GOWAN,-EN	NITHSDALE DIST	MAC GRUER	FRASER
MAC GOWGAN	LOCHABER DIST	MAC GRUER	MAC GREGOR
MAC GOWIN(S)	GOW	MAC GRUTHER,-AR	DRUMMOND
MAC GOWIN(S)	MAC DONALD	MAC GRUTHER,-AR	MAC GREGOR
MAC GOWIN(S)	MAC PHERSON	MAC GUARIE,-Y	MAC QUARRIE
MAC GOWNE	GOW	MAC GUBBIN(S)	BUCHANAN
MAC GOWNE	MAC PHERSON	MAC GUBBIN(S)	CAMPBELL
MAC GRACHIN	MAC NAUGHTEN	MAC GUCKI(A)N	MAC NEIL GIGHA/COLONSAY
MAC GRADE	CLAN CIAN	MAC GUE	MAC KAY
MAC GRADER	STRATHEARN DIST	MAC GUFFIE,-Y	DOUGLAS
MAC GRADY	GRADY	MAC GUFFIE,-Y	MAC FIE
MAC GRAHAM	GRAHAM OF MENTIETH	MAC GUFFIN,-EN	MAC FIE
MAC GRAIL	MAC NEIL	MAC GUFFOCK	DOUGLAS
MAC GRAIME	GRAHAM OF MENTIETH	MAC GUFFOG,-K	MAC FIE

NAME	TARTAN	NAME	TARTAN
MAC GUGAN	MAC NEIL GIGHA/COLONSAY	MAC HAWL	MAC COLL
MAC GUIGAN	MAC NEIL GIGHA/COLONSAY	MAC HAWL	MAC DONALD
MAC GUINNESS	ULSTER TARTAN	MAC HAY	MAC KAY
MAC GUIRE	MAC GUIRE	MAC HAY(E)(S)	HAY
MAC GUIRE	MAC QUARRIE	MAC HAY(E)(S)	SHAW
MAC GUIRE	ULSTER TARTAN	MAC HAYLE	MAC DOUGALL
MAC GUMRIE,-Y	MONTGOMERY	MAC HAYSIE,-Y	HAY
MAC GUNN(I)ON	GALLOWAY DIST	MAC HE(E)VER	MAC IVER
MAC GUNNIGLE	ULSTER TARTAN	MAC HEATH	KEITH
MAC GUNNION	GALLOWAY DIST	MAC HEDDY,-IE	GORDON
MAC GURE	CAMPBELL	MAC HEFFIE,-Y	MAC FIE
MAC GURER	MAC QUARRIE	MAC HELLAN,-EN	MAC LELLEN
MAC GURK	LENNOX DIST	MAC HELLON	MAC LELLEN
MAC GURK	MAC FARLANE	MAC HENDRIE,-Y	HENDERSON
MAC GURL	MAC ORRELL	MAC HENDRIE,-Y	MAC DON OF GLENCOE
MAC GURMAN	STRATHSPEY DIST	MAC HENDRIE,-Y	MAC NAUGHTEN
MAC GURN,-IE,-Y	STRATHEARN DIST	MAC HENISH	MAC INNES
MAC GURTIE,-Y	FORBES	MAC HENRY	MAC DON OF GLENCOE
MAC GUYRT	BUCHANAN	MAC HENRY	MAC NAUGHTEN
MAC GUYRT	MAC WHIRTER	MAC HER(R)	ARRAN DIST
MAC GWIER	MAC GUIRE	MAC HERIOD	ANGUS DIST
MAC GWIER	MAC QUARRIE	MAC HERRAN,-ON	GRANT
MAC GWINE	MAC QUEEN	MAC HERRAN,-ON	MAC DONALD
MAC GYE	MAC KAY	MAC HETCHA	ULSTER TARTAN
MAC GYLE	MAC DOUGALL	MAC HETH	MAC KAY
MAC GYVER	MAC IVER	MAC HETHRICK	MAXWELL
MAC HADDIE,-Y	GORDON	MAC HETT	KEITH
MAC HAFEE,-IE	MAC FIE	MAC HEVER,-OR	MAC IVER
MAC HAFFIE,-EY	MAC FIE	MAC HEY(S)	MAC KAY
MAC HAIG	MAC LEOD	MAC HEYCOURT	ULSTER TARTAN
MAC HAIL	MAC DOUGALL	MAC HIM,-N	FRASER
MAC HALE(S)	MAC DOUGALL	MAC HINTON	MAR DIST
MAC HALL	MAC COLL	MAC HIRR	ARRAN DIST
MAC HALLAM	MALCOLM	MAC HIT(T)	KEITH
MAC HAMIE,-EY	STUART OF BUTE	MAC HIVER,-OR	MAC IVER
MAC HAN(N)	MAC DONALD	MAC HOE	MAC DONALD
MAC HAN(N)	MAC INNES	MAC HOKER	ARRAN DIST
MAC HAN(N)ANICH,-K	BUCHANAN	MAC HOLM(E)	MALCOLM
MAC HANDRIE,-Y	MACKINTOSH	MAC HOMASH	MAC THOMAS
MAC HANISH	MAC CANISH	MAC HOMASH	MACKINTOSH
MAC HANISH	MAC INNES	MAC HOME	MAC THOMAS
MAC HANS	MAC INNES	MAC HOME	MACKINTOSH
MAC HANTIE,-Y	MAC KENZIE	MAC HONAGAN	ARGYLL DIST
MAC HANTIN	MAC KENZIE	MAC HONE	MAC DONELL GLENGARRY
MAC HANTS	MAC INNES	MAC HOO	MAC KAY
MAC HANVICHAR	MAC NAUGHTEN	MAC HORSE	MAC EACHAIN
MAC HAR(R)	ABERDEEN DIST	MAC HOUL(L)	MAC COUL
MAC HARDIE,-Y	CLAN CHATTAN	MAC HOUL(L)	MAC DOUGALL
MAC HARDIE,-Y	FARQUHARSON	MAC HOUSTON	MAC DONALD
MAC HARDIE,-Y	MAC HARDIE	MAC HOWATT	MAC DONALD
MAC HARDIE,-Y	MACKINTOSH	MAC HOWELL	MAC DOUGALL
MAC HARDIE,-Y	MAR DIST	MAC HOWIE,-Y	MAC AULAY
MAC HARG	GALLOWAY DIST	MAC HOWLEY,-IE	MAC AULAY
MAC HARGUE	GALLOWAY DIST	MAC HRAY	MAC RAE
MAC HARL(E)Y,-IE	MAC KENZIE	MAC HUDRIE,-Y	LENNOX DIST
MAC HARNESS	HARKNESS	MAC HUESTON	MAC DONALD
MAC HAROLD	MAC LEOD	MAC HUG	CONNACHT TARTAN
MAC HARRY,-IE	MAC NAUGHTEN	MAC HUGA	EDINBURGH DIST
MAC HAT	CLAN CHATTAN	MAC HUGH	MAC DONALD
MAC HATTAN	CLAN CHATTAN	MAC HUGHEY,-IE	MAC KAY
MAC HATTIE,-Y	CLAN CHATTAN	MAC HULLIE,-Y	GALLOWAY DIST
MAC HATTON	CLAN CHATTAN	MAC HUTCHEN	MAC DONALD
MAC HAUF	MAC AULAY	MAC HUTCHEON	MAC DONALD
MAC HAUL	MAC COLL	MAC HUTCHINSON	MAC DONALD
MAC HAUL	MAC DONALD	MAC IAG	MAC LEOD
MAC HAVER(S)	MAC KEEVER	MAC IAN	GUNN
MAC HAWELL	MAC DOUGALL	MAC IAN	MAC DON ARDNAMURCHAN

NAME	TARTAN
MAC IARGAR	MAC IVER
MAC IASIN	MAC DON CLANRANALD
MAC ICHAN	MAC DONALD
MAC ICHAN	MAC EACHAIN
MAC IDH	MAC KAY
MAC IGGIN(S)	MAC DONALD
MAC IL(L)	MAC GILL
MAC IL(L)RICK	FRASER
MAC IL(L)RICK	MAC DONALD OF SLEAT
MAC ILAHEINEY	ARGYLL DIST
MAC ILARICK	FRASER
MAC ILBOWIE	GLEN LYON DIST
MAC ILBREED	ARGYLL DIST
MAC ILBRIDE	ARGYLL DIST
MAC ILBUIE	MAC DONALD
MAC ILCACHEW	MAR DIST
MAC ILCHENNIE	MAC KENZIE
MAC ILCHERE	ARRAN DIST
MAC ILCRUM	MAC DON ARDNAMURCHAN
MAC ILDEEN	GLASGOW DIST
MAC ILDEWIE,-Y	MAC GREGOR
MAC ILDINNIE,-Y	MAC LEAN
MAC ILDONNIE,-Y	LAMONT
MAC ILDOON	MAC LEAN
MAC ILDOWNIE,-Y	CAMERON
MAC ILDOWNIE,-Y	LAMONT
MAC ILDOWNIE,-Y	MAC GREGOR
MAC ILDOWNIE,-Y	MAC LEAN
MAC ILDUFF	MAC GREGOR
MAC ILDUFF	MAC LEAN
MAC ILDUFF (Irish)	ULSTER TARTAN
MAC ILDUIE	MAC GREGOR
MAC ILDUIN	GLASGOW DIST
MAC ILDUY	MAC GREGOR
MAC ILE	MAC DOUGALL
MAC ILEESE	MAC LEISH
MAC ILEHERE	GRANT
MAC ILELLEN	MAC LELLEN
MAC ILFIE	MAC FIE
MAC ILFREDERIC	COLQUHOUN
MAC ILGORM	GLASGOW DIST
MAC ILHAGGA	EDINBURGH DIST
MAC ILHARGA(A)	EDINBURGH DIST
MAC ILHARGIE,-Y	EDINBURGH DIST
MAC ILHATTON,-AN	CLAN CHATTAN
MAC ILHAYNIE,-Y	MAC DONALD
MAC ILHENNIE,-Y	MAC DONALD
MAC ILHERAN	GRANT
MAC ILHILL	GALLOWAY DIST
MAC ILHON(Y)	GLASGOW DIST
MAC ILHONE	MAC DON OF GLENCOE
MAC ILIN	MAC LEAN
MAC ILLECHUREL	MAC KERRAL
MAC ILLEMARTIN	MAC DONALD
MAC ILLEN,-IN	MAC LEAN
MAC ILLICHRIST	MAC LACHLAN
MAC ILLICHRIST	OGILVIE
MAC ILLIES	GILLIES
MAC ILLIES	MAC PHERSON
MAC ILLIGLAS	ARGYLL DIST
MAC ILLIN	MAC LELLEN
MAC ILLIVRA,-E	MAC GILLIVRAY
MAC ILLIVRACH,-OCH	MAC GILLIVRAY
MAC ILLMALUAG	STUART OF BUTE
MAC ILMARTIN	MAC DONALD
MAC ILMICHAEL	MAC MICHAEL
MAC ILMICHAEL	STUART OF BUTE
MAC ILMONIE,-Y	LAMONT
MAC ILMONIE,-Y	STUART OF BUTE
MAC ILMOON	LAMONT
MAC ILMOON	STUART OF BUTE
MAC ILMORE	MORRISON
MAC ILMOYLE	EDINBURGH DIST
MAC ILMUNIE,-Y	LAMONT
MAC ILMUNIE,-Y	STUART OF BUTE
MAC ILMURCHIE	MAC DONALD
MAC ILMURRAY	MURRAY
MAC ILMURTIE,-Y	MAC DONALD
MAC ILNEW	ARGYLL DIST
MAC ILPATRICK	COLQUHOUN
MAC ILQUHAM	GUNN
MAC ILQUHAM	MAC WILLIAM
MAC ILRA	GRANT
MAC ILRAITH	FRASER
MAC ILRATH	GRANT
MAC ILRAVIE,-Y	MAC GILLIVRAY
MAC ILREACH	FRASER
MAC ILREACH	MAC DONALD OF SLEAT
MAC ILREVIE	MAC DONALD OF SLEAT
MAC ILRICK	FRASER
MAC ILROW	FT. WILLIAM DIST
MAC ILROY	GRANT
MAC ILROY	MAC GILLIVRAY
MAC ILRUTH	MAC GILLIVRAY
MAC ILSHALAM,-OM	MALCOLM
MAC ILTUASH	ARGYLL DIST
MAC ILUDE	GLASGOW DIST
MAC ILVAIN	MAC BAIN
MAC ILVAIN	MAC KAY
MAC ILVAY	CAMPBELL
MAC ILVAY	MAC KELLAR
MAC ILVEEN	MAC BAIN
MAC ILVEIL	MAC MILLAN
MAC ILVENNIE,-Y	MAC BAIN
MAC ILVERA	MAC GILLIVRAY
MAC ILVERN	GRAHAM OF MENTIETH
MAC ILVERNOCH	ARGYLL DIST
MAC ILVERNOG	ARGYLL DIST
MAC ILVERRAN	ARGYLL DIST
MAC ILVOIL	MORRISON
MAC ILVON	MAC BAIN
MAC ILVOR	MORRISON
MAC ILVORA	MAC LEAN
MAC ILVORY	MAC GILLIVRAY
MAC ILVOYLE	MORRISON
MAC ILVRAE	MAC GILLIVRAY
MAC ILVRIDE	MAC DONALD
MAC ILVRONE	FT. WILLIAM DIST
MAC ILWAIN	MAC BAIN
MAC ILWAYNE	MAC BAIN
MAC ILWEE	CAMPBELL
MAC ILWHOM	LAMONT
MAC ILWRAITH	MAC DONALD OF SLEAT
MAC ILWRICK	MAC DONALD
MAC IMMIE,-Y	FRASER
MAC INALLY	BUCHANAN
MAC INALLY	MAC FARLANE
MAC INALLY	MAC KINLAY
MAC INCH	MAC INNES
MAC INDEN	COLQUHOUN
MAC INDEN	MAC DOUGALL
MAC INDEOR	BUCHANAN
MAC INDEOR	MAC ARTHUR
MAC INDEOR	MENZIES

NAME	TARTAN	NAME	TARTAN
MAC INDEWAR	MAC GREGOR	MAC JAMES	GUNN
MAC INDO,-OE	BUCHANAN	MAC JAMES	MAC FARLANE
MAC INER(R)Y	MAC INERY	MAC JAMES	ROBERTSON
MAC INERRY,-IE	MAC NAUGHTEN	MAC JAN(N)ET	GALLOWAY DIST
MAC INESKER	ULSTER TARTAN	MAC JARROW	PAISLEY DIST
MAC INGAN	MAC KINNON	MAC JASPAR,-ER	INVERNESS DIST
MAC INLESTER	FLETCHER	MAC JEDS	ROXBURGH DIST
MAC INLUDE	GLASGOW DIST	MAC JENKIN(S)	STRATHCLYDE DIST
MAC INNES	MAC GREGOR	MAC JERROW	AYRSHIRE DIST
MAC INNES	MAC INNES	MAC JESSICK,-OCK	DAVIDSON
MAC INNIE,-Y	MAC INNIS	MAC JILL	MAC GILL
MAC INNIE,-Y	MAC KENZIE	MAC JILTON	CARRICK DIST
MAC INNON	MAC KINNON	MAC JIMPSEY	GALLOWAY DIST
MAC INREW	ROBERTSON	MAC JISSICK	DAVIDSON
MAC INRIVER	ARGYLL DIST	MAC JOCK(K)IE	GRANT
MAC INROSS	KINROSS	MAC JOR(R)IE,-Y	MAC DONALD
MAC INROY	MAC INROY	MAC JUNKIN	DUNCAN
MAC INROY	MAC INROY OF LUDE	MAC KA(A)	MAC KAY
MAC INROY	ROBERTSON	MAC KAD(D)IE,-Y	FERGUSON
MAC INRUE	ROBERTSON	MAC KAD(D)IE,-Y	GORDON
MAC INRYE	MAC DON OF GLENCOE	MAC KAD(D)IE,-Y	MUNRO
MAC INRYE	MAC NAUGHTEN	MAC KAGUE	FARQUHARSON
MAC INSTALKER	MAC FARLANE	MAC KAGUE	MAC LEOD
MAC INSTALKER	MAC GREGOR	MAC KAI	MAC KAY
MAC INSTER	GALLOWAY DIST	MAC KAIG	FARQUHARSON
MAC INSTRAY,-EY	GALLOWAY DIST	MAC KAIG	MAC LEOD
MAC INTAGGART	MAC TAGGART	MAC KAIL	CAMERON
MAC INTAGGART	ROSS	MAC KAIL	ROTHESAY DIST
MAC INTAYLOR	ARGYLL DIST	MAC KAIN	MAC DON ARDNAMURCHAN
MAC INTIRE	MAC INTYRE	MAC KAIN(S)	MAC DON OF GLENCOE
MAC INTOSH	MACKINTOSH	MAC KAIRNS,-ES	GRANT
MAC INTURF(F)	MAC INTYRE	MAC KALE	CAMERON
MAC INTURNER	LAMONT	MAC KALE	ROTHESAY DIST
MAC INTYRE	MAC INTYRE	MAC KALIP(S)	MAC DON OF GLENCOE
MAC INTYRE	MAC INTYRE OF GLENORCHY	MAC KALIP(S)	MAC DON OF KEPPOCH
MAC INULTIE,-Y	EDINBURGH DIST	MAC KALL	MAC COLL
MAC INVAL	MAC GREGOR	MAC KALL	MAC COLL
MAC INVALLOCH	MAC GREGOR	MAC KALL	ROTHESAY DIST
MAC INVERNEY	ULSTER TARTAN	MAC KALL	STUART OF BUTE
MAC INVILL	ARGYLL DIST	MAC KALLIE,-Y	MAC AULAY
MAC INWILL	ARGYLL DIST	MAC KAMAN	BUCHANAN
MAC IPHIE	MAC FIE	MAC KAMES	GUNN
MAC IRONSIDE	ABERDEEN DIST	MAC KAMEY,-IE	STUART OF BUTE
MAC IRVINE	IRVINE	MAC KANANICH,-K	BUCHANAN
MAC ISALL	MAC KAY	MAC KANDY	MACKINTOSH
MAC ISLE	KYLE	MAC KANE	MAC DON ARDNAMURCHAN
MAC ISSAC(S)	CAMPBELL	MAC KANE	MAC DON OF GLENCOE
MAC ISSAC(S)	MAC DON CLANRANALD	MAC KANNA	MAC INNES
MAC ISSACH	MAC DON CLANRANALD	MAC KARLIE,-EY	MAC KENZIE
MAC IVAR(S)	CAMPBELL	MAC KARRAN	GRANT
MAC IVAR(S)	MAC IVER	MAC KARRICK	CARRICK DIST
MAC IVAR(S)	MAC KEEVER	MAC KASIE,-Y	MAC ASKILL
MAC IVEN	MAC IVER	MAC KASIE,-Y	MAC LEOD
MAC IVER(S)	CAMPBELL	MAC KASKEL	MAC ASKILL
MAC IVER(S)	MAC IVER	MAC KASKEL	MAC LEOD
MAC IVER(S)	MAC KEEVER	MAC KASKILL	MAC ASKILL
MAC IVER(S)	ROBERTSON	MAC KASKILL	MAC LEOD
MAC IVOR(S)	CAMPBELL	MAC KASKLE	MAC ASKILL
MAC IVOR(S)	MAC IVER	MAC KASKLE	MAC LEOD
MAC IVOR(S)	MAC KEEVER	MAC KAUGHAN	MAC DON CLANRANALD
MAC IVOR(S)	ROBERTSON	MAC KAUGHAN	MAC EACHAIN
MAC IVORIE,-Y	MAC IVER	MAC KAVENEY,-IE	MAC KAY
MAC IVORIE,-Y	MAC KENZIE	MAC KAVISH	MAC TAVISH
MAC IVY,-IE	MAC IVER	MAC KAW	MAC KAY
MAC IYE	MAC KAY	MAC KAW	STUART OF BUTE

NAME	TARTAN	NAME	TARTAN
MAC KAY(E)	DAVIDSON	MAC KEKE	MAC KAY
MAC KAY(E)	MAC DONALD	MAC KELDIN	GLASGOW DIST
MAC KAY(E)	MAC KAY	MAC KELL	MAC AULAY
MAC KAY(E)	MAC KAY OF STRATHNAVER	MAC KELL	ROTHESAY DIST
MAC KCOY	MAC KAY	MAC KELL	STUART OF BUTE
MAC KE(E)(S)	MAC KAY	MAC KELL(E)Y	MAC DONALD
MAC KEACHIE,-Y	MAC DONALD	MAC KELLACHIE	MAC DONALD
MAC KEACHRAN	MAC DONALD		
MAC KEACHRAN	MAC EACHAIN	MAC KELLAICH	MAC DONALD
MAC KEAG(UE)	FARQUHARSON	MAC KELLAIG	MAC DONALD
MAC KEAG(UE)	MAC LEOD	MAC KELLAIGH	MAC DONALD
MAC KEAMISH	GUNN	MAC KELLAN	MAC LELLEN
MAC KEAN	GUNN	MAC KELLAR(S)	CAMPBELL
MAC KEAN(E)	MAC DON ARDNAMURCHAN	MAC KELLAR(S)	MAC KELLAR
MAC KEAN(E)	MAC DON OF GLENCOE	MAC KELLEN	MAC LELLEN
MAC KEAN(E)	MAC KEAN	MAC KELLER(S)	CAMPBELL
MAC KEAND	MAC DON ARDNAMURCHAN	MAC KELLER(S)	MAC KELLAR
MAC KEAND	MAC DON OF GLENCOE	MAC KELLICAN	MACKINTOSH
MAC KEAND	MAC KEAN	MAC KELLIE	MAC DONALD
MAC KEARD	MAC HARDIE	MAC KELLIGETT	AYRSHIRE DIST
MAC KEARD	MACKINTOSH	MAC KELLIN(S)	MAC LELLEN
MAC KEARY	MAC GREGOR	MAC KELLIP(S)	MAC DON OF GLENCOE
MAC KEARY	ULSTER TARTAN	MAC KELLIP(S)	MAC KILLOP
MAC KECHAN(S)	MAC DON CLANRANALD	MAC KELLOCH	MAC DONALD
MAC KECHAN(S)	MAC EACHAIN	MAC KELLOG	MAC DONALD
MAC KECHNIE,-Y	MAC DON CLANRANALD	MAC KELLON	MAC LELLEN
MAC KECHNIE,-Y	MAC EACHAIN	MAC KELLOP	MAC DON OF GLENCOE
MAC KEDDIE,-Y	FERGUSON	MAC KELLOP	MAC DON OF KEPPOCH
MAC KEDDIE,-Y	GORDON	MAC KELLOP	MAC KILLOP
MAC KEDDIE,-Y	MUNRO	MAC KELLOR(S)	CAMPBELL
MAC KEEBY,-IE	MAC IVER	MAC KELLOR(S)	MAC KELLAR
MAC KEEGAN	MAC DON CLANRANALD	MAC KELLY,-IE	GALLOWAY DIST
MAC KEEGAN	MAC DONALD	MAC KELLY,-IE	MAC DONALD
MAC KEEHAN	MAC DON ARDNAMURCHAN	MAC KELVAN,-EN,-IN	MAC BAIN
MAC KEEHAN	MAC DON OF GLENCOE	MAC KELVEY	GALLOWAY DIST
MAC KEEHAN	MAC KEAN	MAC KELVIE,-Y	CAMPBELL
MAC KEEL	MAC DONALD	MAC KELVIE,-Y	GALLOWAY DIST
MAC KEEL	MAC GILL	MAC KEM(M)Y,-IE	FRASER
MAC KEEMAN	FRASER	MAC KEN	MAC KENZIE
MAC KEEN(E)	MAC DON OF GLENCOE	MAC KENDO(E)	BUCHANAN
MAC KEEN(E)	MAC DONALD	MAC KENDRICK(S)	MAC KENDRICK
MAC KEEN(E)	MAC KEAN	MAC KENDRICK(S)	MAC NAUGHTEN
MAC KEETCH	KEITH	MAC KENDRIE,-Y	MAC KENDRICK
MAC KEETH	KEITH	MAC KENDRIE,-Y	MAC NAUGHTEN
MAC KEEVER(S)	MAC IVER	MAC KENERICK	MAC KENDRICK
MAC KEEVER(S)	MAC KEEVER	MAC KENERICK	MAC NAUGHTEN
MAC KEEVIE,-Y	MAC IVER	MAC KENERIE,-Y	MAC NAUGHTEN
MAC KEEVLIE,-Y	MAC IVER	MAC KENIBLY	CONNACHT TARTAN
MAC KEG	FARQUHARSON	MAC KENITH	MAC KENZIE
MAC KEG	MAC LEOD	MAC KENNA,-EY	GALLOWAY DIST
MAC KEGGIE,-Y	MACKINTOSH	MAC KENNAN,-EN,-IN	MAC KINNON
MAC KEIAY	MAC KAY	MAC KENNEDY	KENNEDY
MAC KEICHAN(S)	MAC DON CLANRANALD	MAC KENNERIE,-Y	MAC DON OF GLENCOE
MAC KEICHAN(S)	MAC EACHAIN	MAC KENNOCH	MAC KENZIE
MAC KEIGE	MACKINTOSH	MAC KENNY	ULSTER TARTAN
MAC KEIGHN	MAC DON OF GLENCOE	MAC KENRICK	MAC KENDRICK
MAC KEIGHN	MAC KEAN	MAC KENRICK	MAC NAUGHTEN
MAC KEIL	MAC DOUGALL	MAC KENSEE	MAC KENZIE
MAC KEIN	MAC DONALD	MAC KENTHA	MAC KENZIE
MAC KEITCH	MAC PHERSON	MAC KENTHRO	ULSTER TARTAN
MAC KEITH	KEITH	MAC KENTY,-IE	MAC KENZIE
MAC KEITH	MAC PHERSON	MAC KENZEY	APPLECROSS DIST
MAC KEITHAN	KEITH	MAC KENZEY	MAC KENZIE
MAC KEITHAN	MAC DONALD	MAC KENZIE	APPLECROSS DIST
MAC KEIVER	MAC IVER	MAC KENZIE	MAC KENZIE
MAC KEIVER	MAC KEEVER	MAC KENZIER	MAC KENZIE

NAME	TARTAN	NAME	TARTAN
MAC KENZY	APPLECROSS DIST	MAC KEY(S)	MAC KAY
MAC KENZY	MAC KENZIE	MAC KHAN	MAC DONALD
MAC KEOCHAN	MAC DON CLANRANALD	MAC KHAN	MAC INNES
MAC KEOGH	CLAN CIAN	MAC KHEE	MAC KAY
MAC KEOGH	CONNACHT TARTAN	MAC KHONE	MAC EWEN
MAC KEOHNIE,-Y	ANGUS DIST	MAC KIANNAN	MAC KINNON
MAC KEON	MAC EWEN	MAC KIARRON,-AN	GRANT
MAC KEON (Irish)	ULSTER TARTAN	MAC KIARRON,-AN	MAC DONALD
MAC KEOWAN	MAC EWEN	MAC KIARRON,-AN	STUART OF BUTE
MAC KEOWN	MAC EWEN	MAC KIBB(S)	BUCHANAN
MAC KER	MAC KAY	MAC KIBBEN,-IN(S)	GRAHAM OF MENTIETH
MAC KER(R)ACHER	FARQUHARSON	MAC KIBBIN(S)	BUCHANAN
MAC KER(R)Y,-IE	CAMPBELL	MAC KICHAN	MAC DONALD
MAC KERACHER	FARQUHARSON	MAC KICHAN	MAC DOUGALL
MAC KERACHER	MAC DON CLANRANALD	MAC KICHAN	MAC EACHAIN
MAC KERCHER	MAC DON CLANRANALD	MAC KIDDIE,-Y	GORDON
MAC KERLICH	CAMPBELL	MAC KIDDIE,-Y	MUNRO
MAC KERLICH	MAC KENZIE	MAC KIE	MAC KAY
MAC KERLIE	CAMPBELL	MAC KIEHAN	MAC DON ARDNAMURCHAN
MAC KERLIE,-Y	MAC KENZIE	MAC KIER	FIFE DIST
MAC KERN(S)	ROTHESAY DIST	MAC KIERNAN	ULSTER TARTAN
MAC KERNAN	MAC DONALD	MAC KIGGAN(S)	MAC DONALD
MAC KERNIE,-Y	GRANT	MAC KILCHRIST	OGILVIE
MAC KERR	ULSTER TARTAN	MAC KILDUFF	CONNACHT TARTAN
MAC KERRA	FERGUSON	MAC KILE(S)	MAC DOUGALL
MAC KERRAL,-EL	CARRICK DIST	MAC KILGIR	CAMPBELL
MAC KERRAL,-EL	GALLOWAY DIST	MAC KILGIR	KILGORE
MAC KERRAL,-EL	MAC DONALD	MAC KILGUNN	GUNN
MAC KERRAL,-EL	MAC KERRAL	MAC KILL	GALLOWAY DIST
MAC KERRAN,-EN	GRANT	MAC KILL	MAC GILL
MAC KERRAN,-EN	MAC DONALD	MAC KILL	MACKINTOSH
MAC KERRAN,-EN	STUART OF BUTE	MAC KILLAIG	MAC DONALD
MAC KERRAS,-IS	FERGUSON	MAC KILLELLEY	CONNACHT TARTAN
MAC KERRON	GRANT	MAC KILLEN	MAC DONALD
MAC KERRON	MAC DONALD	MAC KILLICAN	MACKINTOSH
MAC KERRON	STUART OF BUTE	MAC KILLIGAN	MACKINTOSH
MAC KERROW	GALLOWAY DIST	MAC KILLIN(S)	MAC DONALD
MAC KERRS	FERGUSON	MAC KILLOP,-IP	MAC DON OF GLENCOE
MAC KERSEY,-IE	FERGUSON	MAC KILLOP,-IP	MAC DON OF KEPPOCH
MAC KERTRICH	MAXWELL	MAC KILLOP,-IP	MAC KILLOP
MAC KES(S)EN	CAMPBELL	MAC KILMORE	MORRISON
MAC KES(S)ON	CAMPBELL	MAC KILMURRAY	MURRAY
MAC KESIE,-Y	CAMPBELL	MAC KILPATRICK	DOUGLAS
MAC KESIE,-Y	MAC DONALD	MAC KILREA	GRANT
MAC KESIND	CAMPBELL	MAC KILROY	GRANT
MAC KESIND	MAC DONALD	MAC KIM(M)	FRASER
MAC KESSACK,-ICK	CAMPBELL	MAC KIMMIE,-Y	FRASER
MAC KESSACK,-ICK	MAC DONALD	MAC KIN(N)	MAC INNES
MAC KESSIE,-Y	CAMPBELL	MAC KINACE	MAC INNES
MAC KESSIE,-Y	MAC DONALD	MAC KINCAIRN	STRATHSPEY DIST
MAC KESSOCK	CAMPBELL	MAC KINCARDY,-IE	STRATHSPEY DIST
MAC KESSOCK	MAC DONALD	MAC KINDELL,-LE	GALLOWAY DIST
MAC KESTER	HAY	MAC KINDEN	COLQUHOUN
MAC KETH	KEITH	MAC KINDEN	MAC DOUGALL
MAC KETH	MAC PHERSON	MAC KINDER	BUCHANAN
MAC KETHRICK	MAXWELL	MAC KINDLAY,-EY	BUCHANAN
MAC KETT	KEITH	MAC KINDLAY,-EY	FARQUHARSON
MAC KETTRICK	MAXWELL	MAC KINDLAY,-EY	MAC KINLAY
MAC KEVENY,-IE	ULSTER TARTAN	MAC KINDLESS	GALLOWAY DIST
MAC KEVIN(S)	ARGYLL DIST	MAC KINDO(E)	BUCHANAN
MAC KEVIT(T)	DAVIDSON	MAC KINH	MAC INNES
MAC KEW	MAC KAY	MAC KINICE	MAC INNES
MAC KEWAN,-EN	MAC EWEN	MAC KINISTRY,-IE	AYRSHIRE DIST
MAC KEWER	MAC IVER	MAC KINLAY	MAC KINLAY
MAC KEWIN	MAC IVER	MAC KINLEY,-IE	BUCHANAN
MAC KEWN	MAC EWEN	MAC KINLEY,-IE	FARQUHARSON
		MAC KINLEY,-IE	MAC KINLAY

NAME	TARTAN	NAME	TARTAN
MAC KINLOCH	MAC KINLOCK	MAC KLISH	MAC LEISH
MAC KINNE	MAC KENZIE	MAC KLOO(S)	STEWART OF APPIN
MAC KINNEL(L)	MAC DONALD	MAC KLOW	MAC LEOD
MAC KINNEY	MAC KENZIE	MAC KLURICH	MAC PHERSON
MAC KINNIE,-Y	GALLOWAY DIST	MAC KNEAL	MAC NEIL
MAC KINNIE,-Y	MAC KENZIE	MAC KNEE	MAC GREGOR
MAC KINNIN	MAC KINNON	MAC KNEFF	GALLOWAY DIST
MAC KINNING(S)	MAC KINNON	MAC KNEITH	MAC GREGOR
MAC KINNIS	MAC INNES	MAC KNELLIE,-Y	MAC NEIL
MAC KINNON	MAC KINNON	MAC KNESS	MAC INNES
MAC KINNOT(T)	MAC KINNON	MAC KNEW	EDINBURGH DIST
MAC KINSIE,-Y	MAC KENZIE	MAC KNIGHT	MAC NAUGHTEN
MAC KINSTER	GALLOWAY DIST	MAC KNITH	MAC GREGOR
MAC KINSTRY,-IE	GALLOWAY DIST	MAC KNO(E)	GALLOWAY DIST
MAC KINTON	MAR DIST	MAC KNOCATER	STEWART OF APPIN
MAC KINTOSH	MACKINTOSH	MAC KNOCKTER	STEWART OF APPIN
MAC KINTY,-IE	MAC KENZIE	MAC KNOON	GALLOWAY DIST
MAC KINTYRE	MAC INTYRE	MAC KNOT	MAC NAUGHTEN
MAC KINVEIL	MAC GREGOR	MAC KNOWN	GALLOWAY DIST
MAC KINVELL	MAC GREGOR	MAC KO(E)	MAC KAY
MAC KINVEN	MAC KINNON	MAC KOAN(E)	GOW
MAC KINVILL(E)	ARGYLL DIST	MAC KOAN(E)	MAC PHERSON
MAC KINVINE	MAC KINNON	MAC KOFFEE,-Y	MAC FIE
MAC KINZEN	MAC KINNON	MAC KOGH	MAC DON CLANRANALD
MAC KINZIE	APPLECROSS DIST	MAC KOGH	MAC KAY
MAC KINZIE	MAC KENZIE	MAC KOLE	MAC COLL
MAC KIPPEN(S)	CAMPBELL	MAC KOLE	MAC DON CLANRANALD
MAC KIRACHAR	HAY	MAC KOM	MAC THOMAS
MAC KIRCHAN	MAC DON CLANRANALD	MAC KONE	COLQUHOUN
MAC KIRCHAN	MAC EACHAIN	MAC KONE	MAC DONELL GLENGARRY
MAC KIRCHEN	MAC DOUGALL	MAC KONKEY,-IE	CAMPBELL
MAC KIRDY,-IE	MAC KIRDY	MAC KONL(E)Y	MAC DONALD
MAC KIRDY,-IE	STUART OF BUTE	MAC KONOCHIE,-Y	GRANT
MAC KIRE	MAC IVER	MAC KONOCHIE,-Y	MAC DOUGALL
MAC KIRGAN	ULSTER TARTAN	MAC KONOCHIE,-Y	ROBERTSON
MAC KIRRECH,-K	ARGYLL DIST	MAC KOO	MAC KAY
MAC KIRRICK	ARGYLL DIST	MAC KOOL	MAC COUL
MAC KIRROCH	ARGYLL DIST	MAC KOOL	MAC LEOD
MAC KISKIE,-Y	MAC ASKILL	MAC KOR(R)EST	PERTHSHIRE DIST
MAC KISSACK	CAMPBELL	MAC KORKLE	MAC CORQUODALE
MAC KISSICK	MAC DONALD	MAC KORLY,-IE	MAC KENZIE
MAC KISSOCK	CAMPBELL	MAC KORREL(L)	MAC ORRELL
MAC KISSON	PERTHSHIRE DIST	MAC KORREST	MAC ORRELL
MAC KISTON	STIRLING DIST	MAC KOSKI(E),-Y	MAC ASKILL
MAC KITCHEN	MAC DONALD	MAC KOSKI(E),-Y	MAC LEOD
MAC KITCHEN	MAC DOUGALL	MAC KOUL	MAC COUL
MAC KITTING	AYRSHIRE DIST	MAC KOUL	MAC LEOD
MAC KITTRICK	DOUGLAS	MAC KOVER	ULSTER TARTAN
MAC KITTRICK	MAXWELL	MAC KOW	GOW
MAC KIVER(S)	MAC IVER	MAC KOW	MAC PHERSON
MAC KIVOR(S)	MAC IVER	MAC KOWGE	CONNACHT TARTAN
MAC KIYE	MAC KAY	MAC KOWN	MAC EWEN
MAC KLAM	MAC LAINE	MAC KOY	MAC KAY
MAC KLANE	MAC LAINE	MAC KREAL	MAC NEIL
MAC KLATCHIE,-Y	AYRSHIRE DIST	MAC KREEL	MAC NEIL
MAC KLE	MAC LEAY	MAC KREETH	MAC RAE
MAC KLELLAND	MAC LELLEN	MAC KREITH	FRASER
MAC KLEM	LAMONT	MAC KREITH	MAC RAE
MAC KLEN	MAC LEAN	MAC KRELL	AYRSHIRE DIST
MAC KLER	CLAN CHATTAN	MAC KRETH	MAC RAE
MAC KLERICH	MAC PHERSON	MAC KRIDE(S)	AYRSHIRE DIST
MAC KLEY	MAC LEAY	MAC KRIDGE	GALLOWAY DIST
MAC KLEY	STEWART OF APPIN	MAC KRILL	MAC RAE
MAC KLEYMORE	MAC LEAY	MAC KRITCHIE,-Y	MACKINTOSH
MAC KLEYMORE	STEWART OF APPIN	MAC KRITH	MAC RAE
MAC KLIN(E)	MAC LEAN	MAC KROKAT	GLASGOW DIST
MAC KLINNAN	MAC LENNAN	MAC KRONE	GALLOWAY DIST

NAME	TARTAN	NAME	TARTAN
MAC KRORY,-IE	MAC DONALD	MAC LARNON	MAC LENNAN
MAC KRORY,-IE	MAC LAREN	MAC LARON	MAC LAREN
MAC KRORY,-IE	MAC RORY	MAC LARTICH,-K	MAC DONALD
MAC KROW	MAC RAE	MAC LARTIE,-Y	MAC DONALD
MAC KUAG	FARQUHARSON	MAC LARY	CLAN CHATTAN
MAC KUB(B)IN(S)	BUCHANAN	MAC LARY	MAC PHERSON
MAC KUE	MAC KAY	MAC LARY	MACKINTOSH
MAC KUHN	MAC EWEN	MAC LASER	MAC GLASHAN
MAC KUID(E)	FARQUHARSON	MAC LASER	MACKINTOSH
MAC KUILIE,-Y	MAC AULAY	MAC LASKIE,-Y	MAC ASKILL
MAC KUIN	MAC EWEN	MAC LASKIE,-Y	MAC LEOD
MAC KULA	MAC AULAY	MAC LATCHIE,-Y	AYRSHIRE DIST
MAC KUNE	MAC EWEN	MAC LAUCHIE	GALLOWAY DIST
MAC KURDY,-IE	MAC KIRDY	MAC LAUCHLAN	MAC LACHLAN
MAC KURDY,-IE	STUART OF BUTE	MAC LAUCHLAN,-IN	MAC LACHLAN
MAC KURRICH,-K	MAC PHERSON	MAC LAUD	MAC LEOD
MAC KUSKIE,-Y	MAC ASKILL	MAC LAUGHLAN(D)	MAC LACHLAN
MAC KUSKIE,-Y	MAC LEOD	MAC LAUGHLIN	MAC LACHLAN
MAC KY	MAC KAY	MAC LAUGHLON	MAC LACHLAN
MAC KY(E)	MAC KAY	MAC LAUREN,-IN	MAC LAREN
MAC KYLE(S)	MAC DONALD	MAC LAURIN	MAC LAURIN
MAC KYLE(S)	MAC DOUGALL	MAC LAUTHLAN,-IN	MAC LACHLAN
MAC KYRE	MAC IVER	MAC LAVE	MAC LEAY
MAC LACHIE,-Y	MAC LACHLAN	MAC LAVE	STEWART OF APPIN
MAC LACHLAN(D)	MAC LACHLAN	MAC LAVERTIE,-Y	MAC DONALD
MAC LACHLEN(D)	MAC LACHLAN	MAC LAWLOR	ULSTER TARTAN
MAC LACHLIN(E)	MAC LACHLAN	MAC LAWRENIE	MAC LAREN
MAC LACKIE,-Y	MAC LACHLAN	MAC LAWRIN	MAC LAREN
MAC LADDIE,-Y	MAC DONALD	MAC LAWS	CAMPBELL
MAC LAE	MAC LEAY	MAC LAWS	MAC THOMAS
MAC LAE	STEWART OF APPIN	MAC LAY	MAC LEAY
MAC LAFFERTY,-IE	MAC DONALD	MAC LAY	STEWART OF APPIN
MAC LAG(G)AN	MAC LAGGAN	MAC LAYNE	MAC LAINE
MAC LAG(G)AN	ROBERTSON	MAC LAYNE	MULL DIST
MAC LAGGER	MAC LAGGAN	MAC LEA	MAC LEAY
MAC LAGHLAN(E)	MAC LACHLAN	MAC LEA	STEWART OF APPIN
MAC LAIM	MAC LAINE	MAC LEAD	MAC LEOD
MAC LAIN(E)	MAC LAINE	MAC LEAF	MAC LEAY
MAC LAINE	MAC LAINE LOCH BUIE	MAC LEAF	STEWART OF APPIN
MAC LAINE	MULL DIST	MAC LEAKEENS	LEAKIE
MAC LAIR(E)	CLAN CHATTAN	MAC LEAKIE,-Y	LEAKIE
MAC LAIR(E)	MAC PHERSON	MAC LEAKIN(S)	LEAKIE
MAC LALLY,-IE	MAC AULAY	MAC LEAN	MAC LEAN
MAC LALOR	ULSTER TARTAN	MAC LEAN	MAC LEAN OF DUART
MAC LAMB	MAC LAINE	MAC LEAN	MULL DIST
MAC LAME	MAC LAINE	MAC LEANAN	MAC LENNAN
MAC LAMMIE,-(E)Y	GALLOWAY DIST	MAC LEAND	MAC LEAN
MAC LAMMIE,-Y	LAMONT	MAC LEAR	CLAN CHATTAN
MAC LAMOND,-T	LAMONT	MAC LEAR	MAX PHERSON
MAC LAMORE	STEWART OF APPIN	MAC LEARAN	MAC LAREN
MAC LAN()DSBOURGH	GALLOWAY DIST	MAC LEARIE,-Y	CLAN CHATTAN
MAC LANACHAN	GALLOWAY DIST	MAC LEARIE,-Y	MAC PHERSON
MAC LANDISH	ANDERSON	MAC LEARIN(S)	MAC LAREN
MAC LANDRISH	ROSS	MAC LEARNAN(D)	ROTHESAY DIST
MAC LANE	MAC LEAN	MAC LEAT(T)Y,-IE	ULSTER TARTAN
MAC LANNIN	MAC LENNAN	MAC LEAVE	MAC LEAY
MAC LANNON	MAC LENNAN	MAC LEAVE	STEWART OF APPIN
MAC LARAN	MAC LAREN	MAC LEAVY	MAC LEAY
MAC LARDY,-IE	MAC DONALD	MAC LEAVY	STEWART OF APPIN
MAC LARE	CLAN CHATTAN	MAC LEAY	LIVINGSTONE
MAC LARE	MAC PHERSON	MAC LEAY	MAC LEAY
MAC LAREN	MAC LAREN	MAC LEAY	STEWART OF APPIN
MAC LARISH	MAC DONALD	MAC LEDDY,-IE	ULSTER TARTAN
MAC LARKEN	CLAN CHATTAN	MAC LEE	MAC KINLAY
MAC LARKEN	MAC PHERSON	MAC LEECE	MAC LEISH
MAC LARKIN(S)	CLAN CHATTAN	MAC LEECE	MAC PHERSON
MAC LARKIN(S)	MAC PHERSON	MAC LEECH	MAC LEISH
		MAC LEECH	MAC LEISH

NAME	TARTAN	NAME	TARTAN
MAC LEEN(E)	MAC LEAN	MAC LINDOWNY,-IE	MAC LEAN
MAC LEERY,-IE	CLAN CHATTAN	MAC LINDSAY	LINDSAY
MAC LEERY,-IE	MAC PHERSON	MAC LINE	MAC LEAN
MAC LEES	MAC LEISH	MAC LINNAN,-EN	MAC LENNAN
MAC LEES	MAC PHERSON	MAC LINNON	MAC LENNAN
MAC LEESBACH,-K	PERTHSHIRE DIST	MAC LINSAY	LINDSAY
MAC LEESH	MAC LEISH	MAC LINTOCK	COLQUHOUN
		MAC LINTOCK	MAC CLINTOCK
MAC LEESH	MAC PHERSON	MAC LINTOCK	MAC DOUGALL
MAC LEGGAN,-EN,-IN	MAC LAGGAN	MAC LINZIE	LINDSAY
MAC LEHOSE	CAMPBELL	MAC LISE	MAC LEISH
MAC LEHOSE	MAC THOMAS	MAC LISE	MAC PHERSON
MAC LEIGH	MAC LEAY	MAC LISH	MAC LEISH
MAC LEIGH	STEWART OF APPIN	MAC LISH	MAC PHERSON
MAC LEIRE	CAMERON	MAC LIVER	CAMPBELL
MAC LEISH	MAC LEISH	MAC LIVER	MAC GREGOR
MAC LEISH	MAC PHERSON	MAC LIVER	MAC IVER
MAC LEISTER	MAC GREGOR	MAC LLELOND	MAC LELLEN
MAC LEITH	LENNOX DIST		
MAC LELLAN(D)	MAC LELLEN		
MAC LELLEN(D)	MAC LELLEN		
MAC LEMMON	LAMONT	MAC LLWAIN	MAC BAIN
MAC LEMORE	STEWART OF APPIN	MAC LOAN	MAC DONALD
MAC LENA(G)HAN	GALLOWAY DIST	MAC LOCHAN	MAC LACHLAN
MAC LENDON	MAC LENNAN	MAC LOCK	MAC FARLANE
MAC LENE	MAC LEAN	MAC LOCKLIN	MAC LACHLAN
MAC LENNA	MAC LENNAN	MAC LOFLIN	MAC LACHLAN
MAC LENNAN,-EN	MAC LENNAN	MAC LONVEY	CAMERON
MAC LENNON	MAC LENNAN	MAC LOO(S)	STEWART OF APPIN
MAC LENZIE	LINDSAY	MAC LOON(E)	GALLOWAY DIST
MAC LEOB	MAC LEOD	MAC LOON(E)	MAC LENNAN
MAC LEOD	MAC LEOD	MAC LORAINE	MAC LAREN
MAC LEOD	MAC LEOD OF ASSYNT	MAC LORAN	MAC LENNAN
MAC LEOD	MAC LEOD OF GESTO	MAC LORG	PAISLEY DIST
MAC LEOD	MAC LEOD OF RAASAY	MAC LORINAN	MAC LENNAN
MAC LEOD	MAC LEOD OF SKYE	MAC LOUD	MAC LEOD
MAC LEON	MAC LAINE	MAC LOUGHLAN,-IN	MAC LACHLAN
MAC LEOSH	MAC LEOD	MAC LOUGHLIN	ULSTER TARTAN
MAC LEOW(D)	MAC LEOD	MAC LOUIS	STUART OF BUTE
MAC LERAN	MAC LAREN	MAC LOUTH	MAC LEOD
MAC LERGA(I)N	MAC LEAN	MAC LOUTHAN	MAC LACHLAN
MAC LERIE,-Y	CLAN CHATTAN	MAC LOW(E)	MAC LEOD
MAC LERIE,-Y	MAC PHERSON	MAC LOWD	MAC LEOD
MAC LERNON	MAC LENNAN	MAC LOWIE,-Y	STUART OF BUTE
MAC LEROY	GRANT	MAC LOWTHEN,-AN	INVERNESS DIST
MAC LEROY	MAC GILLIVRAY	MAC LOY	STUART OF BUTE
MAC LERRON	MAC LAREN	MAC LOYD	MAC LEOD
MAC LES(E)	MAC LEISH	MAC LUCAS	LAMONT
MAC LES(E)	MAC PHERSON	MAC LUCAS	MAC DOUGALL
MAC LESH	MAC PHERSON	MAC LUCKIE,-Y	LAMONT
MAC LESKIE,-Y	MAC ASKILL	MAC LUCKIE,-Y	MAC DOUGALL
MAC LESKIE,-Y	MAC LEOD	MAC LUDE	MAC LEOD
MAC LESTER	MAC ALISTER	MAC LUER	MAC CLURE
MAC LESTER	MAC GREGOR	MAC LUGASH	LAMONT
MAC LETCHIE,-Y	AYRSHIRE DIST	MAC LUGASH	MAC DOUGALL
MAC LEVERTIE,-Y	MAC DONALD	MAC LUHAN	ARGYLL DIST
MAC LEW	STEWART OF APPIN	MAC LUL(L)ICH,-K	MAC DOUGALL
MAC LEWER	MAC CLURE	MAC LUL(L)ICH,-K	MAC LULICH
MAC LEWIN	ARGYLL DIST	MAC LUL(L)ICH,-K	ROSS
MAC LEWIS	STUART OF BUTE	MAC LUMFA	GALLOWAY DIST
MAC LEWISTON	MAC DONALD	MAC LUMPHA(S)	GALLOWAY DIST
MAC LEY	LIVINGSTONE	MAC LUNDIE,-Y	FIFE DIST
MAC LEY	MAC LEAY	MAC LUNG	GALLOWAY DIST
MAC LEY	STEWART OF APPIN	MAC LUNIE,-Y	MAC PHERSON
MAC LIMANS	LAMONT	MAC LURE	MAC CLURE
MAC LIN(N)	MAC LEAN	MAC LURE	MAC LEOD
MAC LINDEN	COLQUHOUN	MAC LURG	AYRSHIRE DIST
MAC LINDEN	MAC DOUGALL	MAC LURG	CARRICK DIST

NAME	TARTAN	NAME	TARTAN
MAC LURKEN,-IN	CLAN CHATTAN	MAC MECHAM	CARRICK DIST
MAC LURKEN,-IN	CLARK	MAC MECUM	CARRICK DIST
MAC LURKEN,-IN	MAC PHERSON	MAC MEEKIN(S)	CARRICK DIST
MAC LUSA	LAMONT	MAC MEEKLE	MAC MICHAEL
MAC LUSKIE,-Y	MAC ASKILL	MAC MEEKLE	STEWART
MAC LUSKIE,-Y	MAC DONALD	MAC MEEN(S)	COLQUHOUN
MAC LUSKIE,-Y	MAC LEOD	MAC MEHEN(S)	CARRICK DIST
MAC LUSTER	MAC DONALD	MAC MEIKAN,-EN	CARRICK DIST
MAC LWAIN	MAC BAIN	MAC MEIN	COLQUHOUN
MAC LWANE	MAC BAIN	MAC MEIN	MENZIES
MAC LWIN	MAC BAIN	MAC MEIRE	MURRAY
MAC LYALL(S)	STEWART	MAC MENAMIN	ULSTER TARTAN
MAC LYLE(S)	STEWART	MAC MENEMY,-IE	GALLOWAY DIST
MAC LYMONT	LAMONT	MAC MENIDE,-Y	ARGYLL DIST
MAC LYN(N)(E)	MAC LEAN	MAC MENIGALL	GALLOWAY DIST
MAC LYSAGHT	CLAN CIAN	MAC MENZIES	MENZIES
MAC MA	MATHESON	MAC MERAMIN	EDINBURGH DIST
MAC MABEN	CARRICK DIST	MAC MERIT	ARGYLL DIST
MAC MACHEN(N)	CARRICK DIST	MAC MICHAEL(S)	MAC MICHAEL
MAC MACKEN	ULSTER TARTAN	MAC MICHAEL(S)	MAC MICHAEL
MAC MAG(G)IS	MAC INNES	MAC MICHAEL(S)	STEWART
MAC MAG(G)NUS	GUNN	MAC MICHAN	CARRICK DIST
MAC MAGH	MATHESON	MAC MICHIE,-Y	MAC DON OF KEPPOCH
MAC MAGUS	GUNN	MAC MICKELL(S)	MAC MICHAEL
MAC MAHEL(S)	MAC MICHAEL	MAC MICKELL(S)	STEWART
MAC MAHEL(S)	STEWART	MAC MICKEN,-AN	CARRICK DIST
MAC MAHILL	MAC MILLAN	MAC MICKIE,-Y	MAC DON OF KEPPOCH
MAC MAHILL(S)	STEWART	MAC MICKING	CARRICK DIST
MAC MAHON	CLAN CIAN	MAC MICKLE(S)	MAC MICHAEL
MAC MAHON	MATHESON	MAC MICKLE(S)	STEWART
MAC MAHON (Irish)	ULSTER TARTAN	MAC MIKEN,-IN	CARRICK DIST
MAC MAIN(E)(S)	COLQUHOUN	MAC MIKLE(S)	MAC MICHAEL
MAC MAIN(E)(S)	GUNN	MAC MIKLE(S)	STEWART
MAC MAIR	MATHESON	MAC MILLAN	MAC MILLAN
MAC MAKEN,-IN(S)	GALLOWAY DIST	MAC MILLAR	AYRSHIRE DIST
MAC MALBRIDE	LENNOX DIST	MAC MILLEN	MAC MILLAN
MAC MALLO(W),-GH	ULSTER TARTAN	MAC MILLER	AYRSHIRE DIST
MAC MALLON,-IN	MAC MILLAN	MAC MILLIAN	MAC MILLAN
MAC MALMURE	LENNOX DIST	MAC MILLIN	MAC MILLAN
MAC MAN(N)	MANSON	MAC MILLION	MAC MILLAN
MAC MANAMY	GALLOWAY DIST	MAC MILLON	MAC MILLAN
MAC MANNIN,-ON	ULSTER TARTAN	MAC MIN(N)	MENZIES
MAC MANNOS	GUNN	MAC MIRRIE,-Y	MURRAY
MAC MANUS	GUNN	MAC MITCHEL(L)	MITCHELL
MAC MAR(R)ISON	MORRISON	MAC MITCHEL(L)	ROSS
MAC MARCUS	MAC DONALD	MAC MO(R)INE	MAC KINNON
MAC MARK	MAC DONALD	MAC MOLAN(D)	MAC MILLAN
MAC MARQUIS	MAC DONALD	MAC MOLBRIDE	LENNOX DIST
MAC MARTIN(E)	CAMERON	MAC MOLLAND	MAC MILLAN
MAC MARVIS	MAC DONALD	MAC MOLLEN	MAC MILLAN
MAC MASTER(S)	BUCHANAN	MAC MON(N)IE,-Y(S)	MENZIES
MAC MASTER(S)	MAC INNES	MAC MONAGHAN	CONNACHT TARTAN
MAC MASTER(S)	MAC MASTER	MAC MONT	AYRSHIRE DIST
MAC MATH	GALLOWAY DIST	MAC MOR(E)LAND	GLASGOW DIST
MAC MATH	MATHESON	MAC MOR(R)AN	MAC KINNON
MAC MATH	NITHSDALE DIST	MAC MOR(R)AN	ULSTER TARTAN
MAC MAUGH	GALLOWAY DIST	MAC MOR(R)Y,-IE	MURRAY
MAC MAURICE	BUCHANAN	MAC MORAINE	ULSTER TARTAN
MAC MAW(E)	MATHESON	MAC MORAY	MURRAY
MAC MAY	MAC DONALD	MAC MORDY,-IE	STUART OF BUTE
MAC MAYBEN	GALLOWAY DIST	MAC MORGAN	MAC KAY
MAC ME(E)CHAN	CARRICK DIST	MAC MORRAN	ARGYLL DIST
MAC ME(E)KEN,-IN	CARRICK DIST	MAC MORRIES	MURRAY
MAC MEAN(S)	COLQUHOUN	MAC MORRIN(E)	GALLOWAY DIST
MAC MEANS	MENZIES	MAC MORRIN(G)	GALLOWAY DIST
MAC MEARTY,-IE	STUART OF BUTE	MAC MORRIS	BUCHANAN

NAME	TARTAN	NAME	TARTAN
MAC MORROW	MURRAY	MAC NATT	MAC FARLANE
MAC MUETRAY	MAC DONALD OF SLEAT	MAC NATT	MAC NAUGHTEN
MAC MUILLE	MULL DIST	MAC NATT	MAC NEIL
MAC MULKEN,-IN	MAC MILLAN	MAC NAUCHTON	MAC NAUGHTEN
MAC MULKEN,-IN	ULSTER TARTAN	MAC NAUGHER	ULSTER TARTAN
MAC MULL(E)	MULL DIST	MAC NAUGHT	MAC NAUGHTEN
MAC MULLAN,-EN(S)	MAC MILLAN	MAC NAUGHTEN	MAC NAUGHTEN
MAC MULLETTE	MAC MILLAN	MAC NAUGHTON	MAC NAUGHTEN
MAC MULLIN(S)	MAC MILLAN	MAC NAUL(L)	GALLOWAY DIST
MAC MULLUN(S)	MAC MILLAN	MAC NAY	MAC GREGOR
MAC MULROON(E)Y	ULSTER TARTAN	MAC NAYER	MAC FARLANE
MAC MUNAGLE	GALLOWAY DIST	MAC NAYER	MAC NAB
MAC MUNN	LAMONT	MAC NAYER	MAC NAUGHTEN
MAC MUNN	STUART OF BUTE	MAC NEA	MAC GREGOR
MAC MURCHIE,-Y	BUCHANAN	MAC NEACE	MAC GREGOR
MAC MURCHIE,-Y	MAC DONALD	MAC NEACHAIL	NICOLSON
MAC MURCHIE,-Y	MAC KENZIE	MAC NEAK	MAC GREGOR
MAC MURDIE,-Y	STUART OF BUTE	MAC NEAL(L)(E)	MAC NEIL
MAC MURDO	MAC DONALD	MAC NEAR	MAC NAB
MAC MURDO	MAC PHERSON	MAC NEAR	MAC NAUGHTEN
MAC MURDOCH	MAC DONALD	MAC NECE	MAC GREGOR
MAC MURDOCH	MAC PHERSON	MAC NECE	STRATHEARN DIST
MAC MURDOW	MAC PHERSON	MAC NEE(S)	MAC GREGOR
MAC MURRAH	MURRAY	MAC NEECE	MAC GREGOR
MAC MURRAY	MURRAY	MAC NEELY,-IE	MAC NEIL
MAC MURRICH,-K	MAC DON CLANRANALD	MAC NEESE	MAC GREGOR
MAC MURRICH,-K	MAC PHERSON	MAC NEICE	MAC GREGOR
MAC MURROW	ULSTER TARTAN	MAC NEICE	STRATHEARN DIST
MAC MURTIE,-Y	MAC KIRDY	MAC NEIF	GALLOWAY DIST
MAC MURTIE,-Y	STUART OF BUTE	MAC NEIGHT	MAC NAUGHTEN
MAC MURTRIE,-Y	MAC DONALD OF SLEAT	MAC NEIL(L((E)	MAC NEIL OF BARRA
MAC MYLLAN(S)	MAC MILLAN	MAC NEIL(L)(E)	MAC NEIL GIGHA/COLONSAY
MAC NAB(B)	MAC ALPINE	MAC NEILAGE	MAC NEIL GIGHA/COLONSAY
MAC NAB(B)	MAC NAB	MAC NEILAGE	MAC NEIL OF BARRA
MAC NABBOW	ARGYLL DIST	MAC NEIR	MAC NAB
MAC NABNEY,-IE	MAC NAB	MAC NEIR	MAC NAUGHTEN
MAC NABO(E)	ARGYLL DIST	MAC NEISH	MAC GREGOR
MAC NABOLA	ARGYLL DIST	MAC NEISH	MAC GREGOR
MAC NACELL	NICOLSON	MAC NEITHAN	KEITH
MAC NACHTAN,-EN	MAC NAUGHTEN	MAC NEIVE	PERTHSHIRE DIST
MAC NACKAIRD	SINCLAIR	MAC NEL(L)IS	MAC NEIL
MAC NAE	MAC GREGOR	MAC NELL	MAC NEIL
MAC NAGEN	MAC NAUGHTEN	MAC NELLEN	STIRLING DIST
MAC NAGHTEN,-IN	MAC NAUGHTEN	MAC NELLIE,-Y	MAC NEIL
MAC NAIN	GALLOWAY DIST	MAC NELT	MAC NEIL
MAC NAIR	LENNOX DIST	MAC NERLIN(E)(D)	ST. ANDREWS DIST
MAC NAIR	MAC FARLANE	MAC NERY,-IE	MAC NAUGHTEN
MAC NAIR	MAC NAB	MAC NESS	MAC GREGOR
MAC NAIR	MAC NAUGHTEN	MAC NESS	MAC INNES
MAC NAIRN	STEWART OF APPIN	MAC NESTRIE,-Y	GALLOWAY DIST
MAC NAIRY	MAC FARLANE	MAC NET(T)	MAC NAUGHTEN
MAC NAIRY	MAC NAB	MAC NETTE	MAC FARLANE
MAC NAIRY	MAC NAUGHTEN	MAC NETTE	MAC NAUGHTEN
MAC NALE	MAC NEIL	MAC NEUR	BUCHANAN
MAC NALLY	GALLOWAY DIST	MAC NEVEN(S)	CAMPBELL
MAC NAMA	ULSTER TARTAN	MAC NEVEN(S)	CUMMING
MAC NAMARA	CLAN CIAN	MAC NEVEN(S)	MAC NAUGHTEN
MAC NAMARA	ULSTER TARTAN	MAC NEVEN(S)	MACKINTOSH
MAC NAMEE	ULSTER TARTAN	MAC NEVIN(S)	CLAN CIAN
MAC NAMELL,-ILL	MAC DOUGALL	MAC NEW	EDINBURGH DIST
MAC NAMELL,-ILL	MAC MILLAN	MAC NEWER	LENNOX DIST
MAC NAMOILE	MAC MILLAN	MAC NEWER	MAC FARLANE
MAC NAMOYLE	MAC MILLAN	MAC NEY	MAC GREGOR
MAC NANAMY,-IE	ULSTER TARTAN	MAC NEZER	MAC GREGOR
MAC NANE	ULSTER TARTAN	MAC NIAL(L)	MAC NEIL
MAC NANNY,-IE	MAC DONALD		
MAC NARY,-IE	MAC NAUGHTEN		

NAME	TARTAN	NAME	TARTAN
MAC NICHOL(S)	CAMPBELL	MAC OLASH	INVERNESS DIST
MAC NICHOL(S)	MAC FIE	MAC OLCHREE	GRANT
MAC NICHOL(S)	MAC LEOD	MAC OLEA	MAC AULAY
MAC NICHOL(S)	NICOLSON	MAC OLESKIE,-Y	MAC ASKILL
MAC NICHOLAS	NICOLSON	MAC OLESKIE,-Y	MAC LEOD
MAC NICKLE(S)	NICOLSON	MAC OLIVE	ULSTER TARTAN
MAC NICOL(L)(S)	CAMPBELL	MAC OLVORY,-IE	ARGYLL DIST
MAC NICOL(L)(S)	MAC FIE	MAC OMBER	STEWART OF APPIN
MAC NICOL(L)(S)	MAC LEOD	MAC OMBRAY,-EY	STEWART OF APPIN
MAC NICOL(L)(S)	NICOLSON	MAC OMIE,-Y	MAC THOMAS
MAC NID(D)ER	MAC FARLANE	MAC OMIE,-Y	MACKINTOSH
MAC NIE	MAC GREGOR	MAC OMISH	GUNN
MAC NIECE	MAC GREGOR	MAC OMISH	MAC THOMAS
MAC NIEL(L)(E)	MAC NEIL	MAC OMISH	MACKINTOSH
MAC NIFF	GALLOWAY DIST	MAC ONACHIE	ROBERTSON
MAC NIGHT	MAC NAUGHTEN	MAC ONACHIE,-Y	CAMPBELL
MAC NINCH	MAC INNES	MAC ONACHIE,-Y	GRANT
MAC NINE	MAC INNES	MAC ONAHAY	HANNA
MAC NINTCH	MAC INNES	MAC ONAHY,-IE	ROBERTSON
MAC NISH	MAC GREGOR	MAC ONCHIE,-Y	GRANT
MAC NISH	MAC INNES	MAC ONCHIE,-Y	ROBERTSON
MAC NISHIE	ROSE	MAC ONICK	ROBERTSON
MAC NIT(T)ER	MAC FARLANE	MAC ONIE,-EY	CAMERON
MAC NITH	MAC INNES	MAC ONION	ULSTER TARTAN
MAC NITT	MAC FARLANE	MAC ORAN	CAMPBELL
MAC NITT	MAC NAUGHTEN	MAC ORE	MAC ORRELL
MAC NIVEN(S)	CAMPBELL	MAC ORIST	MAC ORRELL
MAC NIVEN(S)	CUMMING	MAC ORLY	MAC KENZIE
MAC NIVEN(S)	MAC NAUGHTEN	MAC ORRELL	MAC ORRELL
MAC NIVEN(S)	MAC NIVEN	MAC ORREST	MAC ORRELL
MAC NIVEN(S)	MACKINTOSH	MAC ORRILL	MAC ORRELL
MAC NO(E)	GALLOWAY DIST	MAC ORT	CARRICK DIST
MAC NOBLE	APPLECROSS DIST	MAC OSCAR(S)	ULSTER TARTAN
MAC NOCAIRD	CAMPBELL	MAC OSHEN	MAC DONALD
MAC NOCAIRD	MAC GREGOR	MAC OSKAR	ULSTER TARTAN
MAC NOCKER	ULSTER TARTAN	MAC OSTRIC(H),-K	CAMERON
MAC NOGHER	ULSTER TARTAN	MAC OTTER	MAC ARTHUR
MAC NOHER	ULSTER TARTAN	MAC OU	MAC KAY
MAC NOLL	GALLOWAY DIST	MAC OUAT	FORBES
MAC NOON	GALLOWAY DIST	MAC OUFF	MAC DUFF
MAC NORAVAICH,-K	MUNRO	MAC OUL	MAC DOUGALL
MAC NORMER	AYRSHIRE DIST	MAC OULEY	MAC AULAY
MAC NORTON	MAC NAUGHTEN	MAC OURLIS(H)	CAMERON
MAC NOUGHT	MAC NAUGHTEN	MAC OUTEREY,-IE	GALLOWAY DIST
MAC NOUGHTAN,-ON	MAC NAUGHTEN	MAC OUTRIE,-Y	INVERNESS DIST
MAC NOW	MAC RAE	MAC OVER	ULSTER TARTAN
MAC NOWN	GALLOWAY DIST	MAC OWAN(S)	COLQUHOUN
MAC NOYER	MAC NAB	MAC OWAN(S)	MAC DONELL GLENGARRY
MAC NOYER	MAC NAUGHTEN	MAC OWAN(S)	MAC DOUGALL
MAC NUCATOR	STEWART OF APPIN	MAC OWAN(S)	MAC EWEN
MAC NUCTOR	MAC GREGOR	MAC OWAT	FORBES
MAC NUER	MAC FARLANE	MAC OWEN(S)	COLQUHOUN
MAC NUIR	BUCHANAN	MAC OWEN(S)	MAC DONELL GLENGARRY
MAC NUIR	MAC NAUGHTEN	MAC OWEN(S)	MAC DOUGALL
MAC NULTY	CONNACHT TARTAN	MAC OWEN(S)	MAC EWEN
MAC NULTY	ULSTER TARTAN	MAC OWIN(S)	COLQUHOUN
MAC NUT(T)	MAC NAUGHTEN	MAC OWIN(S)	MAC DONELL GLENGARRY
MAC NUYER	BUCHANAN	MAC OWIN(S)	MAC DOUGALL
MAC NUYER	MAC FARLANE	MAC OWIN(S)	MAC EWEN
MAC NUYER	MAC NAUGHTEN	MAC OWL	MAC DOUGALL
MAC O'SHANNAIG	MAC DONALD	MAC OYD	MAC KAY
MAC OAL	MAC DOUGALL	MAC PADDEN,-IN	MAC FADYEN
MAC OH	MAC KAY	MAC PADDEN,-IN	MAC LAINE
MAC OIK	MAC DONALD	MAC PADIN(E)	MAC FADYEN
MAC OIL	MAC DOUGALL	MAC PADIN(E)	MAC LAINE
MAC OIT	MAC DONALD	MAC PAIK(E)	EDINBURGH DIST
MAC OLANAICH	ARGYLL DIST	MAC PAKE	GALLOWAY DIST

NAME	TARTAN	NAME	TARTAN
MAC PALL	CAMERON	MAC PHILBUN	CONNACHT TARTAN
MAC PALL	MAC PHAIL	MAC PHILP(S)	MAC DON OF GLENCOE
MAC PALL	MACKINTOSH	MAC PHILP(S)	MAC DON OF KEPPOCH
MAC PANT	ULSTER TARTAN	MAC PHILP(S)	MAC KILLOP
MAC PARLAND,-E	MAC FARLANE	MAC PHORICH	LAMONT
MAC PARLON	MAC FARLANE	MAC PHORIE	LAMONT
MAC PARTLAN	ULSTER TARTAN	MAC PHORSAN	MAC PHERSON
MAC PARTLAN(D)	MAC FARLANE	MAC PHUN(N)	CAMPBELL
MAC PARTLIN(E)	MAC FARLANE	MAC PHUN(N)	MAC ARTHUR
MAC PATRICK	LAMONT	MAC PIKE	GALLOWAY DIST
MAC PATRICK	MAC LAREN	MAC PIOT(T)	GRAHAM OF MENTIETH
MAC PAUL	CAMERON	MAC PLOY	STRATHEARN DIST
MAC PAUL	MAC PHAIL	MAC POLAN(D)	CAMERON
MAC PAUL	MACKINTOSH	MAC POLIN	CAMERON
MAC PAY(E)	PERTHSHIRE DIST	MAC POLL	CAMERON
MAC PEAK	GALLOWAY DIST	MAC POLL	MAC PHAIL
MAC PEAT(E)	MAC GREGOR	MAC POLL	MACKINTOSH
MAC PEEK	GALLOWAY DIST	MAC POLLIN(D)	CAMERON
MAC PEETERS	MAC GREGOR	MAC POTTS	GRAHAM OF MENTIETH
MAC PEETERS	MAC LAREN	MAC PRANGLE	ETTRICK DIST
MAC PERTIE,-Y	MAC GREGOR	MAC PRIOR	CAMPBELL
MAC PETER(S)	MAC GREGOR	MAC PROUD(E)	AYRSHIRE DIST
		MAC QUADE	FARQUHARSON
MAC PETIE,-Y	MAC GREGOR	MAC QUADE	MAC DONALD
MAC PETRIE,-Y	MAC GREGOR	MAC QUADE	MAC KAY
MAC PETRIE,-Y	MAC LAREN	MAC QUAID(E)	FARQUHARSON
MAC PHADDAN,-EN	MAC FADYEN	MAC QUAID(E)	MAC DONALD
MAC PHADDAN,-EN	MAC LAINE	MAC QUAIG	MAC NAUGHTEN
MAC PHAIL	CAMERON	MAC QUAIL	EDINBURGH DIST
MAC PHAIL	CLAN CHATTAN	MAC QUAIN(E)	MAC QUEEN
MAC PHAIL	MAC KAY	MAC QUAKE	MAC NAUGHTEN
MAC PHAIL	MAC PHAIL	MAC QUAKER	CAMPBELL
MAC PHAIL	MACKINTOSH	MAC QUAKER	MAC NAUGHTEN
MAC PHAIT	MAC LAREN	MAC QUALL	MANX NATIONAL
MAC PHAL(L)	CAMERON	MAC QUARDY,-IE	MAC KIRDY
MAC PHAL(L)	MAC PHAIL	MAC QUARDY,-IE	STUART OF BUTE
MAC PHAL(L)	MACKINTOSH	MAC QUARN	CAMPBELL
MAC PHALLAIN	MAC FARLANE	MAC QUARRIE,-Y	MAC ALPINE
MAC PHALLIN,-ON	MAC FARLANE	MAC QUARRIE,-Y	MAC QUARRIE
MAC PHARFARLAN	MAC FARLANE	MAC QUART	MAC QUARRIE
MAC PHARLANE,-D	MAC FARLANE	MAC QUARTIE,-Y	MAC KIRDY
MAC PHARLON(D)	MAC FARLANE	MAC QUARTIE,-Y	STUART OF BUTE
MAC PHAT(T)ER	MAC LAREN	MAC QUAT	BUCHANAN
MAC PHATTEN,-ON	MAC FADYEN	MAC QUATE	FARQUHARSON
MAC PHATTEN,-ON	MAC LAINE	MAC QUATE	MAC DONALD
MAC PHAUL	CAMERON	MAC QUATTERS	BUCHANAN
MAC PHAUL	MAC PHAIL	MAC QUATTIE,-Y	BUCHANAN
MAC PHAUL	MACKINTOSH	MAC QUAY	MAC KAY
MAC PHE	MAC FIE	MAC QUE(E)	MAC DONALD
MAC PHEARSON	MAC PHERSON	MAC QUE(E)	MAC KAY
MAC PHEDRAN,-ON	CAMPBELL	MAC QUEEN	CLAN CHATTAN
MAC PHEDRAN,-ON	MAC AULAY	MAC QUEEN	MAC QUEEN
MAC PHEDRAN,-ON	MAC PHERSON	MAC QUEHIE	MAC KAY
MAC PHEE	MAC FIE	MAC QUEIN	NITHSDALE DIST
MAC PHEETERS	MAC GREGOR	MAC QUENNIE,-Y	MAC KENZIE
MAC PHEID	MAC FIE	MAC QUERR(I)ST	BUCHANAN
MAC PHEIR	MAC FIE	MAC QUERRY	MAC QUARRIE
MAC PHERON	GALLOWAY DIST	MAC QUEST(I)ON	MAC DONALD
MAC PHERSON	MAC PHERSON	MAC QUET(T)IE,-Y	GALLOWAY DIST
MAC PHETRES	MAC GREGOR	MAC QUEY	MAC DONALD
MAC PHETRIDGE	MAC LEAN	MAC QUEY	MAC KAY
MAC PHIAL	MAC KAY	MAC QUGH	MAC KAY
MAC PHIE(D)	MAC FIE	MAC QUHEE	MAC KAY
MAC PHIEDRAN,-ON	CAMPBELL	MAC QUHIE	MAC KAY
MAC PHIEDRAN,-ON	MAC AULAY	MAC QUHIRE	MAC GUIRE
MAC PHIER	MAC FIE	MAC QUHIRE	MAC QUARRIE
MAC PHIETRIC	MAC FIE	MAC QUIAN(E)	CLAN CHATTAN
MAC PHIL(L)IP(S)	MAC DON OF GLENCOE	MAC QUIARE	MAC GUIRE
MAC PHIL(L)IP(S)	MAC DON OF KEPPOCH	MAC QUIARE	MAC QUARRIE
MAC PHIL(L)IP(S)	MAC KILLOP		

NAME	TARTAN	NAME	TARTAN
MAC QUID(D)IE,-Y	GALLOWAY DIST	MAC REACHA(I)N	MAC NAUGHTEN
MAC QUIGGAN	GALLOWAY DIST	MAC READIE,-Y	GALLOWAY DIST
MAC QUIKAN	MAC DONALD	MAC REAK,-IE,-Y	EDINBURGH DIST
MAC QUILIKAN,-EN	MAC DONALD	MAC REAL	MAC NEIL
MAC QUILKIN	MACKINTOSH	MAC REARIE,-Y	MAC DONALD
MAC QUILL	MAC WILLIAM	MAC REAVIE,-Y	MAC DONALD OF SLEAT
MAC QUILLAN	ULSTER TARTAN	MAC REDMOND	CONNACHT TARTAN
MAC QUILLAN,-EN	MAC WILLIAM	MAC REE	GRAHAM OF MONTROSE
MAC QUILLIAM	GUNN	MAC REEKIE,-Y	EDINBURGH DIST
MAC QUILLIAM	MAC WILLIAM	MAC REEL	MAC NEIL
MAC QUILLIN(G)	HUNTLY DIST	MAC REIGHT	MAC RAE
MAC QUILLY (Irish)	CONNACHT TARTAN	MAC REITH	MAC RAE
MAC QUILLY,-IE	HUNTLY DIST	MAC RELLIS	MAC NEIL
MAC QUINESS	MAC INNES	MAC RENNIE,-Y	ARGYLL DIST
MAC QUINN	MAC QUEEN	MAC REVIE,-Y	MAC DONALD OF SLEAT
MAC QUINNEY,-IE	MAC KENZIE	MAC REW	MAC GREGOR
MAC QUINTEN	BUCHANAN	MAC REWEN,-AN	MACKINTOSH
MAC QUINTER	BUCHANAN	MAC REY	MAC LEAN OF DUART
MAC QUIRE	MAC GUIRE	MAC REY	MAC RAE
MAC QUIRE	MAC QUARRIE	MAC REYNALDS	MAC DON CLANRANALD
MAC QUIRK(E)	LENNOX DIST	MAC REYNOLD(S)	MAC DON CLANRANALD
MAC QUIRN(S)	CAMPBELL	MAC RIBBON	GRAHAM OF MENTIETH
MAC QUIRN(S)	CAMPBELL	MAC RIDDY,-IE	GALLOWAY DIST
MAC QUIRN(S)	MAC FARLANE	MAC RIDES	GALLOWAY DIST
MAC QUIRT	MAC WHIRTER	MAC RIDGE	GALLOWAY DIST
MAC QUISTON	MAC DONALD	MAC RIE	MAC RAE
MAC QUIT(H)AN,-EN	MAC DONALD	MAC RIGH	GRAHAM OF MONTROSE
MAC QUITSTAN,-EN	MAC DONALD	MAC RIGH	MAC GREGOR
MAC QUITTER	MAC WHIRTER	MAC RIGHT	MAC INTYRE
MAC QUITTY,-IE	GALLOWAY DIST	MAC RILL	MAC RAE
MAC QUIVEY,-IE	MAC IVER	MAC RIMMON	MAC LEOD
MAC QULAY,-EY	MAC AULAY	MAC RIND	MAC DONALD
MAC QUOID	MAC KAY	MAC RINK	ULSTER TARTAN
MAC QUONE	MAC DON OF GLENCOE	MAC RIRIE	MAC DONALD
MAC QUONE	MAC EWEN	MAC RIS(S)	GRAHAM OF MONTROSE
MAC QUORN	CAMPBELL	MAC RISNIE,-EY	MACKINTOSH
MAC QUORQUODALE	MAC CORQUODALE	MAC RITCHIE,-EY	MACKINTOSH
MAC QUOWEN(S)	MAC EWEN	MAC ROAN(E)	GALLOWAY DIST
MAC QUOWN	COWAN	MAC ROARTY	ULSTER TARTAN
MAC QUOY	MAC KAY	MAC ROB(B)	GUNN
MAC RA(CH)	MAC RAE	MAC ROB(B)	INNES
MAC RAB(B)ET,-IT	GALLOWAY DIST	MAC ROB(B)	MAC FARLANE
MAC RABIT(T)	GALLOWAY DIST	MAC ROB(B)	ROBERTSON
MAC RAE	MAC RAE	MAC ROB(B)	STEWART OF APPIN
MAC RAE	MAC RAE OF CONCHRA	MAC ROB(B)IE,-Y	DRUMMOND
MAC RAE	MAC RAE OF INVERINATE	MAC ROB(B)IE,-Y	ROBERTSON
MAC RAFT	GALLOWAY DIST	MAC ROBAS(E)	ROBERTSON
MAC RAIL(D)	MAC LEOD	MAC ROBBIN(S)	ROBERTSON
MAC RAIN(E)	MAC DONALD	MAC ROBBINS	ROBBINSON
MAC RAINIE,-(E)Y	MAC DON CLANRANALD	MAC ROBERT(S)	ROBERTSON
MAC RAINIE,-(E)Y	MAC DONALD	MAC ROBIN	LENNOX DIST
MAC RAITH	MAC DONALD	MAC ROCK	GALLOWAY DIST
MAC RAITH	MAC RAE	MAC RODDY,-IE	GALLOWAY DIST
MAC RAN(N)(E)	MAC DON CLANRANALD	MAC ROE	MAC BETH
MAC RANDLE(S)	MAC DON CLANRANALD	MAC ROFT	GALLOWAY DIST
MAC RANK	MAC LEAN	MAC RONALD	MAC DON CLANRANALD
MAC RANKEN,-IN	MAC LEAN	MAC RONALD	MAC DON OF KEPPOCH
MAC RANNALD(S)	MAC DON CLANRANALD	MAC RONE	GALLOWAY DIST
MAC RATH	MAC RAE	MAC RORY,-IE	MAC LAREN
MAC RAUNDLES	MAC DON CLANRANALD	MAC RORY,-IE	MAC RORY
MAC RAW	MAC LEAN OF DUART	MAC RORYER	MAC RORY
MAC RAW	MAC RAE	MAC ROSKY,-IE	STRATHEARN DIST
MAC RAY	MAC LEAN OF DUART	MAC ROSS	ROSS
MAC RAY	MAC RAE	MAC ROSSAN,-IN	STRATHEARN DIST
MAC RAYNE	MAC DONALD	MAC ROSTIE,-Y	PERTHSHIRE DIST
MAC REA	MAC RAE	MAC ROUN	ROWAN
MAC REA	MAC REA	MAC ROW	MAC RAE

NAME	TARTAN	NAME	TARTAN
MAC ROWAN	ROWAN	MAC SMITH	CLAN CHATTAN
MAC ROY	MAC RAE	MAC SMITH	GOW
MAC RUCK(E)	MAC NAUGHTEN	MAC SMITH	MAC PHERSON
MAC RUDER	DRUMMOND	MAC SMITH	SMITH
MAC RUDER	MAC GREGOR	MAC SOL(E)Y,-IE	MAC DONALD
MAC RUER	DRUMMOND	MAC SON	ULSTER TARTAN
MAC RUM	MAC DONALD	MAC SORLEY,-IE	CAMERON
MAC RUNNEL(L)S	MAC DON CLANRANALD	MAC SORLEY,-IE	LAMONT
MAC RUNNELDS	MAC DON CLANRANALD	MAC SORLEY,-IE	MAC DONALD
MAC RURIE,-Y	MAC DONALD	MAC SORSBY,-IE	CAMERON
MAC RURIE,-Y	MAC LAREN	MAC SORSBY,-IE	MACKINTOSH
MAC RURIE,-Y	MAC RURIE	MAC SOSEN	GALLOWAY DIST
MAC RUVIE,-Y	DUNBLANE DIST	MAC SOUL,-OWL	AYRSHIRE DIST
MAC RYRIE	MAC DONALD	MAC SPADDAN,-EN	AYRSHIRE DIST
MAC SAG(G)ART	MAC TAGGART	MAC SPADDER	CARRICK DIST
MAC SARLAND	MAC FARLANE	MAC SPARRAN,-EN	MAC DONALD
MAC SAUL	AYRSHIRE DIST	MAC SPED(D)ON	CARRICK DIST
MAC SAVAGE	ULSTER TARTAN	MAC SPEFFAN	CARRICK DIST
MAC SAVERY,-IE	AYRSHIRE DIST	MAC SPERRIN,-EN	MAC DONALD
MAC SAY	EDINBURGH DIST	MAC SPIRIT	ARGYLL DIST
MAC SEAVENIE,-Y	MAC QUEEN	MAC SPORRAN	MAC DONALD
MAC SEE	ULSTER TARTAN	MAC SPORRAN	MAC SPORRAN
MAC SEMIS(H)	FRASER	MAC STALKER	ROBERTSON
MAC SETREE	MAXWELL	MAC STAY	MAC GREGOR
MAC SEVENY,-IE	MAC QUEEN	MAC STEA	MAC GREGOR
MAC SHAEFFREY	EDINBURGH DIST	MAC STEPHEN(S)	STEPHENSON
MAC SHAN(E)	MAC DONALD	MAC STEVEN,-S	STEPHENSON
MAC SHANACHAN	MAC DONALD	MAC STEVIN(S)	STEPHENSON
MAC SHANAHAN	MAC DONALD	MAC STOOT(S)	GALLOWAY DIST
MAC SHAND	ABERDEEN DIST	MAC STORE	MAC INTYRE
MAC SHANE	ULSTER TARTAN	MAC STRAVICK	ARGYLL DIST
MAC SHANNOCHAN	MAC DONALD	MAC STRAVOCH,-K	ARGYLL DIST
MAC SHANNOCK	MAC DONALD	MAC STRAWDER	DRUMMOND
MAC SHANNON,-IN	MAC DONALD	MAC STROUL	STRATHCLYDE DIST
MAC SHARRY,-IE	MAC KINNON	MAC STURGEON	GALLOWAY DIST
MAC SHEA,-E	EDINBURGH DIST	MAC SUAY	CLAN CHATTAN
MAC SHEEAN	MAC DONALD	MAC SUAY	MAC QUEEN
MAC SHEEDY	CLAN CIAN	MAC SUET	GALLOWAY DIST
MAC SHEEHY,-IE	MAC DONALD	MAC SUILE	KYLE
MAC SHEEHY,-IE	MAC SHEEHY	MAC SULLA	ULSTER TARTAN
MAC SHEEN	MAC QUEEN	MAC SURDY,-IE	MAC KIRDY
MAC SHEERY,-IE	MAC KINNON	MAC SURDY,-IE	STUART OF BUTE
MAC SHEN(N)OIG	MAC DONALD	MAC SURELY	LAMONT
MAC SHERRIE,-Y	MAC KINNON	MAC SURELY	MAC DONALD
MAC SHERRY (Irish)	ULSTER TARTAN	MAC SURLIE,-Y	LAMONT
MAC SHEWAN	BUCHANAN	MAC SWAIN	CLAN CHATTAN
MAC SHEWLIN	BUCHANAN	MAC SWAIN	MAC QUEEN
MAC SHILE	GRAHAM OF MENTIETH	MAC SWAN	MAC DONALD
MAC SHIMMIE,-Y	FRASER	MAC SWAYED	FARQUHARSON
MAC SHIRLEY	LAMONT	MAC SWED(E)	FARQUHARSON
MAC SHOW(E)N	BUCHANAN	MAC SWEEN,-IE,-Y	CLAN CHATTAN
MAC SHOWLIN(E)	BUCHANAN	MAC SWEEN,-IE,-Y	MAC DONALD
MAC SHUBIN	BUCHANAN	MAC SWEEN,-IE,-Y	MAC QUEEN
MAC SHURLIE,-Y	LAMONT	MAC SWEENY	ULSTER TARTAN
MAC SIM(E)	FRASER	MAC SWEYER	GALLOWAY DIST
MAC SIMON	FRASER	MAC SWIGGIN(S)	ULSTER TARTAN
MAC SIMON	MAC ARTHUR	MAC SWINE	CLAN CHATTAN
MAC SIVER	MAC IVER	MAC SWINE	GRANT
MAC SKEANE	MAC QUEEN	MAC SWINE	MAC QUEEN
MAC SKEEN	MAC QUEEN	MAC SWYNDE	MAC DONALD
MAC SKELLIE,-Y	GALLOWAY DIST	MAC SYMON	FRASER
MAC SKIMMAN,-ON	CUMMING	MAC TAGGART	MAC TAGGART
MAC SKIMMING(S)	FRASER	MAC TAGGART	ROSS
MAC SKULIN	PERTHSHIRE DIST	MAC TAGGETTE	MAC TAGGART
MAC SLAY	PERTHSHIRE DIST	MAC TAGGETTE	ROSS
MAC SLOY	INVERNESS DIST	MAC TAGUE	ROSS

NAME	TARTAN	NAME	TARTAN
MAC TAIR	MAC TIER	MAC ULAN	BUCHANAN
MAC TALIDEFF	ABERDEEN DIST	MAC ULAS(H)	MANX NATIONAL
MAC TAMMIE,-Y	CAMPBELL	MAC ULE	MAC DONALD OF SLEAT
MAC TAMMIE,-Y	MAC TAVISH	MAC ULRIG,-K	CAMERON
MAC TAMNIE,-Y	ARGYLL DIST	MAC ULRIK	CAMERON
MAC TARICH,-K	MAC KENZIE	MAC UMBER	STEWART OF APPIN
MAC TARY	INNES	MAC UR(R)ICH	MAC PHERSON
MAC TASNEY	ULSTER TARTAN	MAC URE	CAMPBELL
MAC TAUSE	CAMPBELL	MAC URE	MAC IVER
MAC TAUSE	MAC TAVISH	MAC VADDIE	MAC FADYEN
MAC TAVISH	CAMPBELL	MAC VADON	MAC FADYEN
MAC TAVISH	FRASER	MAC VADON	MAC LAINE
MAC TAVISH	MAC TAVISH	MAC VAIL	MAC KAY
MAC TAY(E)	PERTHSHIRE DIST	MAC VAIL(E)	CLAN CHATTAN
MAC TEAGUE	ROSS	MAC VAIL(E)	MAC PHAIL
MAC TEAR	MAC TIER	MAC VAIL(E)	MAC PHERSON
MAC TEAR	ROSS	MAC VAIL(E)	MACKINTOSH
MAC TEAY	MAC TIER	MAC VAIN	MAC BAIN
MAC TEE	MAC TIER	MAC VAIN	MAC KAY
MAC TEER	MAC TIER	MAC VALE	CLAN CHATTAN
MAC TEETER(S)	MAC GREGOR	MAC VALE	MAC PHAIL
MAC TEIGUE	ROSS	MAC VALE	MACKINTOSH
MAC TELL	STUART OF BUTE	MAC VAN(N)	MAC BAIN
MAC TENNET(H)	MAC KENZIE	MAC VANE	MAC BAIN
MAC TENTHA	MAC KENZIE	MAC VANE	MAC KAY
MAC TERNAN	EDINBURGH DIST	MAC VANIE,-EY	BUCHANAN
MAC TETH	MAC TIER	MAC VANISH	MAC DON CLANRANALD
MAC TEY(E)	PERTHSHIRE DIST	MAC VANISH	MAC KAY
MAC THAIL	MAC PHAIL	MAC VANNAN,-IN	BUCHANAN
MAC THERLAIC(H)	MAC KENZIE	MAC VANNAN,-IN	MANX NATIONAL
MAC THOM(M)	MAC THOMAS	MAC VANNICH,-ICK	INVERNESS DIST
MAC THOM(M)	MACKINTOSH	MAC VARISH	MAC DONALD
MAC THOMAS	MAC THOMAS	MAC VARNICH	MAC DON CLANRANALD
MAC THOMAS	MACKINTOSH	MAC VARNISH	MAC DON CLANRANALD
MAC THONE	COLQUHOUN	MAC VAUGH	MAC KINNON
MAC THONE	MAC DONELL GLENGARRY	MAC VAY	MAC BETH
MAC TIER	MAC TIER	MAC VAY	MAC DONALD
MAC TIER	ROSS	MAC VAY	MAC LEAN
MAC TIGUE	ROSS	MAC VE(Y)	MAC BETH
MAC TIGUE	ULSTER TARTAN	MAC VE(Y)	MAC LEAN
MAC TIMMON(D)-S	AYRSHIRE DIST	MAC VEA	MAC BETH
MAC TIR	MAC TIER	MAC VEA	MAC DONALD
MAC TISH	MAC TAVISH	MAC VEA	MAC LEAN
MAC TOES	MAC TAVISH	MAC VEAGH	MAC BETH
MAC TOM	MAC THOMAS	MAC VEAGH	MAC DONALD
MAC TOM	MACKINTOSH	MAC VEAGH	MAC LEAN
MAC TOMIL	MAC DONALD	MAC VEAGH	ULSTER TARTAN
MAC TOMINAY	GALLOWAY DIST	MAC VEAN	MAC BAIN
MAC TONNOCHY	ROBERTSON	MAC VEAN	MAC VEAN
MAC TOVERN	ULSTER TARTAN	MAC VEE	MAC FIE
MAC TRAIN	MAC DONALD	MAC VEEKLE	STUART OF BUTE
MAC TRANE	MAC DONALD	MAC VEIGH	MAC BETH
MAC TRETH	MAC RAE	MAC VEIGH	MAC DONALD
MAC TRUSTIE,-Y	FIFE DIST	MAC VEIGH	MAC LEAN
MAC TURK	GALLOWAY DIST	MAC VEITH	MAC BETH
MAC TURNEN	GALLOWAY DIST	MAC VEITH	MAC DONALD
MAC TURNER	GALLOWAY DIST	MAC VEITH	MAC LEAN
MAC TWEED	FRASER	MAC VERLAN(D)	MAC FARLANE
MAC TY(E)IRE	MAC TIER	MAC VERN	ULSTER TARTAN
MAC TYER	MAC TIER	MAC VERRAN	MAC FARLANE
MAC TYGUE	ROSS	MAC VETTIE,-Y	GALLOWAY DIST
MAC UDDEN,-IN	GORDON	MAC VIAN	MAC BAIN
MAC UILL	MAC WILLIAM	MAC VICAR	CAMPBELL
MAC UILLAM,-AN	MAC WILLIAM	MAC VICAR	MAC NAUGHTEN
MAC UIRE	MAC GUIRE	MAC VICKER,-AR(S)	CAMPBELL
MAC ULA(S)	MAC DONALD OF SLEAT	MAC VICKER,-AR(S)	MAC NAUGHTEN

NAME	TARTAN	NAME	TARTAN
MAC VIE	MAC FIE	MAC WEY	MAC KAY
MAC VIG(E)	MAC NAUGHTEN	MAC WHA	MAC RAE
MAC VIN(N)	MAC BAIN	MAC WHA	MANX NATIONAL
MAC VINISH	MAC KENZIE	MAC WHAN	MAC DONALD
MAC VINNIE,-EY	MAC KENZIE	MAC WHAN	MAC QUEEN
MAC VIT(T)IE,-Y	GALLOWAY DIST	MAC WHANNAL,-EL	MAC DONALD
MAC VITE	GALLOWAY DIST	MAC WHARTER	MAC WHIRTER
MAC VODDICH	MAC DON CLANRANALD	MAC WHATIE	BUCHANAN
MAC VOR(H)EIS	INVERNESS DIST	MAC WHAW	MAC RAE
MAC VORICH	MAC DON CLANRANALD	MAC WHEENY	MAC KENZIE
MAC VOY	MAC LEAN	MAC WHEERIE,-Y	MAC QUARRIE
MAC VRACTER	GLEN LYON DIST	MAC WHERTER	BUCHANAN
MAC VRIAN	MAC LEAN	MAC WHERTER	MAC WHIRTER
MAC VRIC(K)	MAC PHERSON	MAC WHERTH	ARGYLL DIST
MAC VRINE	MAC LEAN	MAC WHET(T)IE,-Y	GALLOWAY DIST
MAC VRION	MAC LEAN	MAC WHIDDIE,-Y	GALLOWAY DIST
MAC VRYNE	MAC LEAN	MAC WHINNIE,-EY	MAC KENZIE
MAC VUILLE	MULL DIST	MAC WHIRR	MAC QUARRIE
MAC VULL	MULL DIST	MAC WHIRT	BUCHANAN
MAC VUR(R)ICH	MAC DON CLANRANALD	MAC WHIRT	MAC WHIRTER
MAC VUR(R)ICH	MAC PHERSON	MAC WHIRT(T)ER	BUCHANAN
MAC VURIE	MAC DON CLANRANALD	MAC WHIRT(T)ER	MAC WHIRTER
MAC VURIST	MAC PHERSON	MAC WHISTON	MAC DONALD
MAC VURRAY,-IE	MURRAY	MAC WHITTIE,-Y	GALLOWAY DIST
MAC VYTIE	GALLOWAY DIST	MAC WHOOL	MAC LEOD
MAC WADE	FARQUHARSON	MAC WHORTER	BUCHANAN
MAC WADE	MAC DONALD	MAC WHORTER	MAC WHIRTER
MAC WAIN	CLAN CHATTAN	MAC WHORTHER	BUCHANAN
MAC WAIN	GRANT	MAC WHORTHER	MAC WHIRTER
MAC WAIN	MAC QUEEN	MAC WHYTE	MAC GREGOR
MAC WAL(L)	MANX NATIONAL	MAC WIDDIE,-Y	GALLOWAY DIST
MAC WALDRICK	CAMERON	MAC WIGGIN(S)	INVERNESS DIST
MAC WALDRICK	KENNEDY	MAC WILL	CARRICK DIST
MAC WALRICK	CAMERON	MAC WILLIAM(S)	GUNN
MAC WALRICK	KENNEDY	MAC WILLIAM(S)	MAC FARLANE
MAC WALTER	MAC FARLANE	MAC WILLIAM(S)	MAC KAY
MAC WAM(M)	MANX NATIONAL	MAC WILLIAM(S)	MAC LEOD
MAC WAN	COLQUHOUN	MAC WILLIAM(S)	MAC WILLIAM
MAC WAR(R)ISH	MAC DONALD	MAC WILLIAM(S)	ROBERTSON
MAC WAR(R)ISH	MAC PHERSON	MAC WILLIS	CARRICK DIST
MAC WARAN	MAC FARLANE	MAC WILLY,-IE	HUNTLY DIST
MAC WARAN(S)	CAMPBELL	MAC WILNANE	MAC LENNAN
MAC WARAN(S)	MAC FARLANE	MAC WILNONE	MAC LENNAN
MAC WARD	BAIRD	MAC WILSON	GUNN
MAC WARDY	MAC KIRDY	MAC WILSON	WILSON
MAC WARDY	STUART OF BUTE	MAC WILTON	MAC DONALD
MAC WARN(S)	CAMPBELL	MAC WINEY	MAC KENZIE
MAC WARN(S)	MAC FARLANE	MAC WINNIE,-Y	MAC KENZIE
MAC WARRAN,-EN	CAMPBELL	MAC WIRN(S)	CAMPBELL
MAC WARRAN,-EN	MAC FARLANE	MAC WIRRICH	MAC PHERSON
MAC WAT(T)ERS	FORBES	MAC WIRT	BUCHANAN
MAC WATCH	BUCHANAN	MAC WIRTH	ARGYLL DIST
MAC WATT	FORBES	MAC WITHE(E)	MAC DONALD
MAC WATTIE,-Y	BUCHANAN	MAC WITTIE,-Y	GALLOWAY DIST
MAC WATTIE,-Y	FORBES	MAC WOOD	FARQUHARSON
MAC WAUGHTON	MAC NAUGHTEN	MAC WOOD	MAC DONALD
MAC WAY	MAC LEAN	MAC WOOL	MAC LEOD
MAC WEAN	MAC QUEEN	MAC WOOLIE,-Y	GALLOWAY DIST
MAC WEE	MAC LEAN	MAC WORDIE,-Y	MAC KIRDY
MAC WEED	FARQUHARSON	MAC WORDIE,-Y	STUART OF BUTE
MAC WEEN	MAC QUEEN	MAC WORN(S)	CAMPBELL
MAC WEENIE,-Y	MAC KENZIE	MAC WORN(S)	MAC FARLANE
MAC WEENY	CONNACHT TARTAN	MAC WORTH	ARGYLL DIST
MAC WERICH,-K	ROTHESAY DIST	MAC WORTHER	BUCHANAN
MAC WERTER	BUCHANAN	MAC WRA(I)TH	MAC RAE
MAC WETHEY	GALLOWAY DIST	MAC WRAY	MAC RAE
MAC WETHIE,-Y	GALLOWAY DIST	MAC WRIGHT	MAC INTYRE

NAME	TARTAN	NAME	TARTAN
MAC YAIL	CAMERON	MAGELBY,-IE	CAMPBELL
MAC YALE	CAMERON	MAGELBY,-IE	MAC KELLAR
MAC YANN(I)EL	MAC DONALD	MAGEOWN	GOW
MAC YARGER,-AR	ARGYLL DIST	MAGEOWN	MAC PHERSON
MAC YE	MAC KAY	MAGILL	MAC GILL
MAC YONNEL(L)	MAC DONELL GLENGARRY	MAGINCH	MAC INNES
MAC YULE	MAC DONALD OF SLEAT	MAGINNES	MAC INNES
MAC ZEAL	MAC DOUGALL	MAGINNIS	ULSTER TARTAN
MAC ZEEK	GALLOWAY DIST	MAGLAM(M)ERY,-IE	MONTGOMERY
MAC ZELL	MAC DONALD	MAGLEW	STEWART OF APPIN
MAC ZINC	GALLOWAY DIST	MAGLIN	CLAN CIAN
MAC aLARY (Irish)	CLAN CIAN	MAGNUS	GUNN
MACA	MAC KAY	MAGNUSSON	GUNN
MACALEY	MAC AULAY	MAGOFFIN	MAC FIE
MACHAN(E)	MAC DONALD	MAGOON	MAC EWEN
MACHAN(E)	MAC INNES	MAGOWAN,-EN,-IN	GOW
MACHAR	MAC GREGOR	MAGOWAN,-EN,-IN	MAC PHERSON
MACHEN	MAC KENZIE	MAGRATH	MAC RAE
MACHENZIE	MAC KENZIE	MAGREW	MAC GREGOR
MACHIR	MAC GREGOR	MAGUFFIE,-Y	MAC FIE
MACHRAY	MAC RAE	MAGUIRE	MAC GUIRE
MACHTEY	ROSS	MAGUIRE	ULSTER TARTAN
MACHULA	MUNRO	MAGY	MAC KAY
MACHY,-IE	HOME	MAHAD(D)IE,-Y	FERGUSON
MACIAG	FARQUHARSON	MAHAD(D)IE,-Y	GORDON
MACIESON	MAC KAY	MAHAD(D)IE,-Y	MUNRO
MACINTOSH	MACKINTOSH	MAHAFFIE(E),-Y	MAC FIE
MACK	HOME	MAHAN	CONNACHT TARTAN
MACKALL	STUART OF BUTE	MAHARRY,-IE	MAC RAE
MACKBY	MAC LEAN	MAHER	CLAN CIAN
MACKIE	MAC KAY	MAILER	STRATHEARN DIST
MACKIESON	MACKINTOSH	MAIN(S)	GUNN
MACKININ	MAC KINNON	MAINE(S)	ST. ANDREWS DIST
MACKINTOSH	CLAN CHATTAN	MAINLAND	SINCLAIR
MACKINTOSH	MACKINTOSH	MAIR(S)	MAIR
MACKLAY	MAC LEAY	MAIR(S)	MAR DIST
MACKLAY	STEWART OF APPIN	MAISELS	EDINBURGH DIST
MACKLEEN	MAC LEAN	MAISLETT	DUNBAR DIST
MACKLIN	MAC LEAN	MAISON	EDINBURGH DIST
MACKMAN	MANSON	MAITLAND	LAUDER
MACKMURDO	MAC DONALD	MAITLAND	MAITLAND
MACKMURDO	MAC PHERSON	MAJOR(S)	DUNDEE DIST
MACKOOL	MAC LEOD	MAKAIL	MAC COLL
MACKOUL	MAC COUL	MAKAIL	STUART OF BUTE
MACKOUL	MAC LEOD	MAKALE	MAC COLL
MACKSOUD	MAC LEOD	MAKALE	STUART OF BUTE
MACKWAY,-EY	MAC LEAN	MAKAY	MAC KAY
MACLEY	MAC LEAY	MAKCAW(E)	MAC KAY
MACLEY	STWEART OF APPIN	MAKDUFFIE	MAC FIE
MACOKEY	MAC KAY	MAKE(E)	MAC KAY
MACON(O)CHIE,-Y	ROBERTSON	MAKEE	MAC KAY
MACONCHY,-IE	MAC DOUGALL	MAKER	ROXBURGH DIST
MACONOCHY,-IE	STEWART	MAKERSTOUN,-WN	ROXBURGH DIST
MACOOL	MAC LEOD	MAKFEITHE	MAC FIE
MACOWAN,-EN	GOW	MAKGIE	MAC KAY
MACOWAN,-EN	MAC PHERSON	MAKGILL	MAC GILL
MACOY	MAC KAY	MAKGY(E)	MAC KAY
MACSKEANE	MAC QUEEN	MAKHE	MAC KAY
MADDEN	CONNACHT TARTAN	MAKIA	MAC KAY
MADDEN,-IN	DUNDEE DIST	MAKIE	MAC KAY
MAFEYE	MAC FIE	MAKILL	MAC GILL
MAFFEITH	MAC FIE	MAKY	MAC KAY
MAFFETT	MOFFAT	MALCOLM	MALCOLM
MAGALPIN(E)	MAC ALPINE	MALCOLMSON	MAC LEOD
MAGAN	CLAN CIAN	MALISE	ABERDEEN DIST
MAGAWLEY	MAC AULAY		
MAGEE	MAC KAY		

NAME	TARTAN	NAME	TARTAN
MALL	ROXBURGH DIST	MARVIN	INVERNESS DIST
MALLACE	DUNDEE DIST	MARWICK	CAITHNESS TARTAN
MALLACH,-K	MAC GREGOR	MARWOOD	GLASGOW DIST
MALLAGH	MAC GREGOR	MAS(S)ON	TWEEDSIDE DIST
MALLENY	EDINBURGH DIST	MASHETTE	DRUMMOND
MALLIS(H)	DUNDEE DIST	MASSIE,-Y	MATHESON
MALLISON	DUNDEE DIST	MASTERS	BUCHANAN
MALLOCH,-K	MAC GREGOR	MASTERS	MAC INNES
MALLON	MELVILLE	MASTERSON	BUCHANAN
MALLONIE,-EY	ARGYLL DIST	MASTERSON	MAC INNES
MALLOY	STUART OF BUTE	MATCHES	CALEDONIA TARTAN
MALTMAN	ABERDEEN DIST	MATEER	MAC TIER
MAN(N)	GUNN	MATESON	ABERDEEN DIST
MAN(N)	MANX NATIONAL	MATHER(S)	FIFE DIST
MAN(N)	PERTHSHIRE DIST	MATHESON	MATHESON
MAN(N)SON	GUNN	MATHEWSON	MATHESON
MAN(N)SON	MANSON	MATHIE	MATHESON
MANAUGH	MAC NAUGHTON	MATHIESON	MATHESON
MANDERSON	TWEEDSIDE DIST	MATLACK,-OCK	GLEN LYON DIST
MANDEVILLE	PERTHSHIRE DIST	MATSON	MATHESON
MANEELY	MAC NEIL	MATTERS	ANGUS DIST
MANESON	GUNN	MATTHEW(S)	MATHESON
MANESON	MANSON	MATTIESON	MATHESON
MANNICE	MAC NAUGHTEN	MAU(L)DSLIE,-Y	STRATHCLYDE DIST
MANNIS(E)	MAC NAUGHTEN	MAU(L)DSON	PERTHSHIRE DIST
MANNY,-IE	MANX NATIONAL	MAUCHAN	STRATHCLYDE DIST
MANSELL	ROXBURGH DIST	MAUCHLEN	PAISLEY DIST
MANSEN	MANSON	MAUCHLINE	PAISLEY DIST
MANSFIELD	PERTHSHIRE DIST	MAULE	ANGUS DIST
MANTACH	MAC DON OF KEPPOCH	MAULE	PERTHSHIRE DIST
MANUEL	STIRLING DIST	MAVER,-OR	GORDON
MANWELL	STIRLING DIST	MAVER,-OR	INNES
MANZIE(S)	MENZIES	MAW(E)	TWEEDSIDE DIST
MAPPLEBECK	INVERNESS DIST	MAWER	GORDON
MAR	GORDON	MAWHINNEY,-IE	BUCHANAN
MAR	MAR	MAWHINNEY,-IE	MAC KENZIE
MARCH	EDINBURGH DIST	MAWHITTY,-IE	BUCHANAN
MARCHBANKS	JOHNSTON	MAWSON	PERTHSHIRE DIST
MARCHER	EDINBURGH DIST	MAXON	MAXWELL
MARGACH	STRATHSPEY DIST	MAXTON	MAXTON
MARGADALE	MAC DONALD	MAXTON	MAXWELL
MARGERIE,-ERY	NITHSDALE DIST	MAXWELL	MAXWELL
MARJORIBANKS	JOHNSTON	MAY(S)	MAC DONALD
MARJORYBANKS	JOHNSTON	MAYERS	STRATHEARN DIST
MARK(S)	MAC DONALD	MAYNARD	ST. ANDREWS DIST
MARKINCH	FIFE DIST	MAYNE(S)	ST. ANDREWS DIST
MARKLE	DUNBAR DIST	MAYO	MAC DONALD
MARLEY	INVERNESS DIST	ME(E)KIE,-Y	FORBES
MARMICK	INVERNESS DIST	ME(E)KIE,-Y	MAC DON OF KEPPOCH
MARNIE	ANGUS DIST	MEACHIE,-Y	MAC DON OF KEPPOCH
MARNOCH,-K	INNES	MEADOWS	CAITHNESS TARTAN
MARQUIS(E)	MAC DONALD	MEAGHER	CLAN CIAN
MARR	GORDON	MEALL	ANGUS DIST
MARR	MAR	MEAM(E)	AYRSHIRE DIST
MARRON,-EN	ULSTER TARTAN	MEANIE,-Y	ABERDEEN DIST
MARSH	ROXBURGH DIST	MEANIES	MENZIES
MARSHALL	KEITH	MEANS,-IES	MENZIES
MARSHBURN	TWEEDSIDE DIST	MEANY	CONNACHT TARTAN
MARSTON	INVERNESS DIST	MEAR(E)S	STRATHEARN DIST
MARTEALTO	ANGUS DIST	MEARNS	PAISLEY DIST
MARTIN	MARTIN	MEARSE	ABERDEEN DIST
MARTIN,-E	CAMERON	MEARSON	STIRLING DIST
MARTIN,-E	MAC DONALD	MEARTIE,-Y	STUART OF BUTE
MARTINSON	MAC DONALD	MEASON	BUCHAN DIST
MARTISON	MAC DONALD	MEATH	MATHESON
MARTYN	MAC DONALD	MEBEY	MAC LEAN OF DUART

NAME	TARTAN	NAME	TARTAN
MECALLIE,-Y	MAC AULAY	MEMES	ANGUS DIST
MECAM	MAC LAINE	MENDRUM	DUNDEE DIST
MECAULIE,-Y	MAC AULAY	MENELAWS	ROSS
MECAWLIE,-Y	MAC AULAY	MENGUES	MENZIES
MECAY	MAC KAY	MENMUIR	ANGUS DIST
MECEY,-IE	MAC KAY	MENNICK,-ICH	CALEDONIA TARTAN
MECHIE,-Y	FORBES	MENNICK,-ICH	MINNICK
MECHIE,-Y	MAC DON OF KEPPOCH	MENNIE,-Y	ABERDEEN DIST
MECHLANE	MAC LAINE	MENTIETH	GRAHAM OF MENTIETH
MECUM	MAC LAINE LOCH BUIE	MENTIETH	MENTIETH DIST
MEDLOCK	INVERNESS DIST	MENTIETH	STEWART
MEECHAN	CARRICK DIST	MENTION	EDINBURGH DIST
MEEHAN	CARRICK DIST	MENTIPLAY	FIFE DIST
MEEK(S)	FIFE DIST	MENZIES	MENZIES
MEEKIE,-Y	FORBES	MERC(I)ER	PERTHSHIRE DIST
MEEKIE,-Y	MAC DON OF KEPPOCH	MERCHANT	ANGUS DIST
MEEKIN,-EN	CARRICK DIST	MERCHISTON	EDINBURGH DIST
MEEKISON	FORBES	MERGIE,-Y	FIFE DIST
MEEKISON	MAC DON OF KEPPOCH	MERIAM	GLASGOW DIST
MEEKLE	PERTHSHIRE DIST	MERK(E)	GLASGOW DIST
MEEKLEJOHN	LAMONT	MERLAY	ROXBURGH DIST
MEEME	AYRSHIRE DIST	MERLIE,-Y	MERRILEES
MEENY	CONNACHT TARTAN	MERLIN	EDINBURGH DIST
MEFATT	MOFFAT	MERRICK	GALLOWAY DIST
MEFF	ABERDEEN DIST	MERRILEES	MERRILEES
MEFFAN,-EN	STRATHEARN DIST	MERRILIS	MERRILEES
MEFFET	MOFFAT	MERRY	CARRICK DIST
MEFFIT(T)	MOFFAT	MERRYMAN	CARRICK DIST
MEGALL	STUART OF BUTE	MERRYMOUTH	AYRSHIRE DIST
MEGAW	STUART OF BUTE	MERSER	PERTHSHIRE DIST
MEGGAT,-ET	ETTRICK DIST	MERSON	BUCHAN DIST
MEGGINCH	MAC INNES	MERSTON	DUNBAR DIST
MEGGS	STRATHCLYDE DIST	MERTON	ROXBURGH DIST
MEGINCH	MAC INNES	MESCALL	MAXWELL
MEGUFFIE,-Y	MAC FIE	MESCHIN	STRATHCLYDE DIST
MEHAFF(E)Y	MAC FIE	MESSENGER	GALLOWAY DIST
MEIGGS	STRATHEARN DIST	MESSER	STIRLING DIST
MEIGHAN,-EN	CARRICK DIST	MESTON	ABERDEEN DIST
MEIGLE	PERTHSHIRE DIST	METCALF(E)	METCALF
MEIK(S)	FIFE DIST	METHUN(E)	STRATHEARN DIST
MEIKIE	MAC KAY	METHVEN	STRATHEARN DIST
MEIKLE	ABERDEEN DIST	MEWERS	STRATHCLYDE DIST
MEIKLE(H)AM,-EM	LAMONT	MEWHIRTER	BUCHANAN
MEIKLEJOHN	LAMONT	MEY	SINCLAIR
MEILING	ABERDEEN DIST	MEYNERS	MENZIES
MEIN(E)	ROXBURGH DIST	MHIC LEOID	MAC LEOD
MEIR	ROXBURGH DIST	MICHAEL(S),-SON	MAC DONALD
MEIRN(S)	ANGUS DIST	MICHAELJOHN	LAMONT
MEKAY	MAC KAY	MICHAELSON	MAC MICHAEL
MEKEE(S)	MAC KAY	MICHEY	FORBES
MELBURN(E)	FIFE DIST	MICHEY	MAC DON OF KEPPOCH
MELDON	ROXBURGH DIST	MICHIE,-SON	FORBES
MELDROM(E)	FORBES	MICHIE,-SON	MAC DON OF KEPPOCH
MELDROM(E)	GORDON	MICKEL,-LE	ABERDEEN DIST
MELDRUM(E)	FORBES	MICKEL,-LE	MAC MICHAEL
MELDRUM(E)	GORDON	MICKLEJOHN	LAMONT
MELLAN	ULSTER TARTAN	MICKLESON	MAC MICHAEL
MELLEN,-IN	MELVILLE	MICLAY	MAC LEAY
MELLIS(H)	ABERDEEN DIST	MICLAY,-EY	STEWART OF APPIN
MELLON	MELVILLE	MIDDLAR	ABERDEEN DIST
MELLOR	LORNE DIST	MIDDLEMAS	ROXBURGH DIST
MELLVIE,-Y	MELVILLE	MIDDLEMISS	FIFE DIST
MELROSE	ROXBURGH DIST	MIDDLEMIST	ROXBURGH DIST
MELROSS	ROXBURGH DIST	MIDDLER	ABERDEEN DIST
MELVEEN	GALLOWAY DIST	MIDDLETON	FORBES
MELVILLE	MELVILLE	MIDDLETON	INNES
MELVIN,-EN	MELVILLE	MIDDLETON	MIDDLETON

NAME	TARTAN	NAME	TARTAN
MIDHOPE	ROXBURGH DIST	MOCHAN	DUNDEE DIST
MIL(L)OY	STUART OF BUTE	MOCHRIE,-Y	LENNOX DIST
MILBURN(E)	FIFE DIST	MOD(D(Y,-IE	STEWART
MILBURN(E)	TYNESIDE DIST	MOFFAT	MOFFAT
MILES	ROXBURGH DIST	MOFFET(T)	MOFFAT
MILFORD	CONNACHT TARTAN	MOFFIT(T)	MOFFAT
MILFREDERICK	GALLOWAY DIST	MOFFORD	MOFFAT
MILHOAN	ULSTER TARTAN	MOGGACH	STRATHSPEY DIST
MILIROY	GRANT	MOHAN	CONNACHT TARTAN
MILL(S)	GORDON	MOHAN	ULSTER TARTAN
MILLAN	MAC MILLAN	MOIR	GORDON
MILLANE	MELVILLE	MOIRA	INVERNESS DIST
MILLAR	MAC FARLANE	MOLL(E)	ROXBURGH DIST
MILLAR(D)	ANGUS DIST	MOLLIGAN	ULSTER TARTAN
MILLEN	MAC MILLAN	MOLLINS	GALLOWAY DIST
MILLER	ANGUS DIST	MOLLISON	ABERDEEN DIST
MILLER	MAC FARLANE	MOLLOY	ULSTER TARTAN
MILLESON	ANGUS DIST	MOLONEY	CLAN CIAN
MILLIGAN	NITHSDALE DIST	MOLVIE,-Y	FIFE DIST
MILLIKEN	NITHSDALE DIST	MONA	MAC FARLANE
MILLS	ULSTER TARTAN	MONACH	MAC FARLANE
MILN(E)(S)	GORDON	MONAGHAN	ULSTER TARTAN
MILN(E)(S)	MILNE	MONCHALL	INVERNESS DIST
MILN(E)(S)	OGILVIE	MONCREIFF(E)	MONCRIEFFE
MILNER	GORDON	MONCRIEFF(E)	CRIEFF DIST
MILRAE	GALLOWAY DIST	MONCRIEFF(E)	STRATHEARN DIST
MILROY	GRANT	MONCUR	FIFE DIST
MILROY	MAC GILLIVRAY	MONDELL	EDINBURGH DIST
MILROY	ROBERTSON	MONDIE,-Y	BUCHAN DIST
MILTAN	ARGYLL DIST	MONFRIES	CALEDONIA TARTAN
MILTON	INVERNESS DIST	MONGNEY	MONTGOMERY
MILVAIN	MAC BAIN	MONGRIEVE	MONCRIEFFE
MILVANE	MAC BAIN	MONK(E)	MAC DON KINGSBURGH
MILWAIN	MAC BAIN	MONKTON	EDINBURGH DIST
MILWANE	MAC BAIN	MONLOW	MUNRO
MILWARD	PERTHSHIRE DIST	MONORGAN	PERTHSHIRE DIST
MILWEE	GALLOWAY DIST	MONREITH	MAXWELL
MINDRUM	ROXBURGH DIST	MONRO(E)	MUNRO
MINEELY	MAC NEIL	MONROW	MUNRO
MINER(S)	STRATHCLYDE DIST	MONTAGUE	ULSTER TARTAN
MINIMAN	FIFE DIST	MONTEATH	GRAHAM OF MONTEITH
MINN	MENZIES	MONTEATH	MENTIETH DIST
MINNICK	MINNICK	MONTEITH	GRAHAM OF MONTEITH
MINNICK,-ICH	CALEDONIA TARTAN	MONTEITH	MENTIETH DIST
MINNIS(H)	MENZIES	MONTFORD	ABERDEEN DIST
MINNOCK	MINNICK	MONTGOMERY	MONTGOMERY
MINNUS	MENZIES	MONTIER	EDINBURGH DIST
MINNUS	MENZIES	MONTMORENCY	MONTMORENCY
MINTEER	MAC INTYRE	MONTOOTH	MENTIETH DIST
MINTIE,-Y	STRATHCLYDE DIST	MONTOUR	EDINBURGH DIST
MINTO	ROXBURGH DIST	MONTROSE	GRAHAM OF MONTROSE
MIRE	DUNBAR DIST	MONTROSE	MONTROSE DIST
MIRES	FIFE DIST	MONTROWSE	GRAHAM OF MONTROSE
MIRK	GLASGOW DIST	MONTROWSE	MONTROSE
MIRTEL	GALA WATER DIST	MONWILLIAM(S)	MAC WILLIAM
MITCHAL(L)	MITCHELL	MONYPENNY	FIFE DIST
MITCHAL(L)	ROSS	MONZIE	CRIEFF DIST
MITCHELHILL	TWEEDSIDE DIST	MONZIE	MURRAY
MITCHELL	MITCHELL	MONZIE(S)	MENZIES
MITCHELL	ROSS	MOODIE,-Y	STEWART
MITCHELLSON	MITCHELL	MOON	MURRAY
MITCHELLSON	ROSS	MOON(E)Y	ULSTER TARTAN
MO(O)REHOUSE	GLASGOW DIST	MOOR	GORDON
MOALS	DALZELL	MOOR	MUIR
MOAR	SINCLAIR	MOORE	CAMPBELL
MOAT	MOWAT	MOORE	GORDON
		MOORE	MUIR

NAME	TARTAN	NAME	TARTAN
MOOREHEAD	STRATHCLYDE DIST	MOWBRAY,-EY	FIFE DIST
MOOREHOUSE	GLASGOW DIST	MOWBRAY,-EY	MOWBRAY
MOORMAN	STRATHCLYDE DIST	MOWETT	MOWAT
MOR(R)AY	MURRAY	MOWETT	SUTHERLAND
MOR(R)ISON	BUCHANAN	MOY(S)ES	ABERDEEN DIST
MORAM	ANGUS DIST	MOYES	ANGUS DIST
MORAN	CONNACHT TARTAN	MOYES	FIFE DIST
MORAN	MORAN	MOYHOUSE	FIFE DIST
MORAY	MURRAY	MOYLE	HUNTLY DIST
MORCOT(T)	DUNBAR DIST	MOYNESS	CULLODEN DIST
MORCROFT	TYNESIDE DIST	MUCH,-IE,-Y	STIRLING DIST
MORDENT(E)	MORDENTE	MUCKARSIE,-Y	MAC ARTHUR
MORE	LESLIE	MUCKART	MAC AART
MORE	MUIR	MUCKART	MAC ARTHUR
MORE of Drumcork	GRANT	MUCKEEN	MAC DON ARDNAMURCHAN
MOREBATTLE	ROXBURGH DIST	MUCKEEN	MAC DON OF GLENCOE
MOREBURN	STRATHCLYDE DIST	MUCKEEN	MAC KEAN
MORECROFT	ROXBURGH DIST	MUCKERSIE,-Y	MAC ARTHUR
MORECROFT	TYNESIDE DIST	MUCKLE	TWEEDSIDE DIST
MOREHEARD	STRATHCLYDE DIST	MUCKSTORE	MAC INTYRE
MOREHOUSE	GLASGOW DIST	MUD(D)IE,-Y	STEWART
MORELAND	ANGUS DIST	MUGGAH	STRATHSPEY DIST
MOREVILLE	TWEEDSIDE DIST	MUIL(L)	MULL DIST
MORGAN	MAC KAY	MUIR	CAMPBELL
MORGAN	MORGAN	MUIR	GORDON
MORGUND	MAC KAY	MUIR	MUIR
MORHAM	MUSSELBURGH DIST	MUIRBURN	STRATHCLYDE DIST
MORISON	MORRISON	MUIRDEN	ABERDEEN DIST
MORN(E)	SINCLAIR	MUIRHALL	STRATHCLYDE DIST
MORNINGTON(E)	STRATHCLYDE DIST	MUIRHEAD	STRATHCLYDE DIST
MORPAT	STRATHCLYDE DIST	MUIRHOUSE	GLASGOW DIST
MORPAT	TYNESIDE DIST	MUKURDY	MAC KIRDY
MORRAN	MORAN	MULDONICH	MENTIETH DIST
MORRE	GORDON	MULDOON	ULSTER TARTAN
MORRE	MUIR	MULDOWNEY	CLAN CIAN
MORRELL	ROXBURGH DIST	MULHERRIN	CONNACHT TARTAN
MORREN	MAC KINNON	MULHOLLAND	CONNACHT TARTAN
MORRICE	BUCHANAN	MULHOLLAND	MULHOLLAND
MORRIE,-Y	MURRAY	MULHOLLAND	ULSTER TARTAN
MORRIESON	MORRISON	MULKERRAN	CONNACHT TARTAN
MORRILL	ROXBURGH DIST	MULL	MULL DIST
MORRIN	MAC KINNON	MULLAN (Irish)	ULSTER TARTAN
MORRIS	BUCHANAN	MULLANE	MELVILLE
MORRISON	BUCHANAN	MULLEN	CONNACHT TARTAN
MORRISON	MORRISON	MULLEN(S)	MAC MILLAN
MORROW	ROXBURGH DIST	MULLHALL	ULSTER TARTAN
MORT	PAISLEY DIST	MULLIE,-EY	MULL DIST
MORTHLAND	AYRSHIRE DIST	MULLIGAN	ULSTER TARTAN
MORTIMER	FIFE DIST	MULLIN(S)	MAC MILLAN
MORTON	DOUGLAS	MULLING(S)	MAC MILLAN
MOSCROP	ROXBURGH DIST	MULLION(S)	CRIEFF DIST
MOSES	ABERDEEN DIST	MULLOVER	CONNACHT TARTAN
MOSLIE,-EY	EDINBURGH DIST	MULRAIN	ULSTER TARTAN
MOSS	MAXWELL	MULREADY	CONNACHT TARTAN
MOSSMAN	EDINBURGH DIST	MULREAVY	ULSTER TARTAN
MOTHERALL	STRATHCLYDE DIST	MULREMAN	CONNACHT TARTAN
MOTHERWELL	STRATHCLYDE DIST	MULRENAN	CONNACHT TARTAN
MOUAT	MOWAT	MULRINE	ULSTER TARTAN
MOUAT	SUTHERLAND	MULROE	ULSTER TARTAN
MOUBRAY	EDINBURGH DIST	MULROONEY	CONNACHT TARTAN
MOULTRIE,-Y	TWEEDSIDE DIST	MULROYNE	ULSTER TARTAN
MOUNSIE,-EY	ROXBURGH DIST	MULUNRY	CONNACHT TARTAN
MOUNT(S)	FIFE DIST	MULVAHILL	CONNACHT TARTAN
MOUTRAY	TWEEDSIDE DIST	MULVANAN	ULSTER TARTAN
MOW(E)	ROXBURGH DIST	MULVEY	ULSTER TARTAN
MOWAT(T)	MOWAT	MULVIHILL	CONNACHT TARTAN
MOWAT(T)	SUTHERLAND	MULVIHILL	MELVILLE

NAME	TARTAN	NAME	TARTAN
MULVILLE,-ELL	MELVILLE	MUTCH,-IE,-Y	STIRLING DIST
MULVIN(E)	MELVILLE	MUTRIE,-Y	TWEEDSIDE DIST
MUN	LAMONT	MYAL(L)S	ROXBURGH DIST
MUN	STUART OF BUTE	MYLES	ROXBURGH DIST
MUNCREL(L)(F)	MONCRIEFFE	MYLNE	GORDON
MUNDELL,-LE	GALLOWAY DIST	MYRE	DUNBAR DIST
MUNDIE,-Y	BUCHAN DIST	MYRES	FIFE DIST
MUNDIE,-Y	LAMONT	MYRON	MYRON
MUNDIE,-Y	STUART OF BUTE		
MUNDILL	GALLOWAY DIST		
MUNGALL	STIRLING DIST		
MUNGLE	STIRLING DIST	**N**	
MUNGO	STIRLING DIST		
MUNN	LAMONT		
MUNN	STUART OF BUTE	NACHTEN	MAC NAUGHTEN
MUNNIES,-YS	LAMONT	NAESMITH	ANGUS DIST
MUNNOCH,-K	MAC FARLANE	NAGHTON	MAC NAUGHTEN
MUNRO(E)	MUNRO	NAIL(L)	MAC NEIL
MUNROW	MUNRO	NAIRN(E)	MACKINTOSH
MUNSIE,-EY	ROXBURGH DIST	NAIRN(E)	NAIRN
MUNT	LAMONT	NAISBIT(T)	NISBET
MUNT	STUART OF BUTE	NAISMAITH	ANGUS DIST
MUR(R)IE	MURRAY	NAPIER	MAC FARLANE
MURCHESON	MAC DONALD	NAPIER	NAPIER
MURCHESON	MAC KENZIE	NAPIER	SCOTT
MURCHIE,-Y	BUCHANAN	NAPPER	MAC FARLANE
MURCHIE,-Y	MAC DONALD	NAPPER	NAPIER
MURCHIE,-Y	MAC KENZIE	NAPPER	SCOTT
MURCHISON	BUCHANAN	NASBETT	NISBET
MURCHISON	MAC DONALD	NATTON	MAC NAUGHTEN
MURCHISON	MAC KENZIE	NAUGHTEN,-ON	MAC NAUGHTEN
MURDIE,-Y	MAC KENZIE	NAUGHTIE,-Y	MAC NAUGHTEN
MURDIE,-Y	SUTHERLAND DIST	NAYSMITH,-YTH	ANGUS DIST
MURDO	MAC DONALD	NEAL(E)	MAC NEIL
MURDO	MAC PHERSON	NEAT(E)	INVERNESS DIST
MURDOCH,-CK	MAC DONALD	NEAVE(S)	MURRAY
MURDOCH,-CK	MAC PHERSON	NEAVERY,-IE	PERTHSHIRE DIST
MURDOCH,-CK	MURDOCH	NEC(H)TAN,-EN	MAC NAUGHTEN
MURDOCHSON	MAC DONALD	NEE	GALLOWAY DIST
MURDOCHSON	MAC PHERSON	NEENEY	CLAN CIAN
MURDOSON	MAC DONALD	NEESON	MAC GREGOR
MURDOSON	MAC PHERSON	NEIL(L)	MAC KAY
MURGANE	MAC KAY	NEIL(L)	MAC NEIL
MURIE	PERTHSHIRE DIST	NEILLAND(S)	GALLOWAY DIST
MURIESON	ABERDEEN DIST	NEILSON	GUNN
MURISON	MORRISON	NEILSON	MAC GREGOR
MURK	GLASGOW DIST	NEILSON	MAC KAY
MURPHY	MAC DONALD	NEILSON	MAC NEIL
MURPHY	MURPHY	NEILSON	STUART OF BUTE
MURRAY	MURRAY	NEISH	MAC GREGOR
MURRAY	MURRAY OF ABERCAIRNEY	NEISON	MAC GREGOR
MURRAY	MURRAY OF ATHOLL	NELSON	GUNN
MURRAY	MURRAY OF ELIBANK	NELSON	MAC GREGOR
MURRAY	MURRAY OF TULLIBARDINE	NELSON	MAC NEIL
MURRAY	STRATHEARN DIST	NELSON	STUART OF BUTE
MURRIHY	MURRAY	NELSON (Irish)	ULSTER TARTAN
MURROW	MURRAY	NESBET(T)	DUNBAR
MURRY	MURRAY	NESBET(T)	HOME
MURRY	STRATHEARN DIST	NESBET(T)	NISBET
MURTAGH	MAC PHERSON	NESMITH	ANGUS DIST
MURTIE,-Y	TWEEDSIDE DIST	NESS	FIFE DIST
MUSGRAVE	TYNESIDE DIST	NESSAN,-EN	LOCHABER DIST
MUSHET,-TE	DRUMMOND	NETHERBY,-IE	GRAHAM OF MENTIETH
MUSSELBURGH	MUSSELBURGH DIST	NETHERWOOD	AYRSHIRE DIST
MUSTARD	ANGUS DIST	NETHERY,-IE	GRAHAM OF MENTIETH
MUT(T)ER	STRATHCLYDE DIST	NETTLETON	TYNESIDE DIST

NAME	TARTAN	NAME	TARTAN
NEVAY	ANGUS DIST	NOBEL	MACKINTOSH
NEVERY	GRAHAM OF MENTIETH	NOBLE	APPLECROSS DIST
NEVILLE	DUNDEE DIST	NOBLE	CLAN CHATTAN
NEVIN	CAMPBELL	NOBLE	MACKINTOSH
NEVIN	CUMMING	NOE	GALLOWAY DIST
NEVIN	MAC NAUGHTEN	NOGHER	ULSTER TARTAN
NEVIN	MACKINTOSH	NOLEN	INVERNESS DIST
NEVIN(S)	CLAN CIAN	NOON	ABERDEEN DIST
NEVINSON	CAMPBELL	NOONE	CONNACHT TARTAN
NEVINSON	CUMMING	NOR(H)AM	TWEEDSIDE DIST
NEVINSON	MAC NAUGHTEN	NOR(R)IE	MAC LEOD
NEVINSON	MACKINTOSH	NORMAN(D) (North)	MAC LEOD
NEVISON	CAMPBELL	NORMAN(D) (South)	GALLOWAY DIST
NEVISON	CUMMING	NORMAN(D) (South)	ROXBURGH DIST
NEVISON	MAC NAUGHTEN	NORREY(S)	TWEEDSIDE DIST
NEVISON	MACKINTOSH	NORRIS	TWEEDSIDE DIST
NEWALL	GALLOWAY DIST	NORRY,-IE	MAC LEOD
NEWBERRY	EDINBURGH DIST	NORTHWOOD	ARGYLL DIST
NEWBIE,-Y	TWEEDSIDE DIST	NORVAL(L)	STIRLING DIST
NEWBIGGIN(G)	STRATHCLYDE DIST	NORVIL(L)(E)	STIRLING DIST
NEWBURN	FIFE DIST	NORWELL	STIRLING DIST
NEWCASTLE	EDINBURGH DIST	NORWOOD	ARGYLL DIST
NEWELL	GALLOWAY DIST	NOTMAN	DUNBAR DIST
NEWER	GALLOWAY DIST	NOUGHT	MAC NAUGHTEN
		NOWER	ULSTER TARTAN
NEWHALL	GALLOWAY DIST	NUCATOR	MAC GREGOR
NEWLANDS	GLASGOW DIST	NUCATOR,-ER	MAC NAUGHTEN
NEWLANDS	NEWLANDS	NUDIE	FIFE DIST
NEWTON	EDINBURGH DIST	NUGENT	ULSTER TARTAN
NEYSMITH	ANGUS DIST	NUIR	GALLOWAY DIST
NIBLO(E)	BUCHAN DIST	NUNN	STRATHSPEY DIST
NIC(H)OLSON	MAC LEOD	NUTALL	LORNE DIST
NIC(H)OLSON	NICHOLSON	NUTSHILL	GLASGOW DIST
NICE	MAC GREGOR	NYDIE,-Y	FIFE DIST
NICHOL(L),-S	MAC LEOD		
NICHOL(L),-S	NICHOLSON		
NICKERSON	NICHOLSON		
NICKLE(S)	MAC LEOD		
NICKLE(S)	NICHOLSON	# O	
NICOL(L),-S	MAC LEOD		
NICOL(L),-S	NICHOLSON		
NICOLSON	MAC LEOD		
NICOLSON	NICHOLSON	O'BEICE	CLAN CIAN
NID(D)IE,-Y	ST. ANDREWS DIST	O'BOYD	BOYD
NIDDERIE,-Y	EDINBURGH DIST	O'BOYLE	EDINBURGH DIST
NIDDRY,-AY	EDINBURGH DIST	O'BRADY	CLAN CIAN
NIELANDS	GLASGOW DIST	O'BRENNAN	CLAN CIAN
NIELSON	MAC KAY	O'BRESLIN	CONNACHT TARTAN
NIGEL(L)	GLASGOW DIST	O'BRESLIN	ULSTER TARTAN
NILSON	MAC KAY	O'BRIAIN	CLAN CIAN
NIMMO	NICHOLSON	O'BRIAN	GLASGOW DIST
NINIAN	GALLOWAY DIST	O'BRIEN	ULSTER TARTAN
NISBET(T)	DUNBAR	O'BROCAIN	CLAN CIAN
NISBET(T)	HOME	O'BROLLAGHAN	ULSTER TARTAN
NISBET(T)	NISBET	O'BROLOCHAN	ARGYLL DIST
NISH	MAC GREGOR	O'CAHALAN	CLAN CIAN
NIVEN(S)	CAMPBELL	O'CALLAGHAN	ULSTER TARTAN
NIVEN(S)	CUMMING	O'CANNY	CONNACHT TARTAN
NIVEN(S)	MAC NAUGHTEN	O'CARROL(L)	CLAN CIAN
NIVEN(S)	MACKINTOSH	O'CARRY	CLAN CIAN
NIVISON	CAMPBELL	O'CARTHY	CLAN CIAN
NIVISON	CUMMING	O'CASEY	CONNACHT TARTAN
NIVISON	MAC NAUGHTEN	O'CASEY (Munster)	CLAN CIAN
NIVISON	MACKINTOSH	O'CASSIDY	ULSTER TARTAN
NIXON	ARMSTRONG	O'CASTLES	CLAN CIAN
NOBEL	CLAN CHATTAN	O'CLECKIN	ULSTER TARTAN
		O'COLLINS	CLAN CIAN

NAME	TARTAN	NAME	TARTAN
O'COLTAR	ULSTER TARTAN	O'KENNEDY	ULSTER TARTAN
O'CONCANNON	CONNACHT TARTAN	O'KERIN	CONNACHT TARTAN
O'CONNELL	CLAN CIAN	O'KERRIGAN	CONNACHT TARTAN
O'CONNER	DUNDEE DIST	O'LANACHAN	MAC DONALD
O'CONNOR	CLAN CIAN	O'LANE	MAC DONALD
O'CONNOR	CONNACHT TARTAN	O'LANG	MAC DONALD
O'COOLAHAN	CONNACHT TARTAN	O'LARGIE	ARGYLL DIST
O'COONEY	CLAN CIAN	O'LEARIE,-Y	CLAN CIAN
O'CORMACAN	CLAN CIAN	O'LEARY	ULSTER TARTAN
O'CORRA	CLAN CIAN	O'LENEHAN	CLAN CIAN
O'CREHAN	CONNACHT TARTAN	O'LEONARD	CONNACHT TARTAN
O'CRONANA	CLAN CIAN	O'LONACH	ARGYLL DIST
O'CULLEN	CLAN CIAN	O'LONIE	ARGYLL DIST
O'CURRY	CLAN CIAN	O'LOUGHLIN	ULSTER TARTAN
O'CURRY	ULSTER TARTAN	O'LOUGHNAN	CLAN CIAN
O'DALLON	CLAN CIAN	O'MAHONY	CLAN CIAN
O'DAY	CLANJ CIAN	O'MAY	MAC DONALD
O'DEA	CLAN CIAN	O'MEAGHER	CLAN CIAN
O'DELL	CLAN CIAN	O'MOHAN	CONNACHT TARTAN
O'DONNELL	CONNACHT TARTAN	O'MONAGAN	CONNACHT TARTAN
O'DONNELL	MAC DONALD	O'MULLANEY	CONNACHT TARTAN
O'DONOHUE	CLAN·CIAN	O'MUNNAY	CONNACHT TARTAN
O'DONOVAN	CLAN CIAN	O'NEAL(E)	O'NEIL
O'DORAN	CLAN CIAN	O'NEIL	O'NEIL
O'DOWD	CONNACHT TARTAN	O'NOONAN	CLAN CIAN
O'DRAIN	MAC DONALD	O'QUINN	CLAN CIAN
O'DRANE	MAC DONALD	O'REGAN	CLAN CIAN
O'DRUIM	CLAN CIAN	O'ROURKE	ARGYLL DIST
O'DUIN	CAMPBELL	O'RUANE	CONNACHT TARTAN
O'DUNA	CLAN CIAN	O'SEASNAIN	CLAN CIAN
O'DUNNIE	CAMPBELL	O'SHA(I)G	MAC DONALD
O'EARK	CLAN CIAN	O'SHANNACHAN	MAC DONALD
O'FARREL(L)	O'FARRELL	O'SHANNAHAN	MAC DONALD
O'FELAN	CLAN CIAN	O'SHANNAIG	MAC DONALD
O'FERCINN	CLAN CIAN	O'SHANNICK	MAC DONALD
O'FERGUS	CONNACHT TARTAN	O'SHIEL	ULSTER TARTAN
O'FERREL(L)	O'FARRELL	O'SLATTERY	CLAN CIAN
O'FLANAGAN	CLAN CIAN	O'SPEALAIN	CLAN CIAN
O'GARRA	HAY	O'SULLIVAN	CLAN CIAN
O'GARROW	HAY	O'SWEENY,-IE	MAC QUEEN
O'GILLEEN	CONNACHT TARTAN	O'TOWEY	CONNACHT TARTAN
O'GUILL	CLAN CIAN	O'TRASEY	CLAN CIAN
O'GUNNING	CLAN CIAN	O'hURLEY	CLAN CIAN
O'HAGAN	ULSTER TARTAN	OAG	ABERDEEN DIST
O'HAITHCHIR	CLAN CIAN	OAK(E),-IE	ABERDEEN DIST
O'HALY	CLAN CIAN	OATE(S)	MENTIETH DIST
O'HANDLIE,-LY	MAC DON CLANRANALD	OATMAN	ROXBURGH DIST
O'HANLIE,-Y	MAC DON CLANRANALD	OCHIL(L)TRIE	OCHILTREE
O'HANLON	ULSTER TARTAN	OCHIL(L)TRIE	STEWART
O'HANNA	HANNAY	OCHILTREE,-RY	AYRSHIRE DIST
O'HARA	CLAN CIAN	OCHILTREE,-RY	OCHILTREE
O'HARA	CONNACHT TARTAN	OCHILTREE,-RY	STEWART
O'HARA	ULSTER TARTAN	OCHTERLONIE,-Y	OCHTERLONIE
O'HARE	ULSTER TARTAN	OCKFORD	EDINBURGH DIST
O'HART	CONNACHT TARTAN	OCKMAN	STIRLING DIST
O'HAY	CLAN CIAN	ODDIE,-Y	CAITHNESS TARTAN
O'HAY	HAY	ODEL	CLAN CIAN
O'HEA	HAY	OFFICER	DUNDEE DIST
O'HEANY	ULSTER TARTAN	OGAN	CLAN CIAN
O'HEFFERNAB	CLAN CIAN	OGDAN,-EN	ROXBURGH DIST
O'HEGARTY	CLAN CIAN	OGELBIE,-Y	OGILVIE
O'HEHIR	CLAN CIAN	OGESTON	ANGUS DIST
O'HENEREY	CLAN CIAN	OGG	ABERDEEN DIST
O'HOGAN	CLAN CIAN	OGILBY,-IE	OGILVIE
O'HORA	CLAN CIAN	OGILL	DUNBLANE DIST
O'KEEFE	CLAN CIAN	OGILL	TYNESIDE DIST
O'KEEFE	O'KEEFE	OGILVIE,-Y	OGILVIE
O'KELLAHER	CLAN CIAN	OGILVIE,-Y	OGILVIE OF SKYE

NAME	TARTAN	NAME	TARTAN
OGLE	DUNBLANE DIST	PAD(D)AN	MAC DONALD
OGLE	TYNESIDE DIST	PAD(D)AN	MAC LEAN OF DUART
OGLETREE	OCHILTREE	PAD(D)EN	MAC DONALD
OGLETREE	STEWART	PAD(D)EN	MAC LEAN OF DUART
OGSTON(E),-OUN	BUCHAN DIST	PAD(D)EN	PATEN
OKIL(L)TREE,-IE	OCHILTREE	PAD(D)IE,-Y	GLASGOW DIST
OKIL(L)TREE,-IE	STEWART	PAD(D)ON	MAC DONALD
OLD(S)	TWEEDSIDE DIST	PAD(D)ON	MAC LEAN OF DUART
OLESON	CALEDONIA TARTAN	PAD(D)ON	PATEN
OLIPHANT	OLIPHANT	PADDER	AYRSHIRE DIST
OLIPHANT	SUTHERLAND	PADDOCK	LENNOX DIST
OLIVER	FRASER	PADGEN	EDINBURGH DIST
OLIVER	OLIVER	PADGET	PAGET
OLLASON	CALEDONIA TARTAN	PADSON	LAMONT
OLLESON	CALEDONIA TARTAN	PADYN(E)	GLASGOW DIST
OLONIE	ARGYLL DIST	PAG(G)AN	PAISLEY DIST
OLSSON	CALEDONIA TARTAN	PAGE	FIFE DIST
OLYPHANT	OLIPHANT	PAGET	PAGET
OLYPHANT	SUTHERLAND	PAIGE	FIFE DIST
OMAN(D)	EDINBURGH DIST	PAIN	PAISLEY DIST
ORAM	ABERDEEN DIST	PAINTER	ANGUS DIST
ORCHILLE	GRAHAM	PAIRMAN	ROXBURGH DIST
ORD(E)	ROXBURGH DIST	PAISLEY	PAISLEY DIST
OREM	ABERDEEN DIST	PALFREYMAN	MUSSELBURGH DIST
ORKNEY	ANGUS DIST	PALMER	GLASGOW DIST
ORMISTON	ROXBURGH DIST	PALMER	ROXBURGH DIST
ORMLIE,-LY	CAITHNESS TARTAN	PANNELL	TYNESIDE DIST
ORMOND	SUTHERLAND DIST	PANTER	MONTROSE DIST
ORR	CAMPBELL	PANTON	TWEEDSIDE DIST
ORR	MAC GREGOR	PAPAY	SINCLAIR
ORRICK	FIFE DIST	PAPE	INVERNESS DIST
ORROCK	FIFE DIST	PAPLAY	SINCLAIR
ORTIN	INVERNESS DIST	PAPPEY	SINCLAIR
ORWELL	ABERDEEN DIST	PAPPIL	FALKIRK DIST
OSBORN,-E	PAISLEY DIST	PAPPLE	FALKIRK DIST
OSBOURGH	DUNDEE DIST	PAR(R)IS	GLASGOW DIST
OSBURN,-E	ROXBURGH DIST	PARDEE	GALLOWAY DIST
OSLER	FIFE DIST	PARDOVAN	EDINBURGH DIST
OSTLER	FIFE DIST	PARIS(S)	AYRSHIRE DIST
OSWALD	FIFE DIST	PARK(E)	MAC DON CLANRANALD
OTTER	TWEEDSIDE DIST	PARKER	PERTHSHIRE DIST
OTTERBURN	ROXBURGH DIST	PARKHILL	AYRSHIRE DIST
OUCHTERLONIE,-Y	OCHTERLONIE	PARKINSON	INVERNESS DIST
OURE	MAC EWEN	PARLAN(E)	MAC FARLANE
OUTERSON	ROXBURGH DIST	PARLEY	EDINBURGH DIST
OUTLAW	ANGUS DIST	PARLIN,-ON(E)	MAC FARLANE
OUTRAM	INVERNESS DIST	PARR	PARR
OUTRIE,-AY	INVERNESS DIST	PARRISON	TYNESIDE DIST
OVENS	DUNBAR DIST	PARRY	PERRY
OVER	PERTHSHIRE DIST	PARSON(S)	MAC PHERSON
OWEN(S)	MAC EWEN	PARTICK	STRATHCLYDE DIST
OWENS	CLAN CIAN	PARTRIDGE	MULL DIST
OXLAY,-LEY	STRATHSPEY DIST	PASELIE,-Y	PAISLEY DIST
OYKELL	MAC KAY	PASLEW(E)	PAISLEY DIST
OYNIE	INNES	PASLEY,-IE	PAISLEY DIST
		PASLIG	PAISLEY DIST
		PASSELEWE	PAISLEY DIST
		PASSELY	PAISLEY DIST
		PASTOR	ROXBURGH DIST
		PAT(T)EN	MAC DONALD
		PAT(T)EN	MAC LEAN
		PAT(T)EN	PATEN
		PAT(T)EN	PATEN
PABBIE,-Y	MORRISON	PAT(T)ERSON	CAMPBELL
PABLAY	MORRISON	PAT(T)ERSON	FARQUHARSON
PACE	ROXBURGH DIST	PAT(T)ERSON	LAMONT
PACKER	GLASGOW DIST		

P

NAME	TARTAN	NAME	TARTAN
PAT(T)ERSON	MAC AULAY	PENTLAND	EDINBURGH DIST
PAT(T)ERSON	MAC LAREN	PENTON(E)	GALLOWAY DIST
PAT(T)ON	MAC DONALD	PEOPLES	HAY
PAT(T)ON	MAC LEAN	PEPDIE,-Y	TWEEDSIDE DIST
PAT(T)ON	PATEN	PEPPER	GLASGOW DIST
PATE	FIFE DIST	PERCY	NITHSDALE DIST
PATEY	DUNBAR DIST	PERKIE	EDINBURGH DIST
PATRICK	LAMONT	PERKIN (Irish)	CLAN CIAN
PATRICK	MAC LAREN	PERKINS	GLASGOW DIST
PATTEARSON	CAMPBELL	PERKLE	EDINBURGH DIST
PATTEARSON	FARQUHARSON	PERKS	ROXBURGH DIST
PATTEARSON	LAMONT	PERNESS	STRATHSPEY DIST
PATTEARSON	MAC AULAY	PERRIN(E)	EDINBURGH DIST
PATTIE	FIFE DIST	PERRIS	GLASGOW DIST
PATTINSON	ABERDEEN DIST	PERRONS	LORNE DIST
PATTISON	FARQUHARSON	PERRY,-IE	ANGUS DIST
PATTONSON	ABERDEEN DIST	PERRY,-IE	PERRY
PATULLO	MAC GREGOR	PERSTON	MAC PHERSON
PAUL	CAMERON	PERT	ANGUS DIST
PAUL	CLAN CHATTAN	PERTH	PERTHSHIRE DIST
PAUL	MAC KAY	PERTIE,-RY	MAC GREGOR
PAUL	MACKINTOSH	PERVIS	TWEEDSIDE DIST
PAULIN(E)	ANGUS DIST	PETER(S)	MAC GREGOR
PAULK	MAXWELL	PETERANNA	MAC DON CLANRANALD
PAULK	POLLOCK	PETERKIN	MAC GREGOR
PAULSON	MAC KAY	PETERSON	MAC GREGOR
PAXTANG	TWEEDSIDE DIST	PETERSON	MAC LAREN
PAXTON	TWEEDSIDE DIST	PETRIE,-RY	MAC LAREN
PAYTEN,-ON	PATEN	PETTENRECK,-ICK	SINCLAIR
PEACE	CALEDONIA TARTAN	PETTIE,-Y	ABERDEEN DIST
PEACOCK	MAXWELL	PETTIE,-Y	STRATHCLYDE DIST
PEACOX	MAXWELL	PETTIGREW	STRATHCLYDE DIST
PEARS(T)ON	MAC PHERSON	PETTINAIN	PAISLEY DIST
PEARSON	PEARSON	PETTINGER	FT. WILLIAM DIST
PEASE	ROXBURGH DIST	PETTIT	STRATHCLYDE DIST
PEASTON	EDINBURGH DIST	PEYTON	MAC DONALD
PEAT	MAC GREGOR	PHAIL	MAC PHAIL
PEAT(T)Y,-IE	ANGUS DIST	PHAULL	CAMERON
PEATRIE,-Y	MAC LAREN	PHAULL	MAC PHERSON
PEDDER	FIFE DIST	PHAULL	MACKINTOSH
PEDDIE,-Y	PERTHSHIRE DIST	PHE(E)	MAC FIE
PEDDIN	AYRSHIRE DIST	PHILAN	STRATHCLYDE DIST
PEDEN	AYRSHIRE DIST	PHILIP(P)	LOCHABER DIST
PEEBLES	HAY	PHILIP(P)	MAC DON OF GLENCOE
PEEK	LENNOX DIST	PHILIP(P)	MAC DON OF KEPPOCH
PEEL(E)	GALLOWAY DIST	PHILIP(P)	MAC KILLOP
PEEPLES	HAY	PHILIPSON	LOCHABER DIST
PEET	MAC GREGOR	PHILIPSON	MAC DON OF GLENCOE
PEFFERS	DUNBAR DIST	PHILIPSON	MAC DON OF KEPPOCH
PEGGIE	GALLOWAY DIST	PHILIPSON	MAC KILLOP
PEGLER	ABERDEEN DIST	PHILLANS	STRATHCLYDE DIST
PEN(D)LAND	EDINBURGH DIST	PHILLIP(S)	MAC DON OF GLENCOE
PENDER	GLASGOW DIST	PHILLIP(S)	MAC DON OF KEPPOCH
PENDERG(R)AST	CONNACHT TARTAN	PHILLIP(S)	MAC KILLOP
PENDERG(R)AST	TWEEDSIDE DIST	PHILP(P)	MAC DON OF KEPPOCH
PENDIN	GLASGOW DIST	PHILP(P)	MAC KILLIP
PENDREICH,-GH	STIRLING DIST	PHILPOT	LOCHABER DIST
PENFEATHER	CLAN CIAN	PHILPOT	MAC DON OF GLENCOE
PENMAN	PENMAN	PHILPOT	MAC DON OF KEPPOCH
PENMAN	ROXBURGH DIST	PHILPOT	MAC KILLOP
PENNEFATHER	CLAN CIAN	PHIMISTER	STRATHSPEY DIST
PENNER	EDINBURGH DIST	PHIN(N)	FIFE DIST
PENNERG(R)AST	TWEEDSIDE DIST	PHIPER	MURRAY
PENNET	CULLODEN DIST	PHORICH	LAMONT
PENNIE,-EY	INVERNESS DIST	PHUN(N)	MAC ARTHUR
PENNYCOOK	EDINBURGH DIST	PHYSIL	FRASER
PENNYCUICK	EDINBURGH DIST	PIATT	GRAHAM

NAME	TARTAN	NAME	TARTAN
PICARD	FIFE DIST	POLLOCK	MAXWELL
PICKAN(S)	AYRSHIRE DIST	POLLOCK	POLLOCK
PICKEN(S)	AYRSHIRE DIST	POLLOK	MAXWELL
PICKMAN	FIFE DIST	POLLOK	POLLOCK
PIE	GRAHAM	POLWARTH	TWEEDSIDE DIST
PIERSON	TWEEDSIDE DIST	POMFRET	STRATHCLYDE DIST
PIG(G)OT(T)	TWEEDSIDE DIST	POMPHRAY	STRATHCLYDE DIST
PIL(L)INGER	INVERNESS DIST	PONT	PERTHSHIRE DIST
PILCHIE,-(E)Y	INVERNESS DIST	PONTIE,-Y	INVERNESS DIST
PILLANS	STRATHCLYDE DIST	PONTON	BOYD
PILLING	FIFE DIST	POOK	MAXWELL
PILMER	TWEEDSIDE DIST	POOK	POLLOCK
PILMORE	TWEEDSIDE DIST	POOL(E)	GALLOWAY DIST
PINGLE	GALA WATER DIST	POPE	INVERNESS DIST
PINKERTON	CAMPBELL	PORTAR	GLEN LYON DIST
PINKIE,-Y	EDINBURGH DIST	PORTAS	PORTEOUS
PINKIESLAW	SKENE	PORTEOUS	PORTEOUS
PINMURRY,-AY	MURRAY	PORTER	GLEN LYON DIST
PINNIE,-EY	INVERNESS DIST	PORTER	MAC NAUGHTEN
PIP(P)ER	MURRAY	PORTESSE	PORTEOUS
PIR(R)IE	ABERDEEN DIST	PORTIS	PORTEOUS
PIRNIE,-Y	PERTHSHIRE DIST	POTT(S)	MAC DON OF GLENCOE
PITBLADO	ANGUS DIST	POTT(S)	MAC DON OF KEPPOCH
PITCAIRN	FIFE DIST	POTTER	LENNOX DIST
PITCAIRN	GRAHAM	POTTERFIELD	PAISLEY DIST
PITCAIRN	PITCAIRN	POTTINGER	SINCLAIR
PITCOCK	DUNBAR DIST	POULSON	MAC KAY
PITCOX	DUNBAR DIST	POUND(S)	GLASGOW DIST
PITCULLO	FIFE DIST	POUSTIE,-Y	EDINBURGH DIST
PITH	EDINBURGH DIST	POW(E)	GLASGOW DIST
PITHIE,-Y	ABERDEEN DIST	POWER	CLAN CIAN
PITKEATHLIE,-Y	ANGUS DIST	POWER(S)	CUNNINGHAM
PITKEITHY	STRATHEARN DIST	POWRIE,-Y	ANGUS DIST
PITKETHLY	STRATHEARN DIST	PRAT(T)	GRANT
PITTENDRAY,-EY	CULLODEN DIST	PREACHER	EDINBURGH DIST
PITTENDREIGH	CULLODEN DIST	PRECIOUS	CAITHNESS TARTAN
PITTENWEEM	FIFE DIST	PRENDERGAST	TWEEDSIDE DIST
PITTERKIN	MAC GREGOR	PRENTICE,-ISS	EDINBURGH DIST
PITTIGREW	GLASGOW DIST	PRES(S)LY	ABERDEEN DIST
PITTINGER	FT. WILLIAM DIST	PRESFEN	ROXBURGH DIST
PITULLICH	MAC DON OF KEPPOCH	PRESLAND	CAITHNESS TARTAN
PLATT(E)	PLATT	PRESLIE,-Y	ABERDEEN DIST
PLATTER	ANGUS DIST	PRESTON	EDINBURGH DIST
PLAYFAIR	FIFE DIST	PRESTWICK	AYRSHIRE DIST
PLAYFAIR	PERTHSHIRE DIST	PRETS(W)ELL	TWEEDSIDE DIST
PLENDERLEITH,-LY	ROXBURGH DIST	PRETSELL,-ALL	GALA WATER DIST
PLUM(M)ER	ROXBURGH DIST	PRIDE	PAISLEY DIST
PLUNKET(T)	CLAN CIAN	PRIEST(LY)	ROXBURGH DIST
POAK	MAXWELL	PRIMROSE	FIFE DIST
POAK	POLLACK	PRINCE	BUCHAN DIST
POAN	CLAN CIAN	PRINGLE	GALA WATER DIST
POGUE	MAXWELL	PRIOR(S)	DUNDEE DIST
POGUE	POLLOCK	PROCTOR	ANGUS DIST
POKE	MAXWELL	PROFET(T)	ABERDEEN DIST
POKE	POLLACK	PROPHET	ABERDEEN DIST
POL(L)SON	MAC KAY	PROSSER	ARGYLL DIST
POLE	MAC KAY	PROUDFOOT	TWEEDSIDE DIST
POLES(T)ON	MAC KAY	PROUDIE,-Y	ABERDEEN DIST
POLK	MAXWELL	PROVAN(D)	GLASGOW DIST
POLK	POLLOCK	PROVEN(D)	GLASGOW DIST
POLL	CAMERON	PROVOST	ANGUS DIST
POLL	MACKINTOSH	PRYDE	PAISLEY DIST
POLLACK	MAXWELL	PRYNNE	PAISLEY DIST
POLLACK	POLLOCK	PRYOR	DUNDEE DIST
POLLARD,-ERD	MAC KAY	PUDROCH,-K	MAC GREGOR
POLLO	MAXWELL	PUISLEY	ARGYLL DIST
POLLO	POLLOCK	PUL(L)IG	POLLOCK

NAME	TARTAN	NAME	TARTAN
PULLAR,-ER	PERTHSHIRE DIST		
PUMFRAY	STRATHCLYDE DIST		
PUNDLER	PERTHSHIRE DIST		
PUNN	DUNBAR DIST		
PUNTON	EDINBURGH DIST		
PURCELL	MAC DONALD		
PURDIE,-Y	ROXBURGH DIST		
PURDON,-M	GLASGOW DIST		
PURROCK	DUNDEE DIST		
PURSELL	MAC DONALD		
PURV(I)ES	TWEEDSIDE DIST		
PURVIS	TWEEDSIDE DIST		
PYATT	GRAHAM		
PYE	GRAHAM OF MENTIETH		
PYLE	STRATHCLYDE DIST		
PYOTT	GRAHAM OF MENTIETH		
PYPER	MURRAY		
PYTES	ARGYLL DIST		

R

NAME	TARTAN	NAME	TARTAN
		RAB(B)AN	INVERNESS DIST
		RABB	ROBERTSON
		RAE	MAC RAE
		RAE	RAE
		RAEBURN	BOYD
		RAEBURN	RAEBURN
		RAFF	ABERDEEN DIST
		RAFFAN	STRATHSPEY DIST
		RAFFERTY,-IE	ULSTER TARTAN
		RAFFLES	NITHSDALE DIST
		RAGG	INVERNESS DIST
		RAH	MAC RAE
		RAIBERT	RAIBERT
		RAIGMORE	INVERNESS DIST
		RAIN(E)(S)	GALLOWAY DIST
		RAIN(N)IE,-Y	MAC DON CLANRANALD
		RAINEY	ULSTER TARTAN
		RAINING	NITHSDALE DIST
		RAIT(T)	INVERNESS DIST
		RAITH	AYRSHIRE DIST

Q

NAME	TARTAN	NAME	TARTAN
QUA	MAC KAY	RALSTON	PAISLEY DIST
QUABEN	STEWART	RAMAGE	TWEEDSIDE DIST
QUAID(E)	FARQUHARSON	RAMSAY,-EY	RAMSAY
QUAID(E)	MAC DONALD	RAMSDEN,-ON	ROXBURGH DIST
QUAID(E)	MAC KAY	RAMSON	ABERDEEN DIST
QUAILE	CLAN CIAN	RAN(N)OLDSON	MAC DON CLANRANALD
QUAIN	CLAN CIAN	RANDALL,-ELL	FIFE DIST
QUARLES	TWEEDSIDE DIST	RANDLE(S)	FIFE DIST
QUARRAL(S)	ST. ANDREWS DIST	RANDOLPH	BRUCE
QUARREL(S)	ST. ANDREWS DIST	RANISON	ABERDEEN DIST
QUARRIE,-Y	MAC QUARRIE	RANKE(I)LLOR	FIFE DIST
QUARRIER	CAMPBELL	RANKEN	MAC LEAN
QUATE	FARQUHARSON	RANKEN	RANKIN
QUATE	MAC DONALD	RANKIN(E)	MAC LEAN
QUAY	MAC KAY	RANKIN(E)	RANKIN
QUAYNES	MAC QUEEN	RANNIE,-Y	MAC DON CLANRANALD
QUEEBAN	STEWART	RANNIE,-Y	SKENE
QUEEN	MAC QUEEN	RARITY	AYRSHIRE DIST
QUENTIN	ROXBURGH DIST	RASH	CALEDONIA TARTAN
QUERNE	DUNBAR DIST	RASSIE,-Y	MAC LEOD OF RAASAY
QUEY	MAC KAY	RASSON	CAITHNESS TARTAN
QUIGLEY	CONNACHT TARTAN	RAT(T)CLIFF	BUCHAN DIST
QUIGLEY	ULSTER TARTAN	RAT(T)LIFF	BUCHAN DIST
QUILCAN	MACKINTOSH	RATIGAN	CONNACHT TARTAN
QUILICAN,-KAN	MACKINTOSH	RATTER	CAITHNESS TARTAN
QUILICHAN	MACKINTOSH	RATTRAY	MURRAY
QUILL	CLAN CIAN	RATTRAY	RATTRAY
QUIN(N)	CLAN CIAN	RAVENSHEN	CAITHNESS TARTAN
QUINCY	GLASGOW DIST	RAWDEN	CALEDONIA TARTAN
QUINCY	ULSTER TARTAN	RAWLIN(G)(S)	NITHSDALE DIST
QUINN	GALLOWAY DIST	RAWSON	TWEEDSIDE DIST
QUINN	ULSTER TARTAN	RAY	MAC RAE
QUINON	ROXBURGH DIST	RAY	RAE
QUIRK	CLAN CIAN	RAYBURN	BOYD
QUOID	MAC KAY	RAYBURN	RAEBURN
		RAYNES	GALLOWAY DIST
		REA	MAC KAY
		REA	MAC RAE
		REACH	FARQUHARSON
		READ	REID
		READ	ROBERTSON

NAME	TARTAN	NAME	TARTAN
READIE,-Y	FIFE DIST	REYLIE,-Y	SUTHERLAND DIST
REAY	MAC KAY	REYNELDS	MAC DON CLANRANALD
REBBEN,-IN(S)	MAC QUEEN	REYNOLD(S)	MAC DON CLANRANALD
REBURN	BOYD	RHIND	LINDSAY
REBURN	RAEBURN	RHYND	LINDSAY
RED(D)IE,-Y	ANGUS DIST	RHYS	WELSH NATIONAL
REDDEN(S)	ROXBURGH DIST	RIACH	FARQUHARSON
REDDICK	GRAHAM	RIACH	MAC DONALD OF SLEAT
REDDIN(S)	ROXBURGH DIST	RICE	WELSH NATIONAL
REDDOCK,-H	GRAHAM	RICH	MACKINTOSH
REDFERN	INVERNESS DIST	RICH	RITCH
REDFORD	INNES	RICHAN	CALEDONIA TARTAN
REDLAND(S)	CAITHNESS TARTAN	RICHARDS	STRATHCLYDE DIST
REDNOCK	GRAHAM	RICHARDSON	BUCHANAN
REDPATH	TWEEDSIDE DIST	RICHARDSON	OGILVIE
REE	GALLOWAY DIST	RICHIESON	MUSSELBURGH DIST
REED	REID	RICHMAN	ABERDEEN DIST
REED	ROBERTSON	RICHMOND	STRATHCLYDE DIST
REEKIE,-Y	ANGUS DIST	RICHORDS	STRATHCLYDE DIST
REETH	INVERNESS DIST	RICKART	ABERDEEN DIST
REEVE(S)	STRATHCLYDE DIST	RICKSON	INVERNESS DIST
REGAN	CLAN CIAN	RIDDELL,-LE	ROXBURGH DIST
REGIS	CAITHNESS TARTAN	RIDDET	AYRSHIRE DIST
REIACH	FARQUHARSON	RIDDICK	GRAHAM
REID	REID	RIDDLER	DUNDEE DIST
REID	ROBERTSON	RIDDOCH,-K	GRAHAM
REIDFORD,-URD	INNES	RIDLAND	CAITHNESS TARTAN
REIDPATH	ROXBURGH DIST	RIDLER	ABERDEEN DIST
REIFF	FIFE DIST	RIDLEY	PAISLEY DIST
REITH	ABERDEEN DIST	RIDPATH	ROXBURGH DIST
RELLIE,-Y	TWEEDSIDE DIST	RIED	REID
REMSAY	RAMSAY	RIED	ROBERTSON
REMSON	GLASGOW DIST	RIGG(S)	DUNBAR DIST
RENDALL,-LE	FIFE DIST	RIMMER	STRATHEARN DIST
RENDELL,-LE	FIFE DIST	RIMMON	INVERNESS DIST
RENFREW	PAISLEY DIST	RIMORE	ROXBURGH DIST
RENISON	GLASGOW DIST	RIND(S)	LINDSAY
RENNICK	RENWICK	RING	CLAN CIAN
RENNIE,-Y	MAC DON CLANRANALD	RINNICK	RENWICK
RENNIE,-Y	RENNIE	RINTOUL	MENTIETH DIST
RENNIE,-Y	SKENE	RIP(P)ON	ABERDEEN DIST
RENNIESTON	ROXBURGH DIST	RIPL(I)E,-Y	MACKINTOSH
RENNOCH	NITHSDALE DIST	RIRIE	MAC DONALD
RENOLD(S)	MAC DON CLANRANALD	RISH	MACKINTOSH
RENSHAW	CALEDONIA TARTAN	RISH	RITCH
RENTA	GLASGOW DIST	RISK(IE),(-Y)	BUCHANAN
RENTON	TWEEDSIDE DIST	RISTON	ROXBURGH DIST
RENWICK	RENWICK	RITCH	MACKINTOSH
RENY	MAC RAE	RITCH	RITCH
RENY	RENNIE	RITCHIE	MACKINTOSH
REOCH	FARQUHARSON	RITCHL(E)Y,-IE	AYRSHIRE DIST
REOCH	MAC DONALD OF SLEAT	RITSON	GALLOWAY DIST
REPER	ABERDEEN DIST	RITTLER	ABERDEEN DIST
RESTON	DUNBAR DIST	RIVIE,-EY	MAC DONALD OF SLEAT
RESTON	TWEEDSIDE DIST	RIX	PERTHSHIRE DIST
RETSON	GALLOWAY DIST	ROACH	ARGYLL DIST
REUEL	FIFE DIST	ROADVILLE	ROXBURGH DIST
REVAN(S)	MAC QUEEN	ROAN	ROWAN
REVEN(S)	MAC QUEEN	ROARK	CALEDONIA TARTAN
REVICH,-K	GLASGOW DIST	ROARK(E)	ULSTER TARTAN
REVIE,-Y	FRASER	ROAST	ABERDEEN DIST
REVIE,-Y	MAC DONALD OF SLEAT	ROB(B)	MAC FARLANE
REW	ANGUS DIST	ROB(B)	ROBERTSON
REW	MONTROSE DIST	ROB(B)	STEWART OF APPIN
REWCASTLE	ROXBURGH DIST	ROB(I)SON	ROBERTSON
REWELL	FIFE DIST	ROBBIE,-Y	ROBERTSON
REYBURN	RAEBURN		

NAME	TARTAN	NAME	TARTAN
ROBBINS	ROBBINS	ROSS	ROSE
ROBBINS	ROBERTSON	ROSS	ROSS
ROBERSON	ROBERTSON	ROSSE(Y)	MAC LEOD OF RAASAY
ROBERTON	STRATHCLYDE DIST	ROSSIE,-(E)Y	MAC LEOD OF RAASAY
ROBERTS	ROBERTSON	ROSSITER	GALLOWAY DIST
ROBERTSON	ROBERTSON	ROSWELL	EDINBURGH DIST
ROBERTSON	ROBERTSON OF KINDEACE	ROTHESAY	ROTHESAY DIST
ROBESON	ROBERTSON	ROTHNIE,-NEY	ABERDEEN DIST
ROBINS	ROBBINS	ROUGH	STRATHCLYDE DIST
ROBINSON	GUNN	ROUGHAN	CLAN CIAN
ROBINSON	ROBBINS	ROUGHHEAD	TWEEDSIDE DIST
ROBINSON	ROBERTSON	ROULL	TURNBULL
ROBISON	GUNN	ROULSTON	ULSTER TARTAN
ROBISON	ROBERTSON	ROURKE	ULSTER TARTAN
ROBSON	GUNN	ROUSAY	MAC LEOD OF RAASAY
ROBSON	TYNESIDE DIST	ROUST	RUST
ROCHE	EDINBURGH DIST	ROUTLEDGE	ROXBURGH DIST
ROCK	EDINBURGH DIST	ROW(E)	LENNOX DIST
ROCKALL	NITHSDALE DIST	ROWAN(D)	ROWAN
ROD(D)AN	NITHSDALE DIST	ROWAT(T)	GLASGOW DIST
RODDAM	BERWICK DIST	ROWEN,-IN(S)	ROWAN
RODDIE	INVERNESS DIST	ROWHAN	CLAN CIAN
RODDY,-IE	GALLOWAY DIST	ROWLAND	INVERNESS DIST
RODEAK	GALLOWAY DIST	ROWLAND	ROXBURGH DIST
RODERICK	MAC DONALD	ROWNIE,-Y	INVERNESS DIST
RODGER(S)	ANGUS DIST	ROWSAY	MAC LEOD OF RAASAY
RODGIE,-Y	ABERDEEN DIST	ROWZIE	MAC LEOD OF RAASAY
RODMAN	AYRSHIRE DIST	ROXBORO	ROXBURGH DIST
ROE	ARGYLL DIST	ROXBURGH	ROXBURGH DIST
ROGER(S)	ANGUS DIST	ROY	MAC GILLIVRAY
ROGERSON	ABERDEEN DIST	ROY(E)	ROBERTSON
ROGIE	INVERNESS DIST	ROYDEN	PAISLEY DIST
ROLAN	CONNACHT TARTAN	ROYDS	FIFE DIST
ROLL	ABERDEEN DIST	ROYLE	CALEDONIA TARTAN
ROLLAN(D)	ABERDEEN DIST	RUANE	CONNACHT TARTAN
ROLLIN(G)S	ROXBURGH DIST	RUARK(E)	CALEDONIA TARTAN
ROLLO	ROLLO	RUBISLAW	SKENE
ROLLOCK,-H	ROLLO	RUCASTLE	ROXBURGH DIST
ROLSON	ANGUS DIST	RUCKBIE,-Y	ROXBURGH DIST
ROLSTON	ULSTER TARTAN	RUD(D)IMAN	ABERDEEN DIST
ROMAIN	TWEEDSIDE DIST	RUDDERFORD	ROXBURGH DIST
ROMAN(S)	ROXBURGH DIST	RUDDOCH	ABERDEEN DIST
ROMANES	ROXBURGH DIST	RUDDOCK	GALLOWAY DIST
ROME	GALLOWAY DIST	RUDGE	INVERNESS DIST
RON(N)AN	LOCHABER DIST	RUFF	STRATHCLYDE DIST
RON(N)EY	TWEEDSIDE DIST	RUFFUS	TWEEDSIDE DIST
RONALD	MAC DON OF KEPPOCH	RUGG	ABERDEEN DIST
RONALDSON	MAC DON OF KEPPOCH	RUHL	TURNBULL
RONAN	CONNACHT TARTAN	RULE	TURNBULL
RONEY	GALLOWAY DIST	RULSTON(E)	ARGYLL DIST
ROOK(E)S	SUTHERLAND DIST	RUMBOLD	STRATHSPEY DIST
ROOM(E)	ARGYLL DIST	RUMGAY	FIFE DIST
ROONEY	ULSTER TARTAN	RUNCI(E)MAN	ROXBURGH DIST
ROOPTON	AYRSHIRE DIST	RUNCIE,-Y	BUCHAN DIST
ROOT(E)	GALLOWAY DIST	RUNNELL(S)	MAC DON CLANRANALD
ROPER	ABERDEEN DIST	RUNNICK	RENWICK
RORI(E)SON	MAC DONALD	RUPTON	AYRSHIRE DIST
RORI(E)SON	MAC LAREN	RUSK	BUCHANAN
RORI(E)SON	MAC RORY	RUSKIE,-Y	PERTHSHIRE DIST
RORIE,-Y	MAC DONALD	RUSKIN	BUCHANAN
RORIE,-Y	MAC LAREN	RUSLAND	CALEDONIA TARTAN
RORIE,-Y	MAC RORY	RUSSEL(L)	CUMMING
ROSE	ROSE	RUSSEL(L)	RUSSELL
ROSEWELL	EDINBURGH DIST	RUST(E)	ABERDEEN DIST
ROSIE,-EY	CAITHNESS TARTAN	RUST(E)	RUST
ROSLIN,-YN	EDINBURGH DIST	RUTHERFORD,-URD	ROXBURGH DIST

NAME	TARTAN	NAME	TARTAN
RUTHERGLEN	STRATHCLYDE DIST	SAYDE	MAC QUEEN
RUTHVEN	RUTHVEN	SCABIE,-EY	MAC KAY
RUTLEDGE	ROXBURGH DIST	SCADDAN	GALLOWAY DIST
RUTLEDGE (Irish)	ULSTER TARTAN	SCADLOCK	PAISLEY DIST
RUXTON	ABERDEEN DIST	SCALES	GALLOWAY DIST
RYBURN	RAEBURN	SCALLIE,-Y	ARGYLL DIST
RYDER	DUNDEE DIST	SCALPIE,-Y	MAC LEOD
RYE	ABERDEEN DIST	SCANLAN,-ON	CLAN CIAN
RYMORE,-OUR	TWEEDSIDE DIST	SCANNELL	CONNACHT TARTAN
RYND(S)	LINDSAY	SCARLETT	NITHSDALE DIST
RYRIE	MAC DONALD	SCARTH	CAITHNESS TARTAN
RYSLAND	AYRSHIRE DIST	SCENSE	SKENE
RYSTO(U)N	ROXBURGH DIST	SCHAW(E)	SHAW OF TORDARROCH
		SCHENSE	SKENE
		SCHOOLBREAD	FIFE DIST
		SCIATER	SINCLAIR
		SCLATER	ABERDEEN DIST
# S		SCOB(B)IE,-Y	MAC KAY
		SCOBBE	MAC KAY
		SCOLLAY,-EY	CAITHNESS TARTAN
SA(U)CHIE	CRIEFF DIST	SCONE	PERTHSHIRE DIST
SABISTON	CAITHNESS TARTAN	SCOON	PERTHSHIRE DIST
SAD(D)LER	ROXBURGH DIST	SCORGIE,-Y	ABERDEEN DIST
SADLIER	ROXBURGH DIST	SCOTLAND	ANGUS DIST
SAFELY	GALLOWAY DIST	SCOTT	SCOTT
SAGE	FIFE DIST	SCOTTLAWN	ANGUS DIST
SAICH	CALEDONIA TARTAN	SCOUGAL(L)	MUSSELBURGH DIST
SALKELD	TYNESIDE DIST	SCOULER	GLASGOW DIST
SALKRIG(E)	TWEEDSIDE DIST	SCRIBNER	CLARK
SALMON(D)	PERTHSHIRE DIST	SCRIMGEOUR	SCRYMGEOUR
SALTER	MUSSELBURGH DIST	SCRIMMIGER	SCRYMGEOUR
SALTO(U)N	FRASER	SCRIV(E)NER	CLARK
SAM(P)SON	STRATHCLYDE DIST	SCROGGIE,-Y	DUNDEE DIST
SAMUEL	MAC DONALD	SCROGGINS	DUNDEE DIST
SAND(E)MAN	PERTHSHIRE DIST	SCROGGS	ROXBURGH DIST
SAND(I)LANDS	DOUGLAS	SCROLL	CLARK
SAND(S)	FIFE DIST	SCRULTON	ABERDEEN DIST
SANDALL	ROXBURGH DIST	SCRYMGEOUR	SCRYMGEOUR
SANDER(S)	MAC ALISTER	SCULLIE,-Y	CAITHNESS TARTAN
SANDER(S)	MAC DONELL GLENGARRY	SCUNY	FIFE DIST
SANDERSON	MAC ALISTER	SEARLE(S)	DUNDEE DIST
SANDERSON	MAC DONELL GLENGARRY	SEAT	SHAW OF TORDARROCH
SANDESON	MAC ALISTER	SEAT(T)ER	CAITHNESS TARTAN
SANDESON	MAC DONELL GLENGARRY	SEATH	SHAW OF TORDARROCH
SANDFORD	FIFE DIST	SEATON	SETON
SANDIE	MAC DONELL GLENGARRY	SEATOR	CAITHNESS TARTAN
SANDILANDS	DALZELL	SEATTER	CAITHNESS TARTAN
SANDIN	DOUGLAS	SEELER	ROXBURGH DIST
SANDISON	GUNN	SEGGIE,-Y	FIFE DIST
SANDLIN,-AN(S)	DOUGLAS	SEIRVIN(E)	GLASGOW DIST
SANDOCK	EDINBURGH DIST	SELBOURNE	STRATHSPEY DIST
SANDS	FIFE DIST	SELBY,-IE	TWEEDSIDE DIST
SANER	EDINBURGH DIST	SELBY,-IE	TYNESIDE DIST
SANG	ABERDEEN DIST	SELCRAIG	GALLOWAY DIST
SANGSTER	ABERDEEN DIST	SELKIRK	ROXBURGH DIST
SANKIE,-Y	ROXBURGH DIST	SELKIRK	SELKIRK
SANQUHAR	AYRSHIRE DIST	SELLAR(S),-ER(S)	ABERDEEN DIST
SAUCER	STIRLING DIST	SELLAR(S),-ER(S)	SELLAR
SAUNDERS	MAC ALISTER	SELVIN	GLASGOW DIST
SAUNDERS	MAC DONELL GLENGARRY	SEMPLE,-ILL	PAISLEY DIST
SAUSER	STIRLING DIST	SENIOR	ANGUS DIST
SAVAGE	ULSTER TARTAN	SERJEANT	GRAHAM
SAVIDGE	EDINBURGH DIST	SERLE(S)	PERTHSHIRE DIST
SAWYEAR	SAWYER	SERVICE	MENTIETH DIST
SAWYER	GLASGOW DIST	SERVICE	SERVICE
SAWYER	SAWYER	SESSOR	DUNBAR DIST

NAME	TARTAN	NAME	TARTAN
SETH	SHAW OF TORDARROCH	SHORT(E)	STIRLING DIST
SETON	SETON	SHORTER	AYRSHIRE DIST
SEWALL,-ELL	ROXBURGH DIST	SHORTHOUSE	FIFE DIST
SEYBOLD	FIFE DIST	SHORTREED	ROXBURGH DIST
SEYMORE	DUNDEE DIST	SHORTRIDGE	NITHSDALE DIST
SHAD	TYNESIDE DIST	SHOWAN,-EN	ABERDEEN DIST
SHADDON,-EN	GLASGOW DIST	SHUME	HOME
SHADE	EDINBURGH DIST	SHUNGER	ANGUS DIST
SHADFORTH	CALEDONIA TARTAN	SHUTTARD	CALEDONIA TARTAN
SHAFTO(E)	EDINBURGH DIST	SIBBALD	FIFE DIST
SHAK(E)LOCK	ANGUS DIST	SIBBALL	FIFE DIST
SHAKLE	BUCHAN DIST	SIBBULD	FIFE DIST
SHALE	EDINBURGH DIST	SIDIE,-EY	PERTHSHIRE DIST
SHALLCROSS	CAITHNESS TARTAN	SIDNEY	CLAN CIAN
SHAND	ABERDEEN DIST	SIEVEWRIGHT	MACKINTOSH
SHANK(S)	EDINBURGH DIST	SILK(E)	CLAN CIAN
SHANLIN	CAITHNESS TARTAN	SILLARS,-ERS	ARRAN DIST
SHANNEN,-ON	MAC DONALD	SILVER	ANGUS DIST
SHARKEY	ULSTER TARTAN	SILVERTON	FIFE DIST
SHARON	INVERNESS DIST	SILVESTER	ST. ANDREWS DIST
SHARP(E)	MAC DONALD	SILVIE,-Y	ANGUS DIST
SHARP(E)	STUART OF BUTE	SIM(E)(S)	FRASER
SHAW	SHAW OF TORDARROCH	SIM(E)SON	FRASER
SHAY	ARGYLL DIST	SIMMINGTON	STRATHCLYDE DIST
SHEA	LORNE DIST	SIMON(S)	FRASER
SHEACH	SHAW OF TORDARROCH	SIMOND(S)	FRASER
SHEAD	CAMPBELL	SIMONDSON	FRASER
SHEARER,-AR	ABERDEEN DIST	SIMPKINS	FRASER
SHED	CAMPBELL	SIMPSON	CAMPBELL-SIMPSON
SHEDDEN,-AN,-ON	AYRSHIRE DIST	SIMPSON	FRASER
SHEED	EDINBURGH DIST	SINCLAIR	SINCLAIR
SHEEDY	CLAN CIAN	SINCLARE	SINCLAIR
SHELDRICK	ARGYLL DIST	SINGLETON	EDINBURGH DIST
SHELLIE,-EY	STRATHSPEY DIST	SINKLER	SINCLAIR
SHELMERDINE	GALLOWAY DIST	SINTON	GALLOWAY DIST
SHENNAN	MAC DONALD	SIROWAN	GRAHAM
SHEPHERD,-ARD	ROXBURGH DIST	SIVAS,-ES	ABERDEEN DIST
SHEPLIE,-Y	TYNESIDE DIST	SIVEWRIGHT	MACKINTOSH
SHERAR,-ER	ABERDEEN DIST	SIWES	EDINBURGH DIST
SHERET	ABERDEEN DIST	SKAE	CAITHNESS TARTAN
SHERIDAN	ULSTER TARTAN	SKAINS	SKENE
SHERIF(F)SON	DUNBAR DIST	SKAIR	ABERDEEN DIST
SHERLAW	STRATHCLYDE DIST	SKEA	CAITHNESS TARTAN
SHERRAT(T)	ABERDEEN DIST	SKEAN(S)	SKENE
SHERRIE,-Y	MAC KINNON	SKED(D)	MUSSELBURGH DIST
SHERRIF(F)(S)	ABERDEEN DIST	SKEEN(E)(S)	SKENE
SHERWIN	ABERDEEN DIST	SKEG(G)IE,-Y	GLASGOW DIST
SHEWAN,-EN	ABERDEEN DIST	SKELDON	AYRSHIRE DIST
SHEY	ARGYLL DIST	SKELLIE,-Y	GALLOWAY DIST
SHIACH	SHAW OF TORDARROCH	SKENE	SKENE
SHIEL(L)(S)	ROXBURGH DIST	SKEOCH	AYRSHIRE DIST
SHIELD(S)	EDINBURGH DIST	SKERVINE	IRVINE
SHIERLAW	STRATHCLYDE DIST	SKEY	STRATHCLYDE DIST
SHILESTON	NITHSDALE DIST	SKIDDIE,-Y	MAC LEOD
SHILLINGLAW	TWEEDSIDE DIST	SKIMMING	GALLOWAY DIST
SHIPLAW	TWEEDSIDE DIST	SKINNER	MAC GREGOR
SHIPLEY,-LY	TYNESIDE DIST	SKIPPER	ABERDEEN DIST
SHIRAR	AYRSHIRE DIST	SKRIMMIGER	SCRYMGEOUR
SHIRLAW	STRATHCLYDE DIST	SLACK	ROXBURGH DIST
SHIRLEY	STRATHCLYDE DIST	SLAINS	HAY
SHIRRAS	ABERDEEN DIST	SLAT(T)ER	ABERDEEN DIST
SHIRREF(S)	ABERDEEN DIST	SLATTERY	CLAN CIAN
SHISH	CALEDONIA TARTAN	SLAY	ABERDEEN DIST
SHIVAS,-ES	ABERDEEN DIST	SLEIGH	ABERDEEN DIST
SHIVES	ABERDEEN DIST	SLESSER,-OR	ABERDEEN DIST
SHONER	FIFE DIST	SLIGHT	EDINBURGH DIST
SHONIE,-EY	FIFE DIST	SLIMON	DUNDEE DIST

NAME	TARTAN	NAME	TARTAN
SLOAN(E)	GALLOWAY DIST	SPAD(D)EN	ABERDEEN DIST
SLORA	DAVIDSON	SPAIN	EDINBURGH DIST
SLORIE,-Y	DAVIDSON	SPALDING	MURRAY
SLOSS	AYRSHIRE DIST	SPANG	GLASGOW DIST
SLOVEWRIGHT	PERTHSHIRE DIST	SPANKIE,-Y	DUNDEE DIST
SLOWAN	NITHSDALE DIST	SPARK(E)(S)	ABERDEEN DIST
SLYMON	DUNDEE DIST	SPE(E)DEN,-IN	FIFE DIST
SMA(I)RT	MAC KENZIE	SPEDDIN(G)	GALA WATER DIST
SMAIL	MURRAY	SPEED	ANGUS DIST
SMALE	MURRAY	SPEEDIE,-Y	FIFE DIST
SMALL	MURRAY	SPEID	ANGUS DIST
SMALLEY	GLASGOW DIST	SPEIRS	STIRLING DIST
SMALLWOOD	PAISLEY DIST	SPEL(L)MAN	CONNACHT TARTAN
SMART	MAC KENZIE	SPELAINE	CLAN CIAN
SMEALL	MURRAY	SPELLAN	CLAN CIAN
SMEATON	SMEATON	SPELLMAN (Irish)	CLAN CIAN
SMELLIE,-Y	STRATHCLYDE DIST	SPENCE	MAC DUFF
SMETON	SMEATON	SPENCE	SPENS
SMIBERT	EDINBURGH DIST	SPENCER	SPENCER
SMILLIE,-EY	PAISLEY DIST	SPENS	MAC DUFF
SMISON	CALEDONIA TARTAN	SPENS	SPENS
SMITH	CLAN CHATTAN	SPERLING	PAISLEY DIST
SMITH	GOW	SPERLINS	PAISLEY DIST
SMITH	MAC PHERSON	SPIERS	BOYD
SMITH (Hebridean)	SMITH	SPILEMAN	ABERDEEN DIST
SMOLLETT	LENNOX DIST	SPILMAN	CLAN CIAN
SMYLIE,-EY	ARGYLL DIST	SPINK(S)	ABERDEEN DIST
SMYTH	GOW	SPIRLING	PAISLEY DIST
SMYTH	MAC PHERSON	SPITTAL,-EL,-LE	BUCHANAN
SNADDEN	TWEEDSIDE DIST	SPOLLEN	CLAN CIAN
SNAPE	STRATHCLYDE DIST	SPOORS	GLASGOW DIST
SNEDDAN,-EN,-ON	TWEEDSIDE DIST	SPORRAN	MAC DONALD
SNELL	GLASGOW DIST	SPOT(I)SWOOD	TWEEDSIDE DIST
SNODDIE,-Y	CAITHNESS TARTAN	SPOTT(S)	DUNBAR DIST
SNODGRASS	IRVINE	SPOWATT	FIFE DIST
SNODGRASS	SNODGRASS	SPRING(ER)	ABERDEEN DIST
SNOWDEN,-ON	TWEEDSIDE DIST	SPROAT	GALLOWAY DIST
SNYPE	GLASGOW DIST	SPROTT	GALLOWAY DIST
SOFFLEY	NITHSDALE DIST	SPROUL	MAC FARLANE
SOFTLY	GALLOWAY DIST	SPROUNT	ANGUS DIST
SOM(M)ERS	LINDSAY	SPRUELL	MAC FARLANE
SOM(M)ERVILLE	SOMERVILLE	SPRUNT	FIFE DIST
SOMYR(S)	LINDSAY	SQUAIR	FIFE DIST
SONDAILANDS	DOUGLAS	SQUIRE	FIFE DIST
SONGSTER	ABERDEEN DIST	ST. CLAIR	SINCLAIR
SORBIE,-Y	GALLOWAY DIST	ST. MARTIN	TYNESIDE DIST
SORLEYSON	AYRSHIRE DIST	STABLE(S)	ANGUS DIST
SORLIE,-EY	CAMERON	STACK	MAC DONALD OF SLEAT
SORLIE,-EY	LAMONT	STACK	MAC DONALD OF STAFFA
SORLIE,-EY	MAC DONALD	STAFFIN	GALLOWAY DIST
SOTHERAN	TYNESIDE DIST	STAIG	NITHSDALE DIST
SOTHERN	TYNESIDE DIST	STAIN	STRATHCLYDE DIST
SOUDER	CARRICK DIST	STAINES	STEPHENSON
SOUDIE,-Y	INVERNESS DIST	STAIR(S)	AYRSHIRE DIST
SOULE	DOUGLAS	STALKER	MAC FARLANE
SOUNESS	TWEEDSIDE DIST	STALKER	MAC GREGOR
SOUPER	ABERDEEN DIST	STANFIELD	EDINBURGH DIST
SOUTAR	CARRICK DIST	STANFORD	GLASGOW DIST
SOUTER	NITHSDALE DIST	STANHOPE	TWEEDSIDE DIST
SOUTHERLAND	SUTHERLAND	STANLEY	EDINBURGH DIST
SOUTHHOUSE	EDINBURGH DIST	STAPLETON	TYNESIDE DIST
SOUTHLAND	SUTHERLAND DIST	STARK	ROBERTSON
SOUTHWICK	GALLOWAY DIST	STARRET(T)	AYRSHIRE DIST
SOWDEN,-AN	ROXBURGH DIST	STATER	BERWICK DIST
SOWNESS	TWEEDSIDE DIST	STAVERT	TWEEDSIDE DIST
SOWTER	GALLOWAY DIST	STEDMAN	ANGUS DIST

NAME	TARTAN	NAME	TARTAN
STEEDMAN	ANGUS DIST	STRANACK	ABERDEEN DIST
STEEL(E)	TWEEDSIDE DIST	STRANG(E)	ANGUS DIST
STEEN(S)	STEPHENSON	STRANGE(R)	MAC GREGOR
STEENSON	STEPHENSON	STRAT(T)ON	EDINBURGH DIST
STEILL	TWEEDSIDE DIST	STRATH	ABERDEEN DIST
STEIN(S)	STEPHENSON	STRATHARN	STRATHEARN DIST
STENHOUSE	BRUCE	STRATHEARN	STRATHEARN DIST
STEPHENS	STEPHENSON	STRATHENDRY	FIFE DIST
STEPHENSON	STEPHENSON	STRATHIE,-Y	CRIEFF DIST
STERET(T)	AYRSHIRE DIST	STRATHIE,-Y	PERTHSHIRE DIST
STERN(S)	GLASGOW DIST	STRATOUN	EDINBURGH DIST
STERRETT	DOUGLAS	STRAUGHAN	MAR DIST
STERRIT(T)	AYRSHIRE DIST	STRAWN	MAR DIST
STEUART	STEWART	STRICKLAND(S)	DUNBAR DIST
STEVENS	STEPHENSON	STRICKLAND(S)	PAISLEY DIST
STEVENSON	STEPHENSON	STRICKLE(R)	GLASGOW DIST
STEVENSON	STEVENSON	STRINGER	MAC GREGOR
STEWARD	STEWART	STROAK	STURROCK
STEWART	STEWART (CLAN)	STROCK	STURROCK
STEWART	STEWART OF APPIN	STROKE	STURROCK
STEWART	STEWART OF ARDSHIEL	STRON	MAR DIST
STEWART	STEWART OF ATHOLL	STRONACH	STRATHSPEY DIST
STEWART	STEWART OF FINGASK	STROTHER	TWEEDSIDE DIST
STEWART	STEWART OF GALLOWAY	STROWAN,-EN	GRAHAM
STEWART	STEWART OF URRAND	STROYAN	GALLOWAY DIST
STILL	MUSSELBURGH DIST	STRUTHERS	TWEEDSIDE DIST
STILLIE,-Y	MUSSELBURGH DIST	STUART	STEWART
STINSON	STEPHENSON	STUART	STUART OF BUTE
STINSON	STINSON	STUPERT	AYRSHIRE DIST
STIRIE,-EY	AYRSHIRE DIST	STURGEON	MAXWELL
STIRK(S)	FIFE DIST	STURRICK	ANGUS DIST
STIRLING	STIRLING DIST	STURRICK	STURROCK
STIRRAT	AYRSHIRE DIST	STURROCK	ANGUS DIST
STIRTON	FIFE DIST	STURROCK	STURROCK
STITCHEL	ROXBURGH DIST	SUITOR	CARRICK DIST
STITT	ETTRICK DIST	SULLIVAN	CLAN CIAN
STIVEN	STEPHENSON	SUMMERHILL	TWEEDSIDE DIST
STIVENSON	STEPHENSON	SUMMERS	LINDSAY
STOB	PERTHSHIRE DIST	SUMNER	LINDSAY
STOB(B)IE,-Y	TWEEDSIDE DIST	SUMPTER	PERTHSHIRE DIST
STOBART	TYNESIDE DIST	SUNDERLAND	TYNESIDE DIST
STOBHILL	EGLINTON DIST	SUSTER	PAISLEY DIST
STOBIE,-Y	MAC KAY	SUTHERLAND	SUTHERLAND
STOBO	GLASGOW DIST	SUTHERLINE	SUTHERLAND
STODDART,-ERT	GALLOWAY DIST	SUTTER	CARRICK DIST
STOKER,-AR	ABERDEEN DIST	SUTTIE,-(E)Y	GRANT
STOLCARE	MAC GREGOR	SUTTON	GALLOWAY DIST
STONE	CLAN CIAN	SWAN(N)	GUNN
STONE	ROXBURGH DIST	SWAN(N)	MAC QUEEN
STONIER	INVERNESS DIST	SWANNIE,-EY	GUNN
STONYER	INVERNESS DIST	SWANSON	GUNN
STOR(R)Y,-IE	OGILVIE	SWANSTON(E)	EDINBURGH DIST
STORER	CULLODEN DIST	SWANTON	EGLINTON DIST
STORM	CULLODEN DIST	SWEENIE,-Y	GUNN
STORMONT	FIFE DIST	SWEENIE,-Y	MAC QUEEN
STORRAR	CULLODEN DIST	SWELLIE,-Y	GLASGOW DIST
STORRIE,-EY	OGILVIE	SWENSON	GUNN
STORY	TYNESIDE DIST	SWINBURNE	TYNESIDE DIST
STOTT	ABERDEEN DIST	SWINFORD	GLASGOW DIST
STOW(E)	EDINBURGH DIST	SWINGER	CALEDONIA TARTAN
STRACHAN	DEESIDE DIST	SWINHOE	AYRSHIRE DIST
STRACHAN	MAR DIST	SWINTON	TWEEDSIDE DIST
STRACHAN	STRATHSPEY DIST	SWIT(E)	EDINBURGH DIST
STRACKAN,-EN	MAR DIST	SWORD	PERTHSHIRE DIST
STRADE	ABERDEEN DIST	SYARE	GLASGOW DIST
STRAITON	PERTHSHIRE DIST	SYDE	FIFE DIST
STRALOCH	ABERDEEN DIST	SYDIE,-Y	PERTHSHIRE DIST

NAME	TARTAN	NAME	TARTAN
SYLVESTER	ST. ANDREWS DIST	TAVNEY	CLAN CIAN
SYLVIE	ANGUS DIST	TAW(E)S	FARQUHARSON
SYM(E)(S)	FRASER	TAWES(S)ON	CAMPBELL
SYM(M)ER	LINDSAY	TAWSESON	MAC TAVISH
SYMINGTON	DOUGLAS	TAY(E)S	FARQUHARSON
SYMON(S)	FRASER	TAYLOR,-ER	CAMERON
SYMPSON	FRASER	TAYLOR,-ER	TAYLOR
		TAYMAN	PERTHSHIRE DIST
		TEACHER	LENNOX DIST
T		TEAL(L)ING	ANGUS DIST
		TEALL	GORDON
		TEALL	TEALL
		TEDDLIE,-LY	ARGYLL DIST
TABURNER	EDINBURGH DIST	TEES	GLASGOW DIST
TACKET	PERTHSHIRE DIST	TEETER(S)	MAC GREGOR
TAF(F)EY	CONNACHT TARTAN	TELFER	ROXBURGH DIST
TAGGART	ROSS	TELFER	STRATHCLYDE DIST
TAIG	INVERNESS DIST	TELFORD	STRATHCLYDE DIST
TAILOR	CAMERON	TELLER	DUNBAR DIST
TAILOR	TAYLOR	TEMAN	ABERDEEN DIST
TAILYOUR	CAMERON	TEMPLE	MUSSELBURGH DIST
TAILYOUR	TAYLOR	TEMPLEAND	GALLOWAY DIST
TAIR	MAC TIER	TEMPLEMAN	EDINBURGH DIST
TAIT(E)	EDINBURGH DIST	TEMPLETON	AYRSHIRE DIST
TALBERT	ABERDEEN DIST	TEND(E)MAN	PERTHSHIRE DIST
TALFER	STRATHCLYDE DIST	TENDER	ANGUS DIST
TALLIDEFF	ABERDEEN DIST	TENLER	DUNBAR DIST
TALLIE,-EY	EDINBURGH DIST	TENNANT	STIRLING DIST
TAM	MAC THOMAS	TENNANT	TENNANT
TAM(E)SON	MAC THOMAS	TENNENT	STIRLING DIST
TAM(E)SON	MACKINTOSH	TENNENT	TENNANT
TAM(E)SON	STRATHSPEY DIST	TENNIE,-Y	TENNANT
TAM(M)ANY	CLAN CIAN	TERRAS,-IS	INVERNESS DIST
TAME	EDINBURGH DIST	TERRELL	MACKINTOSH
TAMMES	MAC THOMAS	TERRIS	INVERNESS DIST
TAMMES	MACKINTOSH	TERRY	MONTROSE DIST
TAMMIE,-Y	MAC THOMAS	TERSE	ABERDEEN DIST
TANDERSON	CALEDONIA TARTAN	TERSIE,-Y	ABERDEEN DIST
TANKARD,-ERD	CALEDONIA TARTAN	TESTARD	ABERDEEN DIST
TANNACH	CUMBERNAULD DIST	TESTOR,-ER	ABERDEEN DIST
TANNAHILL	AYRSHIRE DIST	TEUN(I)ON	BUCHAN DIST
TANNER	TWEEDSIDE DIST	TEVIOTDALE	ROXBURGH DIST
TANNIEL(L)	MAC DONELL GLENGARRY	TEWNION	BUCHAN DIST
TANNIS	PERTHSHIRE DIST	THACKER	ABERDEEN DIST
TANNOCK,-H	AYRSHIRE DIST	THAIL	DALZELL
TANNYHILL	AYRSHIRE DIST	THAIN(E)	STIRLING DIST
TANPARD(E)	GLASGOW DIST	THAIN(E)	THAIN
TARBERT	CAMPBELL	THALL(I)ON	FIFE DIST
TARLACHSON	MAC KENZIE	THANYN(E)	STIRLING DIST
TARLASON	MAC KENZIE	THANYN(E)	THAIN
TARPEY	CONNACHT TARTAN	THAW(E)(S)	ABERDEEN DIST
TARRAS	INVERNESS DIST	THAYN(E)	THAIN
TARRELL	ROSS	THAYNE	STIRLING DIST
TARRELL,-ILL	MACKINTOSH	THEMAN	ABERDEEN DIST
TARVES,-IS	BUCHAN DIST	THEOBALD	ST. ANDREWS DIST
TARVETT	FIFE DIST	THIERRY	STIRLING DIST
TARVIT	FIFE DIST	THIN	TWEEDSIDE DIST
TASKER	DUNDEE DIST	THIRD	ABERDEEN DIST
TASKER	TWEEDSIDE DIST	THIRLSTANE,-STON	TWEEDSIDE DIST
TASKILL,-ELL	MAC ASKILL	THOM(P)SON	CAMPBELL
TASKILL,-ELL	MAC LEOD	THOM(P)SON	MAC TAVISH
TASSIE,-Y	GLASGOW DIST	THOM(P)SON	THOMPSON
TASTARD	ABERDEEN DIST	THOM(S)	MAC THOMAS
TATE	EDINBURGH DIST	THOM(S)	MACKINTOSH
TATENEL(L)	ABERDEEN DIST	THOMAS	CAMPBELL
TAVERNER,-OUR	EDINBURGH DIST	THOMAS	MAC THOMAS
		THOMAS	MACKINTOSH

NAME	TARTAN	NAME	TARTAN
THOMAS(S)ON	CAMPBELL	TOMISON	MAC THOMAS
THOMASON	MAC FARLANE	TOMISON	MACKINTOSH
THOMIE,-Y	MAC THOMAS	TOMLIN(E)	LOCH LAGGAN DIST
THOMIE,-Y	MACKINTOSH	TOMSON	MAC THOMAS
THOMLING	GALLOWAY DIST	TONE	ULSTER TARTAN
THOMSON	MAC THOMAS	TONER	MULL DIST
THOMSON	MACKINTOSH	TONER	ULSTER TARTAN
THOMSON	THOMPSON	TONG(U)E	INVERNESS DIST
THORBURN	ROXBURGH DIST	TONNACHIE,-Y	ROBERTSON
THORN(E)SON	GLASGOW DIST	TONNOCH(Y)	ROBERTSON
THORNE	SUTHERLAND DIST	TONSON	FIFE DIST
THORNHILL	NITHSDALE DIST	TOOKE	EDINBURGH DIST
THORNTON	ANGUS DIST	TOOT(E)	GALLOWAY DIST
THORPE	ABERDEEN DIST	TOOTH	TOOTH
THORS	ABERDEEN DIST	TOP(P)	ABERDEEN DIST
THORSKLE	PERTHSHIRE DIST	TOPLADY	TYNESIDE DIST
THOW(E)(S)	ABERDEEN DIST	TOPLESS	INVERNESS DIST
THREFALL	ARGYLL DIST	TOPLIE,-Y	GLASGOW DIST
THRIEPLAND	TWEEDSIDE DIST	TOPLIS	INVERNESS DIST
THRIFT	EDINBURGH DIST	TORBAIN	FIFE DIST
THRIST	LENNOX DIST	TORBETT	CAMPBELL
THROWLESS	ANGUS DIST	TORBURN(E)	GALLOWAY DIST
THYNE	STRATHCLYDE DIST	TORK(E)	MAC LEOD
TIBBERMORE	MULL DIST	TORKIL(D)SON	MAC LEOD
TID(D)Y,-IE	CALEDONIA TARTAN	TORLAN	MAC DONALD OF SLEAT
TILER	DUNBAR DIST	TORMON(D/T)SON	MAC LEOD
TILLERY	ABERDEEN DIST	TORMONT,-D	MAC LEOD
TILLIE,-Y	TWEEDSIDE DIST	TORN	ABERDEEN DIST
TILLMAN	TYNESIDE DIST	TORN(E)BULL	TURNBULL
TILLOTSON	INVERNESS DIST	TORR	FIFE DIST
TIMMONS	TWEEDSIDE DIST	TORRANCE	EDINBURGH DIST
TIMPSON	INVERNESS DIST	TORRENCE	EDINBURGH DIST
TIN(E)DALL	TYNESIDE DIST	TORRENS	CLAN CIAN
TINDELL,-LE	ANGUS DIST	TORRIE,-Y	CAMPBELL OF CAWDOR
TINKLER	PERTHSHIRE DIST	TOSH	MACKINTOSH
TINLIN(E)	ROXBURGH DIST	TOSHACH	MACKINTOSH
TINMAN	PAISLEY DIST	TOUCH(E)	ABERDEEN DIST
TINNING	NITHSDALE DIST	TOUGH,-Y	ABERDEEN DIST
TINNISWOOD	ROXBURGH DIST	TOUNG	INVERNESS DIST
TINNOCK	STRATHCLYDE DIST	TOURNER	LAMONT
TINNON	BUCHAN DIST	TOWARD,-T	LAMONT
TINSLIE,-LY	CALEDONIA TARTAN	TOWER	ABERDEEN DIST
TINSMAN	AYRSHIRE DIST	TOWERS	EDINBURGH DIST
TINTO	STRATHCLYDE DIST	TOWIE	BARCLAY
TIRWIT(T)	TYNESIDE DIST	TOWN(S)	EDINBURGH DIST
TIVERTON	FIFE DIST	TOWNEND	INVERNESS DIST
TOBBERMORE	MULL DIST	TOWRIE	ARGYLL DIST
TOCHER	ABERDEEN DIST	TOWSON	MAC TAVISH
TOCK	EDINBURGH DIST	TOWSON	MAC THOMAS
TOD(D)	GORDON	TOWSON	MACKINTOSH
TODDIE,-Y	EGLINTON DIST	TOYLE	PERTHSHIRE DIST
TODRICK	EDINBURGH DIST	TRABOUN	TWEEDSIDE DIST
TODSHALL,-ELL	EDINBURGH DIST	TRACEY	CLAN CIAN
TOFTS	ROXBURGH DIST	TRAIL(L)	FIFE DIST
TOISH	MACKINTOSH	TRAIN	MAC DONALD
TOLBERT	ABERDEEN DIST	TRAINER,-OR	FIFE DIST
TOLLER,-AR	GLASGOW DIST	TRAQUIR	TWEEDSIDE DIST
TOLLERAN	CONNACHT TARTAN	TRASEY	CLAN CIAN
TOLLIE,-EY	BARCLAY	TRAYLE	ABERDEEN DIST
TOLLUM	MAC LEOD	TREBUN(E)	TWEEDSIDE DIST
TOLME(Y)	MAC LEOD	TREMBLIE,-Y	ANGUS DIST
TOLMIE,-Y	MAC LEOD	TRENANT,-ENT	EDINBURGH DIST
TOM(S)	MAC THOMAS	TRENCH	TWEEDSIDE DIST
TOMELTY	ULSTER TARTAN	TRENT	FIFE DIST
TOMIE,-Y	MAC LEOD	TREVOR	PERTHSHIRE DIST

NAME	TARTAN	NAME	TARTAN
TREW	PERTHSHIRE DIST	TWEED	TWEEDSIDE DIST
TREWIT(T)	TYNESIDE DIST	TWEED(D)ALE	FRASER
TREWMAN	ROXBURGH DIST	TWEED(D)ALE	HAY
TREWNOT	GALLOWAY DIST	TWEEDIE,-Y	FRASER
TRICE	DALZELL	TWEEDMAN	BERWICK DIST
TRICKETT	CAITHNESS TARTAN	TWINDALE	PAISLEY DIST
TRIMBLE	TURNBULL	TWORT	ARGYLL DIST
TROD(D)IE,-Y	PERTHSHIRE DIST	TYGART	ROSS
TROLLOPE	PERTHSHIRE DIST	TYGRT	ROSS
TROOP(E)	GORDON	TYLER	DUNBAR DIST
TROTTER	EDINBURGH DIST	TYNDRUM	TYNDRUM
TROTTER	TWEEDSIDE DIST	TYNEMOUTH	TYNESIDE DIST
TROUP(E)	DOUGLAS	TYNINGHAM(E)	DUNBAR DIST
TROUP(E)	GORDON	TYRE	MAC INTYRE
TRU(E)BULL	TURNBULL	TYREE,-IE	PERTHSHIRE DIST
TRU(E)MAN	ROXBURGH DIST	TYSON	ROXBURGH DIST
TRUBUCK	DALZELL	TYTLER	EDINBURGH DIST
TRUBUL	TURNBULL		
TRUITT	TYNESIDE DIST		
TRUM(M)ELL	TURNBULL		
TRUMBLE	TURNBULL		
TRUMBUL(L)	TURNBULL		
TRUMLAND	CALEDONIA TARTAN		
TRUMPE(N)TON	CALEDONIA TARTAN		

U

NAME	TARTAN	NAME	TARTAN
TRUSTIE,-Y	GALLOWAY DIST	UDNEY,-IE	ABERDEEN DIST
TRUWHITT	TYNESIDE DIST	UDSTON(E)	STRATHCLYDE DIST
TRYWHITT	TYNESIDE DIST	ULBRAND	PAISLEY DIST
TUACH	INVERNESS DIST	ULRICK	SINCLAIR
TUCKETT	TYNESIDE DIST	UMPHRAY,-EY	PERTHSHIRE DIST
TUCKS	BUCHAN DIST	UMPHRAYSON	ABERDEEN DIST
TUDHOPE	ROXBURGH DIST	UNDERWOOD	AYRSHIRE DIST
TUKE	EDINBURGH DIST	UNES	GALLOWAY DIST
TULIBO	ABERDEEN DIST	UNWIN(E)	ROXBURGH DIST
TULL(I)O	ROSS	UR(R)	MAC IVER
TULLAR,-ER	FIFE DIST	UR(R)ICH	MAC PHERSON
TULLEMIE,-Y	MAC LEOD	UR(R)IE,-Y	URQUHART
TULLIDEFF,-PH	ABERDEEN DIST	URCHILL	PERTHSHIRE DIST
TULLIE,-Y	BARCLAY	URCHLE	PERTHSHIRE DIST
TULLIS	FIFE DIST	URE	CAMPBELL
TULLOCH,-K	ROSS	URE	MAC IVER
TUMASON	MAC THOMAS	URIE,-EY	MAC IVER
TUMASON	MACKINTOSH	URQUHART	URQUHART
TUNNOCK	ROXBURGH DIST	URRELL,-ALL	MAC ORRELL
TUNSTALL	HUNTLY DIST	URRIE,-Y	KEITH
TURBETT	LENNOX DIST	URWELL	INVERNESS DIST
TURCAN	FIFE DIST	USDIN,-EN	MAC DONALD
TURFUS	GLASGOW DIST	USHER	ANGUS DIST
TURING	ABERDEEN DIST	UTTERSON	EDINBURGH DIST
TURK(E)	GALLOWAY DIST		
TURNBERRY	TURNBERRY		
TURNBULL	TURNBULL		
TURNER	LAMONT		
TURNET	ROXBURGH DIST		
TURPIE	ANGUS DIST		
TURPIE	TYNESIDE DIST		
TURPIN	ANGUS DIST		

V

NAME	TARTAN	NAME	TARTAN
TURPNEY	CALEDONIA TARTAN	VAIL	CLAN CHATTAN
TURRIFF,-EFF	HAY	VAIL	MAC PHAIL
TURSE	ABERDEEN DIST	VAIR	ROXBURGH DIST
TUSKER	INVERNESS DIST	VALE	GALLOWAY DIST
TUTHILL	STRATHSPEY DIST	VALENTE	LOCHABER DIST
TWAD(D)ELL,-LE	FRASER	VALLANCE	ANGUS DIST
TWAD(D)ELL,-LE	HAY	VALLANCE	FIFE DIST
TWATT	CALEDONIA TARTAN	VALLENTINE,-YNE	ANGUS DIST
TWED(D)ALE	FRASER	VAN(N)	MANX NATIONAL
TWED(D)ALE	HAY	VAN(N)ACH	MANX NATIONAL
TWEDDEL(L)	FRASER	VAN(N)ICH	MANX NATIONAL
		VANCE	GALLOWAY DIST

NAME	TARTAN	NAME	TARTAN
VANNAN,-IN	ANGUS DIST	WALCAR(E)	PERTHSHIRE DIST
VANNAN,-IN	MANX NATIONAL	WALCAR(E)	WALKER
VANS	GALLOWAY DIST	WALCER	WALKER
VARGUS	FERGUSON	WALCH	TWEEDSIDE DIST
VASS	MUNRO	WALDEVE	ROXBURGH DIST
VASS	ROSS	WALDGRAVE	ABERDEEN DIST
VASSAND	CALEDONIA TARTAN	WALDIE,-Y	ROXBURGH DIST
VASSAR,-IR	AYRSHIRE DIST	WALDRON	ROXBURGH DIST
VAUGHN	ABERDEEN DIST	WALES	WALLACE
VAUS(S)	MUSSELBURGH DIST	WALFORD	ROXBURGH DIST
VE(I)TCH	TWEEDSIDE DIST	WALKAR,-OR	WALKER
VEIGH	MAC LEAN OF DUART	WALKER	MAC GREGOR
VEITCH	STRATHSPEY DIST	WALKER	STEWART OF APPIN
VENNAL	ABERDEEN DIST	WALKER	WALKER
VENTERS	FIFE DIST	WALKIN(G)SHAW	PAISLEY DIST
VERDON	VERDON	WALKUP	GALLOWAY DIST
VERE	HOPE-VERE	WALLACE	WALLACE
VERGUS	FERGUSON	WALLACE	WALLACE OF DUNDEE
VERLE	ROXBURGH DIST	WALLACH	ST. ANDREWS DIST
VERNEL	LORNE DIST	WALLET	NITHSDALE DIST
VERNER	EDINBURGH DIST	WALLINGFORD	ROXBURGH DIST
VERNON	CALEDONIA TARTAN	WALLIS	WALLACE
VERT(H)	EDINBURGH DIST	WALLOCH	ST. ANDREWS DIST
VERT(T)Y,-IE	ABERDEEN DIST	WALLRAND	ROXBURGH DIST
VERT(T)Y,-IE	ANGUS DIST	WALLS	WALLACE
VESSIE,-Y	STRATHCLYDE DIST	WALLSEND	BERWICK DIST
VETCH	ROXBURGH DIST	WALLSON	GUNN
VICARS	ROXBURGH DIST	WALLSON	MAC KAY
VICKERMAN	GALLOWAY DIST	WALLSON	WILSON
VICKERS	ROXBURGH DIST	WALPOLE	GLASGOW DIST
VIG(U)ERS	CORNISH TARTAN	WALSH	ROXBURGH DIST
VIGUS	CORNISH TARTAN	WALSIN	GUNN
VILE	GALLOWAY DIST	WALSIN	MAC KAY
VILLIE	HUNTLY DIST	WALSIN	WILSON
VILLIE	MAC WILLIAM	WALSTON	EDINBURGH DIST
VINT	GALLOWAY DIST	WALTER(S)	BUCHANAN
VIPONT(E)	VIPONT	WALTER(S)	FORBES
VOCAT	ABERDEEN DIST	WALTERSON	MAC FARLANE
VOGAN	ROXBURGH DIST	WALTHEW	ROXBURGH DIST
VOLLAR,-ER	ABERDEEN DIST	WALTON	LORNE DIST
VOLUME	ANGUS DIST	WAN(N)S,-CE	ST. ANDREWS DIST
VURICH	MAC PHERSON	WANDERSON	FIFE DIST
VURIST	MAC PHERSON	WANLESS,-ISS	TWEEDSIDE DIST
		WANN	EDINBURGH DIST
		WAR(R)IE,-EY	MAC QUARRIE
		WARD	ROXBURGH DIST
		WARDEN	FIFE DIST
		WARDHAUGH	ROXBURGH DIST
		WARDHAWK,-OOK	GALLOWAY DIST
		WARDLAW	MAXWELL

W

NAME	TARTAN	NAME	TARTAN
WADDEL(L),-LE	EDINBURGH DIST	WARDLE	ABERDEEN DIST
WADDELL	FIFE DIST	WARDRAP	ABERDEEN DIST
WADDIE,-Y	ROXBURGH DIST	WARDROP(E)	ABERDEEN DIST
WADKINS	BUCHANAN	WARDROP(ER)	FIFE DIST
WADKINS	FORBES	WARE(S)	WEIR
WADSWORTH(ER)	BUCHAN DIST	WARIN	LENNOX DIST
WAFERER	STRATHCLYDE DIST	WARINER	GLASGOW DIST
WAGGERALL,-ELL	WAGGERALL	WARK	TWEEDSIDE DIST
WAGHORN	LENNOX DIST	WARNER	GLASGOW DIST
WAID(E)	FARQUHARSON	WARNES	LENNOX DIST
WAID(E)	MAC DONALD	WARNOCK,-H	GLASGOW DIST
WAIT(E)	FARQUHARSON	WARRACK	ABERDEEN DIST
WAIT(E)	MAC DONALD	WARRAND	INVERNESS DIST
WAKE	GALLOWAY DIST	WARREN	FIFE DIST
WAKELIN	FIFE DIST	WARRENDER	FIFE DIST
WAKERIE,-Y	ANGUS DIST	WARRICK,-H	ABERDEEN DIST
WAKERS	WALKER	WARROCK	ABERDEEN DIST

120

NAME	TARTAN	NAME	TARTAN
WARTLEY,-IE	AYRSHIRE DIST	WELLAND(S)	ANGUS DIST
WARWICK	GALLOWAY DIST	WELLINGTON	WELLINGTON
WAS(S)ON	BUCHANAN	WELLS	ABERDEEN DIST
WAS(S)ON	FORBES	WELLWOOD	FIFE DIST
WASFORD	CARRICK DIST	WELSH	ROXBURGH DIST
WASHINGTON	DUNBAR	WEMYSS	MAC DUFF
WASS	MUNRO	WEMYSS	WEMYSS
WASS	ROSS	WENTON	INVERNESS DIST
WASSON	BUCHANAN	WEST	BUCHAN DIST
WASSON	WATSON	WESTALL,-ELL	ABERDEEN DIST
WASTIE,-Y	FIFE DIST	WESTBURN	FIFE DIST
WAT(T)SON	WATSON	WESTBURY	EDINBURGH DIST
WATCHMAN	FIFE DIST	WESTFALL	ABERDEEN DIST
WATERS	BUCHANAN	WESTGARTH	EDINBURGH DIST
WATERS	FORBES	WESTLAND(S)	HUNTLY DIST
WATERS	ROSS	WESTMAN	INVERNESS DIST
WATERSON	ANGUS DIST	WESTON,-EN	GALLOWAY DIST
WATERSTO(U)N	ANGUS DIST	WESTRAY	CALEDONIA TARTAN
WATHERSTON(E)	ANGUS DIST	WESTWATER	FIFE DIST
WATKINS	BUCHANAN	WESTWOOD	FIFE DIST
WATKINS	FORBES	WEYMES	WEMYSS
WATRET	GALLOWAY DIST	WHAIR	SUTHERLAND DIST
WATSON	BUCHANAN	WHAMMOND	BUCHAN DIST
WATSON	FORBES	WHANNEL	GALLOWAY DIST
WATSON	WATSON	WHARRIE,-Y	MAC QUARRIE
WATT(S)	BUCHANAN	WHATMOUGH	CALEDONIA TARTAN
WATT(S)	FORBES	WHE(E)LAN(S)	ROXBURGH DIST
WATTERS	BUCHANAN	WHEATLANDS	DALZELL
WATTERS	FORBES	WHEATLY	DALLZELL
WATTERS	ROSS	WHEELWRIGHT	ROXBURGH DIST
WATTIE,-EY	FORBES	WHENT	ABERDEEN DIST
WATTIE,-Y	BUCHANAN	WHIG(H)AM	TWEEDSIDE DIST
WATTIE,-Y	ROSS	WHIGHT	GALLOWAY DIST
WATTSON	BUCHANAN	WHILLAN(S)	ROXBURGH DIST
WATTSON	FORBES	WHIN	GALLOWAY DIST
WATTSON	WATSON	WHINNEY,-IE	MAC KENZIE
WAUCHOPE	ROXBURGH DIST	WHIPPO	STRATHCLYDE DIST
WAUGH	ROXBURGH DIST	WHITBY	TWEEDSIDE DIST
WAUGHTON	EDINBURGH DIST	WHITE	LAMONT
WEAR	WEIR	WHITE	MAC GREGOR
WEATHERHEAD	TWEEDSIDE DIST	WHITEBURN(E)	EDINBURGH DIST
WEATHERLY	DUNBAR DIST	WHITECROSS	ABERDEEN DIST
WEATHERSTON(E)	TWEEDSIDE DIST	WHITEFIELD	SINCLAIR
WEAVER	MAC FARLANE	WHITEFORD	AYRSHIRE DIST
WEAVER	STIRLING DIST	WHITEHALL	GLASGOW DIST
WEBSTER	MAC FARLANE	WHITEHEAD	DUNBAR DIST
WEDDELL,-LE	EDINBURGH DIST	WHITEHILL	PERTHSHIRE DIST
WEDDERBO(U)RN(E)	HOME	WHITEHOPE	ROXBURGH DIST
WEDDERBURN	HOME	WHITELAW	DUNBAR DIST
WEDDERLIE	TWEEDSIDE DIST	WHITELOCK	EDINBURGH DIST
WEDDOW	ANGUS DIST	WHITESIDE	STRATHCLYDE DIST
WEDOW	STRATHCLYDE DIST	WHITESMITH	EDINBURGH DIST
WEEDEN,-ON	ROXBURGH DIST	WHITESON	WHITSON
WEEK(S)	CALEDONIA TARTAN	WHITEWELL	GALLOWAY DIST
WEEMS	MAC DUFF	WHITFIELD	TYNESIDE DIST
WEEMS	WEMYSS	WHITFORD	AYRSHIRE DIST
WEENY,-IE	MAC KENZIE	WHITHERSPOON	WITHERSPOON
WEEPERS	FIFE DIST	WHITING	EDINBURGH DIST
WEER	WEIR	WHITL(E)Y,-IE	CALEDONIA TARTAN
WEIGHTON	ANGUS DIST	WHITLAW	ROXBURGH DIST
WEIR	BUCHANAN	WHITLOCK	DALZELL
WEIR	WEIR	WHITSLADE	ROXBURGH DIST
WEL(L)HAM	GALLOWAY DIST	WHITSON,-UN	WHITSON
WELCH	EDINBURGH DIST	WHITTEN,-IN	GLASGOW DIST
WELIVER	MAC GREGOR	WHITTEN,-IN	ROXBURGH DIST
WELL(E)SLEY	WELLINGTON	WHITTER	INVERNESS DIST

121

NAME	TARTAN	NAME	TARTAN
WHITTING	EDINBURGH DIST	WINLAW	STRATHCLYDE DIST
WHITTINGHAM(E)	MUSSELBURGH DIST	WINNING	MAC LENNAN
WHITTON,-UN	ROXBURGH DIST	WINSETT	INVERNESS DIST
WHOLECOT,-CUT	ROXBURGH DIST	WINT	TWEEDSIDE DIST
WHYMAN,-MON	BUCHAN DIST	WINTER(S)	TWEEDSIDE DIST
WHYSON	WHITSON	WINTHROP(E)	ROXBURGH DIST
WHYTE	LAMONT	WINTIE,-Y	ABERDEEN DIST
WHYTE	MAC GREGOR	WINTO(U)N	MUSSELBURGH DIST
WHYTICK,-OCK	EDINBURGH DIST	WINTOUR(S)	TWEEDSIDE DIST
WHYTSON	WHITSON	WIPER	GALLOWAY DIST
WICK	CAITHNESS TARTAN	WISE	ABERDEEN DIST
WICKEM,-UM	EDINBURGH DIST	WISEHART	MAR DIST
WICKENDEN	GALLOWAY DIST	WISEMAN	ANGUS DIST
WICKETSHAW	EDINBURGH DIST	WISHART	ABERDEEN DIST
WICKHAM	EDINBURGH DIST	WISHAW	STRATHCLYDE DIST
WIDDRINGTON	TYNESIDE DIST	WISTON	STRATHCLYDE DIST
WIDOW	STRATHCLYDE DIST	WITHER	GALLOWAY DIST
WIER	WEIR	WITHERSPOON	WITHERSPOON
WIGHAM(E)	ROXBURGH DIST	WITTER	INVERNESS DIST
WIGHT	EDINBURGH DIST	WITTET	INVERNESS DIST
WIGHTMAN	TWEEDSIDE DIST	WITTON	ROXBURGH DIST
WIGHTON	ANGUS DIST	WO(U)LFSON	INVERNESS DIST
WIGMORE	EDINBURGH DIST	WODDROP	ETTRICK DIST
WILD(E)	ABERDEEN DIST	WOLF(E)	DUNDEE DIST
WILDRIDGE	EDINBURGH DIST	WOLF(E) (Irish)	CLAN CIAN
WILDSMITH	EDINBURGH DIST	WOLLER	ROXBURGH DIST
WILEY	HUNTLY DIST	WOLLOX	GLASGOW DIST
WILGUS	ABERDEEN DIST	WONDER(S)	ANGUS DIST
WILKIE,-Y	FIFE DIST	WOOD	ROXBURGH DIST
WILKIE,-Y	MAC DONALD	WOODALL	GALLOWAY DIST
WILKIN(S)	MAC DONALD	WOODBOURNE	AYRSHIRE DIST
WILKINSON	MAC DONALD	WOODBURN	AYRSHIRE DIST
WILL(S)	GUNN	WOODCOCK	GLASGOW DIST
WILL(S)	MAC KAY	WOODELL	GALLOWAY DIST
WILLANS	MAC DONALD	WOODFIELD	NITHSDALE DIST
WILLARD	FIFE DIST	WOODFORD	ROXBURGH DIST
WILLET(S)	CARRICK DIST	WOODHALL,-AW	EDINBURGH DIST
WILLET(S)	INVERNESS DIST	WOODHEAD	STRATHCLYDE DIST
WILLGOOK	BUCHAN DIST	WOODMAN	ABERDEEN DIST
WILLIAM(S)	GUNN	WOODROW	GLASGOW DIST
WILLIAM(S)	MAC KAY	WOODRUFF	GLASGOW DIST
WILLIAM(S)	MAC WILLIAM	WOODSIDE	AYRSHIRE DIST
WILLIAMSON	GUNN	WOODSON	TWEEDSIDE DIST
WILLIAMSON	MAC KAY	WOODWARD	INVERNESS DIST
WILLIAMSON	MAC LEOD	WOOLDRI(D)GE	EDINBURGH DIST
WILLIAMSON	MAC WILLIAM	WOOLEY	CALEDONIA TARTAN
WILLIAMSON	ROBERTSON	WORDIE,-Y	STIRLING DIST
WILLIE	HUNTLY DIST	WORK	CALEDONIA TARTAN
WILLIS	GALLOWAY DIST	WORKMAN	FIFE DIST
WILLIS(S)ON	GALLOWAY DIST	WORMET	FIFE DIST
WILLOCK(S)	ABERDEEN DIST	WORSFIELD	INVERNESS DIST
WILLOCK(S)	AYRSHIRE DIST	WOTHERSPOON	WITHERSPOON
WILLOX(S)	ABERDEEN DIST	WRANGHAM	ROXBURGH DIST
WILLSHOT	EDINBURGH DIST	WRANGHOLM(E)	ROXBURGH DIST
WILSON	GUNN	WRANNOCK	STIRLING DIST
WILSON	INNES	WRAY	MAC RAE
WILSON	MAC KAY	WREN	ARGYLL DIST
WILSON	WILSON	WRIGHT	MAC INTYRE
WILTON	ROXBURGH DIST	WRIGHTSON	MAC INTYRE
WIM(M)S	WEMYSS	WYATT	ANGUS DIST
WIN(D)RAM	STRATHCLYDE DIST	WYETH	ABERDEEN DIST
WIN(N)AN	MAC LENNAN	WYL(L)IE,-EY	GUNN
WINCHELL	TWEEDSIDE DIST	WYL(L)IE,-EY	MAC FARLANE
WINCHESTER	STRATHCLYDE DIST	WYLD(E)	ANGUS DIST
WINDRAM	STRATHCLYDE DIST	WYMAN	STRATHSPEY DIST
WINGATE	GLASGOW DIST	WYMBS	WEMYSS
WINGO	ABERDEEN DIST	WYMES	WEMYSS
WINK	ABERDEEN DIST		

NAME	TARTAN
WYMOND	TWEEDSIDE DIST
WYMS	WEMYSS
WYND(E)	ANGUS DIST
WYNES(S)	ABERDEEN DIST
WYNN(E)	FT. WILLIAM DIST
WYPER(S)	STRATHCLYDE DIST
WYSE	ABERDEEN DIST
WYTH(E)	ABERDEEN DIST
WYVILL(E)	TWEEDSIDE DIST

Y, Z

NAME	TARTAN
YAIR	MUSSELBURGH DIST
YARROW	ETTRICK DIST
YATES	GALLOWAY DIST
YEAMAN	DUNDEE DIST
YEATS	GALLOWAY DIST
YEATS (Irish)	CONNACHT TARTAN
YELL	DALZELL
YELL	SKENE
YELLOWER	GALLOWAY DIST
YELLOWLEE(S)	EDINBURGH DIST
YELLOWLIE,-EY	ST. ANDREWS DIST
YELTO(U)N	STRATHCLYDE DIST
YENSTAY	CALEDONIA TARTAN
YEOMAN	DUNDEE DIST
YERROW	GALLOWAY DIST
YESTER	HAY
YETHAM	ROXBURGH DIST
YETTS	GALLOWAY DIST
YOOL	BUCHANAN
YORK	ROXBURGH DIST
YORKSTON	EDINBURGH DIST
YORSTAN	EDINBURGH DIST
YORSTO(U)N	EDINBURGH DIST
YOTSO(U)N	EDINBURGH DIST
YOUNG(E)	DOUGLAS
YOUNG(E)	YOUNG
YOUNGER	FIFE DIST
YOUNGHUSBAND	INVERNESS DIST
YOUNGSON	MAR DIST
YOUNIE,-Y	INNES
YOURSTAN	EDINBURGH DIST
YOURSTOUN	EDINBURGH DIST
YUILL	BUCHANAN
YUIR	CAMPBELL
YULE	BUCHANAN
YULLO	STRATHCLYDE DIST
YUNNIE,-Y	INNES
ZELL	DALZELL
ZUILL	BUCHANAN

ADDENDA and NOTES

BUSSEY	FIFE DIST
CASTEL(L)AW	GALLOWAY DIST
CASTELLO(W/E)	GALLOWAY DIST
CASTLEL(L)AW	GALLOWAY DIST
CHAVERS	ABERDEEN DIST
CHAVIS	ABERDEEN DIST
CHAVOUS	ABERDEEN DIST
CRANNA	ANGUS DIST
CRENNA	ANGUS DIST
GEFFERS	FIFE DIST
GOFFERS	FIFE DIST
GUES(S)(T)	TYNESIDE DIST
HUSTON	MAC DONALD
LOFLAN	MAC LACHLAN
MA(Y)BERRY	TYNESIDE DIST
MAC ALEESE	STEWART OF APPIN
MAC BURRICH,-K	MAC PHERSON
MAC BURRICH,-K	MAC DON CLANRANALD
MAC CLEOUD	MAC LEOD
MAC COLLUM	MAC CALUM
MAC COURTIE	MAC KIRDY
MAC CRANIE,-Y	MAC DON CLANRANALD
MAC KEM(M)Y	FRASER
MAC LOFAN	MAC LACHLAN
MAC LOFLAN	MAC LACHLAN
MAC LORI	GALLOWAY DIST
MAC STRUMER	MAC STRUMER
MALES	DEESIDE DIST
MELTON	TWEEDSIDE DIST
MILLIN	CONNACHT TARTAN
NEEL	MAC NEIL
STRAWHORN	DEESIDE DIST
STRAWHORN	MAR DIST
WHITMELL	TYNESIDE DIST

About the Author

Philip D. Smith, Jr., Professor of Languages and Linguistics, is a former university dean and associate-provost in the Pennsylvania State System of Higher Education. He holds the BA in Spanish, the MA in History, and the PhD in Foreign Language Education with a certificate of advanced studies in Gaelic. Dr. Smith is a member of the Guild of Tartan Scholars and a Fellow of the Scottish Tartans Society. He is a Fellow of the Society of Antiquaries of Scotland. Professor Smith teaches Gaelic and lectures internationally on tartan, Scottish hisory and Gaelic culture. He is the co-author, with Dr. D. Gordon Teall, of **District Tartans** (London: Shepheard-Walwyn, 1992).